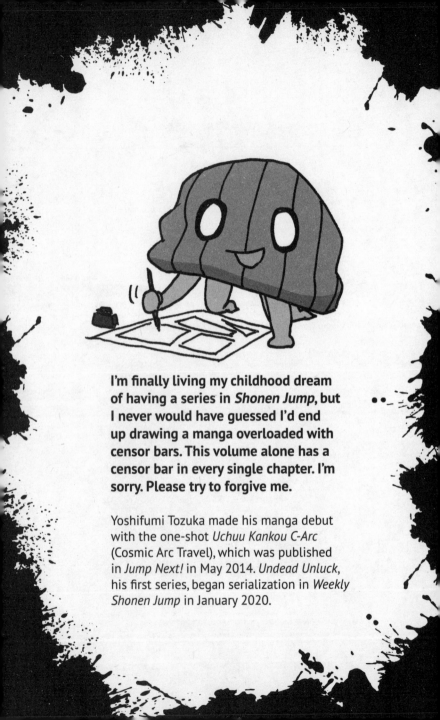

I'm finally living my childhood dream of having a series in *Shonen Jump*, but I never would have guessed I'd end up drawing a manga overloaded with censor bars. This volume alone has a censor bar in every single chapter. I'm sorry. Please try to forgive me.

Yoshifumi Tozuka made his manga debut with the one-shot *Uchuu Kankou C-Arc* (Cosmic Arc Travel), which was published in *Jump Next!* in May 2014. *Undead Unluck*, his first series, began serialization in *Weekly Shonen Jump* in January 2020.

UNDEAD UNLUCK

Volume 1

Shonen Jump Edition

STORY AND ART BY

Yoshifumi Tozuka

Translation: **David Evelyn**
Touch-Up Art & Lettering: **Michelle Pang**
Design: **Kam Li**
Editor: **Karla Clark**

First published in Japan in 2020 by SHUEISHA Inc., Tokyo.
English translation rights arranged by SHUEISHA Inc.

Printed in the U.S.A.

Published by VIZ Media, LLC
P.O. Box 77010
San Francisco, CA 94107

10 9 8 7 6 5 4 3 2 1
First printing, May 2021

RATED T+ OLDER TEEN ratings.viz.com

PARENTAL ADVISORY
UNDEAD UNLUCK is rated T+ for Older Teen and is recommended for ages 16 and up. This volume contains suggestive themes, crude humor and violence.

VIZ MEDIA
viz.com

SHONEN JUMP

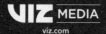

UNDEAD UNLUCK

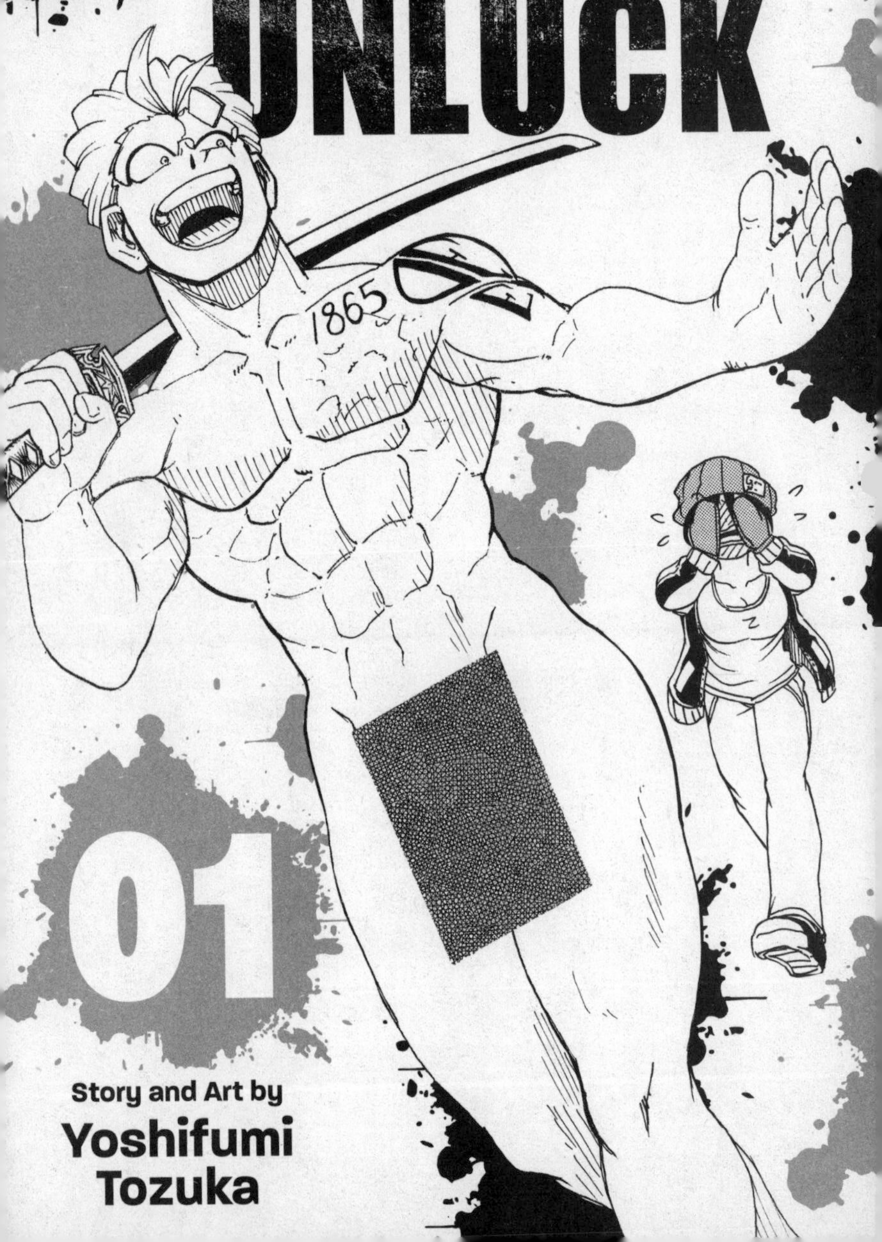
1865

01

Story and Art by
Yoshifumi Tozuka

UNDEAD UNLUCK

01

No. 001 Undead and Unluck

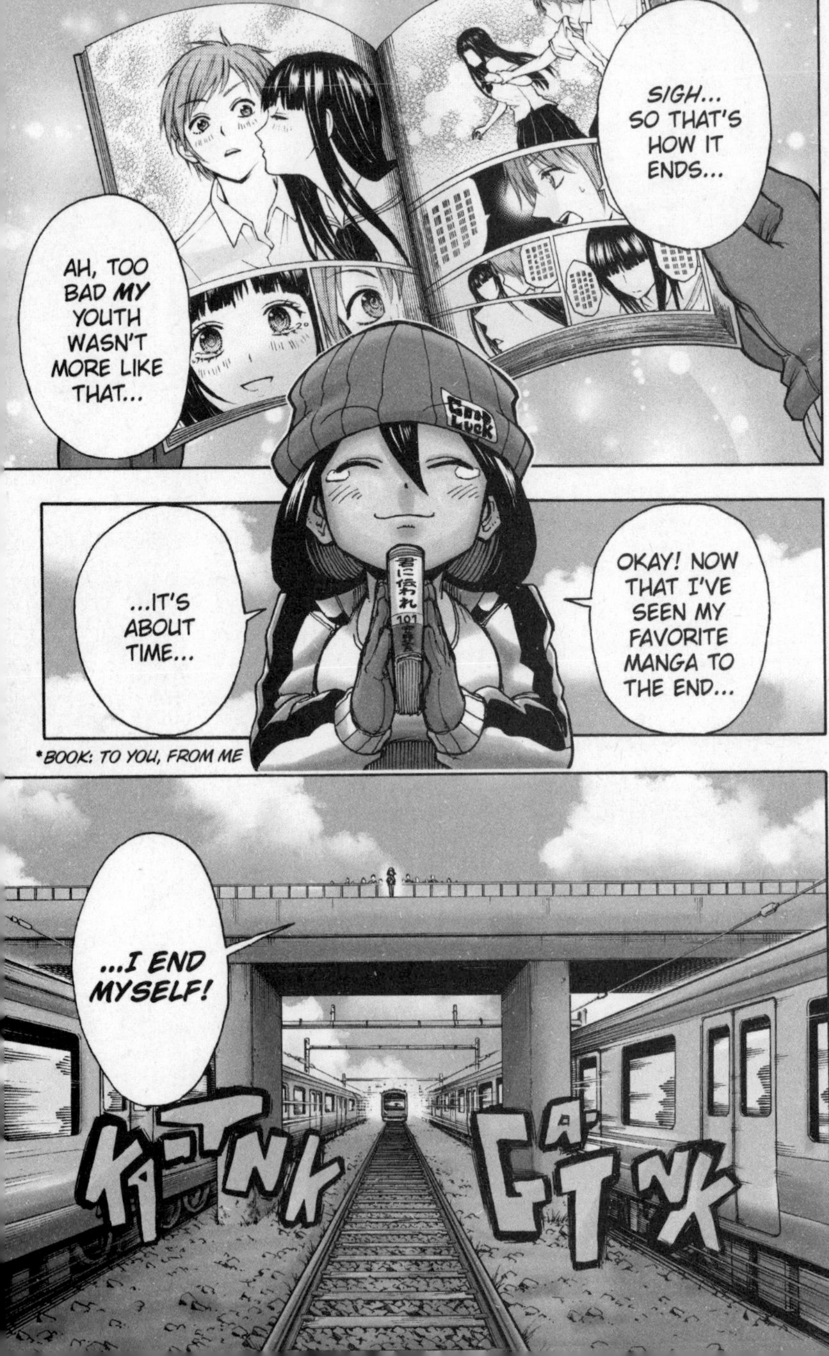
SIGH... SO THAT'S HOW IT ENDS...
AH, TOO BAD *MY* YOUTH WASN'T MORE LIKE THAT...
GOOD LUCK
君に伝われ
101
OKAY! NOW THAT I'VE SEEN MY FAVORITE MANGA TO THE END...
...IT'S ABOUT TIME...
...I END MYSELF!
GA-TNK
KA-TNK

*BOOK: TO YOU, FROM ME

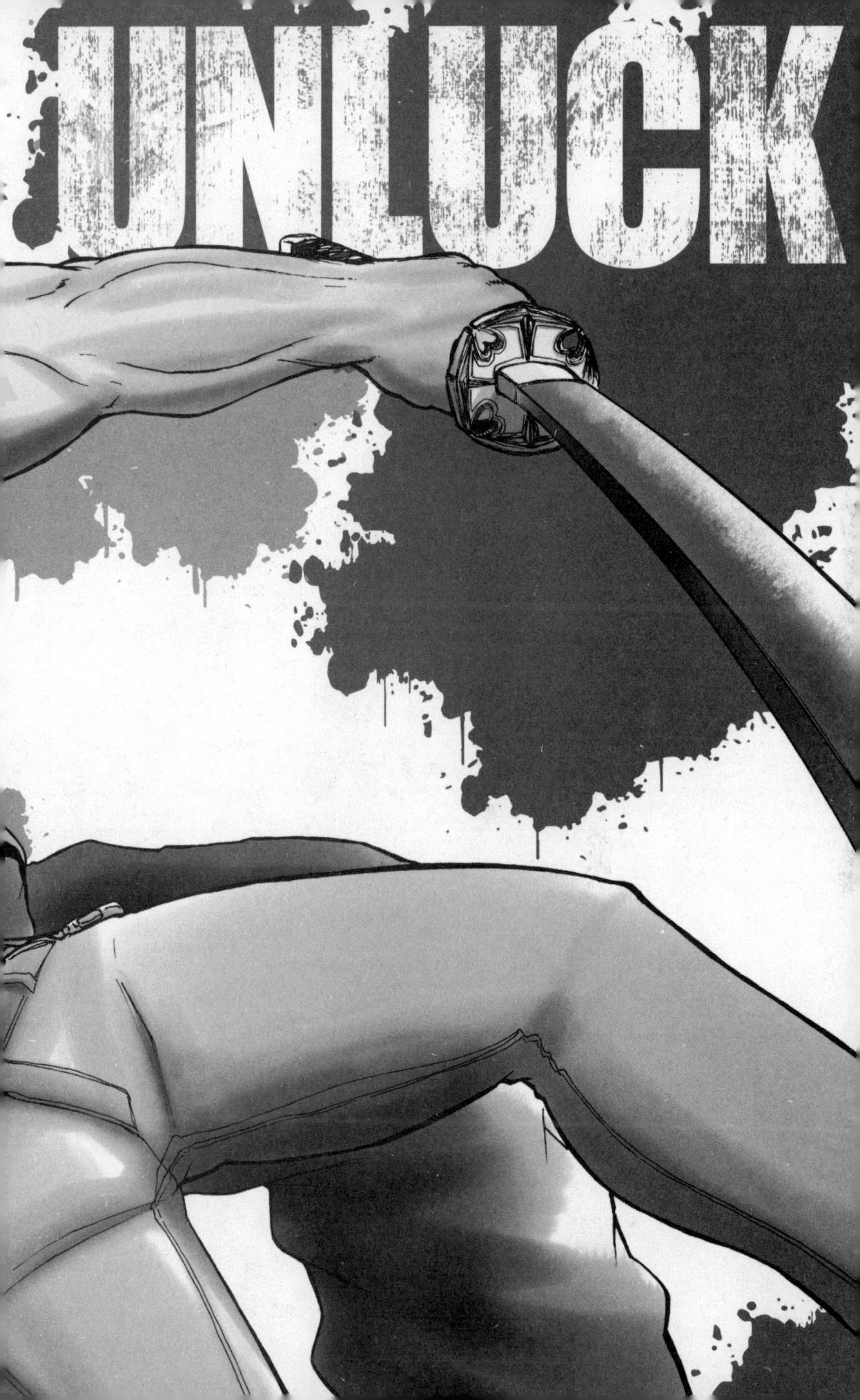
UNLUCK

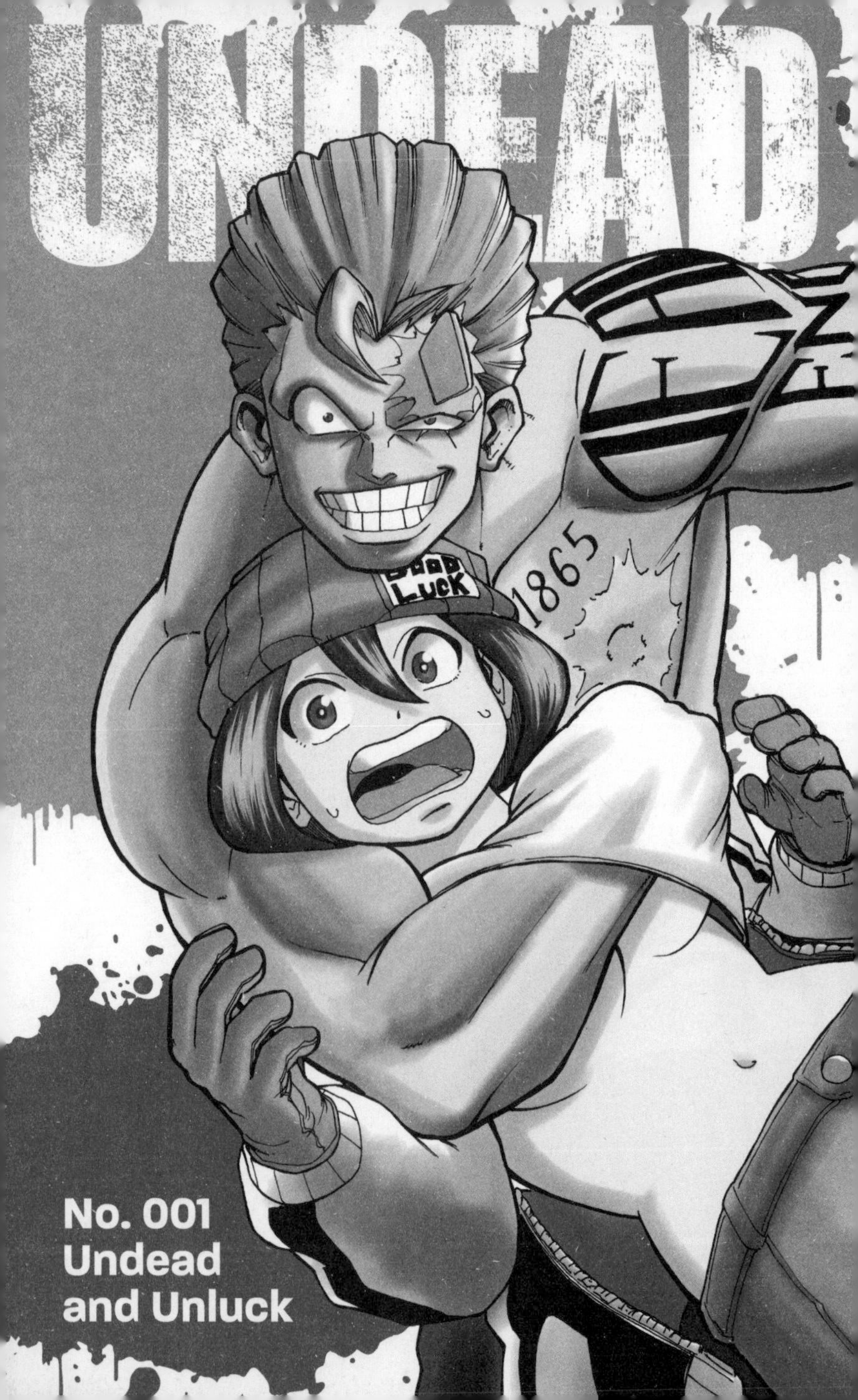
UNDEAD
LUCK
1865

No. 001 Undead and Unluck

UNDEAD
UNLUCK

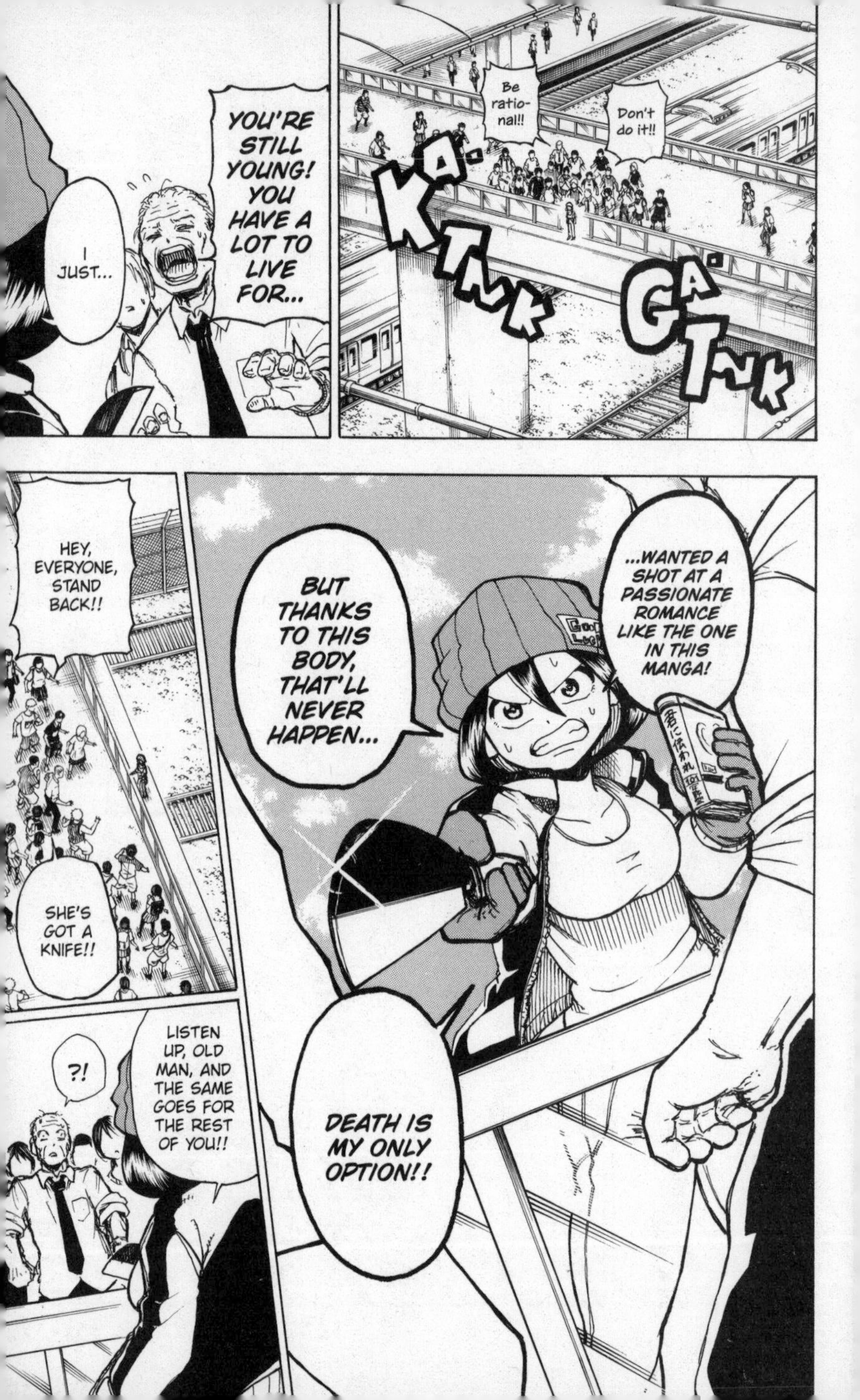
Don't do it!!
Be rational!!
KA-TNK
GA-TNK
YOU'RE STILL YOUNG! YOU HAVE A LOT TO LIVE FOR...
I JUST...
...WANTED A SHOT AT A PASSIONATE ROMANCE LIKE THE ONE IN THIS MANGA!
BUT THANKS TO THIS BODY, THAT'LL NEVER HAPPEN...
DEATH IS MY ONLY OPTION!!
HEY, EVERYONE, STAND BACK!!
SHE'S GOT A KNIFE!!
?!
LISTEN UP, OLD MAN, AND THE SAME GOES FOR THE REST OF YOU!!

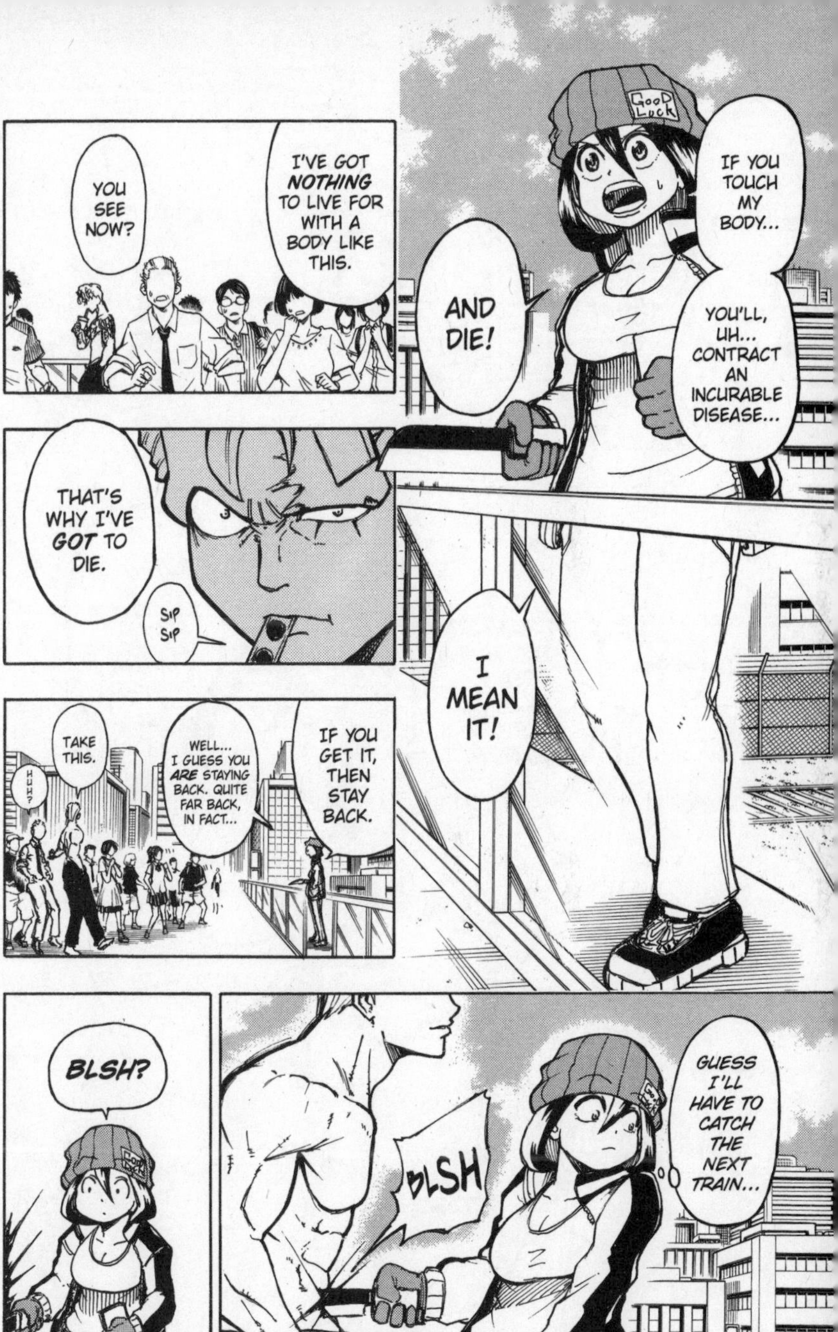
GOOD LUCK
IF YOU TOUCH MY BODY...
YOU'LL, UH... CONTRACT AN INCURABLE DISEASE...
AND DIE!
I MEAN IT!
I'VE GOT NOTHING TO LIVE FOR WITH A BODY LIKE THIS.
YOU SEE NOW?
THAT'S WHY I'VE GOT TO DIE.
SIP SIP
IF YOU GET IT, THEN STAY BACK.
WELL... I GUESS YOU ARE STAYING BACK. QUITE FAR BACK, IN FACT...
TAKE THIS.
HUH?
GUESS I'LL HAVE TO CATCH THE NEXT TRAIN...
BLSH
BLSH?

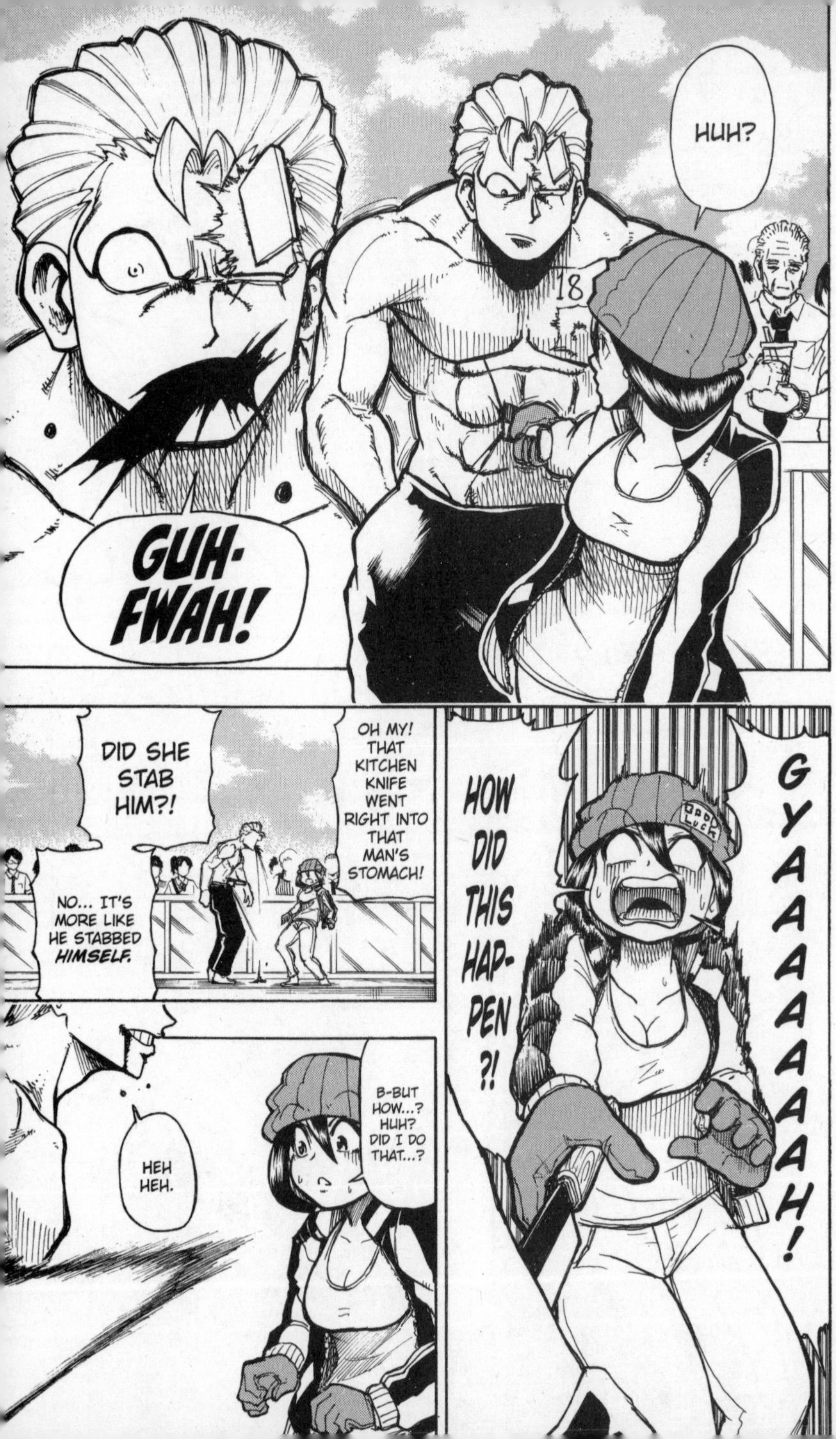
HUH?
GUH-FWAH!
GYAAAAAAAAAH!
HOW DID THIS HAP-PEN?!
OH MY! THAT KITCHEN KNIFE WENT RIGHT INTO THAT MAN'S STOMACH!
DID SHE STAB HIM?!
NO... IT'S MORE LIKE HE STABBED *HIMSELF.*
B-BUT HOW...? HUH? DID I DO THAT...?
HEH HEH.

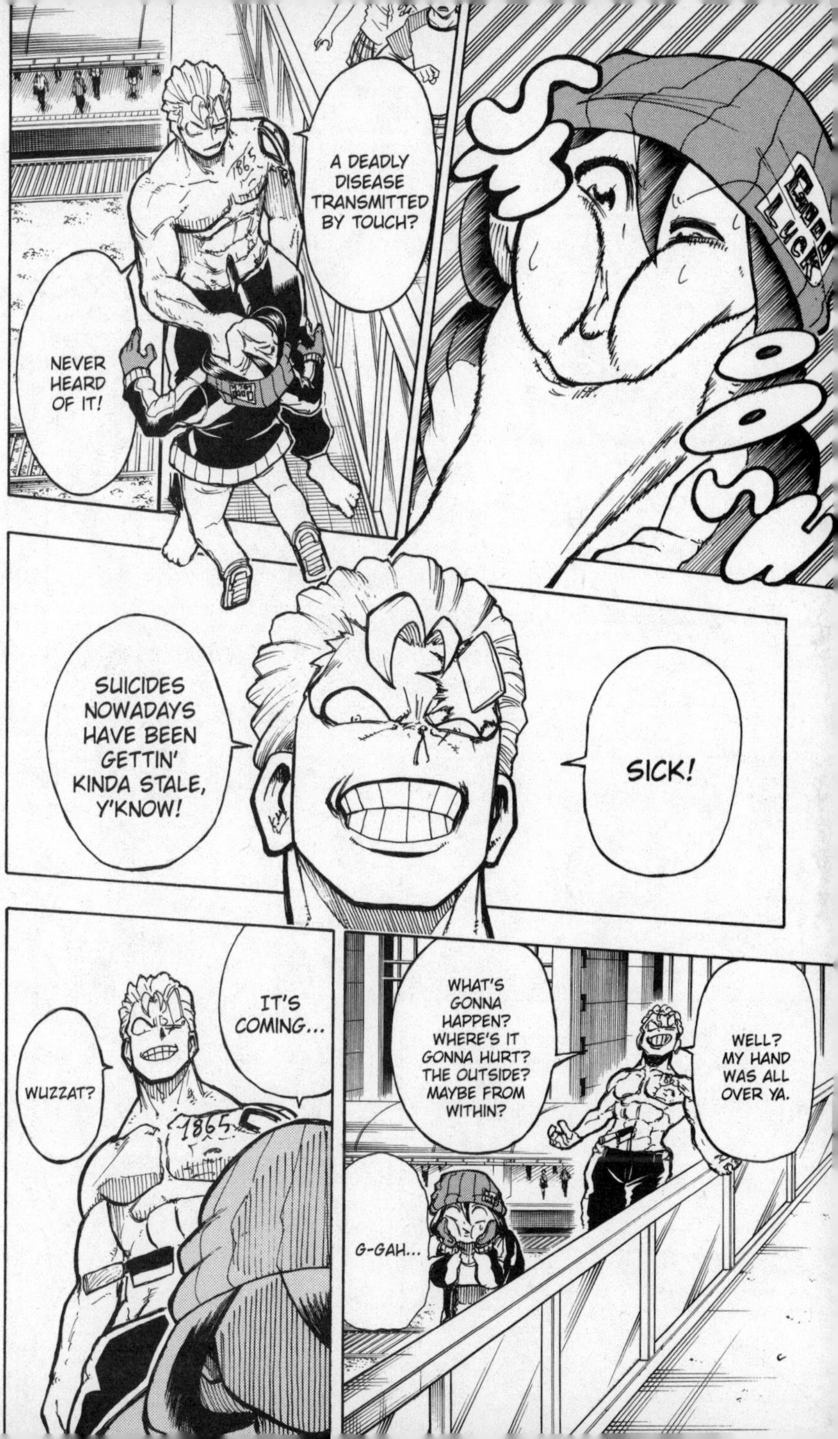
A DEADLY DISEASE TRANSMITTED BY TOUCH?
NEVER HEARD OF IT!
SICK!
SUICIDES NOWADAYS HAVE BEEN GETTIN' KINDA STALE, Y'KNOW!
WELL? MY HAND WAS ALL OVER YA.
WHAT'S GONNA HAPPEN? WHERE'S IT GONNA HURT? THE OUTSIDE? MAYBE FROM WITHIN?
G-GAH...
IT'S COMING...
WUZZAT?

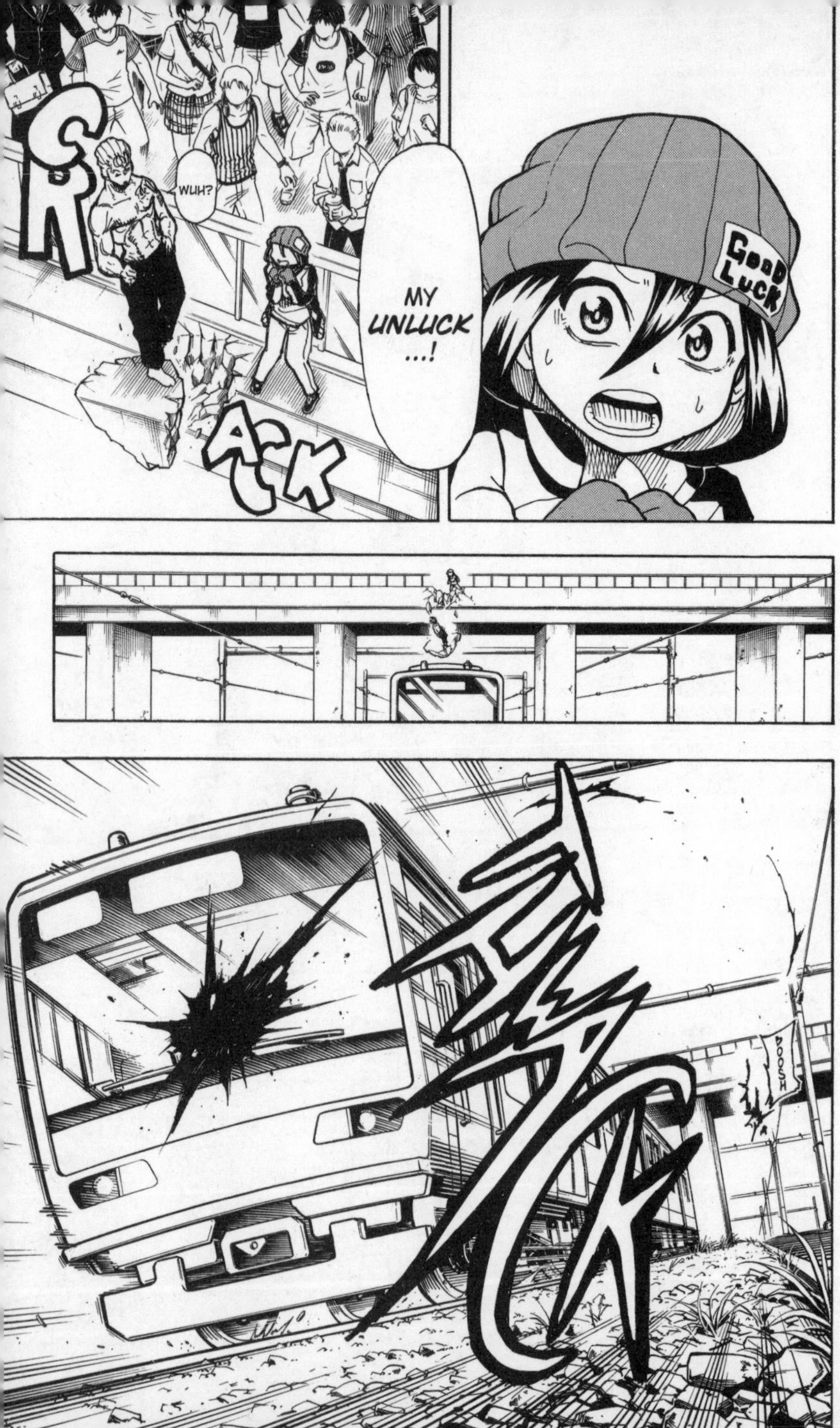
MY UNLUCK ...!
CRACK
WUH?
DOOSH

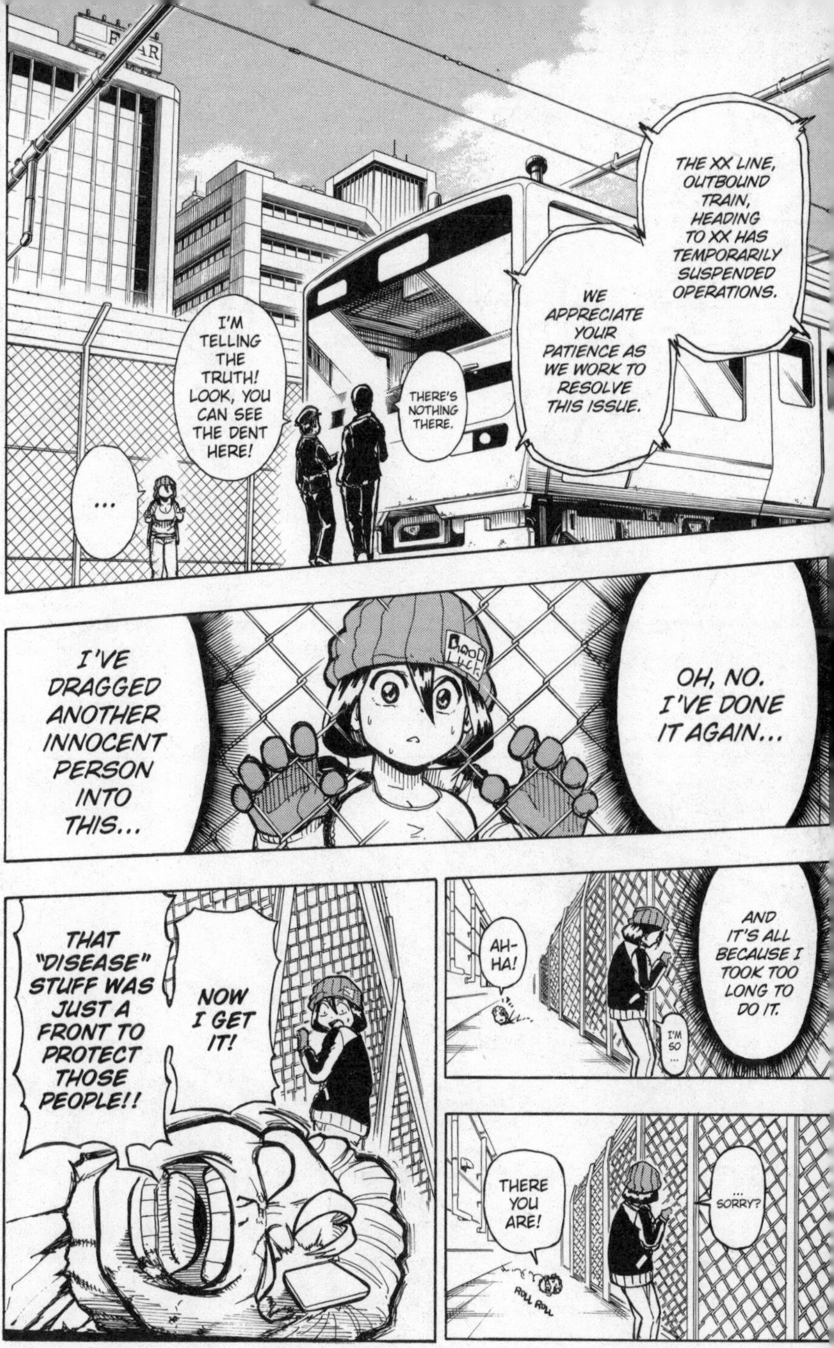
THE XX LINE, OUTBOUND TRAIN, HEADING TO XX HAS TEMPORARILY SUSPENDED OPERATIONS.
WE APPRECIATE YOUR PATIENCE AS WE WORK TO RESOLVE THIS ISSUE.
THERE'S NOTHING THERE.
I'M TELLING THE TRUTH! LOOK, YOU CAN SEE THE DENT HERE!
...
OH, NO. I'VE DONE IT AGAIN...
I'VE DRAGGED ANOTHER INNOCENT PERSON INTO THIS...
AND IT'S ALL BECAUSE I TOOK TOO LONG TO DO IT.
I'M SO ...
AH-HA!
... SORRY?
THERE YOU ARE!
ROLL ROLL
NOW I GET IT!
THAT "DISEASE" STUFF WAS JUST A FRONT TO PROTECT THOSE PEOPLE!!

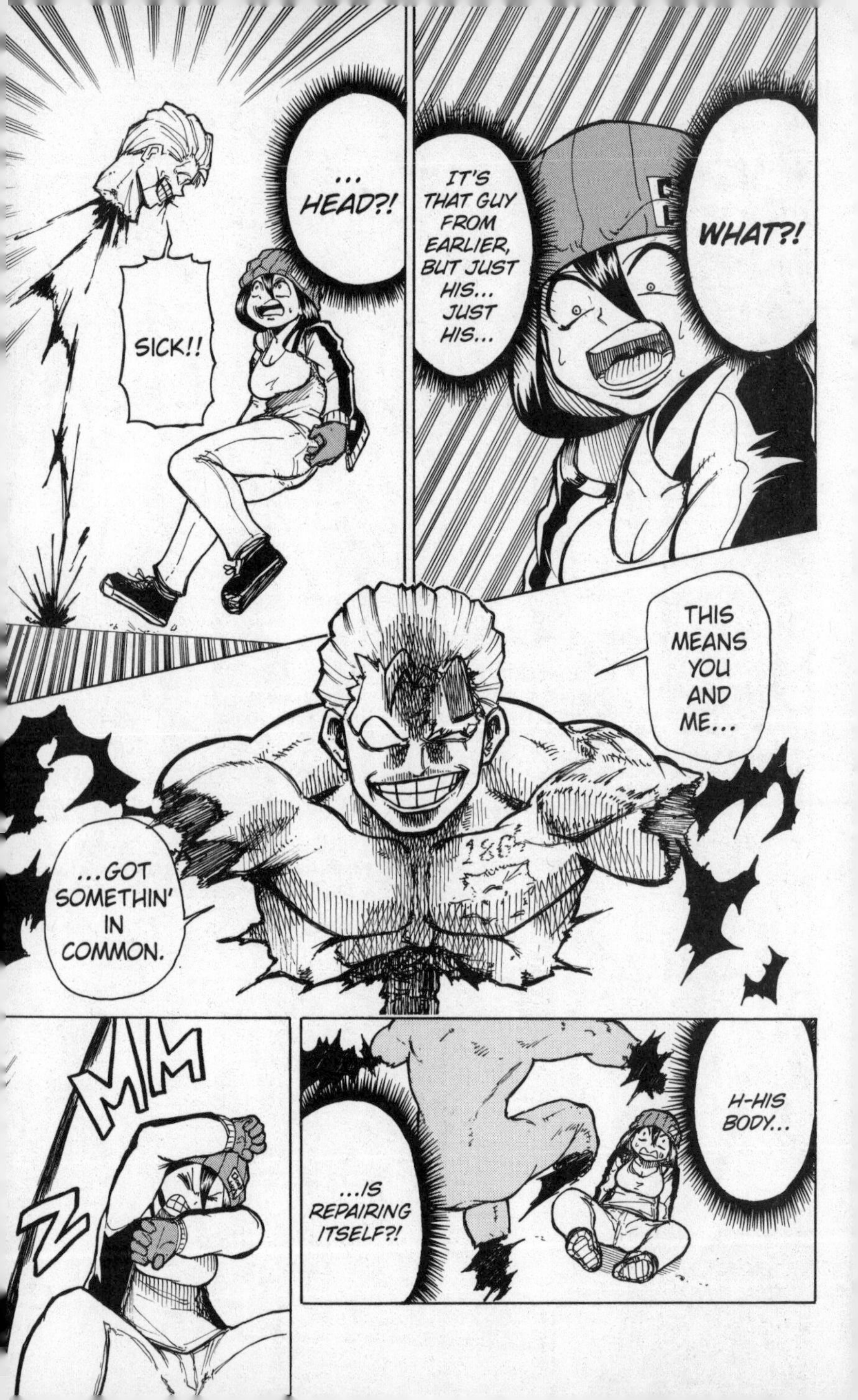
WHAT?!
IT'S THAT GUY FROM EARLIER, BUT JUST HIS... JUST HIS...
... HEAD?!
SICK!!
THIS MEANS YOU AND ME...
...GOT SOMETHIN' IN COMMON.
H-HIS BODY...
...IS REPAIRING ITSELF?!
ZMMM

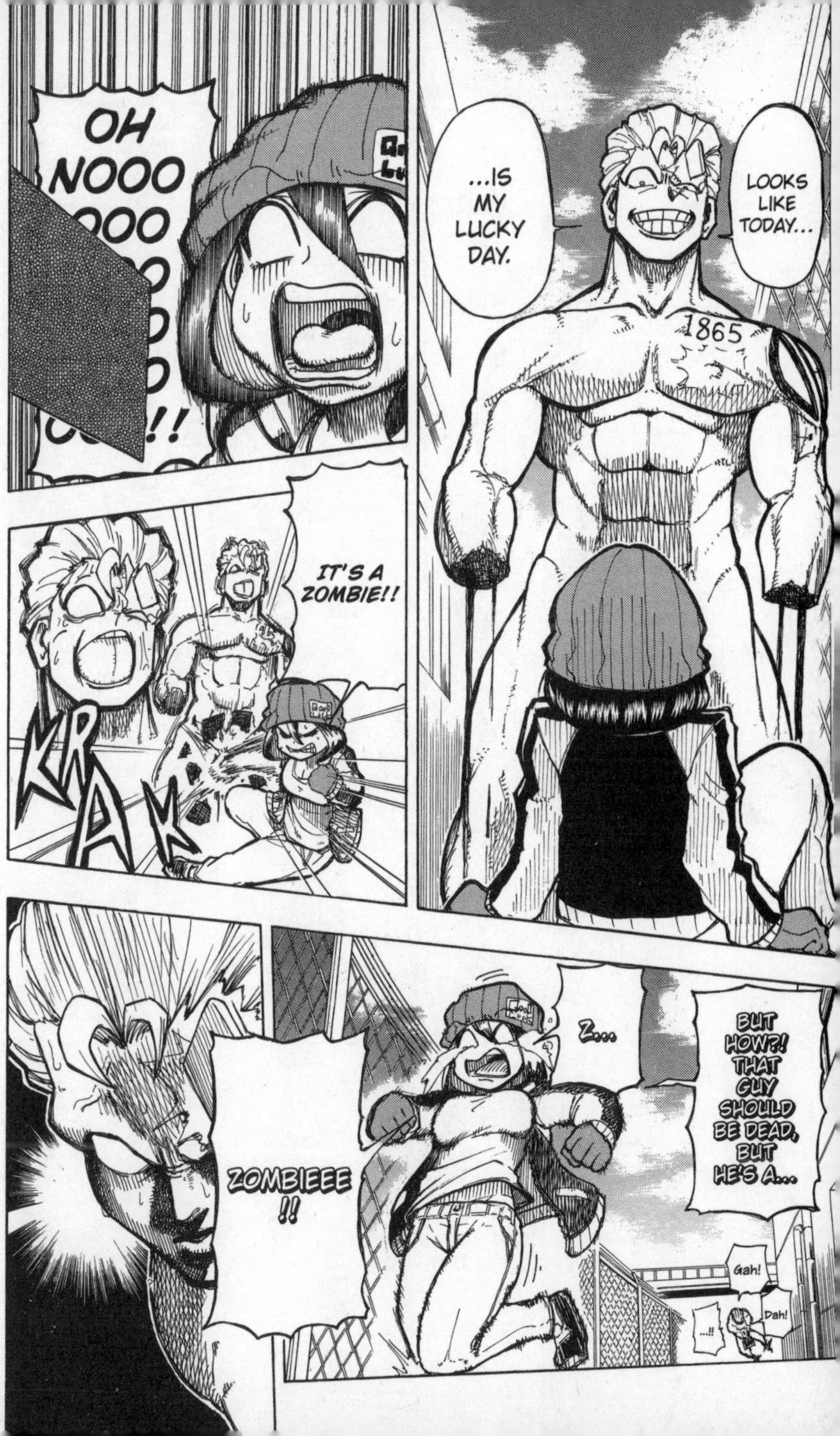
LOOKS LIKE TODAY...
...IS MY LUCKY DAY.
1865
OH NOOOOOOOOOOOO!!
IT'S A ZOMBIE!!
KRAK
BUT HOW?! THAT GUY SHOULD BE DEAD, BUT HE'S A...
Z...
Gah!
Dah!
...!!
ZOMBIEEE!!

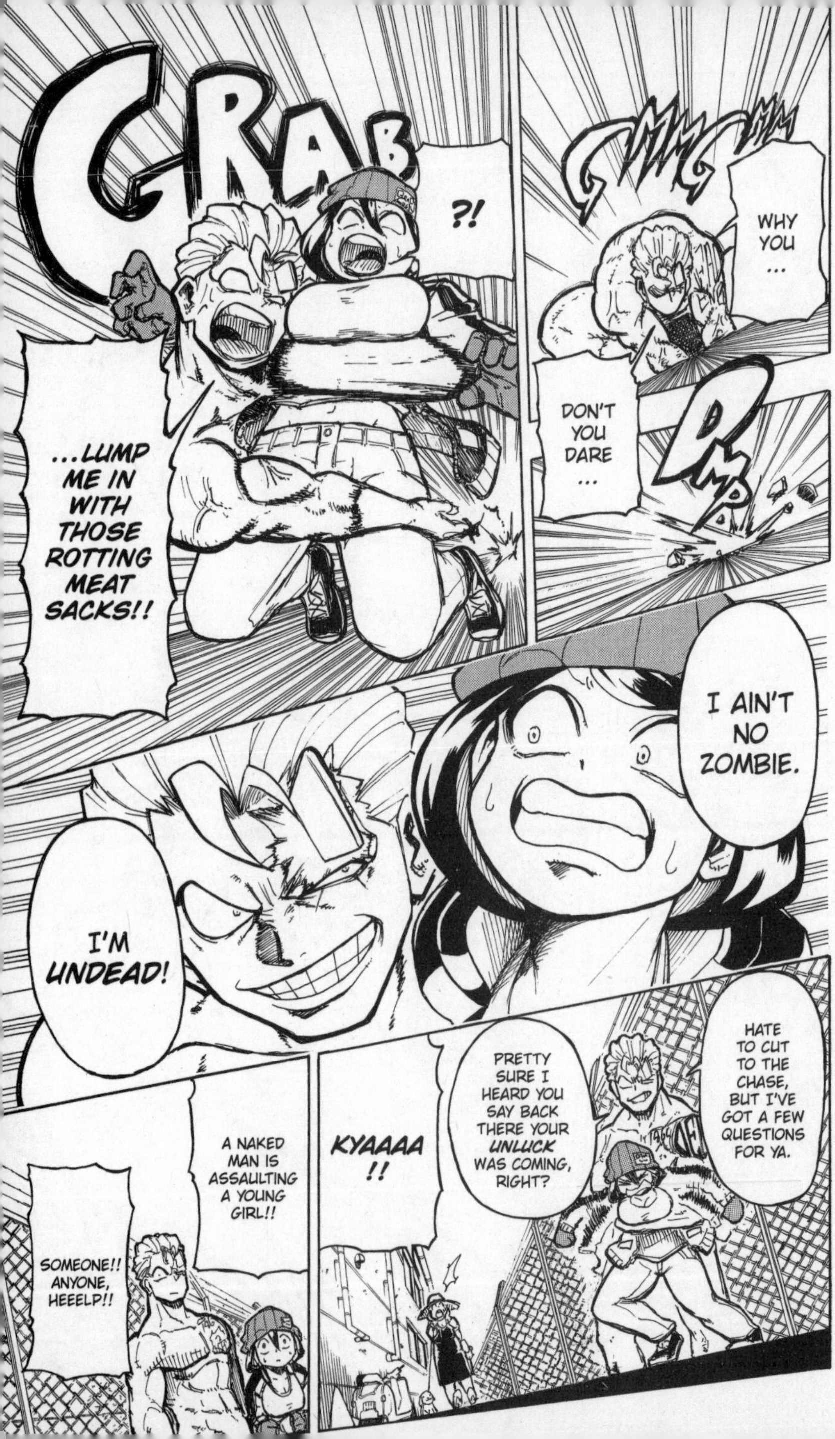
WHY YOU ...
DON'T YOU DARE ...
GRAB
?!
...LUMP ME IN WITH THOSE ROTTING MEAT SACKS!!
I AIN'T NO ZOMBIE.
I'M UNDEAD!
HATE TO CUT TO THE CHASE, BUT I'VE GOT A FEW QUESTIONS FOR YA.
PRETTY SURE I HEARD YOU SAY BACK THERE YOUR UNLUCK WAS COMING, RIGHT?
KYAAAA!!
A NAKED MAN IS ASSAULTING A YOUNG GIRL!!
SOMEONE!! ANYONE, HEEELP!!

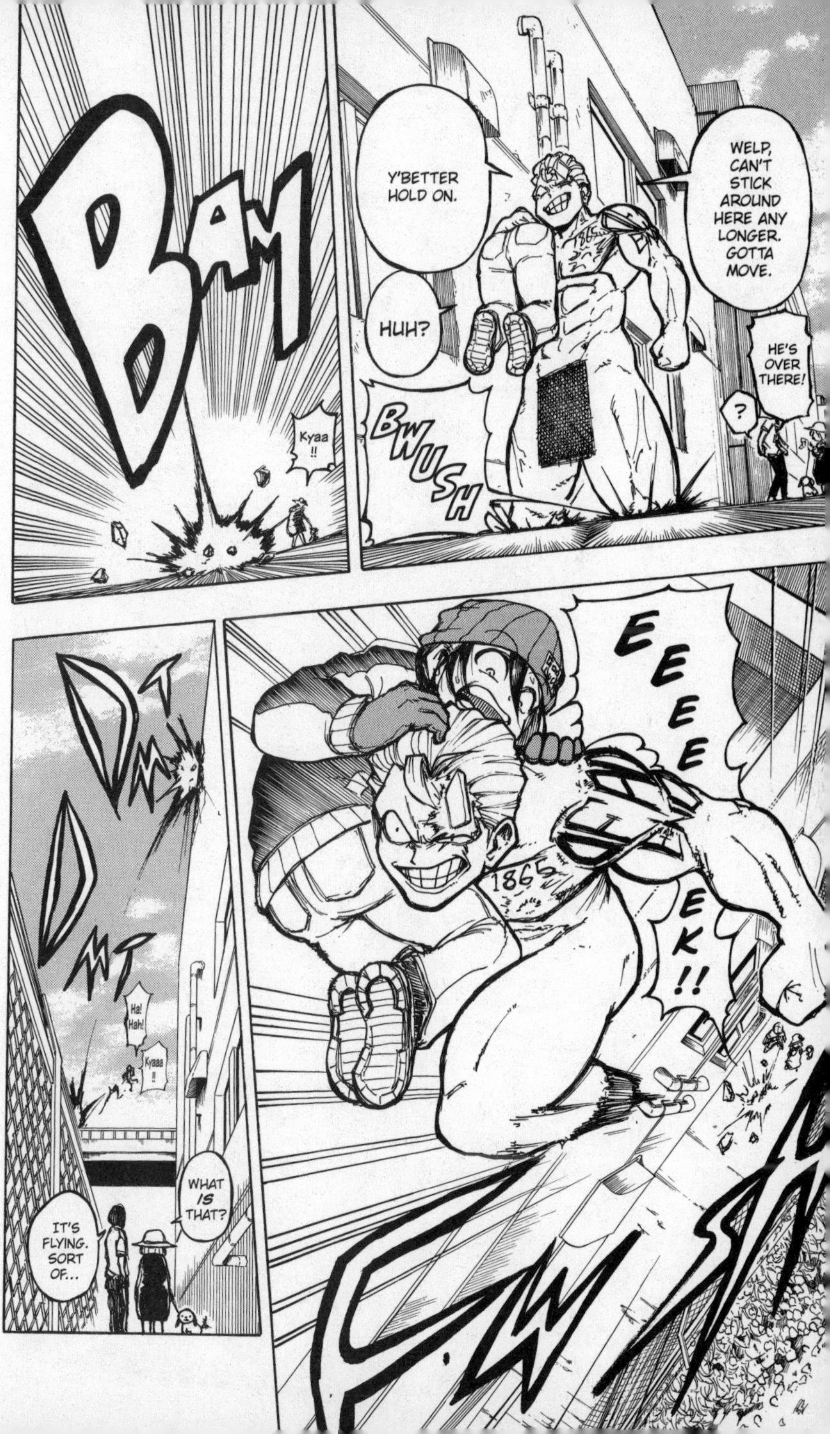
WELP, CAN'T STICK AROUND HERE ANY LONGER. GOTTA MOVE.
Y'BETTER HOLD ON.
HE'S OVER THERE!
HUH?
?
BWUSH
BAM
Kyaa!!
EEEEEK!!
Ha! Hah!
Kyaaa!!
WHAT IS THAT?
IT'S FLYING. SORT OF...

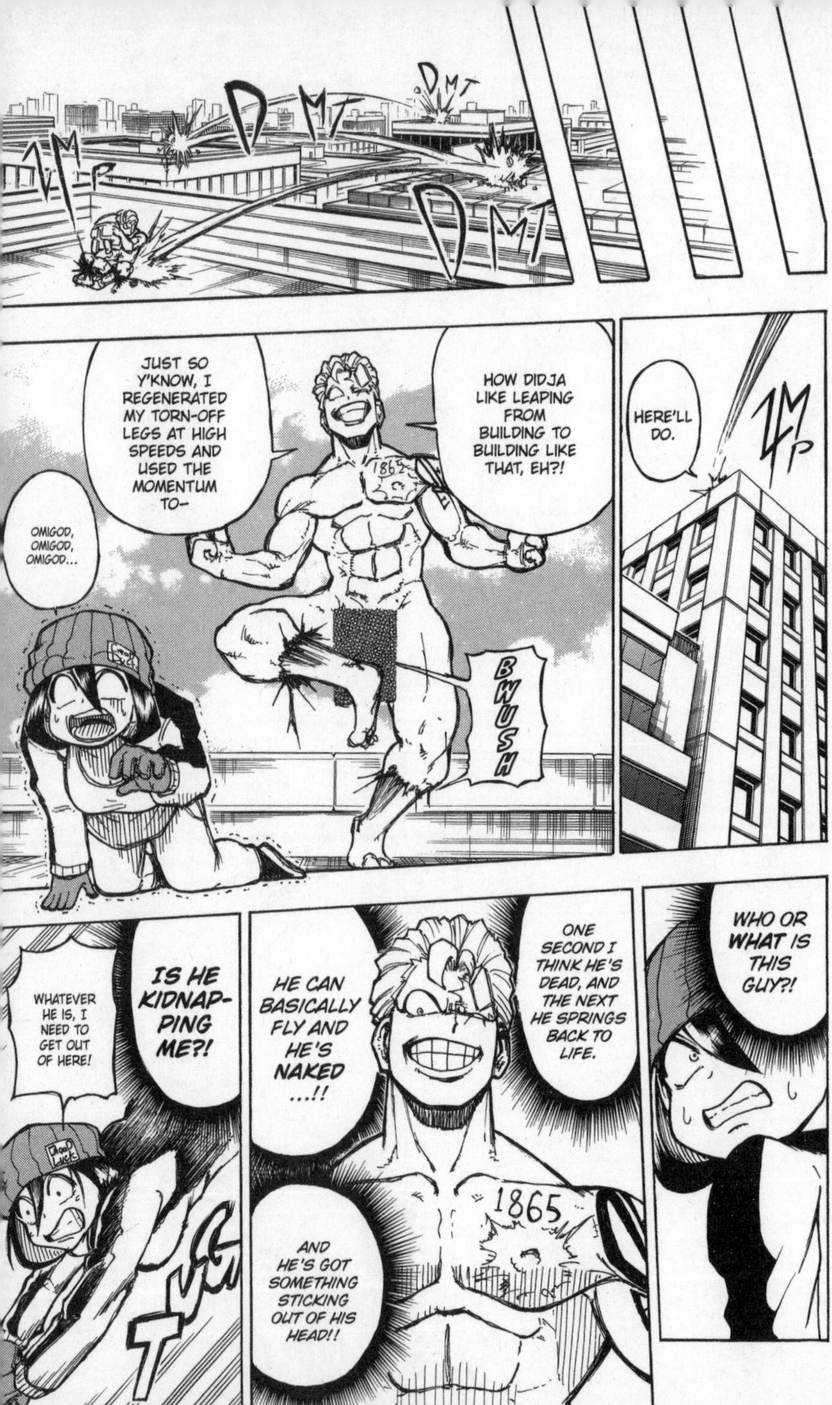
DMT
DMT
DMT
ZMP
HERE'LL DO.
ZMP
HOW DIDJA LIKE LEAPING FROM BUILDING TO BUILDING LIKE THAT, EH?!
JUST SO Y'KNOW, I REGENERATED MY TORN-OFF LEGS AT HIGH SPEEDS AND USED THE MOMENTUM TO—
OMIGOD, OMIGOD, OMIGOD...
BWUSH
WHO OR WHAT IS THIS GUY?!
ONE SECOND I THINK HE'S DEAD, AND THE NEXT HE SPRINGS BACK TO LIFE.
HE CAN BASICALLY FLY AND HE'S NAKED ...!!
1865
AND HE'S GOT SOMETHING STICKING OUT OF HIS HEAD!!
IS HE KIDNAPPING ME?!
WHATEVER HE IS, I NEED TO GET OUT OF HERE!
GOOD LUCK

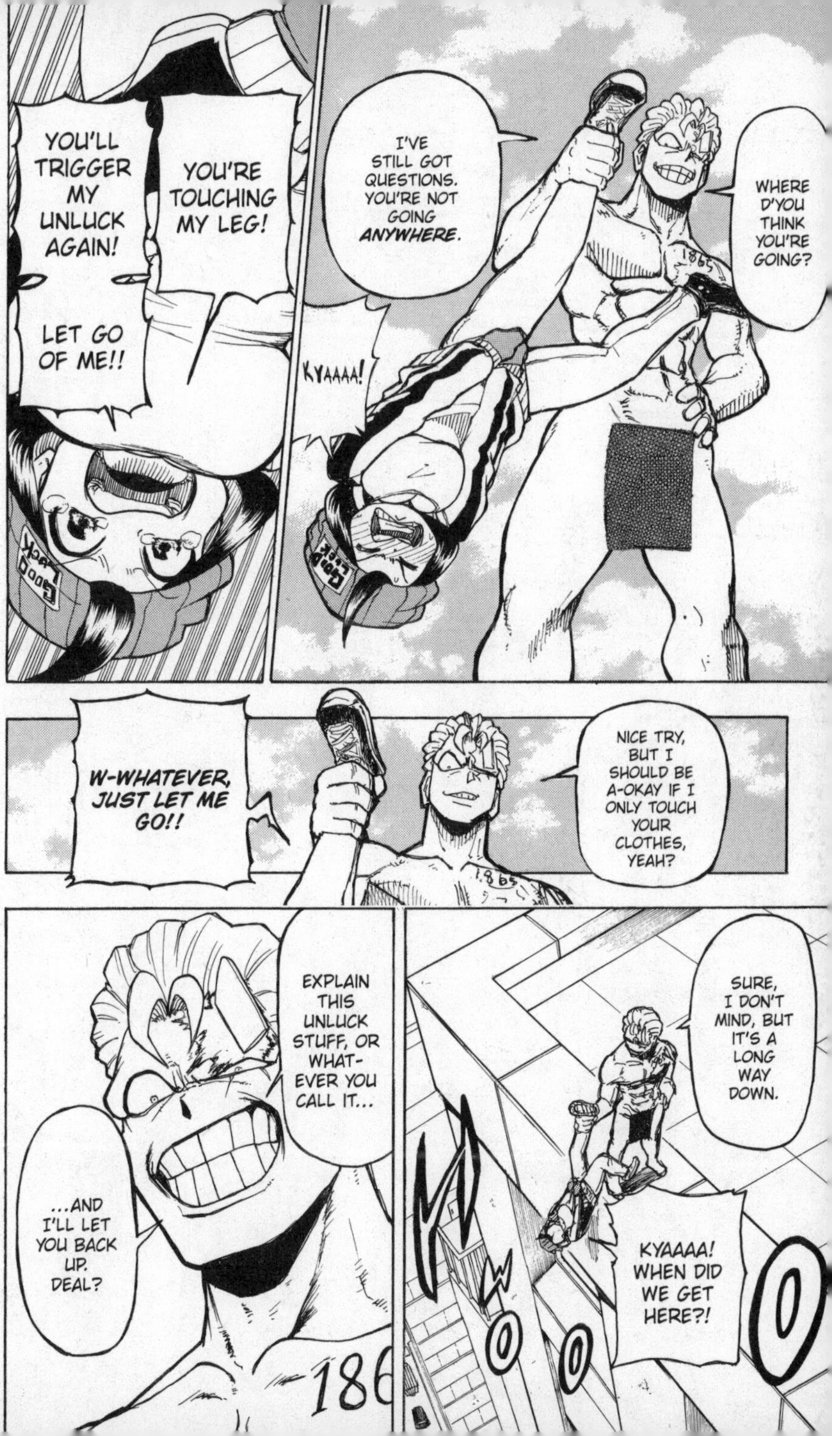
WHERE D'YOU THINK YOU'RE GOING?
I'VE STILL GOT QUESTIONS. YOU'RE NOT GOING *ANYWHERE*.
KYAAAA!
YOU'RE TOUCHING MY LEG!
YOU'LL TRIGGER MY UNLUCK AGAIN!
LET GO OF ME!!
NICE TRY, BUT I SHOULD BE A-OKAY IF I ONLY TOUCH YOUR CLOTHES, YEAH?
W-WHATEVER, JUST LET ME GO!!
SURE, I DON'T MIND, BUT IT'S A LONG WAY DOWN.
KYAAAA! WHEN DID WE GET HERE?!
EXPLAIN THIS UNLUCK STUFF, OR WHAT-EVER YOU CALL IT...
...AND I'LL LET YOU BACK UP. DEAL?

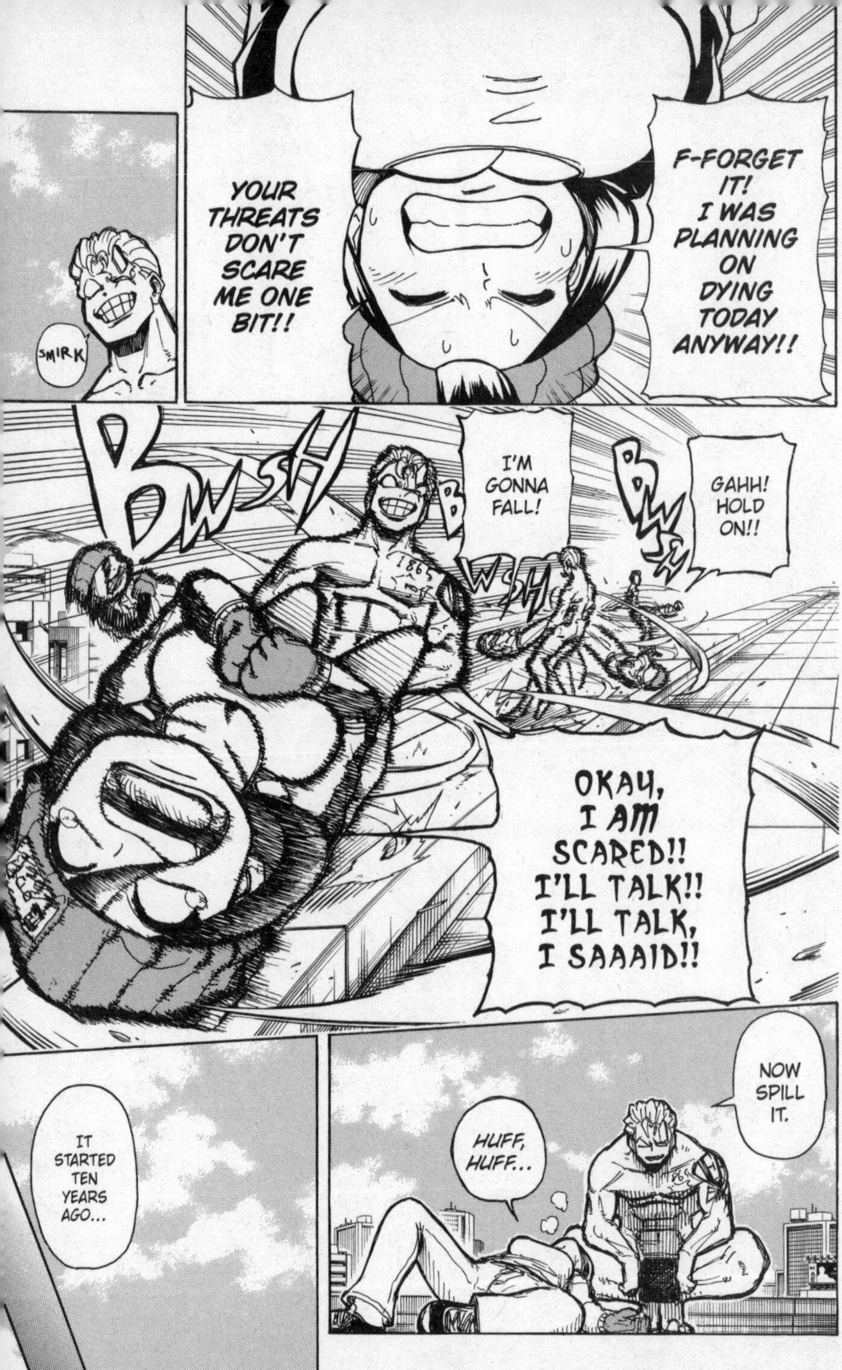
F-FORGET IT! I WAS PLANNING ON DYING TODAY ANYWAY!!
YOUR THREATS DON'T SCARE ME ONE BIT!!
SMIRK
GAHH! HOLD ON!!
BWSH
I'M GONNA FALL!
BWSH
BWSH
OKAY, I AM SCARED!! I'LL TALK!! I'LL TALK, I SAAAID!!
NOW SPILL IT.
HUFF, HUFF...
IT STARTED TEN YEARS AGO...

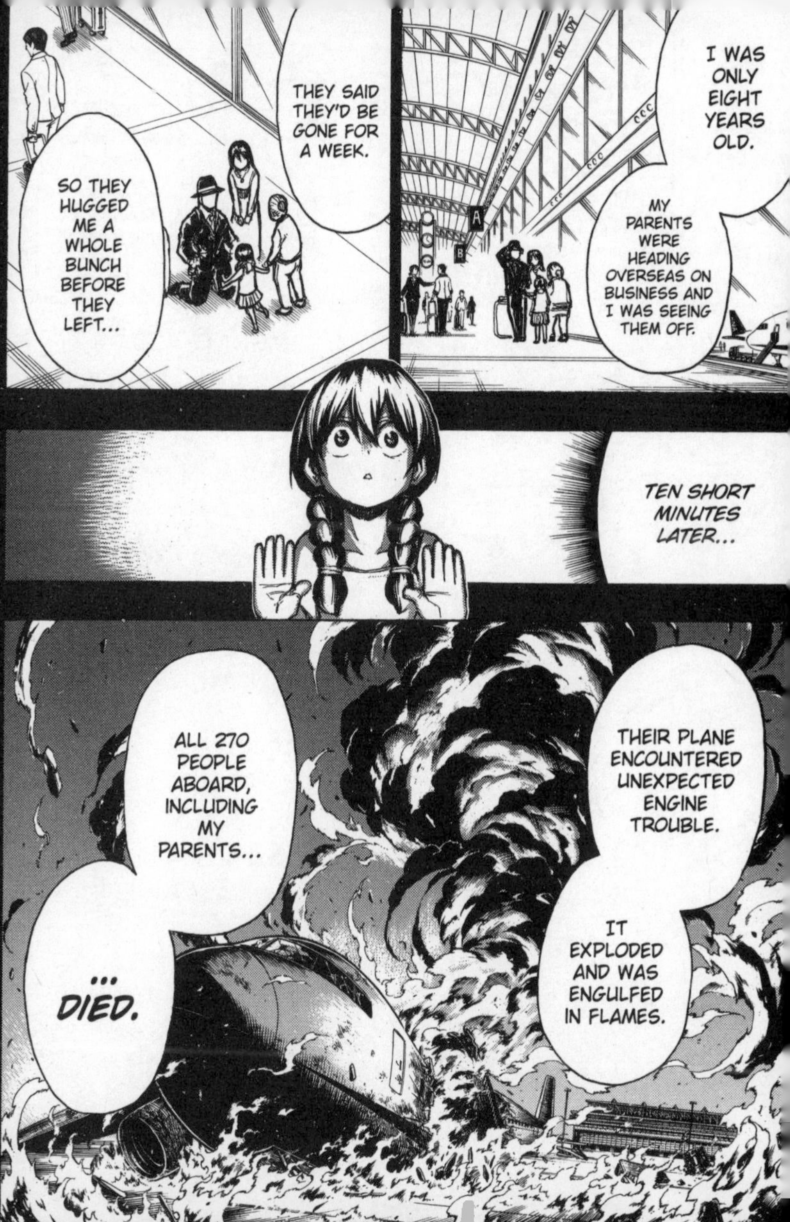
I WAS ONLY EIGHT YEARS OLD.
MY PARENTS WERE HEADING OVERSEAS ON BUSINESS AND I WAS SEEING THEM OFF.
THEY SAID THEY'D BE GONE FOR A WEEK.
SO THEY HUGGED ME A WHOLE BUNCH BEFORE THEY LEFT...
TEN SHORT MINUTES LATER...
THEIR PLANE ENCOUNTERED UNEXPECTED ENGINE TROUBLE.
IT EXPLODED AND WAS ENGULFED IN FLAMES.
ALL 270 PEOPLE ABOARD, INCLUDING MY PARENTS...
...DIED.

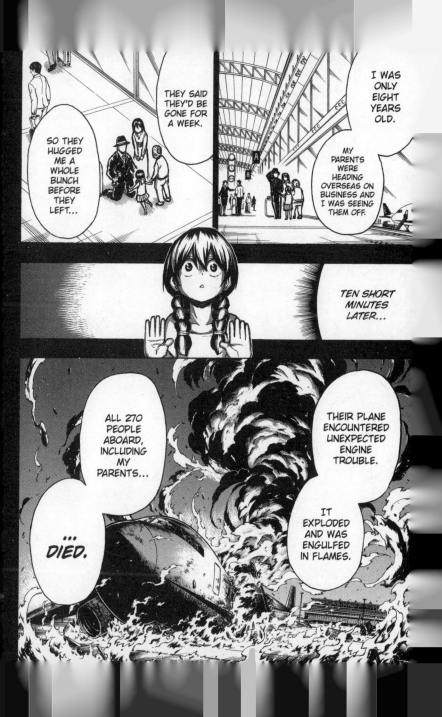

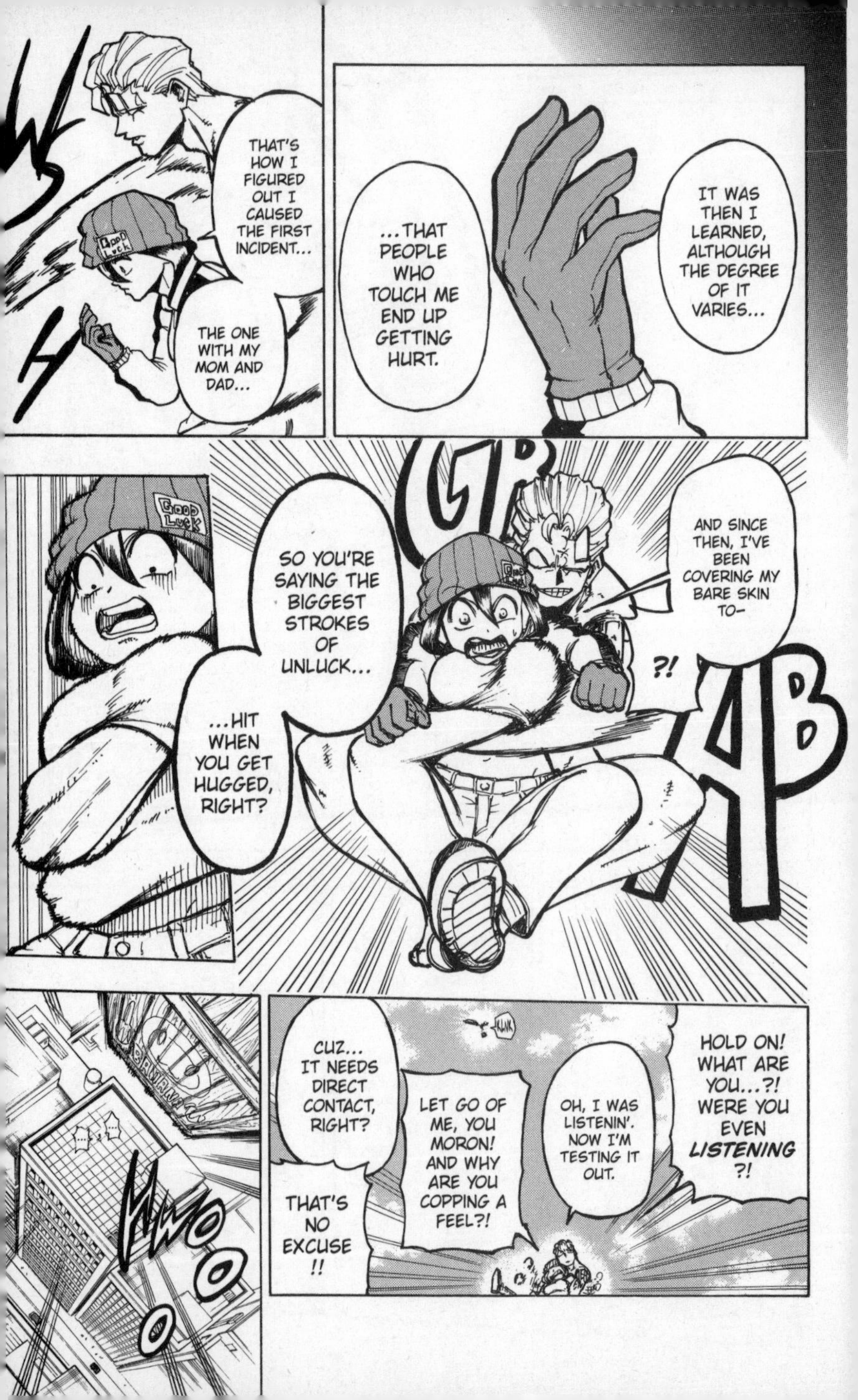
IT WAS THEN I LEARNED, ALTHOUGH THE DEGREE OF IT VARIES...
...THAT PEOPLE WHO TOUCH ME END UP GETTING HURT.
THAT'S HOW I FIGURED OUT I CAUSED THE FIRST INCIDENT...
THE ONE WITH MY MOM AND DAD...
AND SINCE THEN, I'VE BEEN COVERING MY BARE SKIN TO–
?!
GRAB
SO YOU'RE SAYING THE BIGGEST STROKES OF UNLUCK...
...HIT WHEN YOU GET HUGGED, RIGHT?
HOLD ON! WHAT ARE YOU...?! WERE YOU EVEN *LISTENING*?!
OH, I WAS LISTENIN'. NOW I'M TESTING IT OUT.
LET GO OF ME, YOU MORON! AND WHY ARE YOU COPPING A FEEL?!
CUZ... IT NEEDS DIRECT CONTACT, RIGHT?
THAT'S NO EXCUSE!!

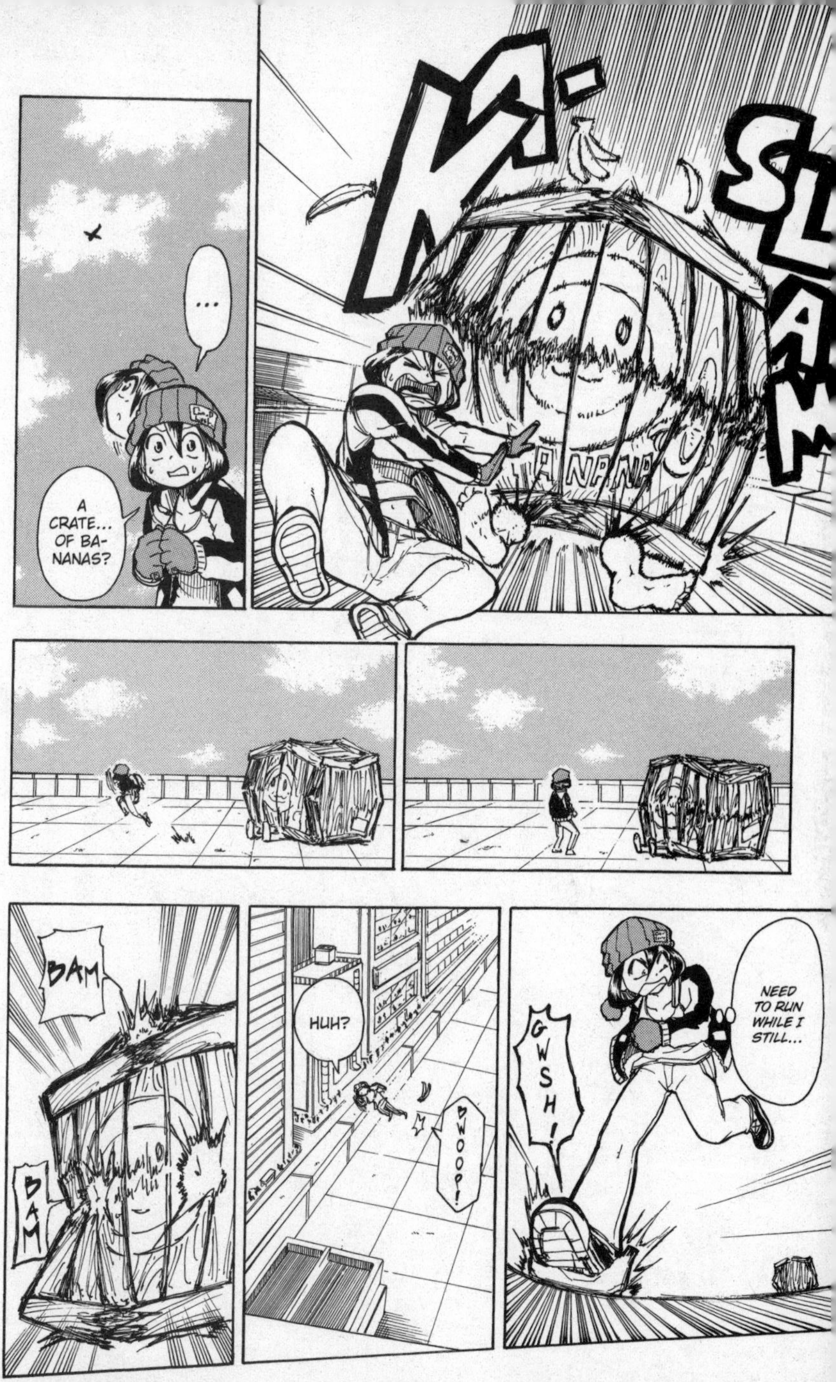
KA-
SLAM
...
A CRATE... OF BA-NANAS?
NEED TO RUN WHILE I STILL...
GWSH!
HUH?
BWOOP!
BAM
BAM

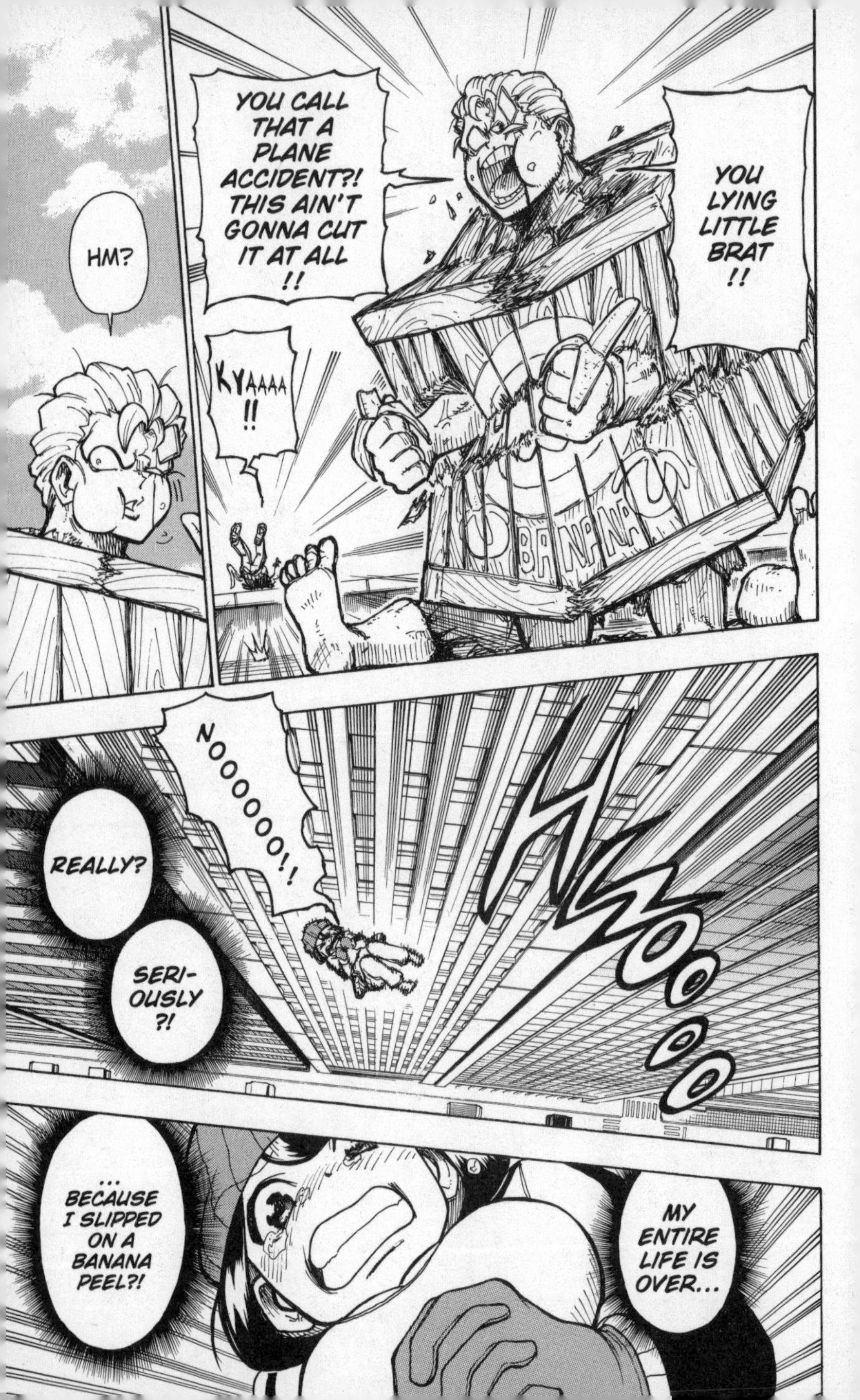
YOU LYING LITTLE BRAT !!
YOU CALL THAT A PLANE ACCIDENT?! THIS AIN'T GONNA CUT IT AT ALL !!
BANANA
KYAAAA !!
HM?
NOOOOOOO!!
REALLY?
SERI-OUSLY ?!
MY ENTIRE LIFE IS OVER...
...BECAUSE I SLIPPED ON A BANANA PEEL?!

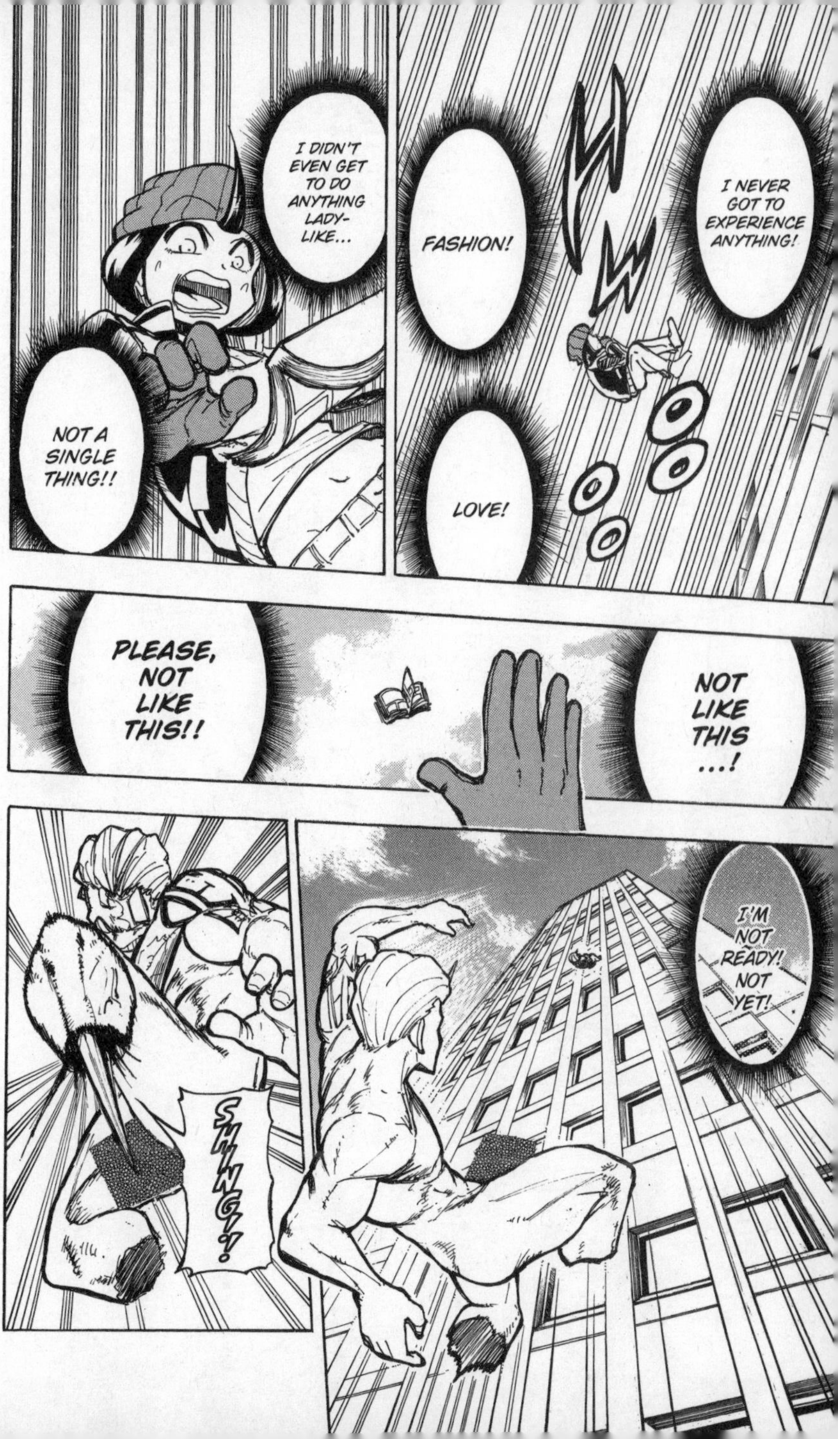
I NEVER GOT TO EXPERIENCE ANYTHING!
FASHION!
LOVE!
I DIDN'T EVEN GET TO DO ANYTHING LADY-LIKE...
NOT A SINGLE THING!!
NOT LIKE THIS...!
PLEASE, NOT LIKE THIS!!
I'M NOT READY! NOT YET!
SHING!?!

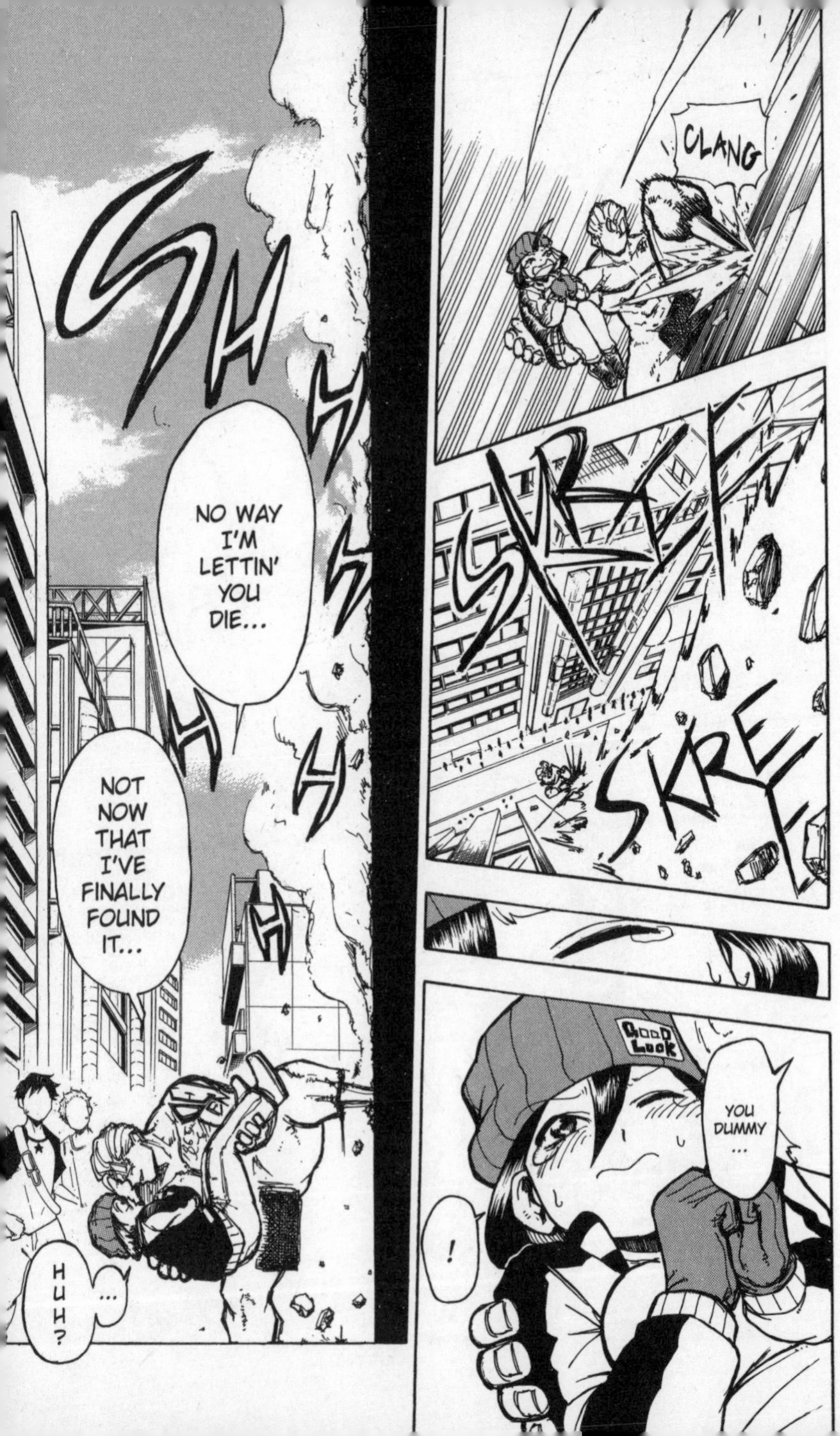
CLANG
SKREE
YOU DUMMY...
!
NO WAY I'M LETTIN' YOU DIE...
NOT NOW THAT I'VE FINALLY FOUND IT...
HUH...?

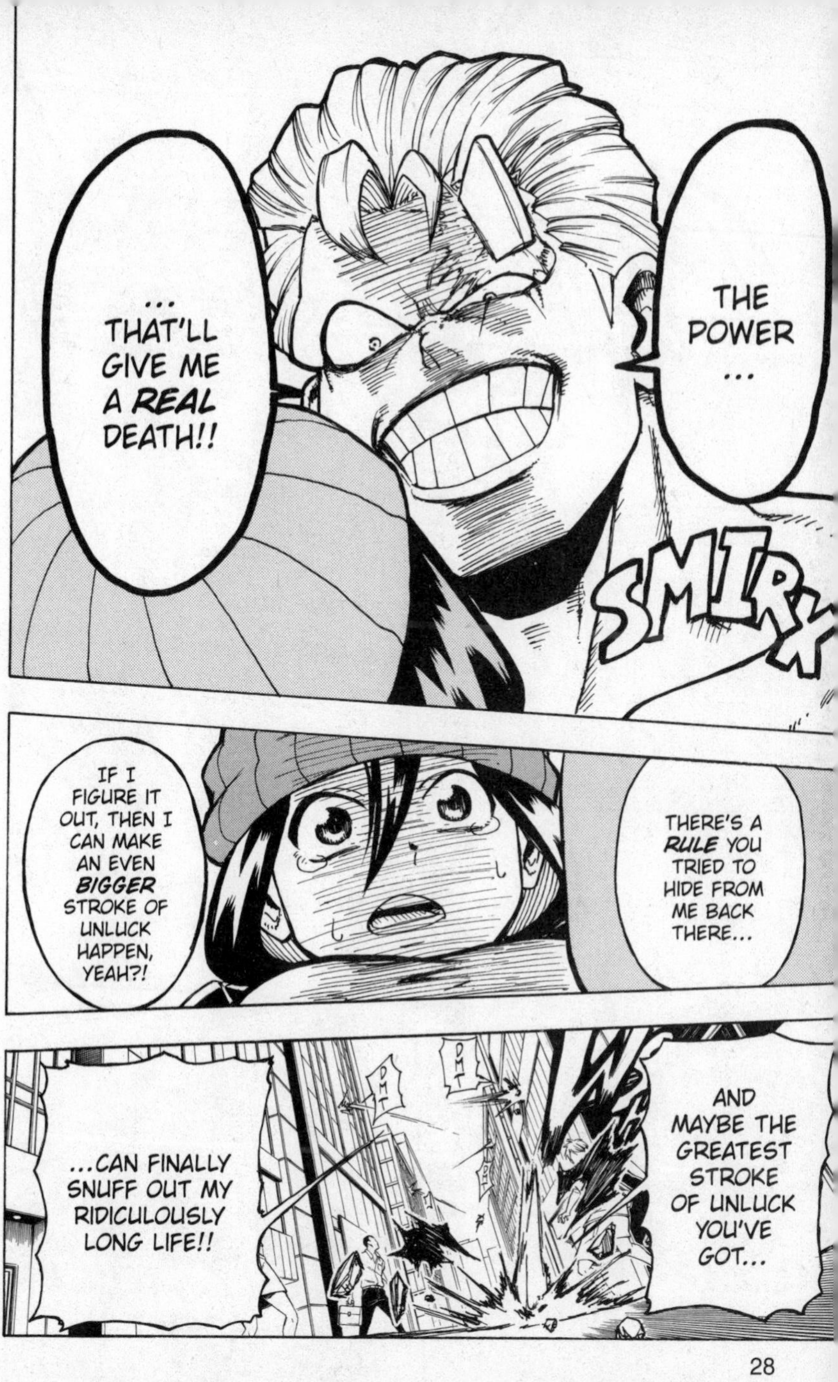
THE POWER ...
... THAT'LL GIVE ME A REAL DEATH!!
SMIRK
THERE'S A RULE YOU TRIED TO HIDE FROM ME BACK THERE...
IF I FIGURE IT OUT, THEN I CAN MAKE AN EVEN BIGGER STROKE OF UNLUCK HAPPEN, YEAH?!
AND MAYBE THE GREATEST STROKE OF UNLUCK YOU'VE GOT...
...CAN FINALLY SNUFF OUT MY RIDICULOUSLY LONG LIFE!!

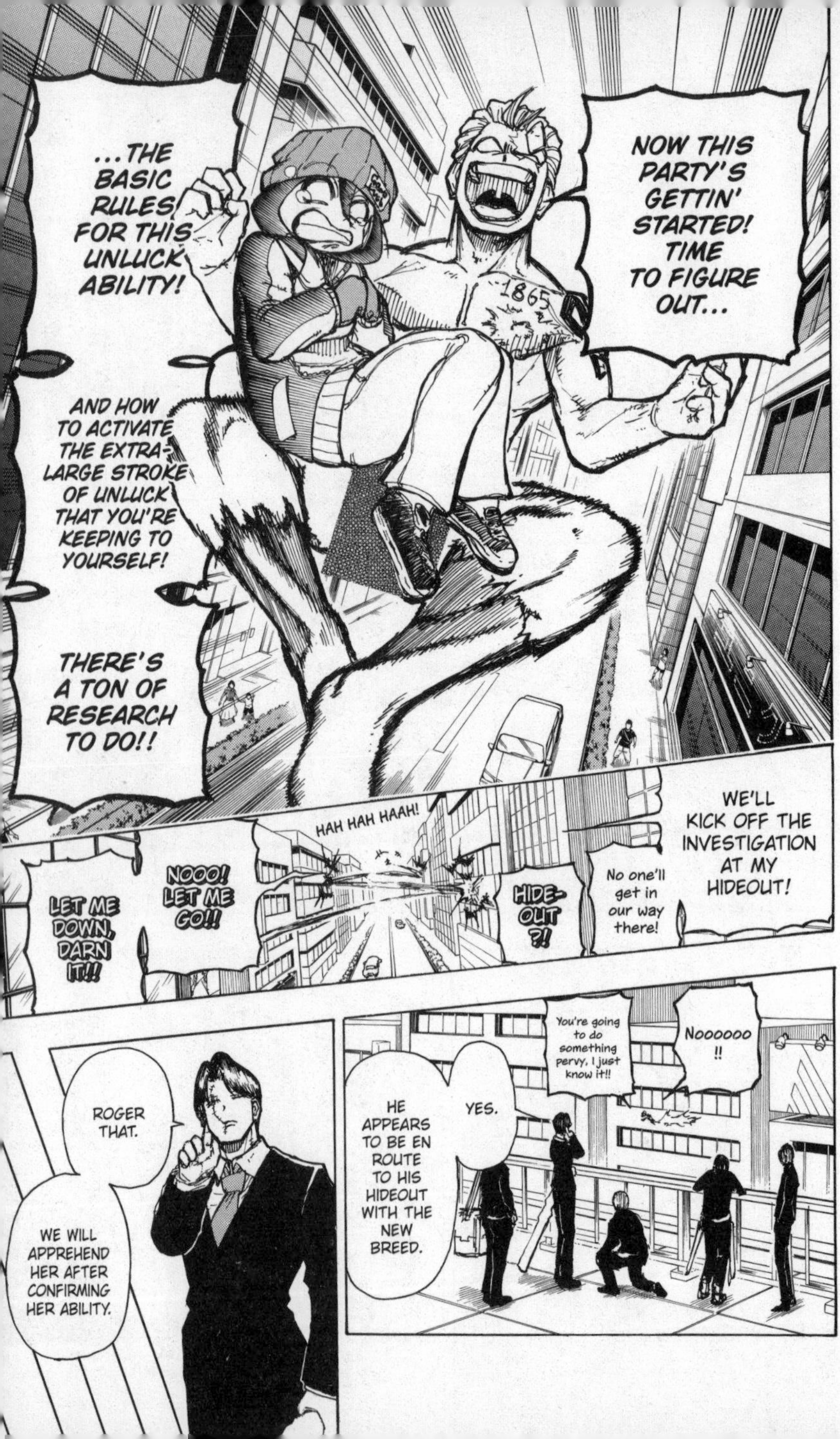
NOW THIS PARTY'S GETTIN' STARTED! TIME TO FIGURE OUT...
...THE BASIC RULES FOR THIS UNLUCK ABILITY!
AND HOW TO ACTIVATE THE EXTRA-LARGE STROKE OF UNLUCK THAT YOU'RE KEEPING TO YOURSELF!
THERE'S A TON OF RESEARCH TO DO!!
WE'LL KICK OFF THE INVESTIGATION AT MY HIDEOUT!
No one'll get in our way there!
HIDE-OUT ?!
HAH HAH HAAH!
NOOO! LET ME GO!!
LET ME DOWN, DARN IT!!
Noooooo !!
You're going to do something pervy, I just know it!!
YES.
HE APPEARS TO BE EN ROUTE TO HIS HIDEOUT WITH THE NEW BREED.
ROGER THAT.
WE WILL APPREHEND HER AFTER CONFIRMING HER ABILITY.

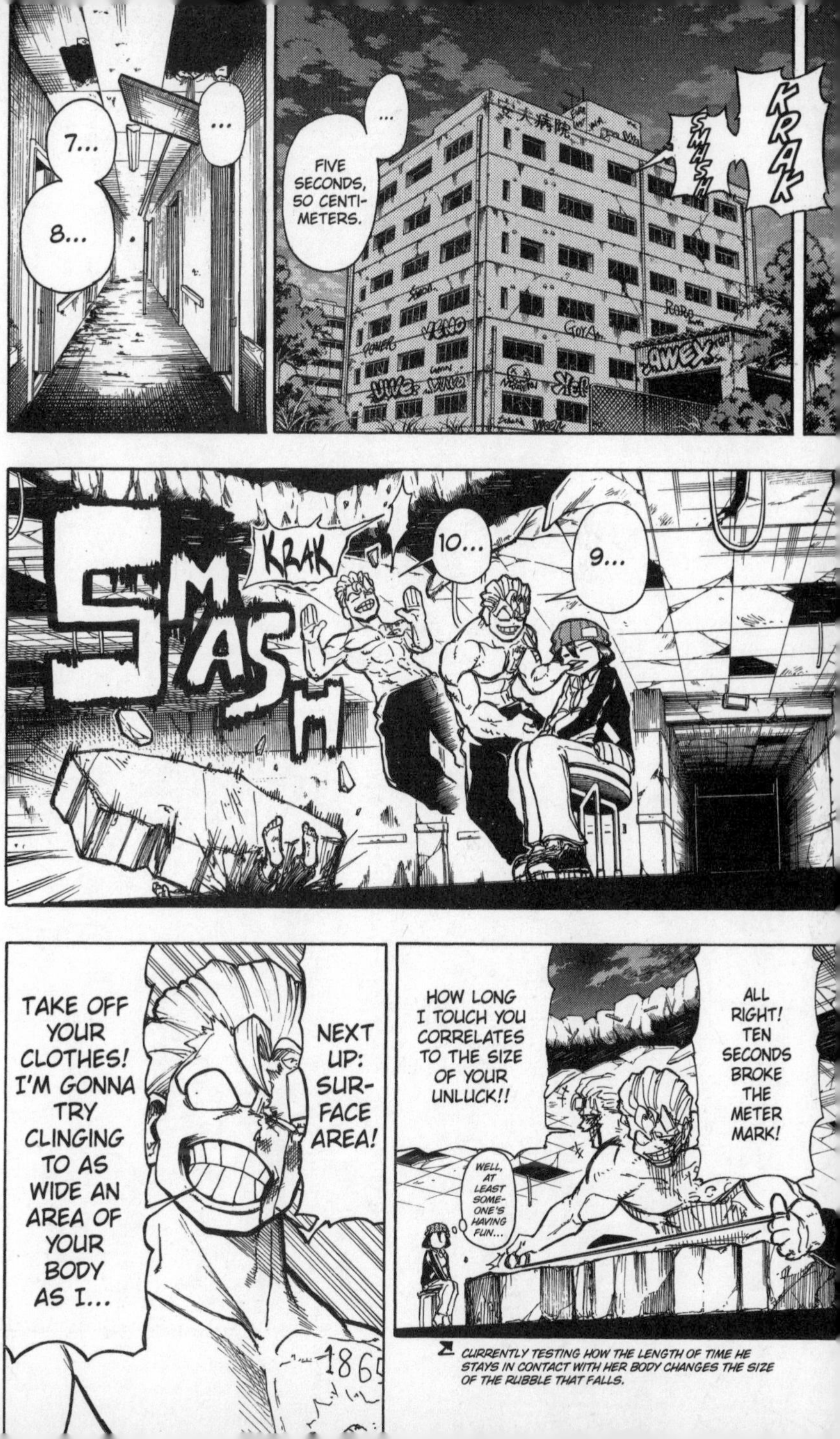
KRAK
SMASH
...
FIVE SECONDS, 50 CENTIMETERS.
...
7...
8...
9...
10...
KRAK
SMASH
ALL RIGHT! TEN SECONDS BROKE THE METER MARK!
HOW LONG I TOUCH YOU CORRELATES TO THE SIZE OF YOUR UNLUCK!!
WELL, AT LEAST SOME-ONE'S HAVING FUN...
NEXT UP: SUR-FACE AREA!
TAKE OFF YOUR CLOTHES! I'M GONNA TRY CLINGING TO AS WIDE AN AREA OF YOUR BODY AS I...

CURRENTLY TESTING HOW THE LENGTH OF TIME HE STAYS IN CONTACT WITH HER BODY CHANGES THE SIZE OF THE RUBBLE THAT FALLS.

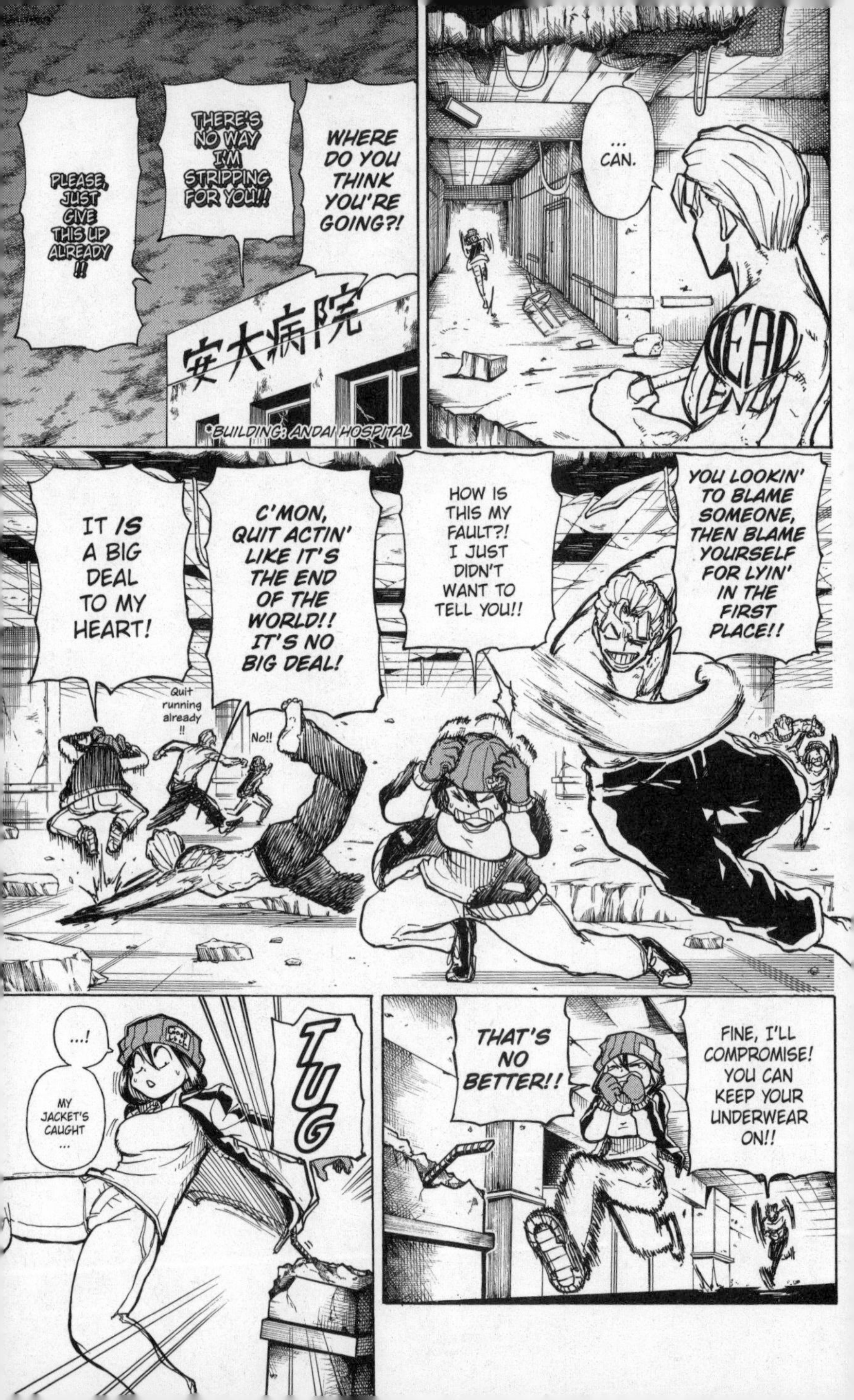
... CAN.
WHERE DO YOU THINK YOU'RE GOING?!
THERE'S NO WAY I'M STRIPPING FOR YOU!!
PLEASE, JUST GIVE THIS UP ALREADY!!
安大病院
*BUILDING: ANDAI HOSPITAL
YOU LOOKIN' TO BLAME SOMEONE, THEN BLAME YOURSELF FOR LYIN' IN THE FIRST PLACE!!
HOW IS THIS MY FAULT?! I JUST DIDN'T WANT TO TELL YOU!!
C'MON, QUIT ACTIN' LIKE IT'S THE END OF THE WORLD!! IT'S NO BIG DEAL!
IT IS A BIG DEAL TO MY HEART!
No!!
Quit running already!!
FINE, I'LL COMPROMISE! YOU CAN KEEP YOUR UNDERWEAR ON!!
THAT'S NO BETTER!!
TUG
...!
MY JACKET'S CAUGHT...

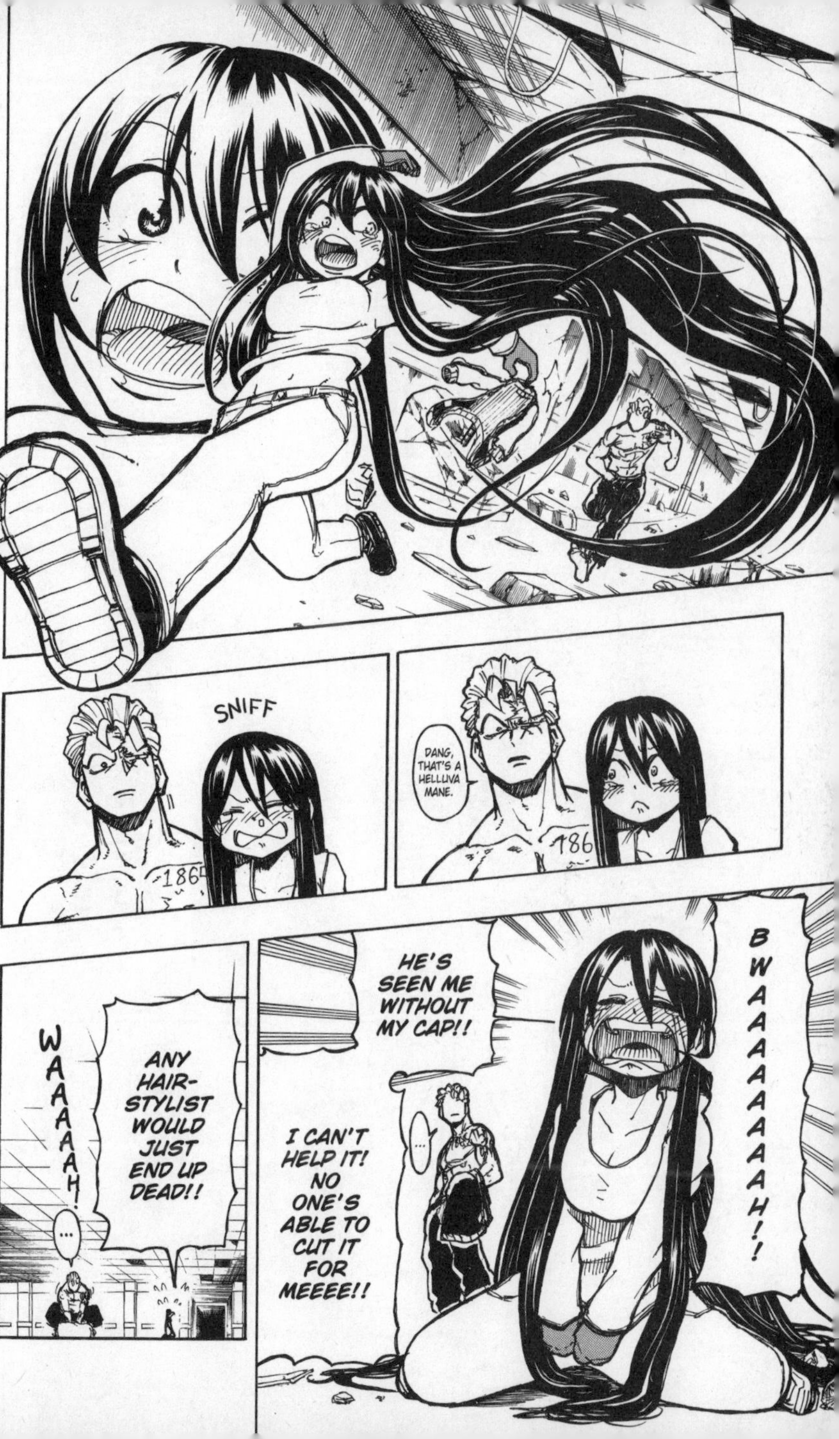
DANG, THAT'S A HELLUVA MANE.
SNIFF
BWAAAAAAAAH!!
HE'S SEEN ME WITHOUT MY CAP!!
I CAN'T HELP IT! NO ONE'S ABLE TO CUT IT FOR MEEEE!!
...
ANY HAIR-STYLIST WOULD JUST END UP DEAD!!
WAAAAAH!
...

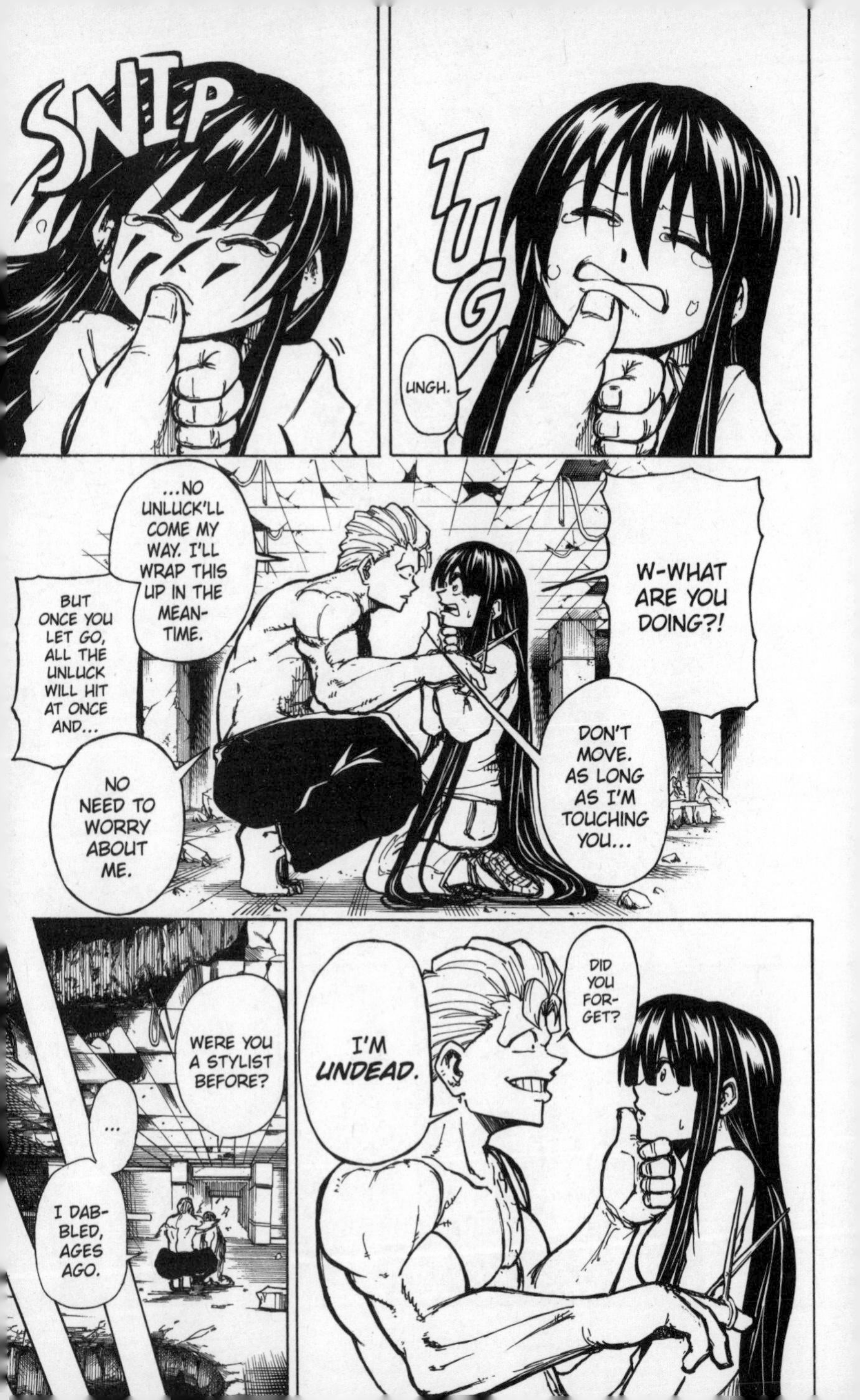
TUG
UNGH.
SNIP
W-WHAT ARE YOU DOING?!
DON'T MOVE. AS LONG AS I'M TOUCHING YOU...
BUT ONCE YOU LET GO, ALL THE UNLUCK WILL HIT AT ONCE AND...
NO NEED TO WORRY ABOUT ME.
...NO UNLUCK'LL COME MY WAY. I'LL WRAP THIS UP IN THE MEAN-TIME.
DID YOU FOR-GET?
I'M *UNDEAD.*
WERE YOU A STYLIST BEFORE?
...
I DAB-BLED, AGES AGO.

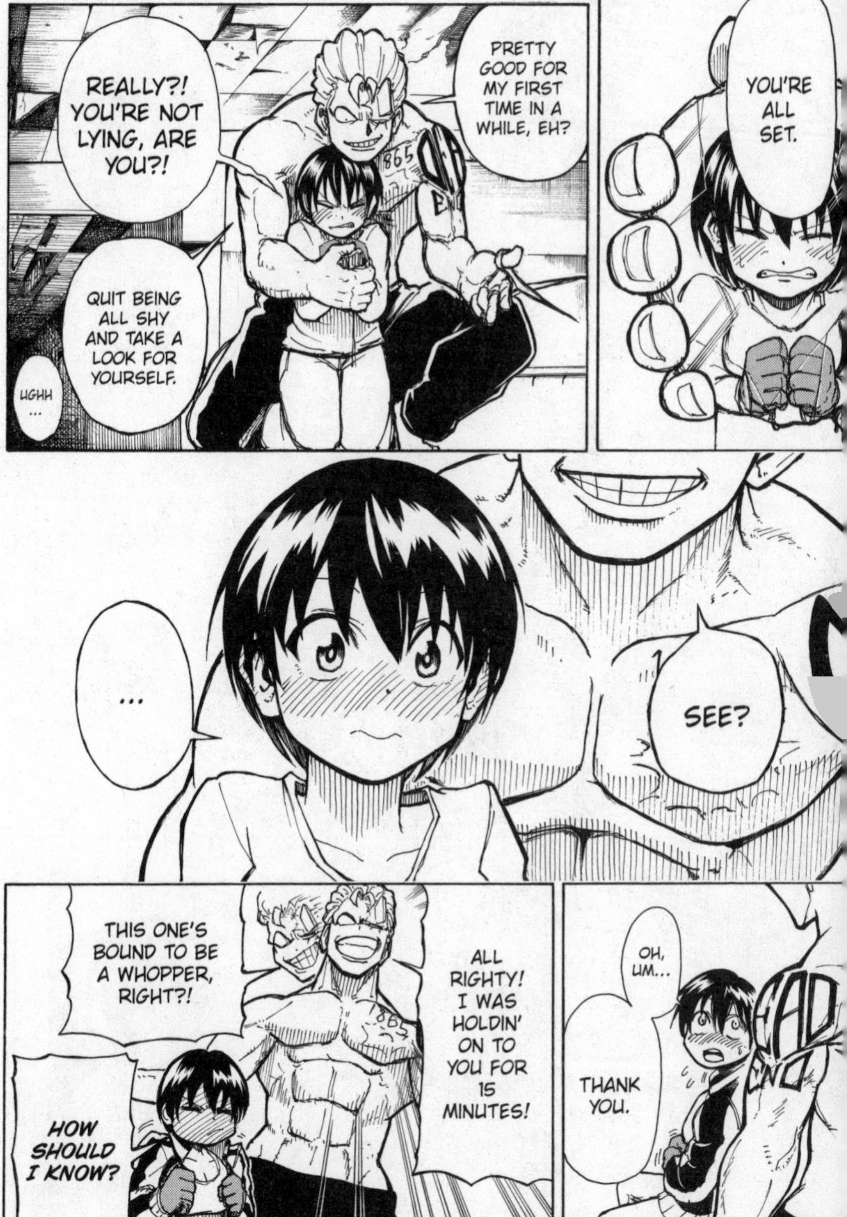
YOU'RE ALL SET.
PRETTY GOOD FOR MY FIRST TIME IN A WHILE, EH?
REALLY?! YOU'RE NOT LYING, ARE YOU?!
QUIT BEING ALL SHY AND TAKE A LOOK FOR YOURSELF.
UGHH ...
SEE?
...
OH, UM...
THANK YOU.
ALL RIGHTY! I WAS HOLDIN' ON TO YOU FOR 15 MINUTES!
THIS ONE'S BOUND TO BE A WHOPPER, RIGHT?!
HOW SHOULD I KNOW?

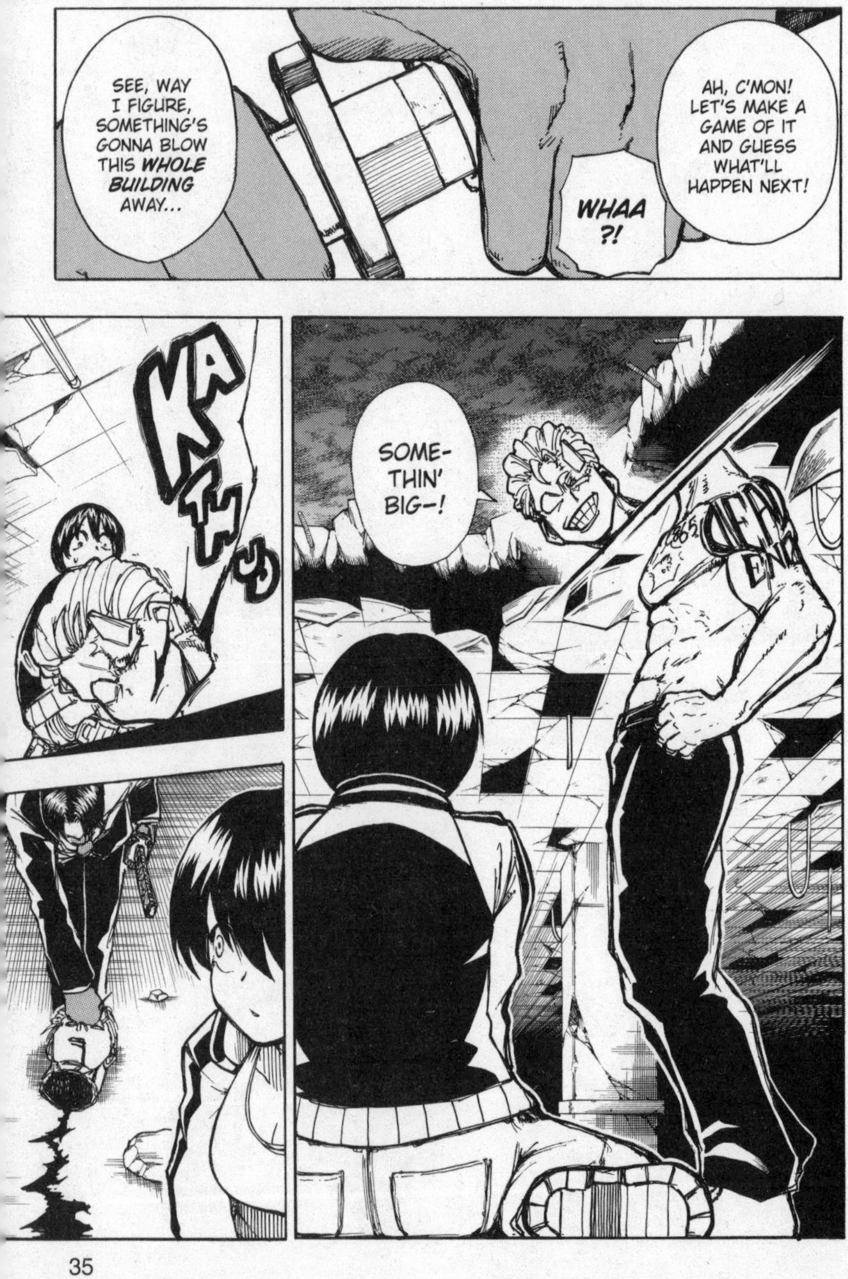
AH, C'MON! LET'S MAKE A GAME OF IT AND GUESS WHAT'LL HAPPEN NEXT!
WHAA ?!
SEE, WAY I FIGURE, SOMETHING'S GONNA BLOW THIS ***WHOLE BUILDING*** AWAY...
SOME-THIN' BIG-!
KATHUD

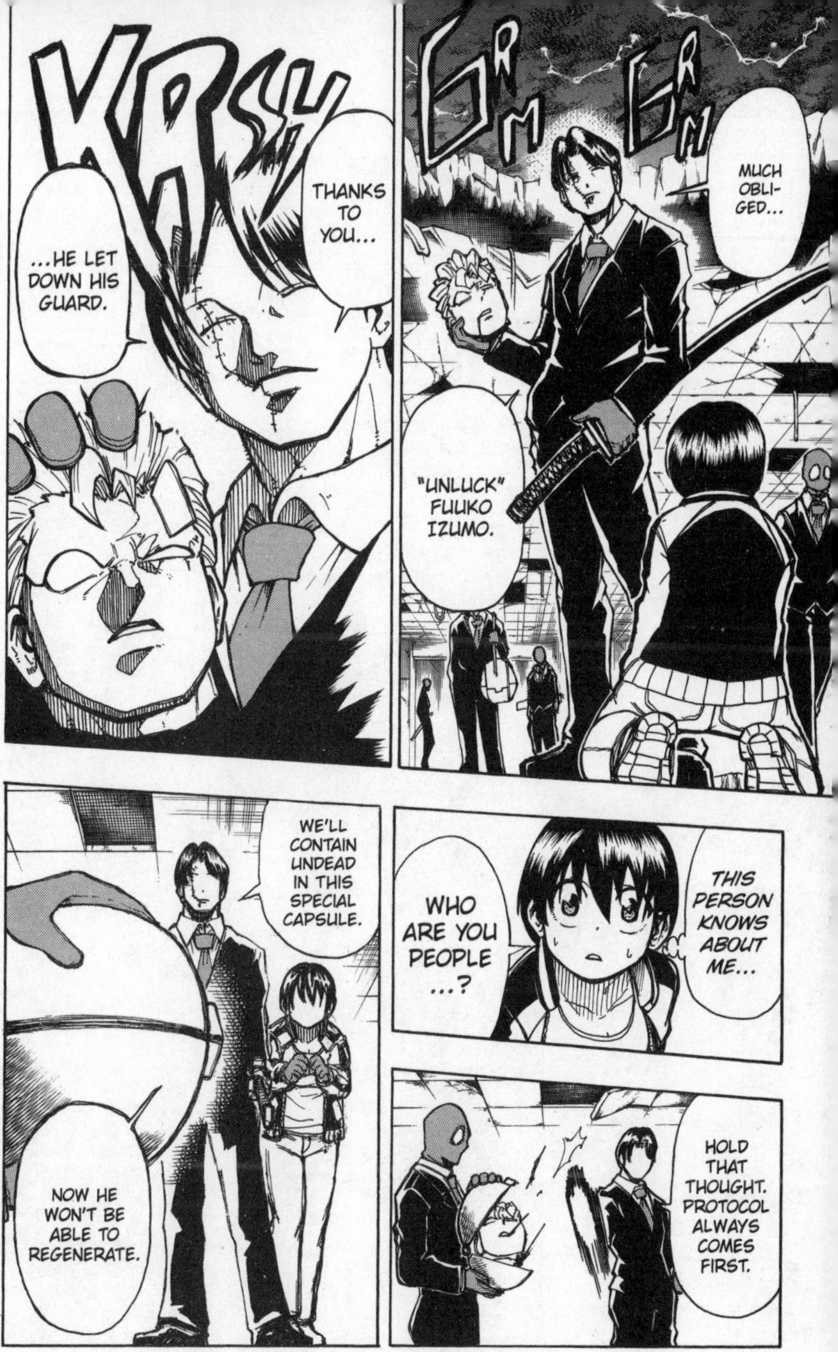
GRM GRM
MUCH OBLIGED...
"UNLUCK" FUUKO IZUMO.
KRSSH
THANKS TO YOU...
...HE LET DOWN HIS GUARD.
THIS PERSON KNOWS ABOUT ME...
WHO ARE YOU PEOPLE ...?
HOLD THAT THOUGHT. PROTOCOL ALWAYS COMES FIRST.
WE'LL CONTAIN UNDEAD IN THIS SPECIAL CAPSULE.
NOW HE WON'T BE ABLE TO REGENERATE.

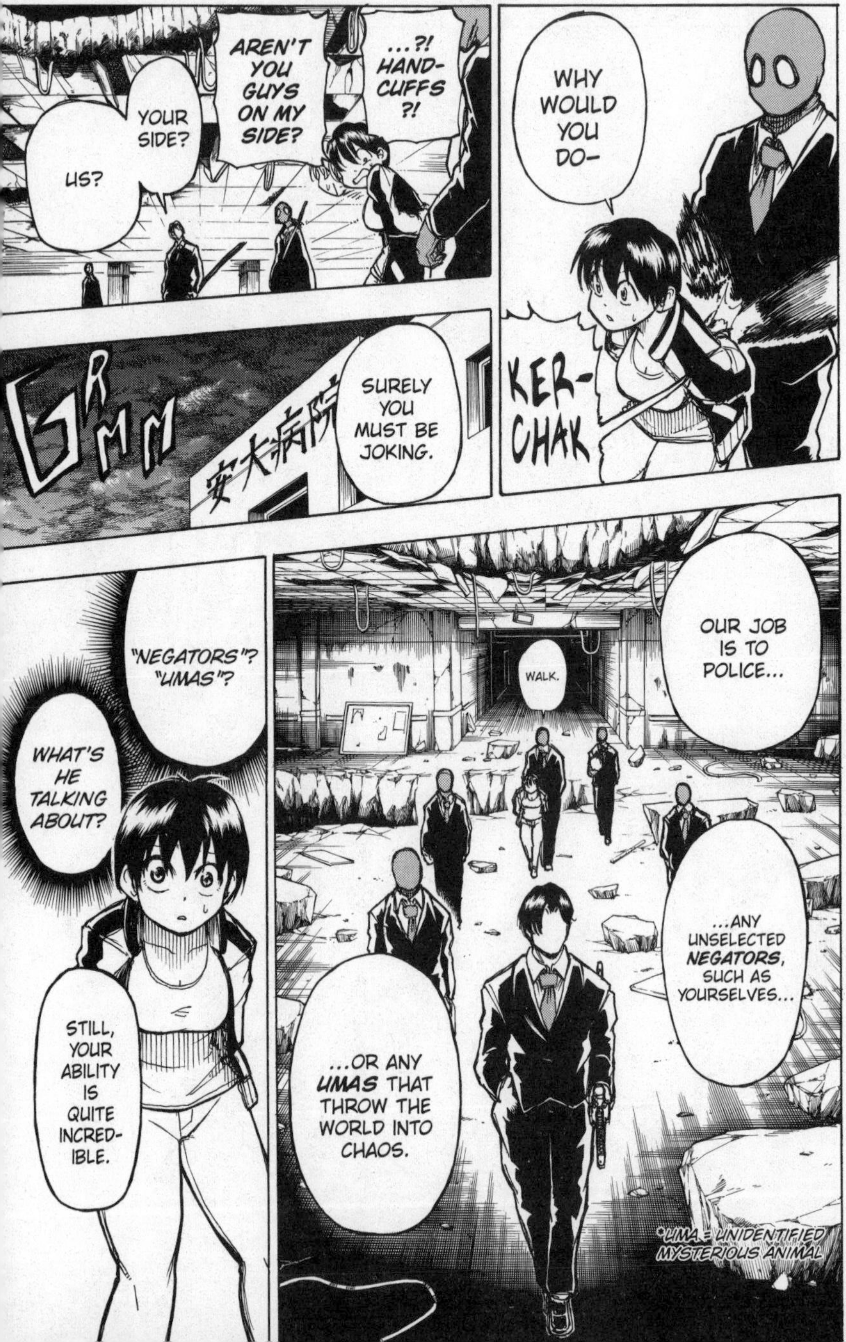
WHY WOULD YOU DO-
...?! HANDCUFFS?!
AREN'T YOU GUYS ON MY SIDE?
YOUR SIDE?
US?
KER-CHAK
SURELY YOU MUST BE JOKING.
安大病院
GRMM
OUR JOB IS TO POLICE...
WALK.
...ANY UNSELECTED NEGATORS, SUCH AS YOURSELVES...
...OR ANY UMAS THAT THROW THE WORLD INTO CHAOS.
*UMA = UNIDENTIFIED MYSTERIOUS ANIMAL
"NEGATORS"? "UMAS"?
WHAT'S HE TALKING ABOUT?
STILL, YOUR ABILITY IS QUITE INCREDIBLE.

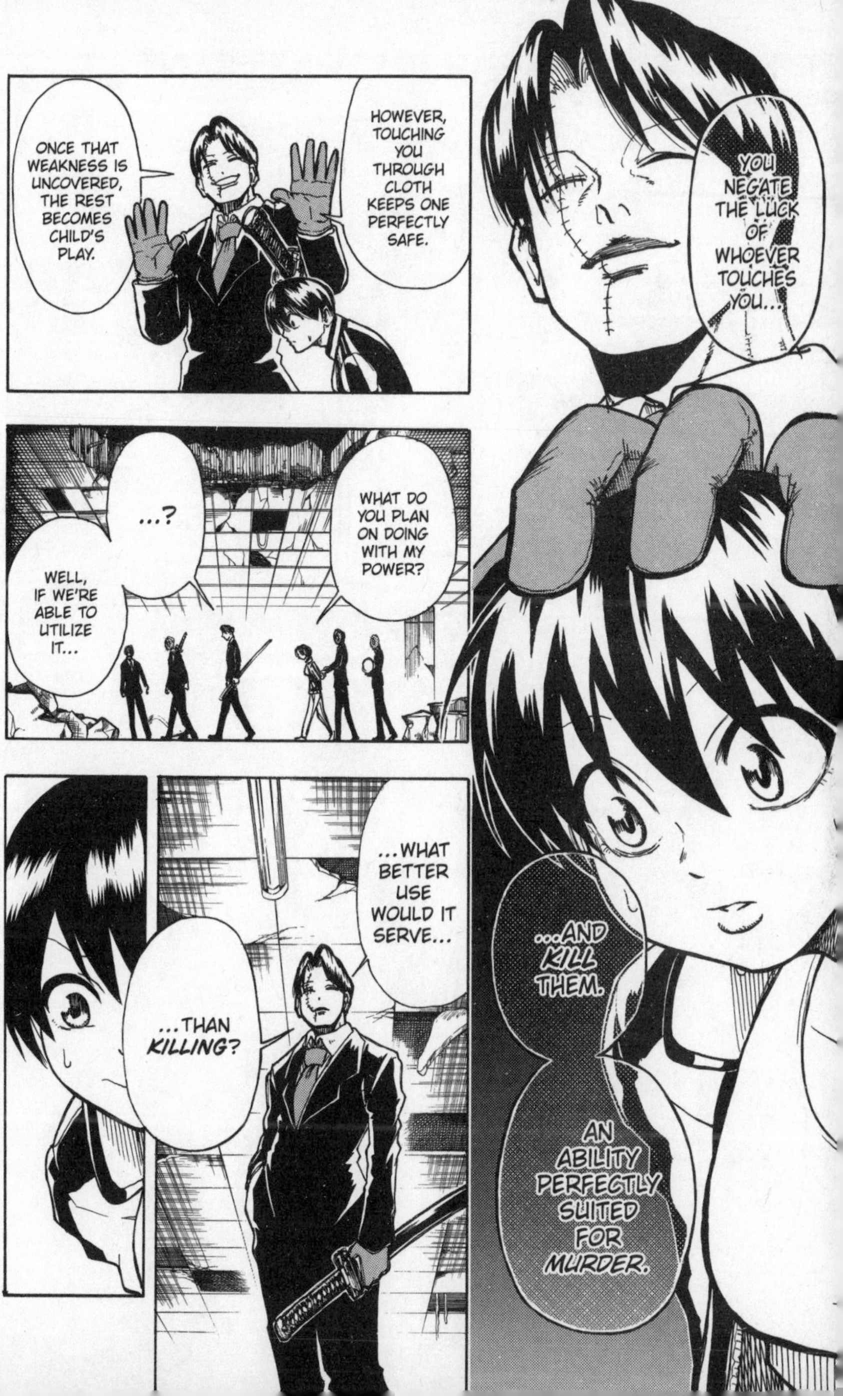
YOU NEGATE THE LUCK OF WHOEVER TOUCHES YOU...
...AND *KILL* THEM.
AN ABILITY PERFECTLY SUITED FOR *MURDER*.
HOWEVER, TOUCHING YOU THROUGH CLOTH KEEPS ONE PERFECTLY SAFE.
ONCE THAT WEAKNESS IS UNCOVERED, THE REST BECOMES CHILD'S PLAY.
WHAT DO YOU PLAN ON DOING WITH MY POWER?
...?
WELL, IF WE'RE ABLE TO UTILIZE IT...
...WHAT BETTER USE WOULD IT SERVE...
...THAN *KILLING*?

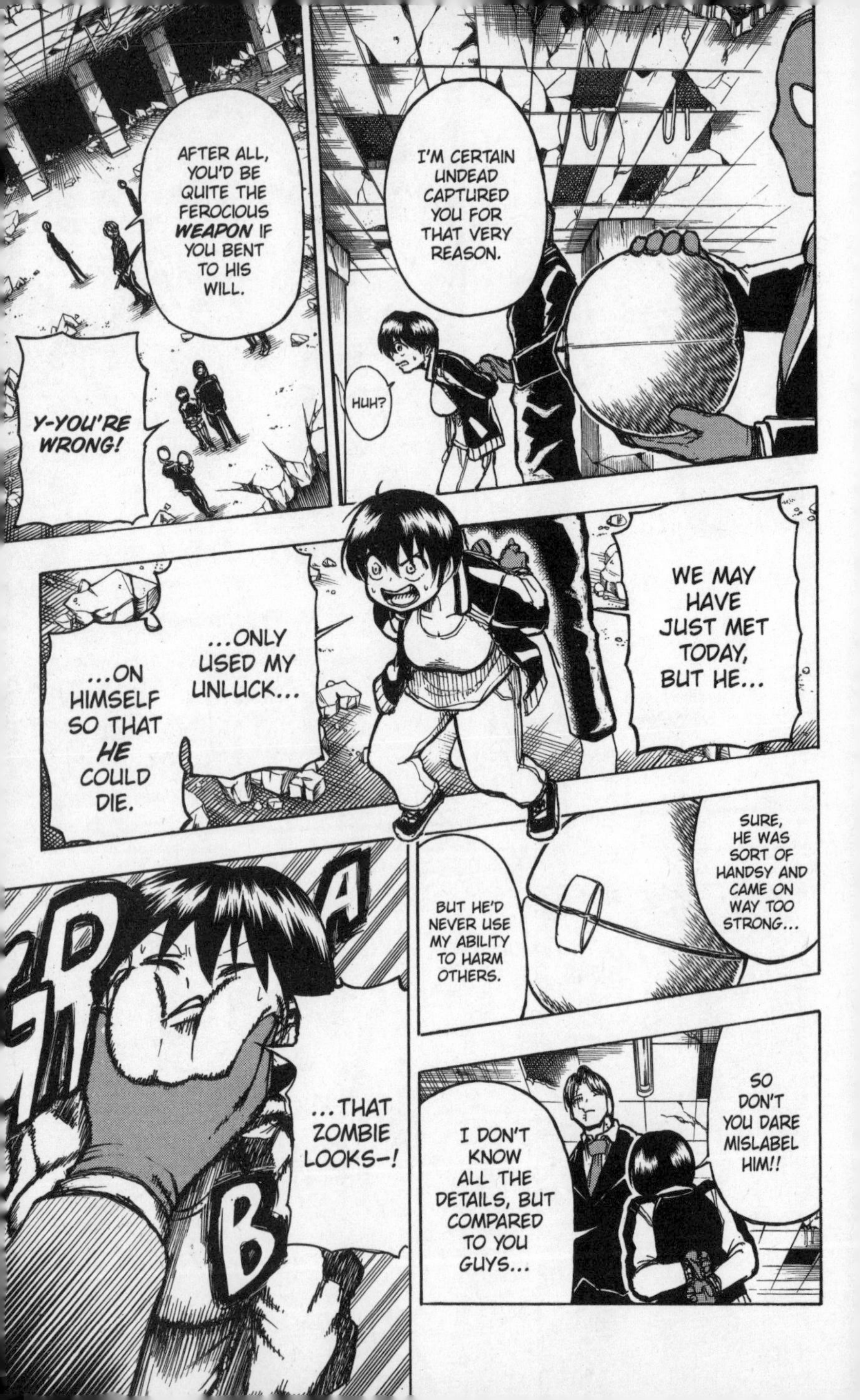
I'M CERTAIN UNDEAD CAPTURED YOU FOR THAT VERY REASON.
HUH?
AFTER ALL, YOU'D BE QUITE THE FEROCIOUS WEAPON IF YOU BENT TO HIS WILL.
Y-YOU'RE WRONG!
WE MAY HAVE JUST MET TODAY, BUT HE...
...ONLY USED MY UNLUCK...
...ON HIMSELF SO THAT HE COULD DIE.
SURE, HE WAS SORT OF HANDSY AND CAME ON WAY TOO STRONG...
BUT HE'D NEVER USE MY ABILITY TO HARM OTHERS.
SO DON'T YOU DARE MISLABEL HIM!!
I DON'T KNOW ALL THE DETAILS, BUT COMPARED TO YOU GUYS...
...THAT ZOMBIE LOOKS-!

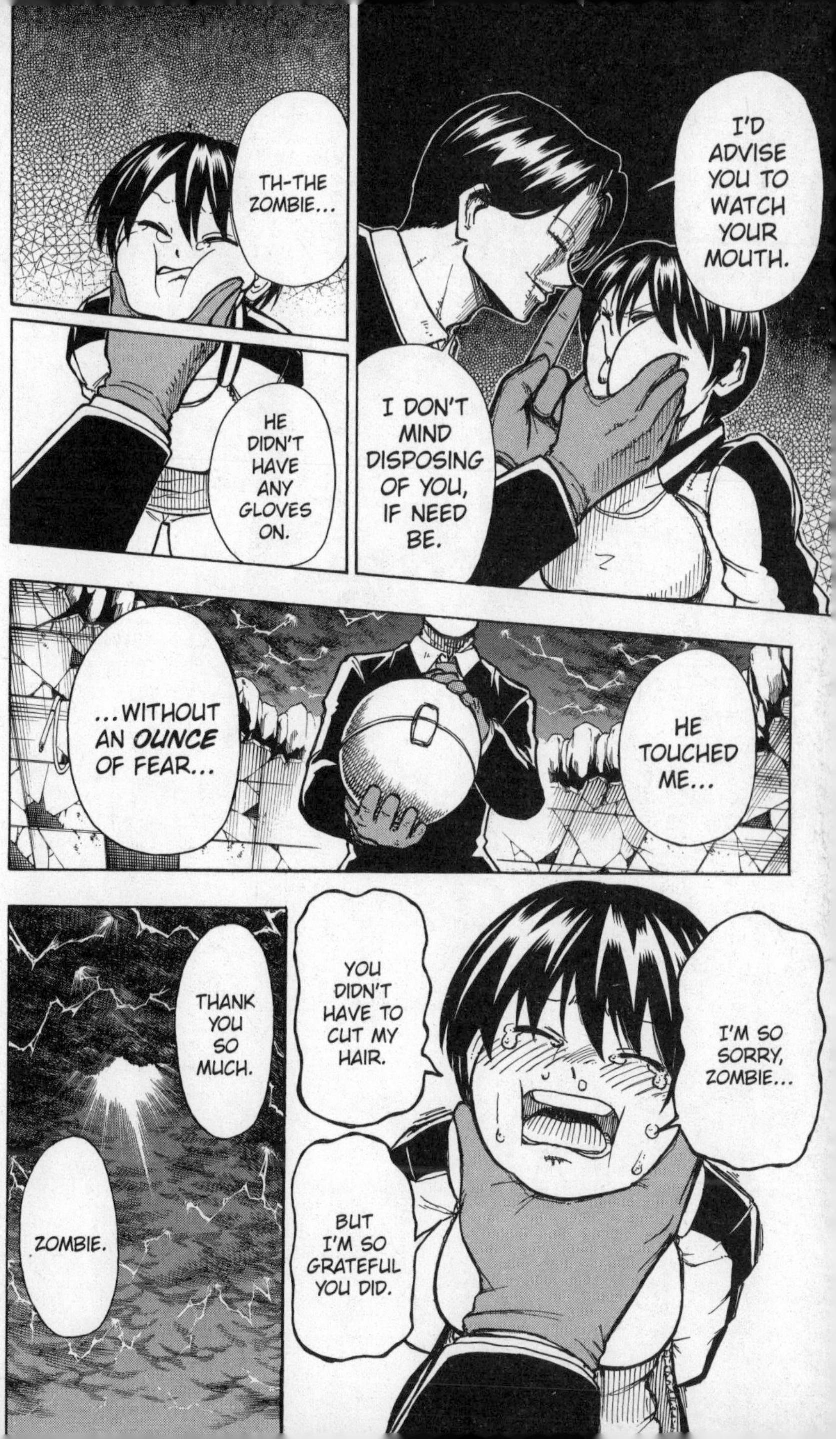
I'D ADVISE YOU TO WATCH YOUR MOUTH.
I DON'T MIND DISPOSING OF YOU, IF NEED BE.
TH-THE ZOMBIE...
HE DIDN'T HAVE ANY GLOVES ON.
HE TOUCHED ME...
...WITHOUT AN *OUNCE* OF FEAR...
I'M SO SORRY, ZOMBIE...
YOU DIDN'T HAVE TO CUT MY HAIR.
BUT I'M SO GRATEFUL YOU DID.
THANK YOU SO MUCH.
ZOMBIE.

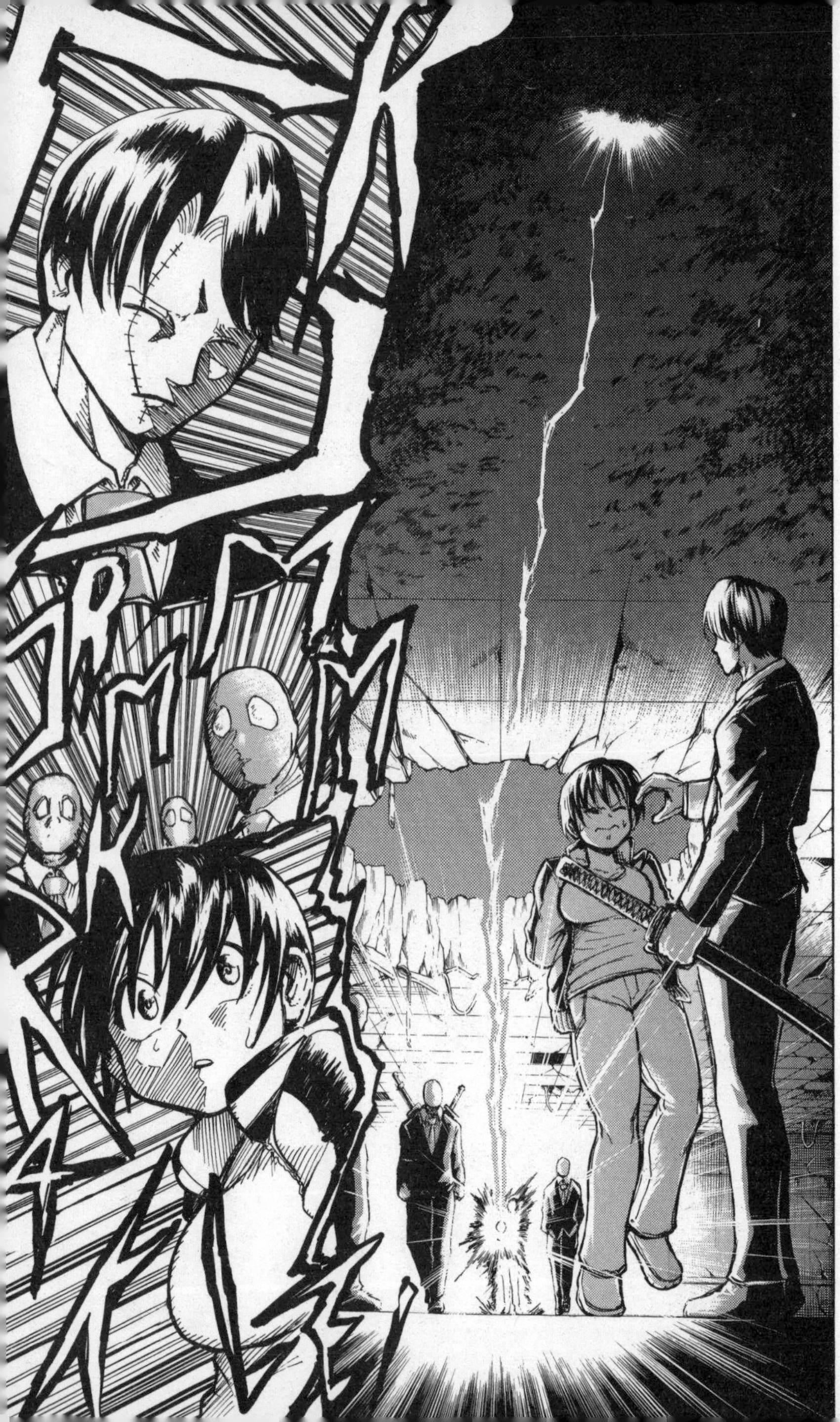

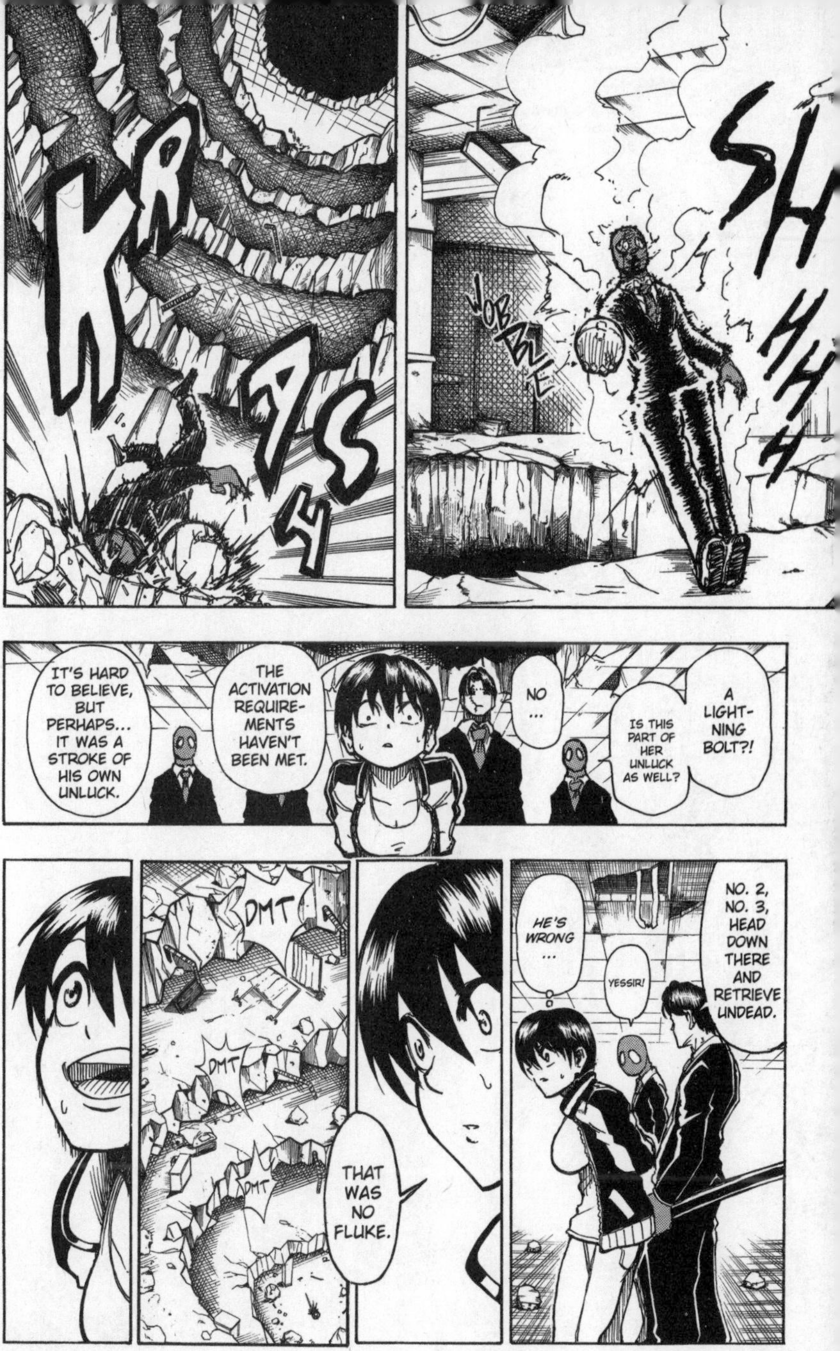
SHHHHH
WOBBLE
KRASH
A LIGHTNING BOLT?!
IS THIS PART OF HER UNLUCK AS WELL?
NO ...
THE ACTIVATION REQUIREMENTS HAVEN'T BEEN MET.
IT'S HARD TO BELIEVE, BUT PERHAPS... IT WAS A STROKE OF HIS OWN UNLUCK.
NO. 2, NO. 3, HEAD DOWN THERE AND RETRIEVE UNDEAD.
YESSIR!
HE'S WRONG ...
THAT WAS NO FLUKE.
DMT
DMT
DMT

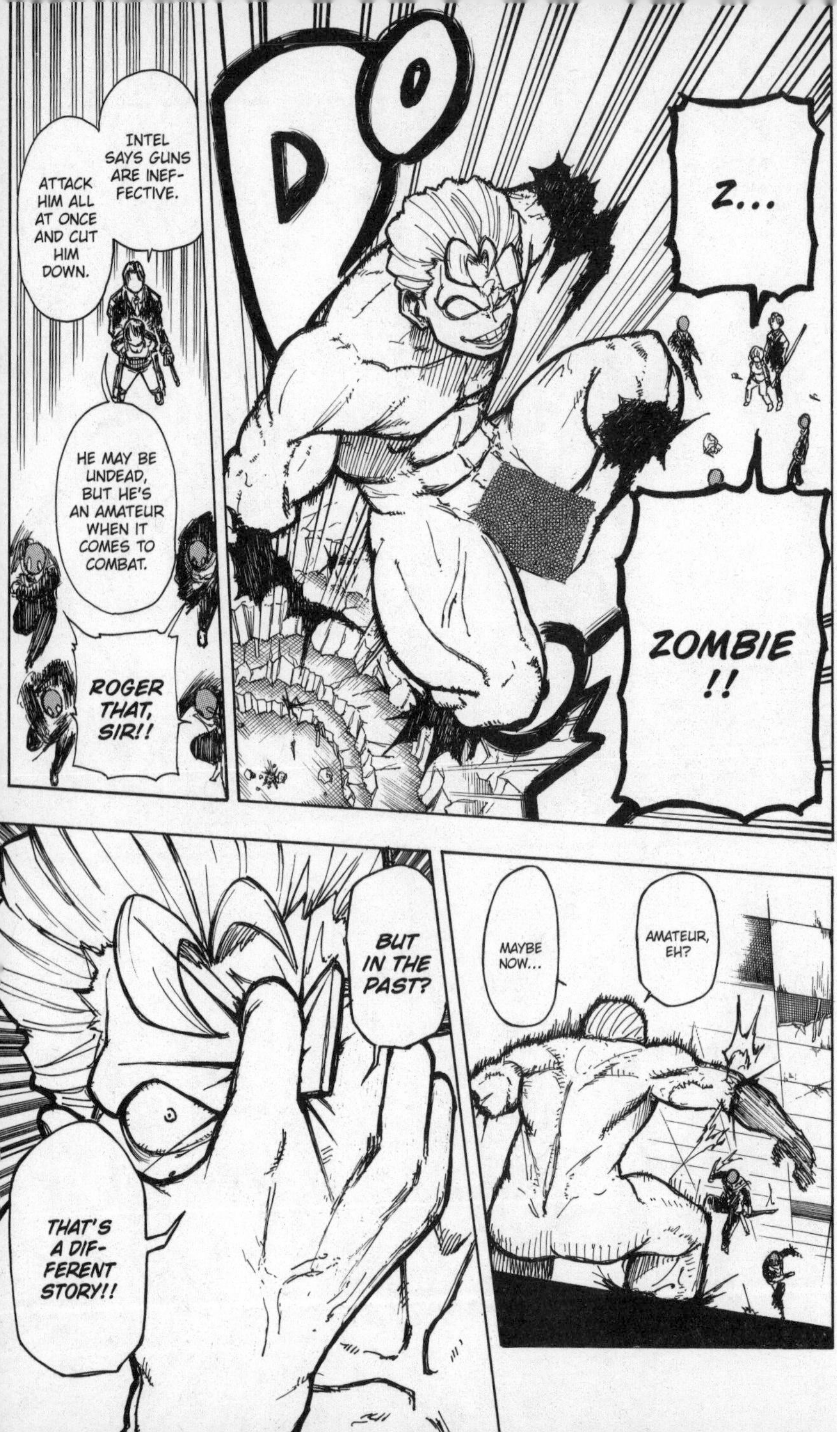
DO
Z...
ZOMBIE !!
INTEL SAYS GUNS ARE INEF-FECTIVE.
ATTACK HIM ALL AT ONCE AND CUT HIM DOWN.
HE MAY BE UNDEAD, BUT HE'S AN AMATEUR WHEN IT COMES TO COMBAT.
ROGER THAT, SIR!!
AMATEUR, EH?
MAYBE NOW...
BUT IN THE PAST?
THAT'S A DIF-FERENT STORY!!

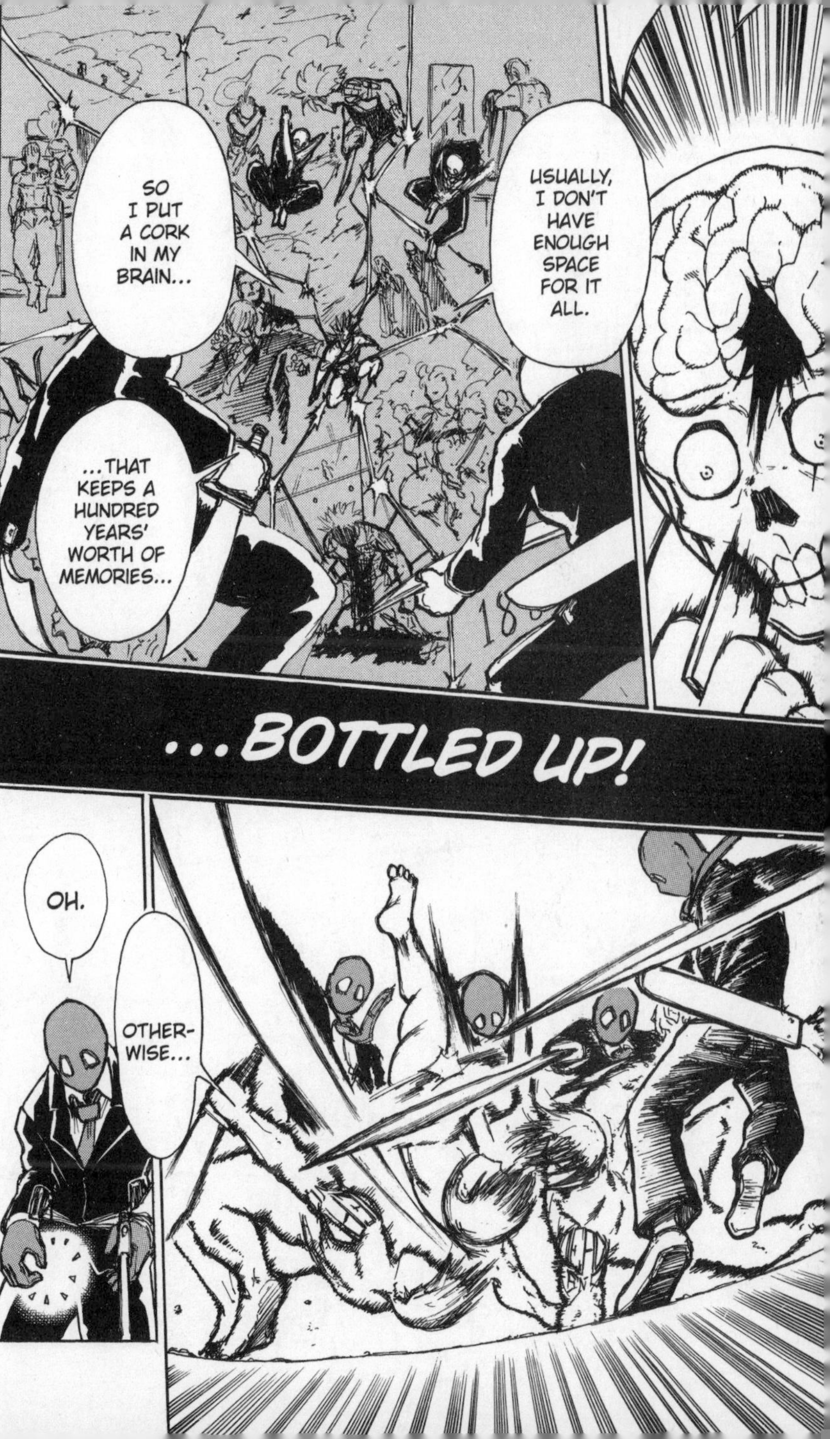
USUALLY, I DON'T HAVE ENOUGH SPACE FOR IT ALL.
SO I PUT A CORK IN MY BRAIN...
...THAT KEEPS A HUNDRED YEARS' WORTH OF MEMORIES...
...BOTTLED UP!
OTHER-WISE...
OH.

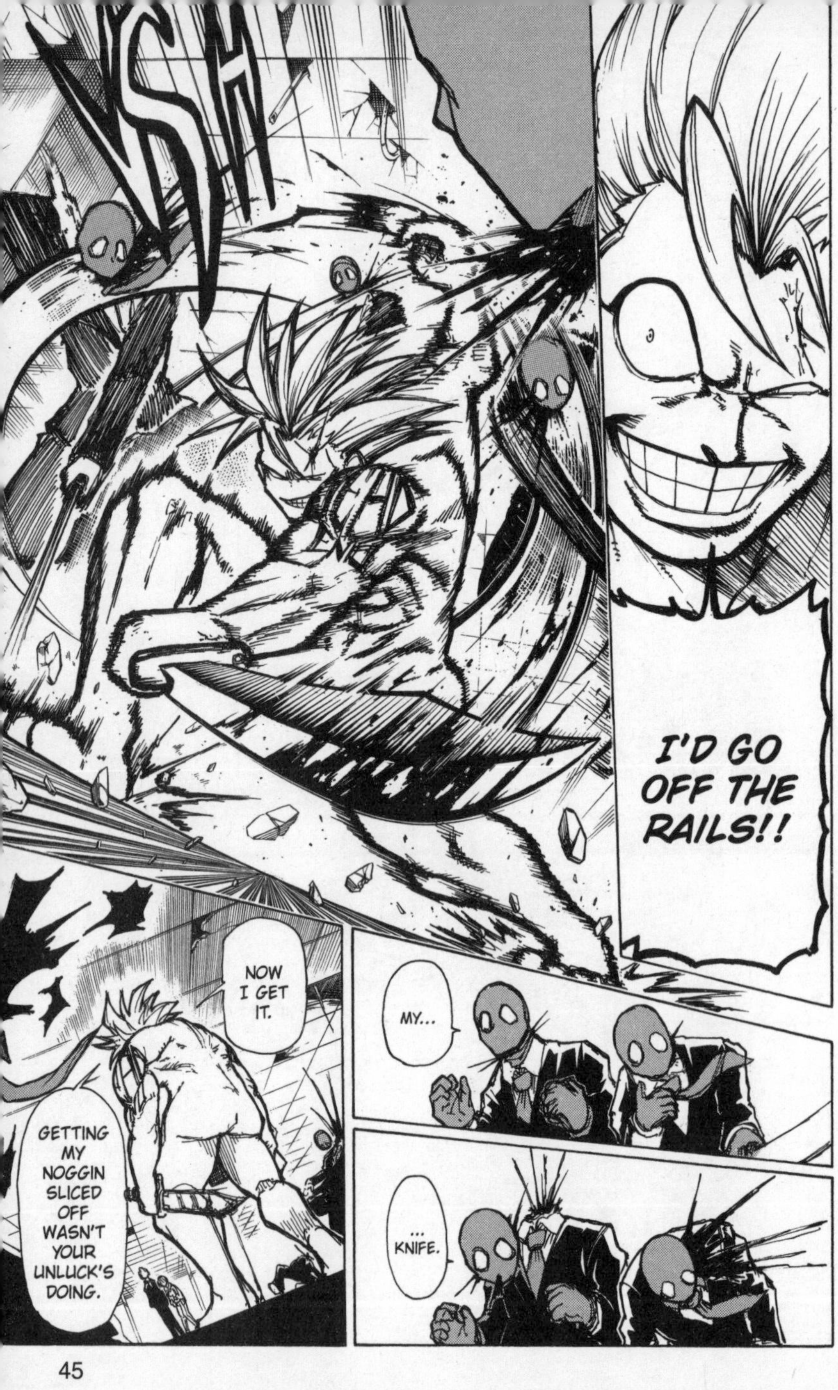
I'D GO OFF THE RAILS!!
VSH
MY...
... KNIFE.
NOW I GET IT.
GETTING MY NOGGIN SLICED OFF WASN'T YOUR UNLUCK'S DOING.

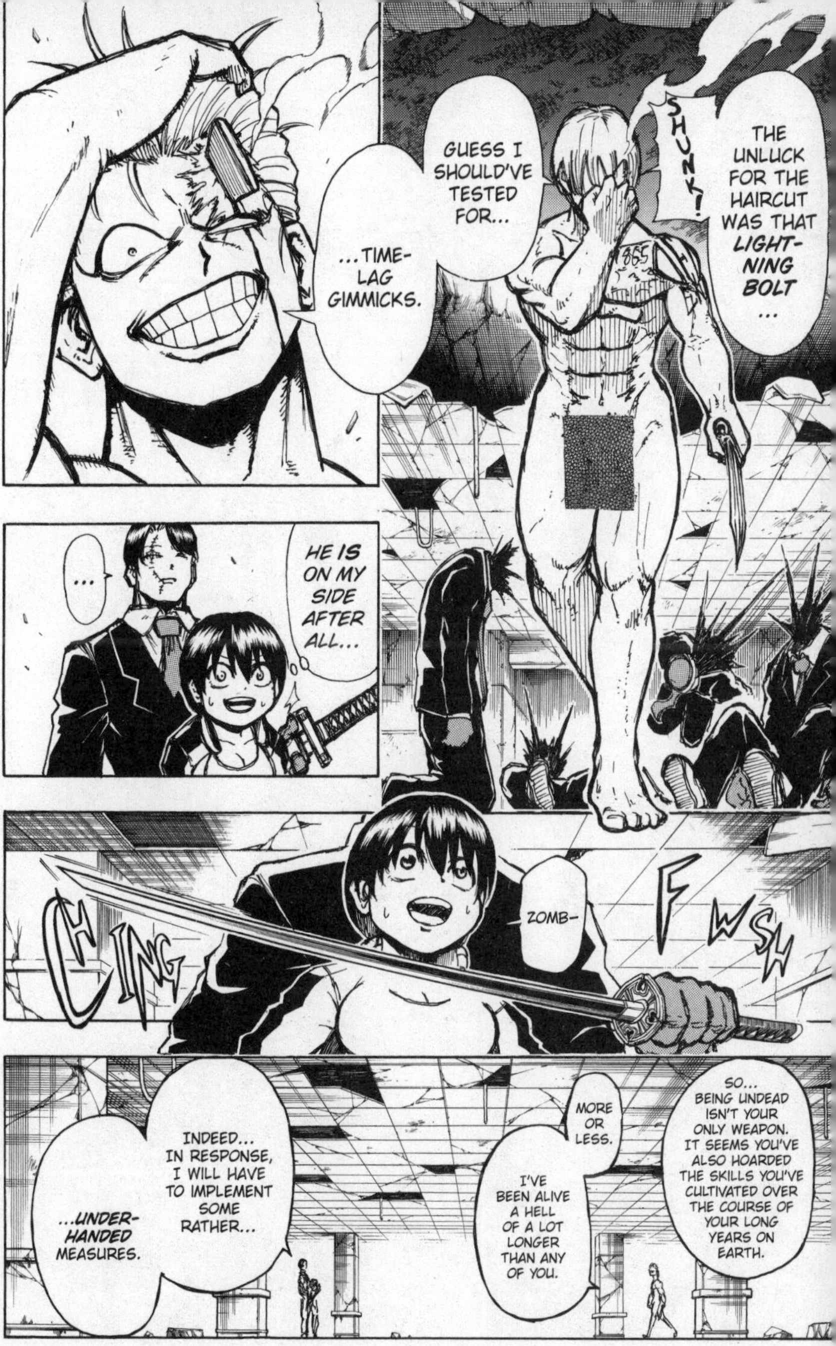
SHUNK!
THE UNLUCK FOR THE HAIRCUT WAS THAT LIGHTNING BOLT...
GUESS I SHOULD'VE TESTED FOR...
...TIME-LAG GIMMICKS.
HE IS ON MY SIDE AFTER ALL...
...
FWSH
ZOMB-
CHING
SO... BEING UNDEAD ISN'T YOUR ONLY WEAPON. IT SEEMS YOU'VE ALSO HOARDED THE SKILLS YOU'VE CULTIVATED OVER THE COURSE OF YOUR LONG YEARS ON EARTH.
MORE OR LESS.
I'VE BEEN ALIVE A HELL OF A LOT LONGER THAN ANY OF YOU.
INDEED... IN RESPONSE, I WILL HAVE TO IMPLEMENT SOME RATHER...
...UNDERHANDED MEASURES.

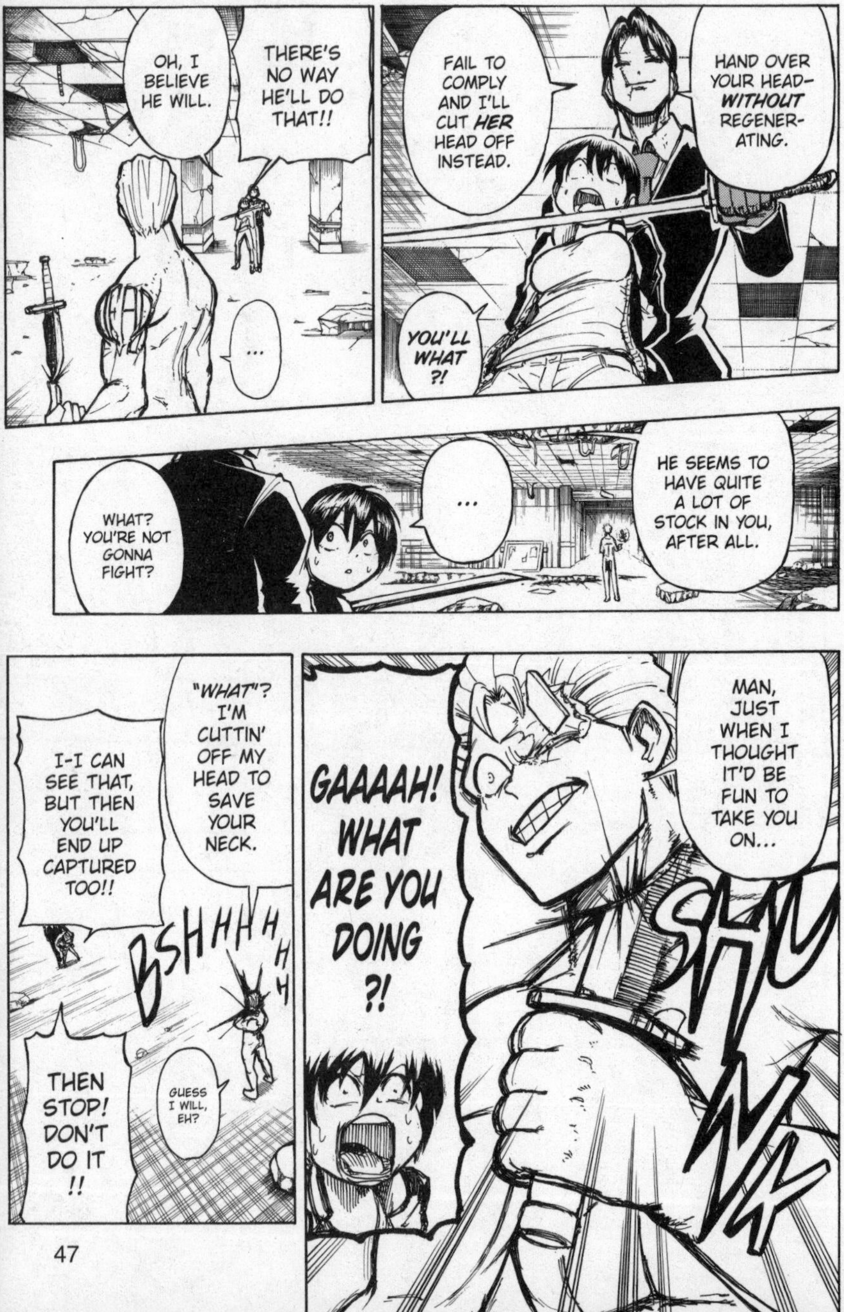

HAND OVER YOUR HEAD—*WITHOUT* REGENERATING.
FAIL TO COMPLY AND I'LL CUT *HER* HEAD OFF INSTEAD.
YOU'LL WHAT ?!
THERE'S NO WAY HE'LL DO THAT!!
OH, I BELIEVE HE WILL.
...
HE SEEMS TO HAVE QUITE A LOT OF STOCK IN YOU, AFTER ALL.
...
WHAT? YOU'RE NOT GONNA FIGHT?
MAN, JUST WHEN I THOUGHT IT'D BE FUN TO TAKE YOU ON...
SHUNK
GAAAAH! WHAT ARE YOU DOING ?!
"*WHAT*"? I'M CUTTIN' OFF MY HEAD TO SAVE YOUR NECK.
I-I CAN SEE THAT, BUT THEN YOU'LL END UP CAPTURED TOO!!
BSHHHHHHH
GUESS I WILL, EH?
THEN STOP! DON'T DO IT !!

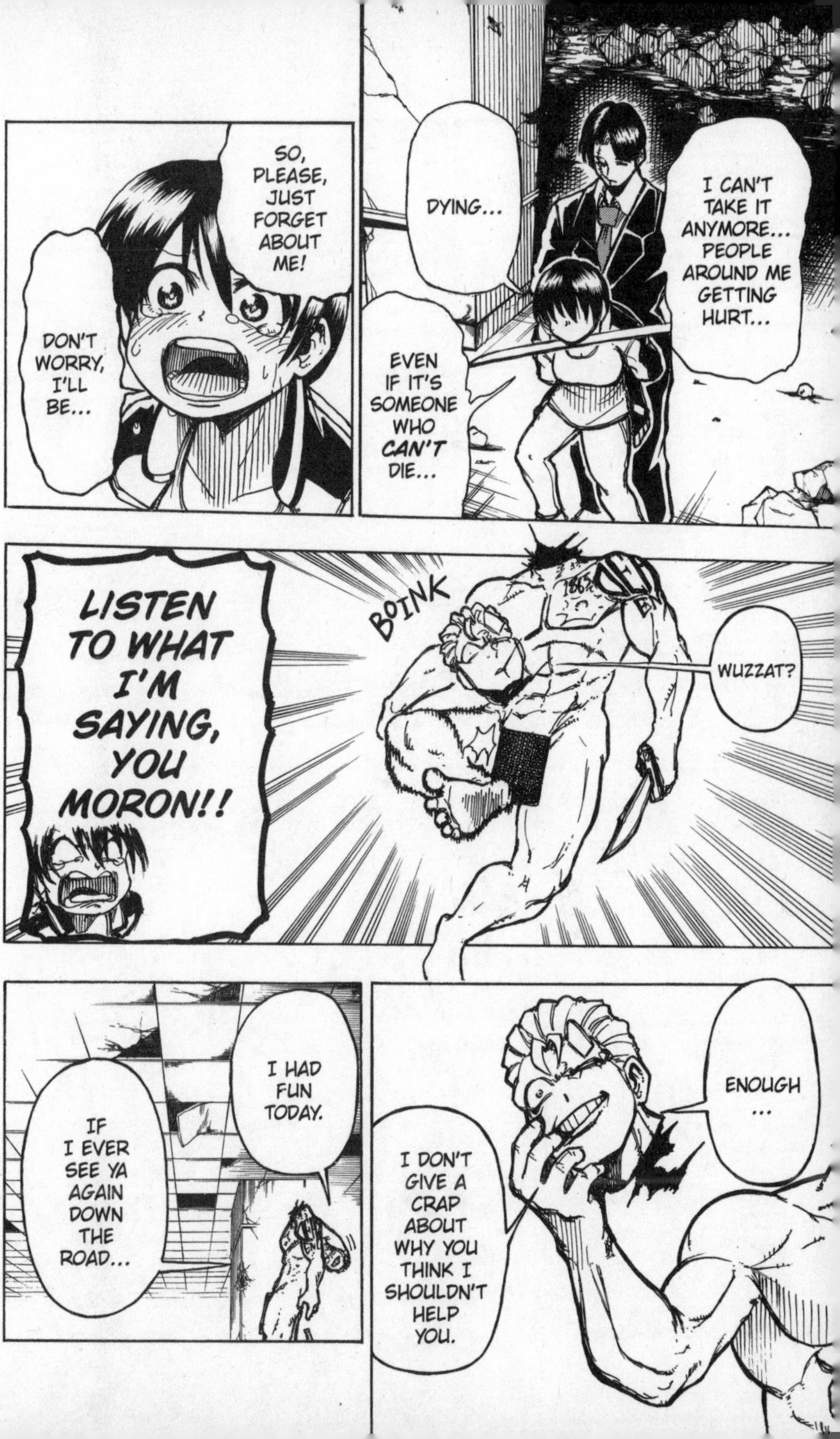
I CAN'T TAKE IT ANYMORE... PEOPLE AROUND ME GETTING HURT...
DYING...
EVEN IF IT'S SOMEONE WHO CAN'T DIE...
SO, PLEASE, JUST FORGET ABOUT ME!
DON'T WORRY, I'LL BE...
BOINK
WUZZAT?
LISTEN TO WHAT I'M SAYING, YOU MORON!!
ENOUGH...
I DON'T GIVE A CRAP ABOUT WHY YOU THINK I SHOULDN'T HELP YOU.
I HAD FUN TODAY.
IF I EVER SEE YA AGAIN DOWN THE ROAD...

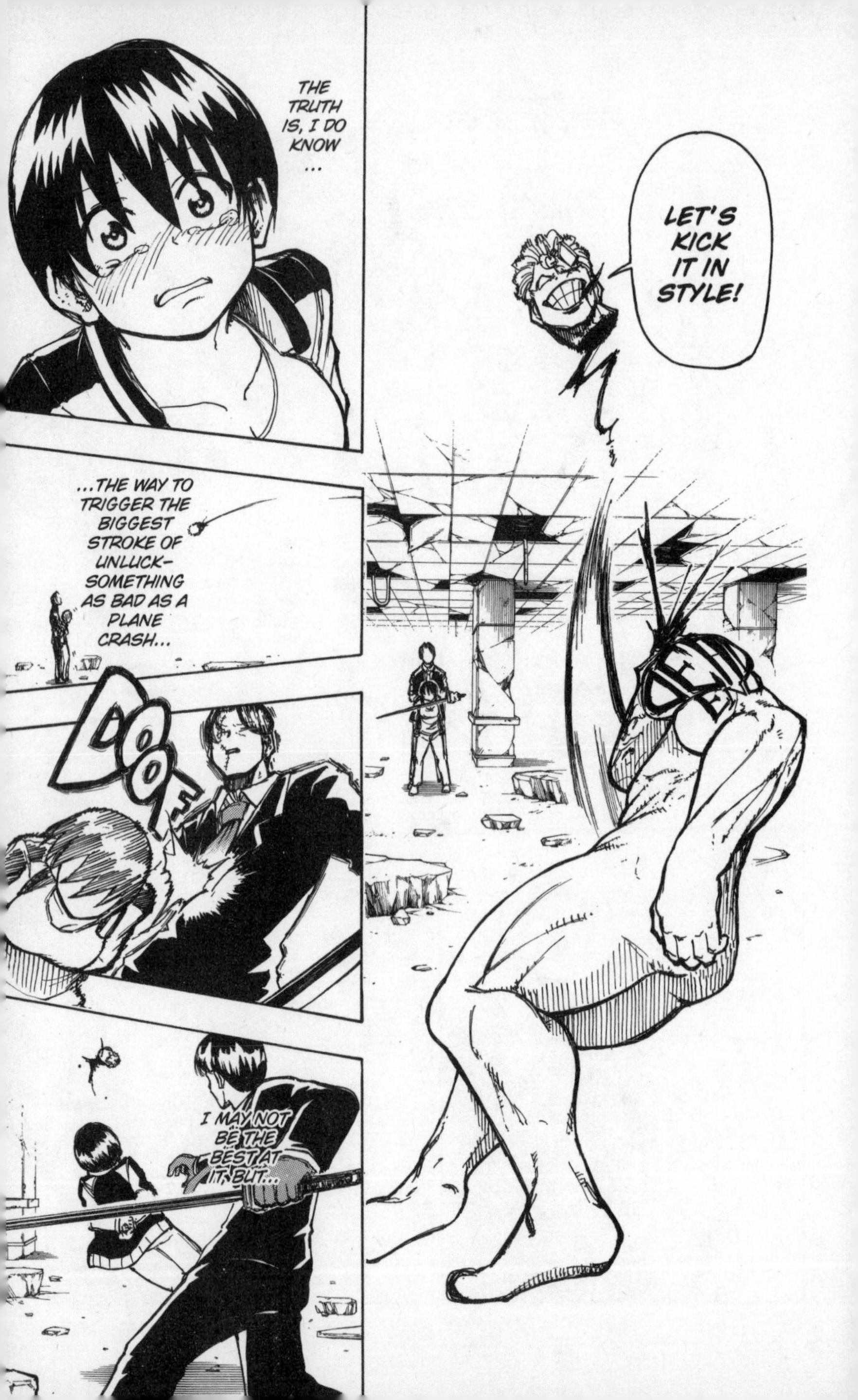
LET'S KICK IT IN STYLE!
THE TRUTH IS, I DO KNOW ...
...THE WAY TO TRIGGER THE BIGGEST STROKE OF UNLUCK—SOMETHING AS BAD AS A PLANE CRASH...
DOOF
I MAY NOT BE THE BEST AT IT, BUT...

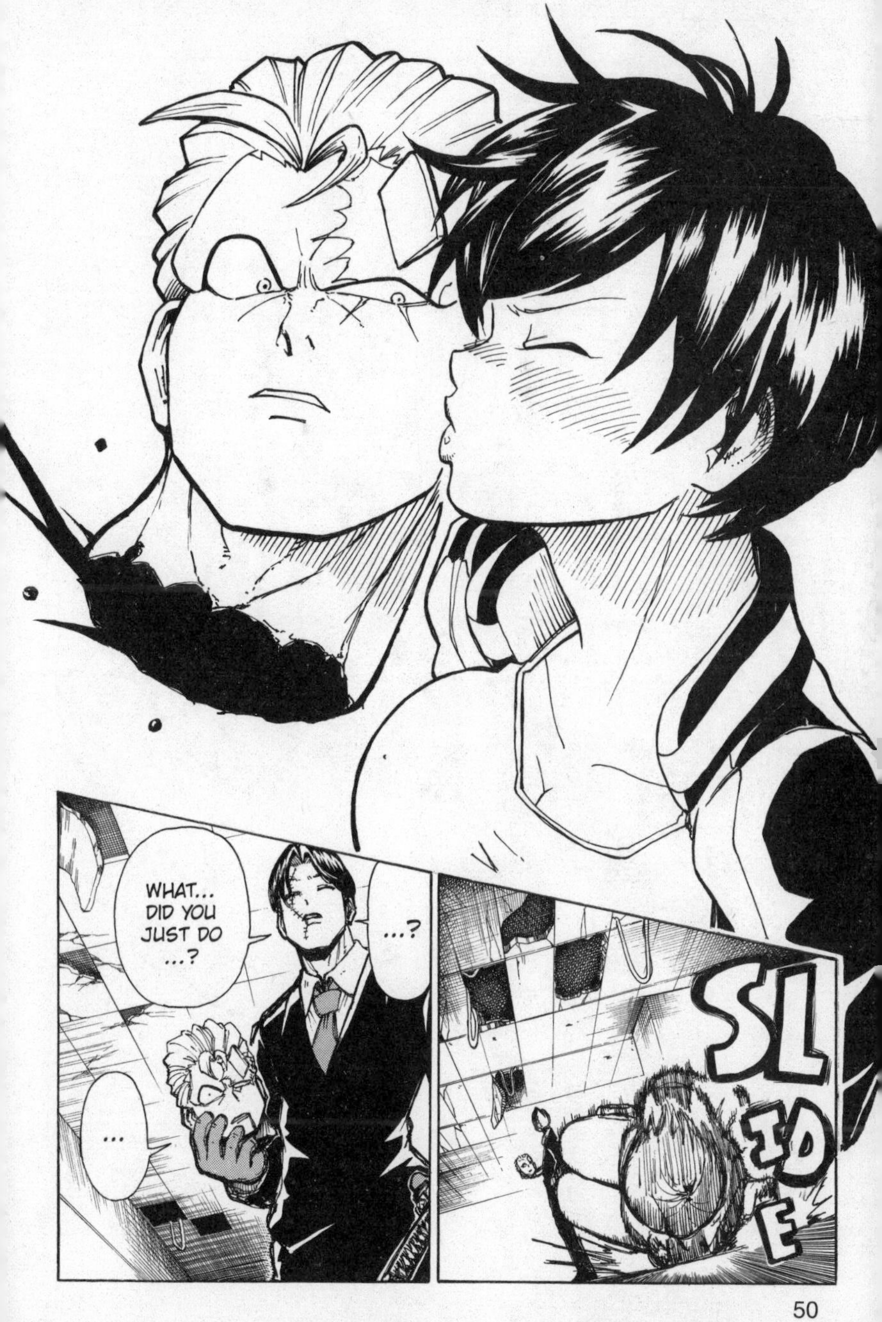
SLIDE
...?
WHAT... DID YOU JUST DO ...?
...

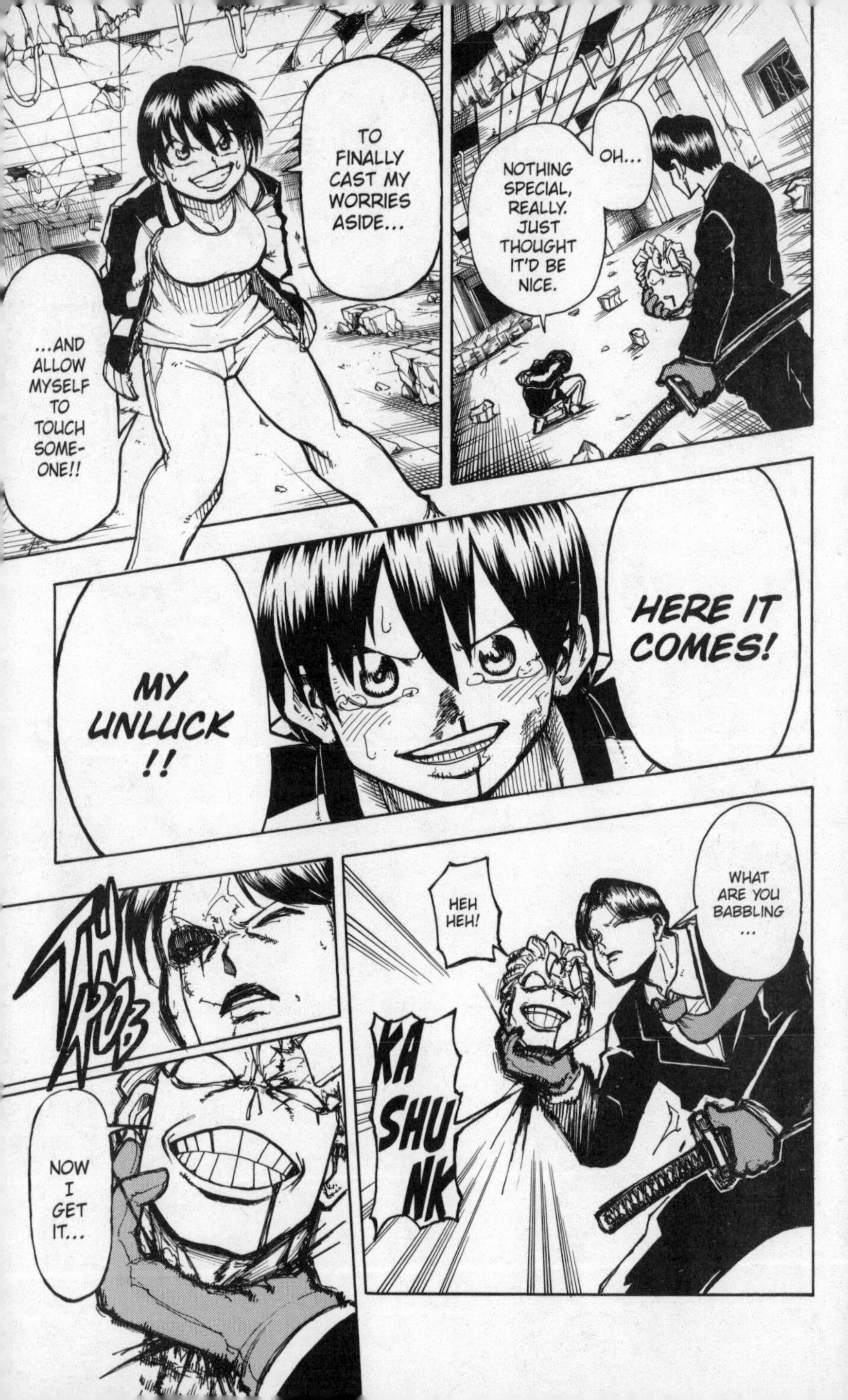
OH...
NOTHING SPECIAL, REALLY. JUST THOUGHT IT'D BE NICE.
TO FINALLY CAST MY WORRIES ASIDE...
...AND ALLOW MYSELF TO TOUCH SOME-ONE!!
HERE IT COMES!
MY UNLUCK!!
WHAT ARE YOU BABBLING...
HEH HEH!
KASHUNK
THROB
NOW I GET IT...

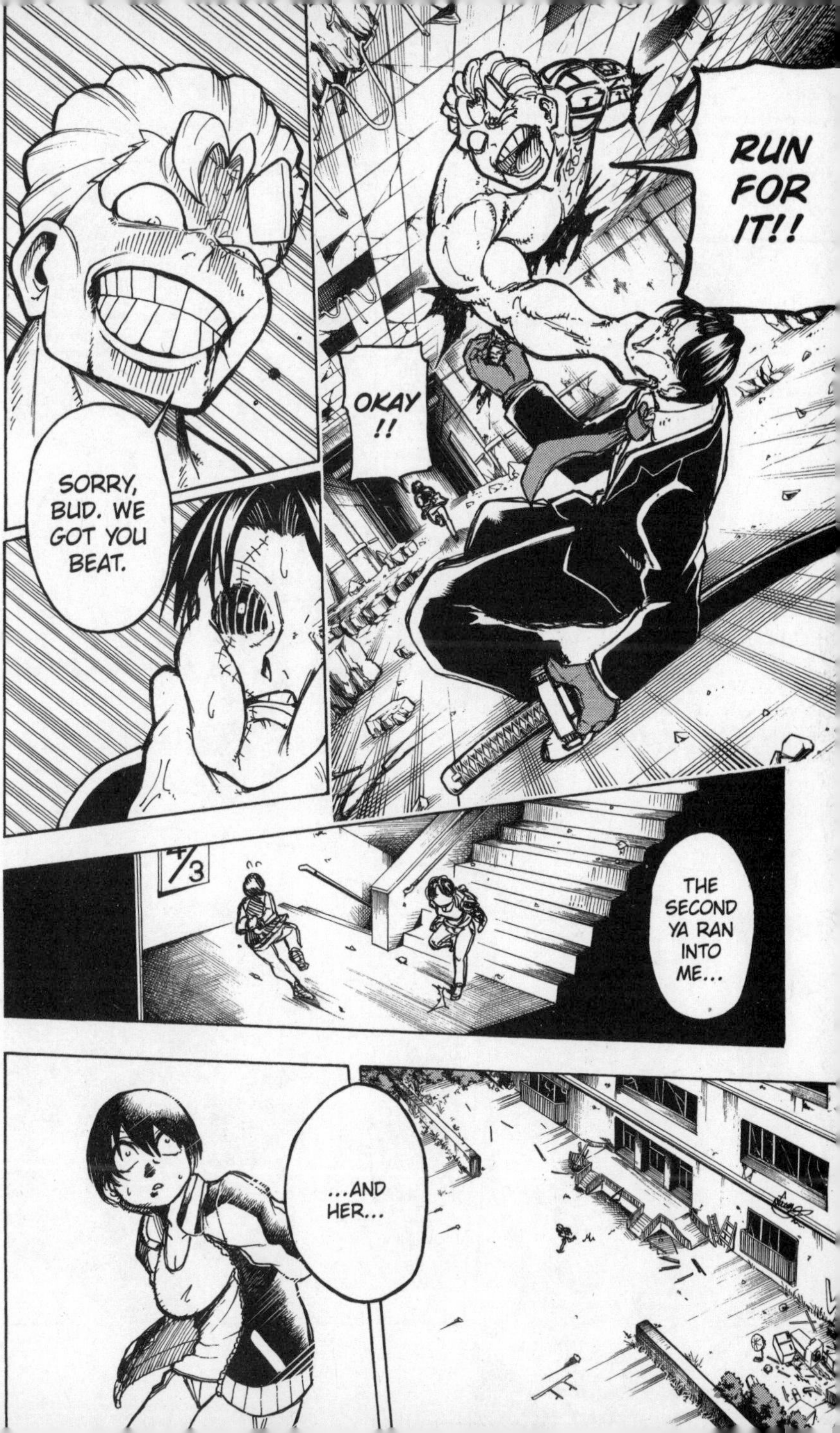
RUN FOR IT!!
OKAY!!
SORRY, BUD. WE GOT YOU BEAT.
THE SECOND YA RAN INTO ME...
...AND HER...

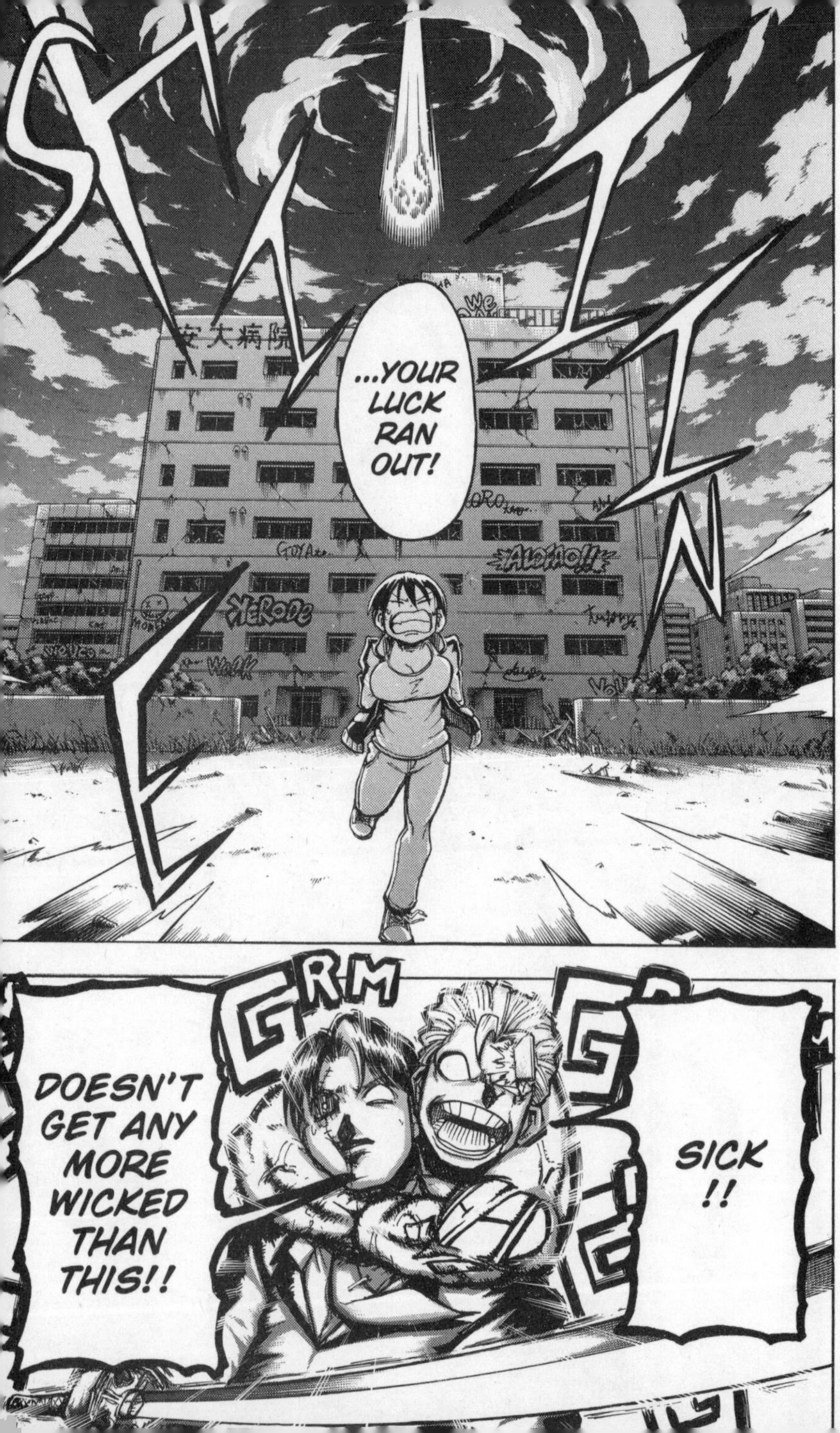
...YOUR LUCK RAN OUT!
SICK!!
GRM
DOESN'T GET ANY MORE WICKED THAN THIS!!

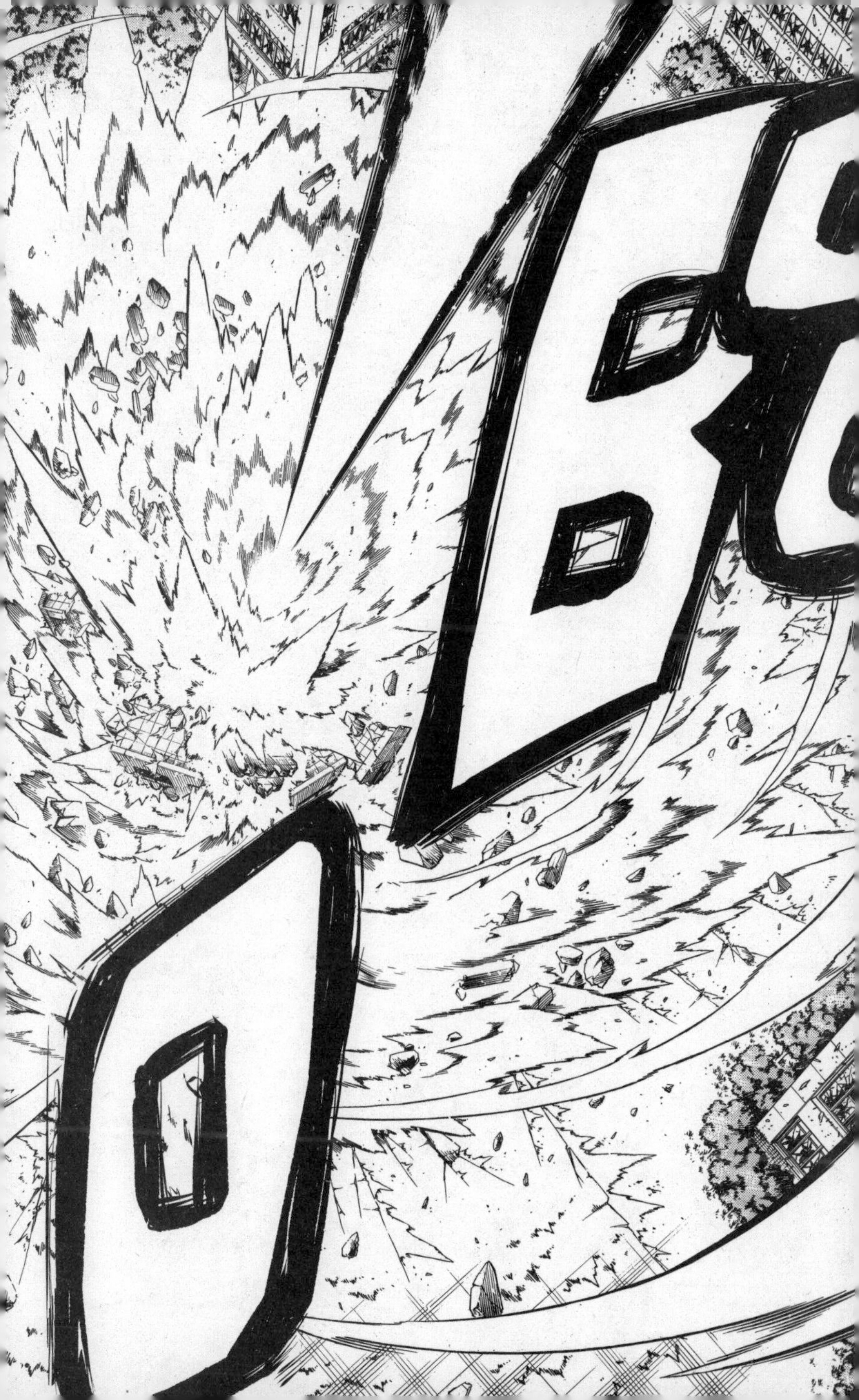

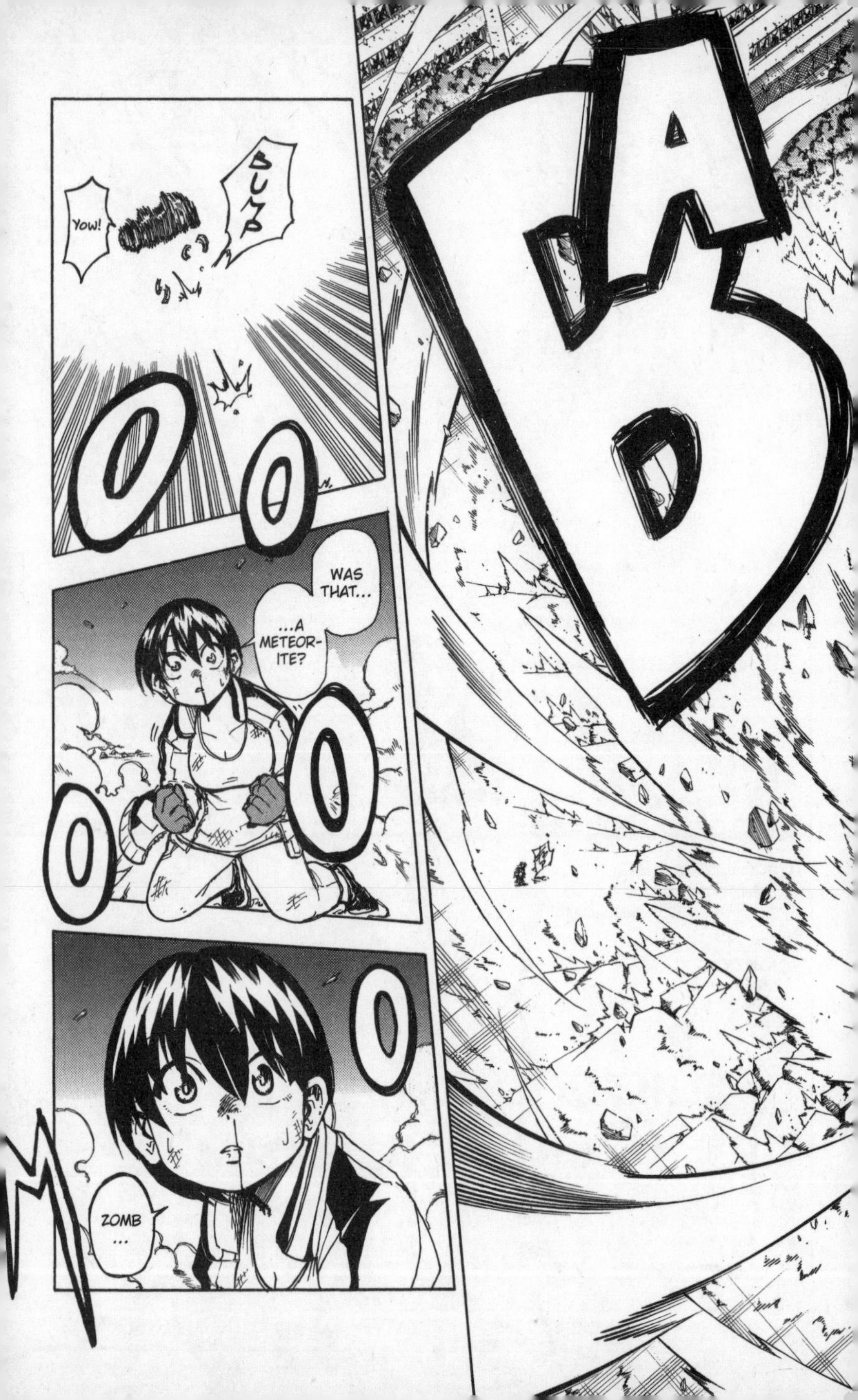
BUMP
YOW!
WAS THAT...
...A METEORITE?
ZOMB ...

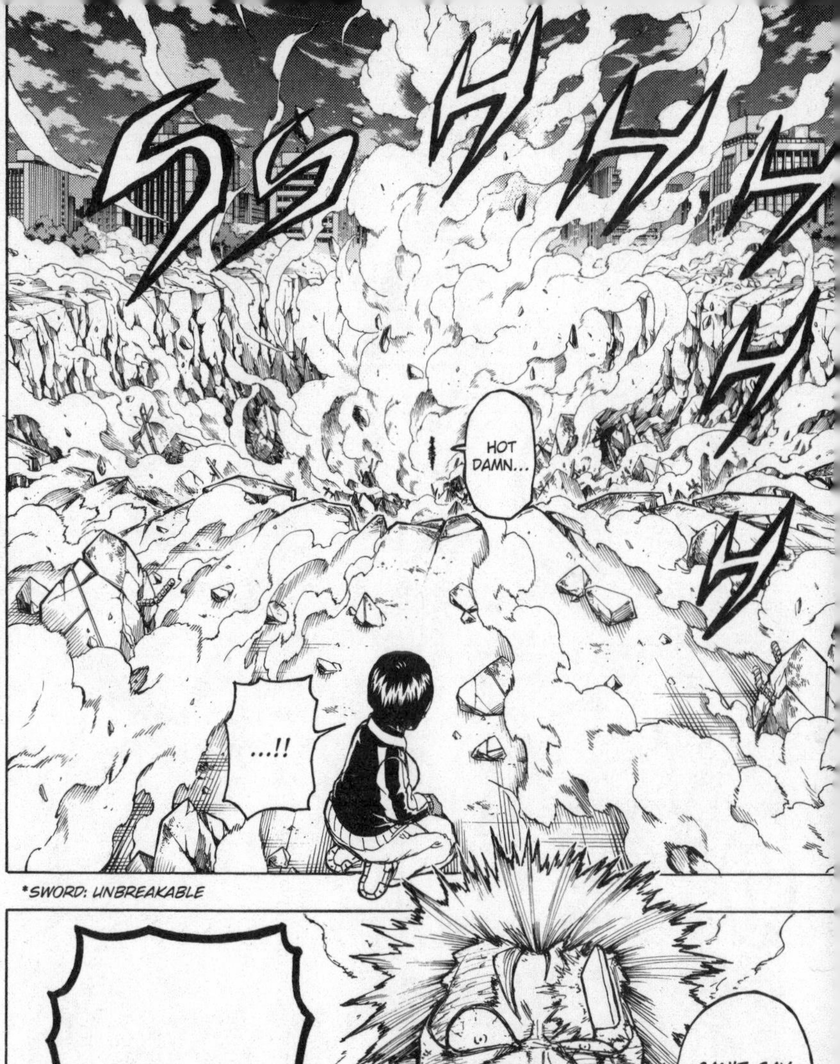
HOT DAMN...
...!!

*SWORD: UNBREAKABLE

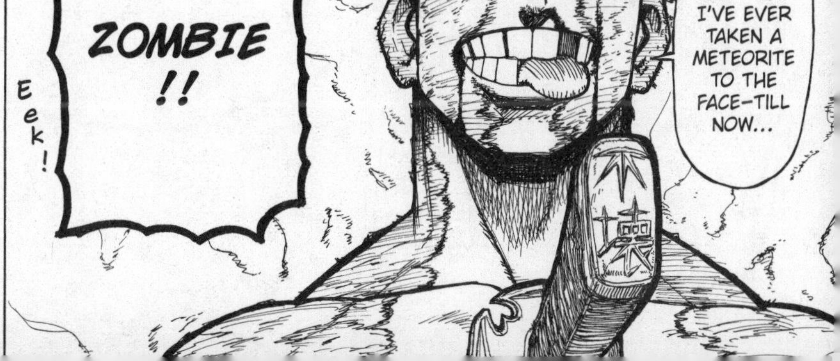
CAN'T SAY I'VE EVER TAKEN A METEORITE TO THE FACE–TILL NOW...
ZOMBIE !!
Eek!

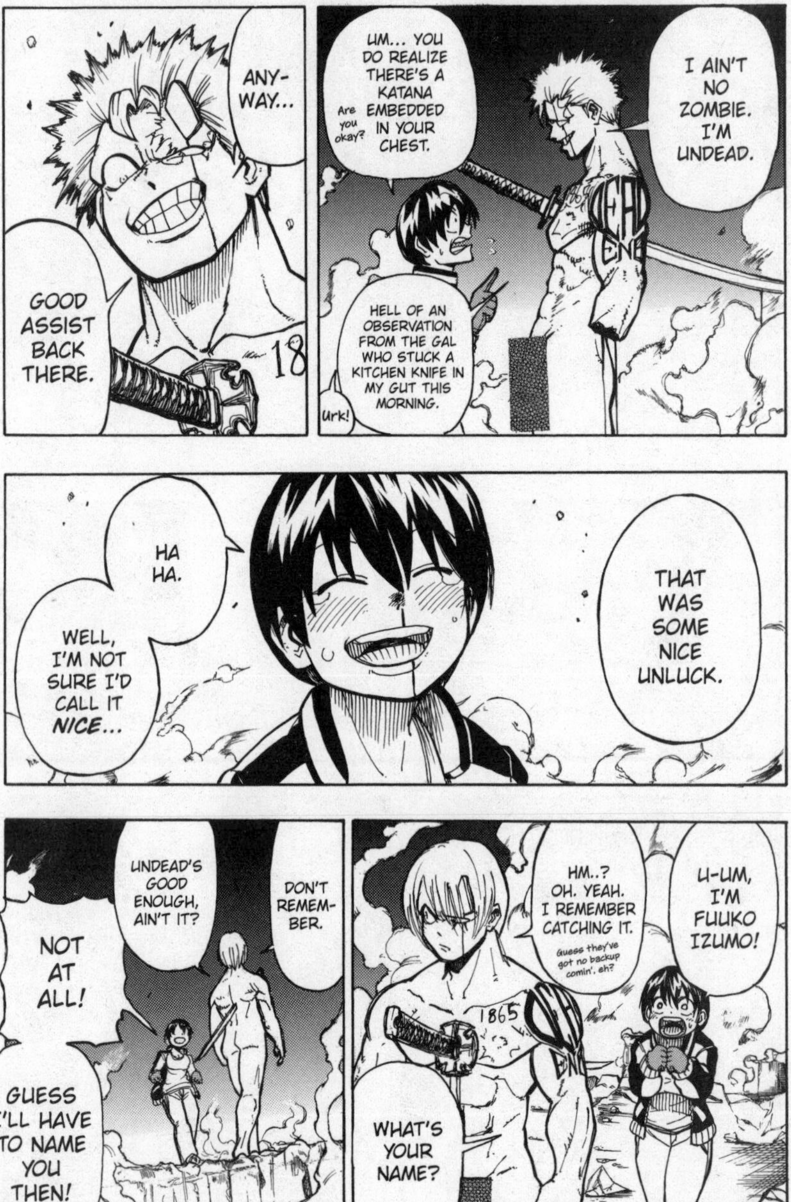
I AIN'T NO ZOMBIE. I'M UNDEAD.
UM... YOU DO REALIZE THERE'S A KATANA EMBEDDED IN YOUR CHEST.
Are you okay?
HELL OF AN OBSERVATION FROM THE GAL WHO STUCK A KITCHEN KNIFE IN MY GUT THIS MORNING.
Urk!
ANY-WAY...
GOOD ASSIST BACK THERE.
18
THAT WAS SOME NICE UNLUCK.
HA HA.
WELL, I'M NOT SURE I'D CALL IT *NICE*...
U-UM, I'M FUUKO IZUMO!
HM..? OH. YEAH. I REMEMBER CATCHING IT.
Guess they've got no backup comin', eh?
1865
WHAT'S YOUR NAME?
DON'T REMEMBER.
UNDEAD'S GOOD ENOUGH, AIN'T IT?
NOT AT ALL!
GUESS I'LL HAVE TO NAME YOU THEN!

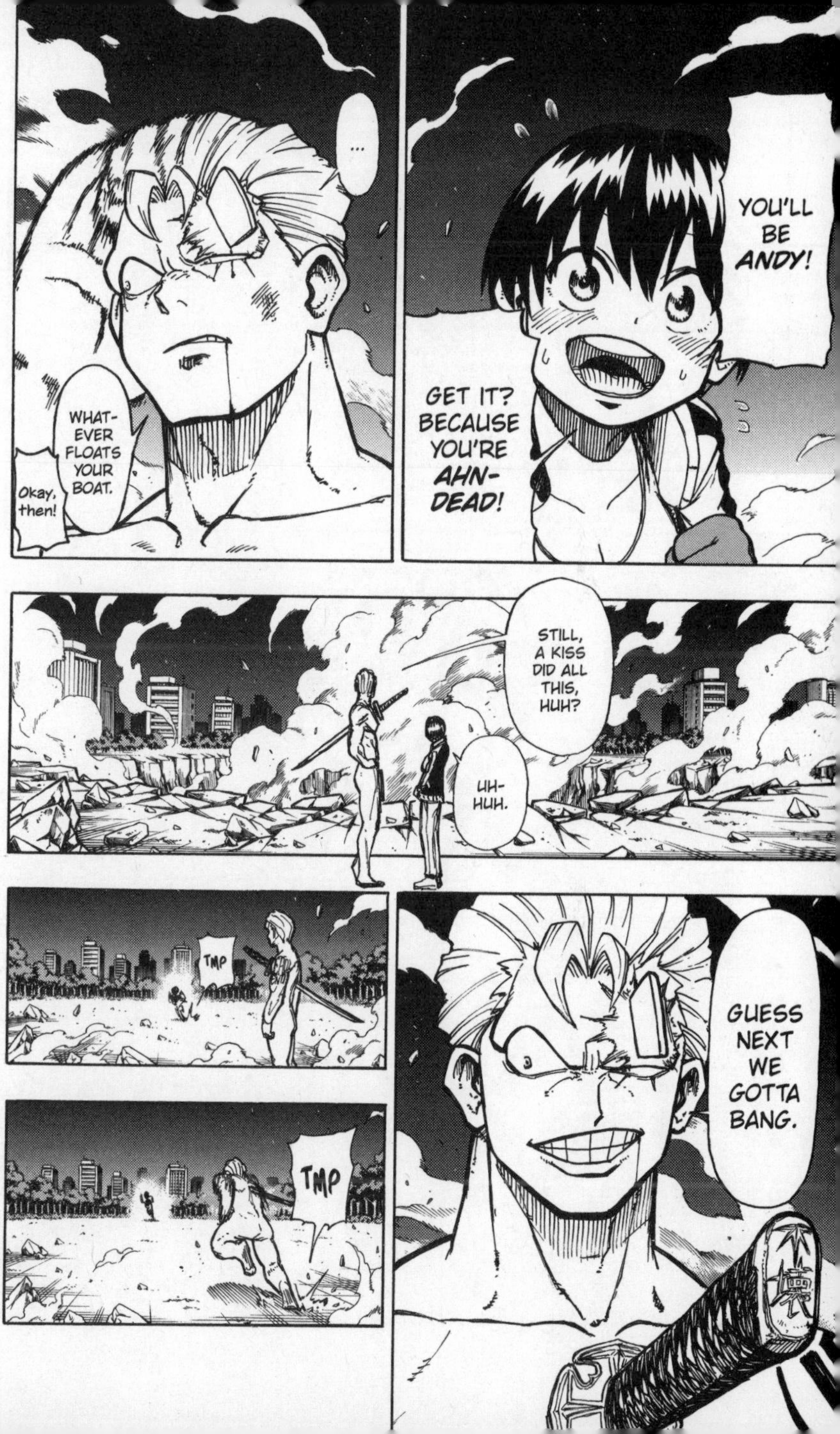
YOU'LL BE ANDY!
GET IT? BECAUSE YOU'RE AHN-DEAD!
...
WHAT-EVER FLOATS YOUR BOAT.
Okay, then!
STILL, A KISS DID ALL THIS, HUH?
UH-HUH.
GUESS NEXT WE GOTTA BANG.
TMP
TMP

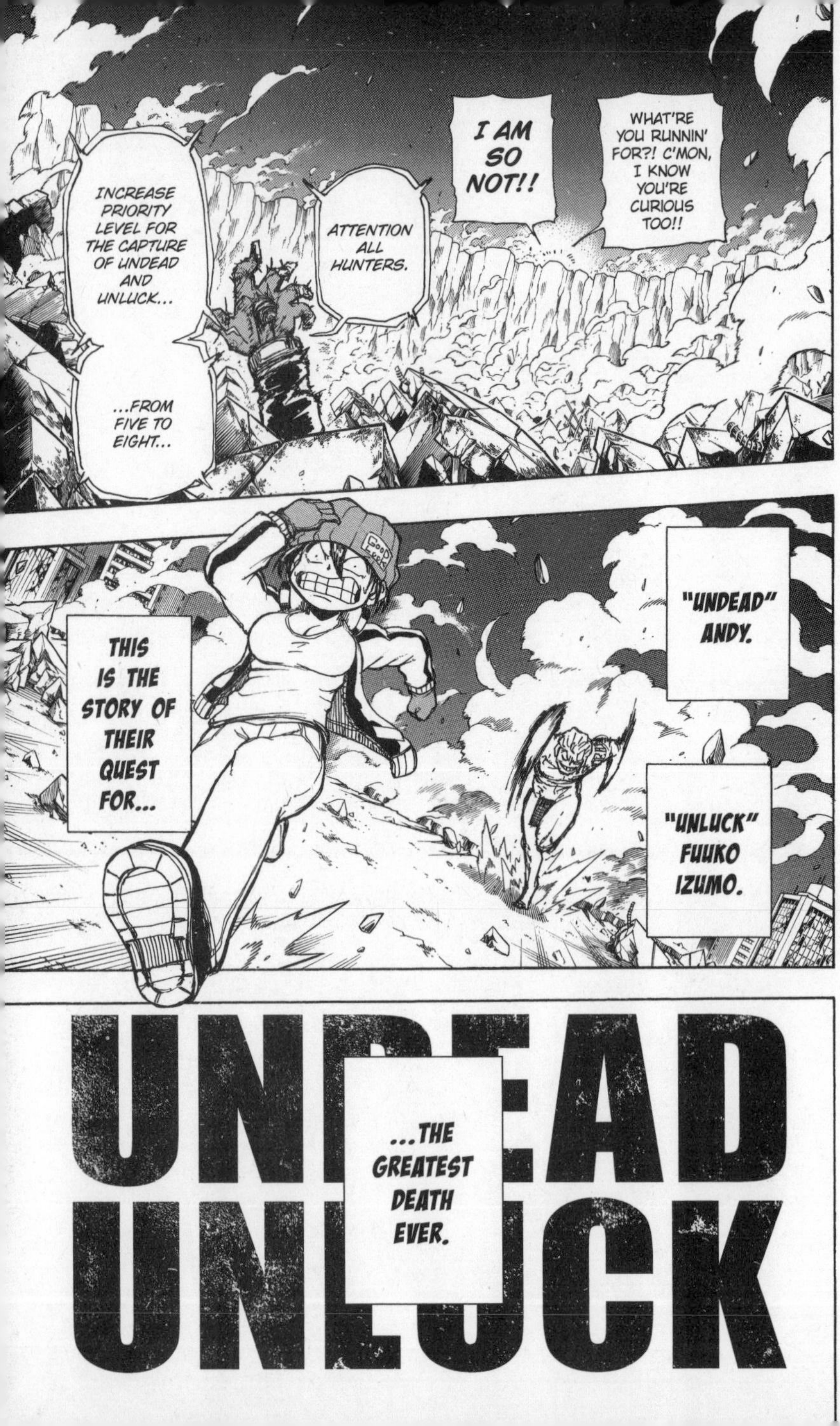
WHAT'RE YOU RUNNIN' FOR?! C'MON, I KNOW YOU'RE CURIOUS TOO!!
I AM SO NOT!!
ATTENTION ALL HUNTERS.
INCREASE PRIORITY LEVEL FOR THE CAPTURE OF UNDEAD AND UNLUCK...
...FROM FIVE TO EIGHT...
"UNDEAD" ANDY.
"UNLUCK" FUUKO IZUMO.
THIS IS THE STORY OF THEIR QUEST FOR...
...THE GREATEST DEATH EVER.
UNDEAD UNLUCK

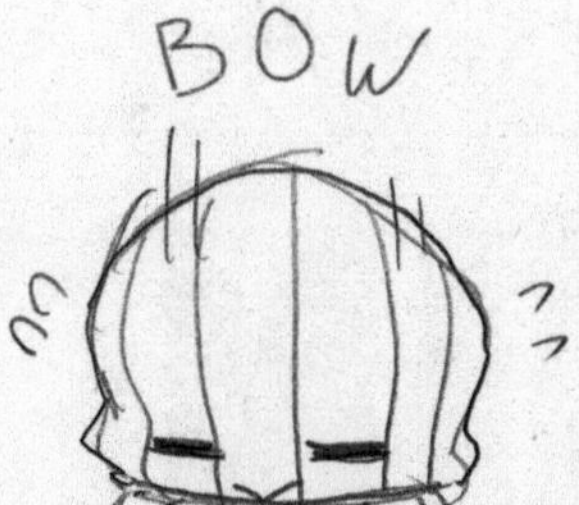
BOW

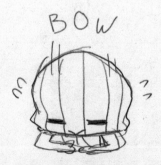

Thank you very much
for buying volume 1.

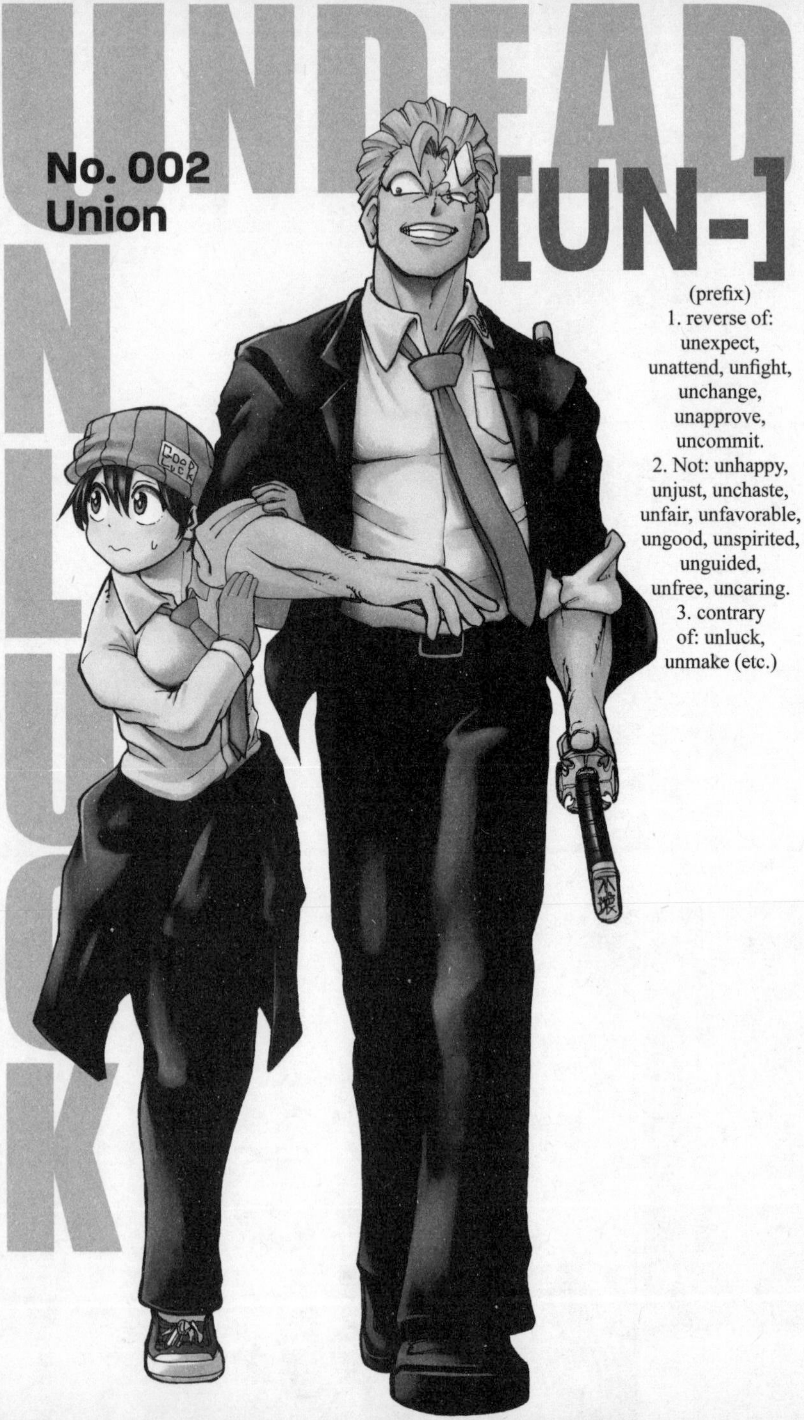
UNDEAD
UNLUCK
No. 002
Union
[UN-]
(prefix)
1. reverse of: unexpect, unattend, unfight, unchange, unapprove, uncommit.
2. Not: unhappy, unjust, unchaste, unfair, unfavorable, ungood, unspirited, unguided, unfree, uncaring.
3. contrary of: unluck, unmake (etc.)

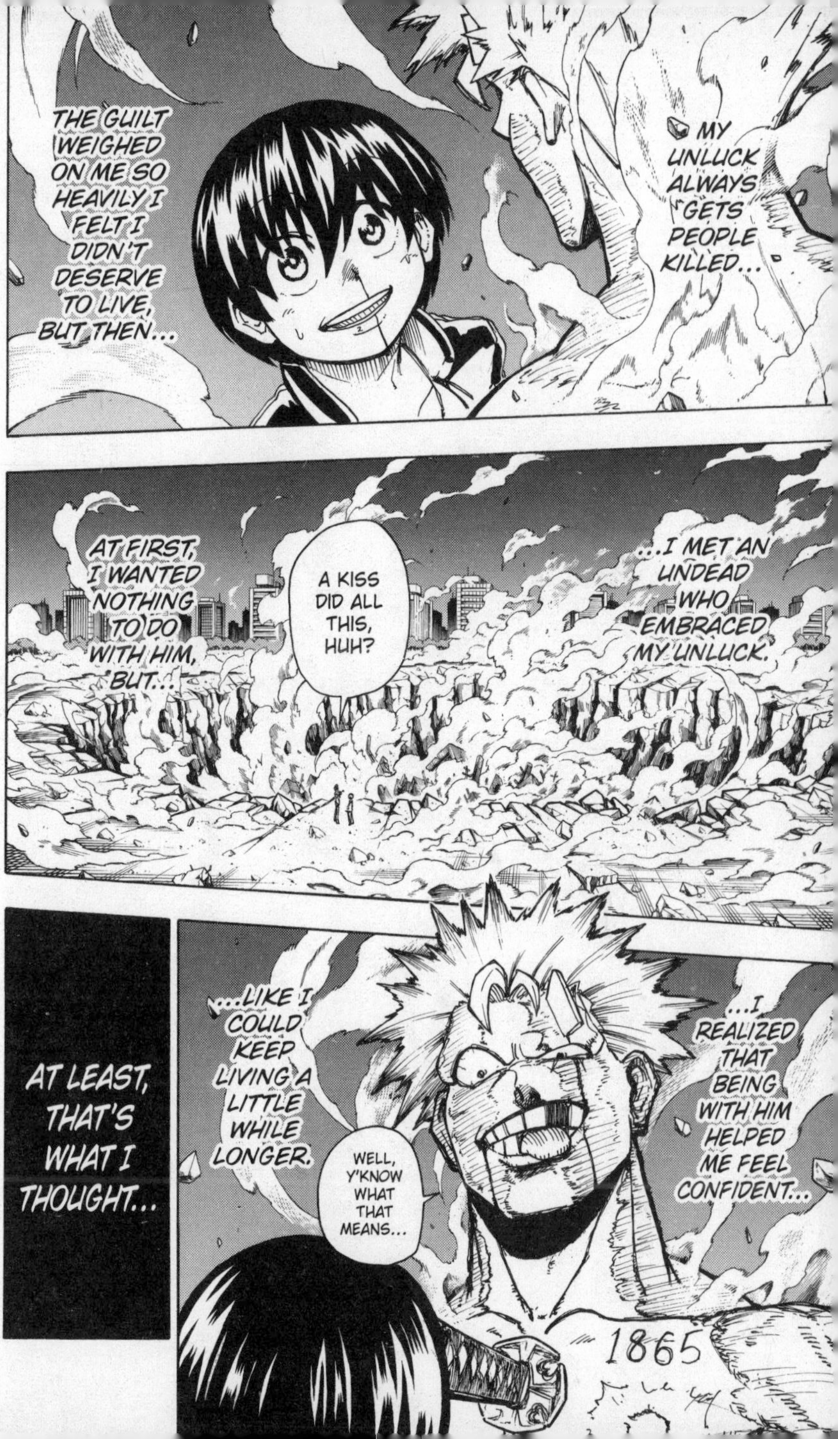
MY UNLUCK ALWAYS GETS PEOPLE KILLED...
THE GUILT WEIGHED ON ME SO HEAVILY I FELT I DIDN'T DESERVE TO LIVE, BUT THEN...
...I MET AN UNDEAD WHO EMBRACED MY UNLUCK.
A KISS DID ALL THIS, HUH?
AT FIRST, I WANTED NOTHING TO DO WITH HIM, BUT...
...I REALIZED THAT BEING WITH HIM HELPED ME FEEL CONFIDENT...
...LIKE I COULD KEEP LIVING A LITTLE WHILE LONGER.
WELL, Y'KNOW WHAT THAT MEANS...
1865
AT LEAST, THAT'S WHAT I THOUGHT...

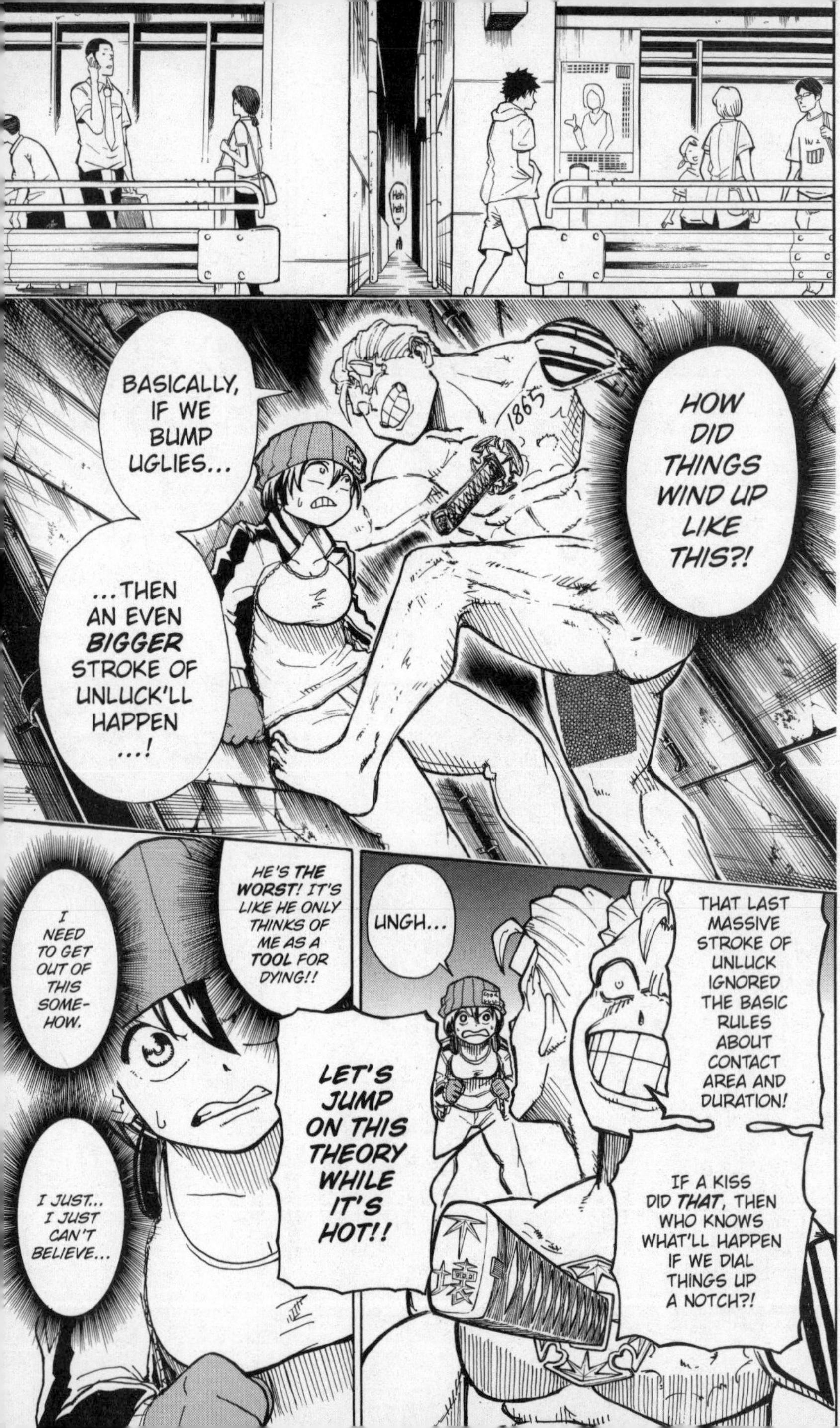
Heh heh
HOW DID THINGS WIND UP LIKE THIS?!
BASICALLY, IF WE BUMP UGLIES...
...THEN AN EVEN BIGGER STROKE OF UNLUCK'LL HAPPEN...!
THAT LAST MASSIVE STROKE OF UNLUCK IGNORED THE BASIC RULES ABOUT CONTACT AREA AND DURATION!
UNGH...
IF A KISS DID THAT, THEN WHO KNOWS WHAT'LL HAPPEN IF WE DIAL THINGS UP A NOTCH?!
LET'S JUMP ON THIS THEORY WHILE IT'S HOT!!
HE'S THE WORST! IT'S LIKE HE ONLY THINKS OF ME AS A TOOL FOR DYING!!
I NEED TO GET OUT OF THIS SOME-HOW.
I JUST... I JUST CAN'T BELIEVE...

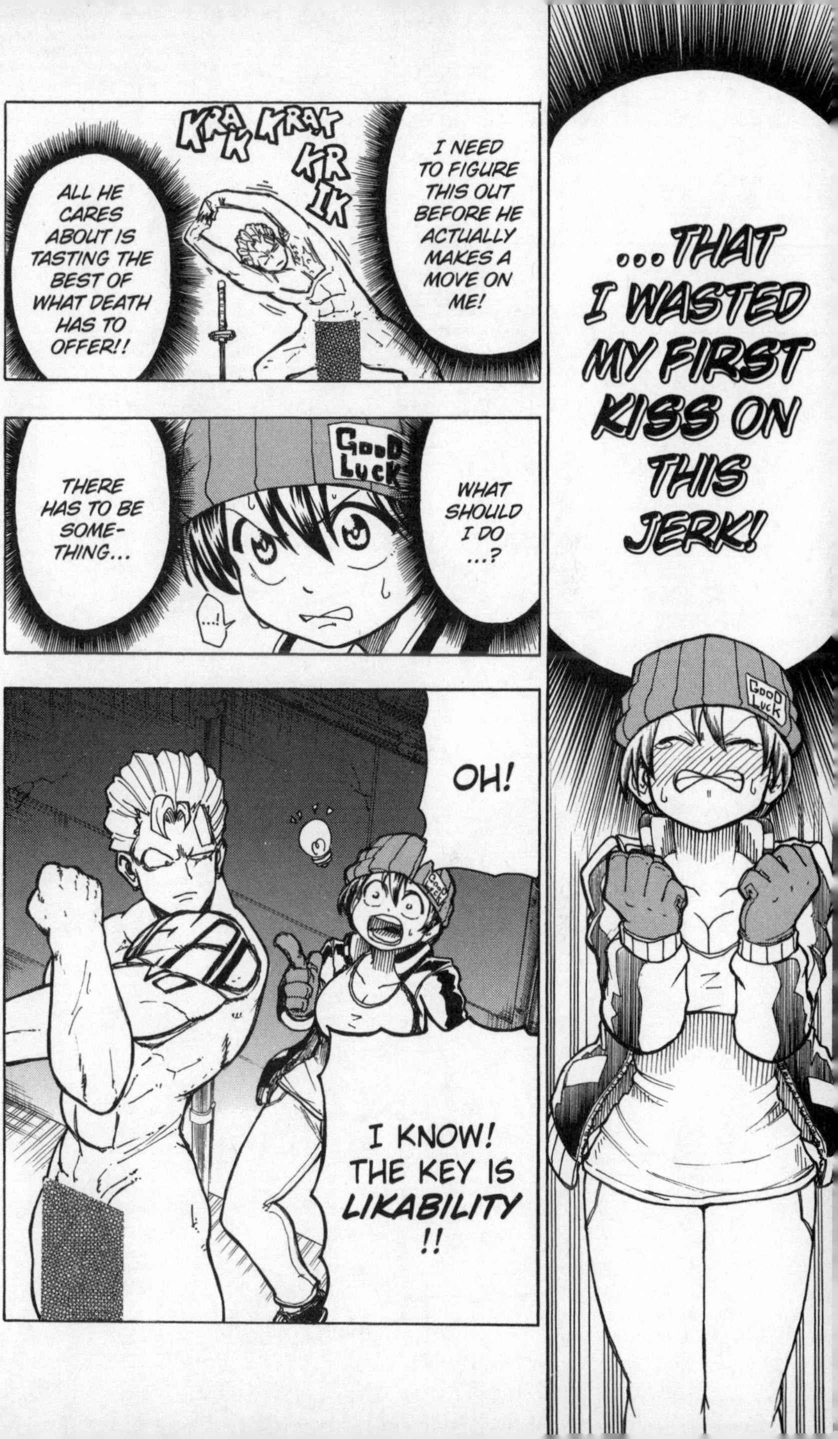
...THAT I WASTED MY FIRST KISS ON THIS JERK!
I NEED TO FIGURE THIS OUT BEFORE HE ACTUALLY MAKES A MOVE ON ME!
KRAK KRAK KRIK
ALL HE CARES ABOUT IS TASTING THE BEST OF WHAT DEATH HAS TO OFFER!!
GOOD LUCK
WHAT SHOULD I DO ...?
THERE HAS TO BE SOME-THING...
...!
OH!
GOOD LUCK
I KNOW! THE KEY IS *LIKABILITY* !!

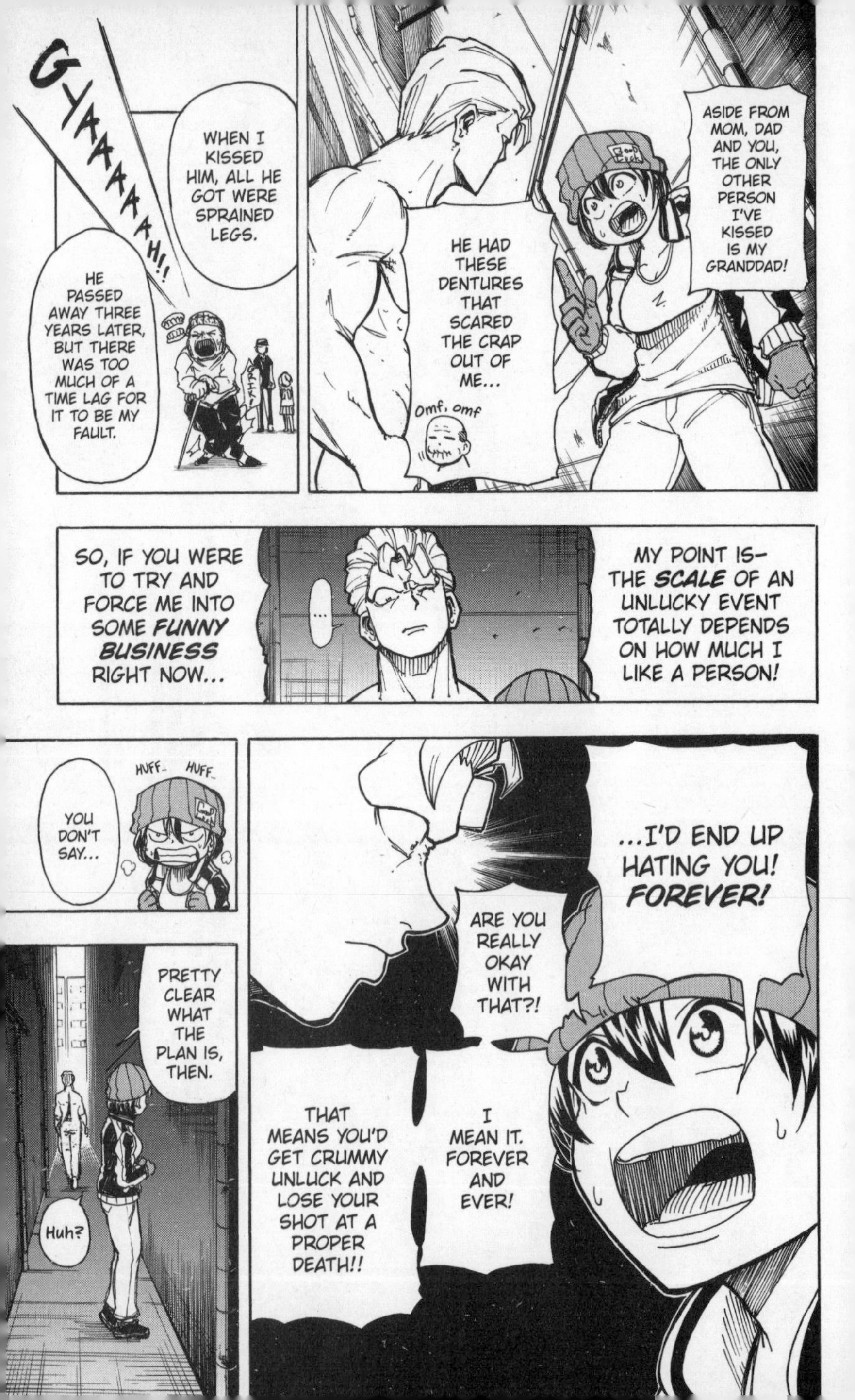
ASIDE FROM MOM, DAD AND YOU, THE ONLY OTHER PERSON I'VE KISSED IS MY GRANDDAD!
HE HAD THESE DENTURES THAT SCARED THE CRAP OUT OF ME...
Omf, omf
WHEN I KISSED HIM, ALL HE GOT WERE SPRAINED LEGS.
GYAAAAAAH!!
HE PASSED AWAY THREE YEARS LATER, BUT THERE WAS TOO MUCH OF A TIME LAG FOR IT TO BE MY FAULT.
MY POINT IS— THE *SCALE* OF AN UNLUCKY EVENT TOTALLY DEPENDS ON HOW MUCH I LIKE A PERSON!
...
SO, IF YOU WERE TO TRY AND FORCE ME INTO SOME *FUNNY BUSINESS* RIGHT NOW...
...I'D END UP HATING YOU! *FOREVER!*
ARE YOU REALLY OKAY WITH THAT?!
I MEAN IT. FOREVER AND EVER!
THAT MEANS YOU'D GET CRUMMY UNLUCK AND LOSE YOUR SHOT AT A PROPER DEATH!!
HUFF... HUFF...
YOU DON'T SAY...
PRETTY CLEAR WHAT THE PLAN IS, THEN.
Huh?

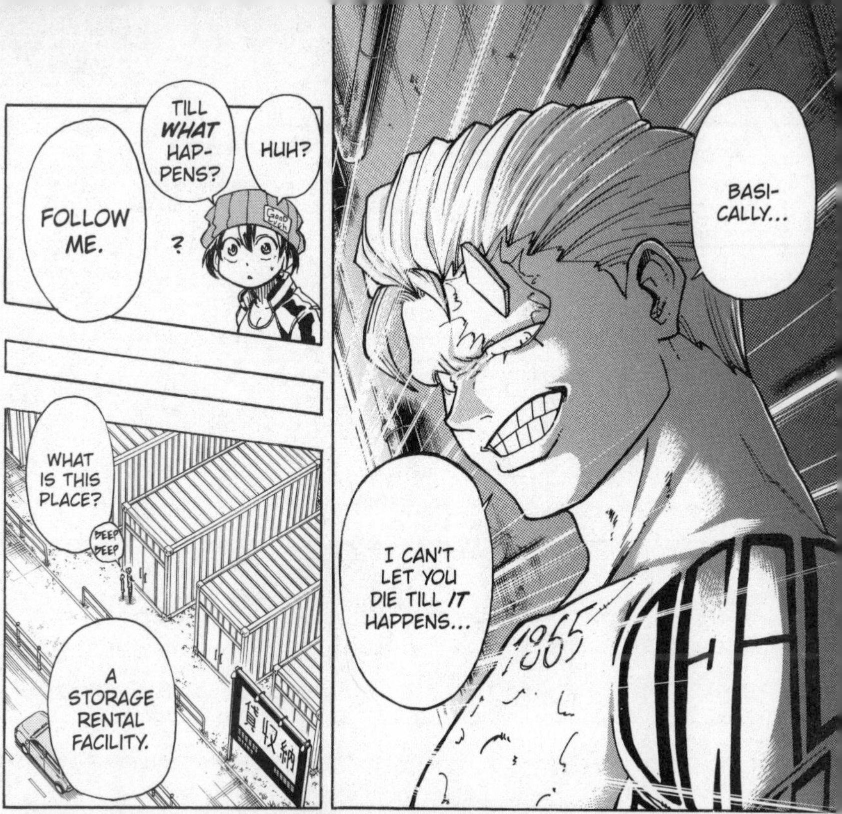
BASI-CALLY...
I CAN'T LET YOU DIE TILL *IT* HAPPENS...
HUH?
TILL ***WHAT*** HAP-PENS?
FOLLOW ME.
?
WHAT IS THIS PLACE?
BEEP BEEP
A STORAGE RENTAL FACILITY.
貸収納

SIGN: STORAGE RENTAL

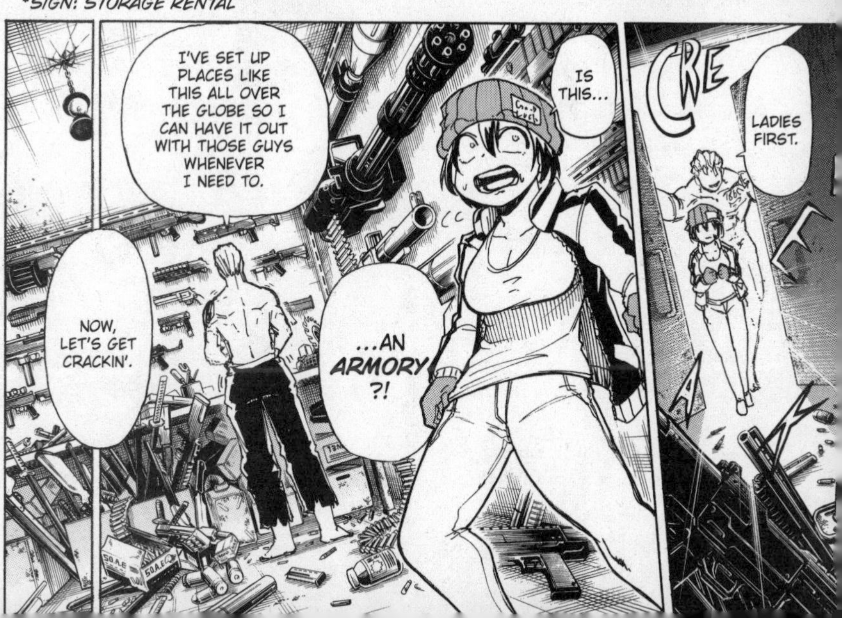
CRE
LADIES FIRST.
IS THIS...
...AN ***ARMORY*** ?!
I'VE SET UP PLACES LIKE THIS ALL OVER THE GLOBE SO I CAN HAVE IT OUT WITH THOSE GUYS WHENEVER I NEED TO.
NOW, LET'S GET CRACKIN'.

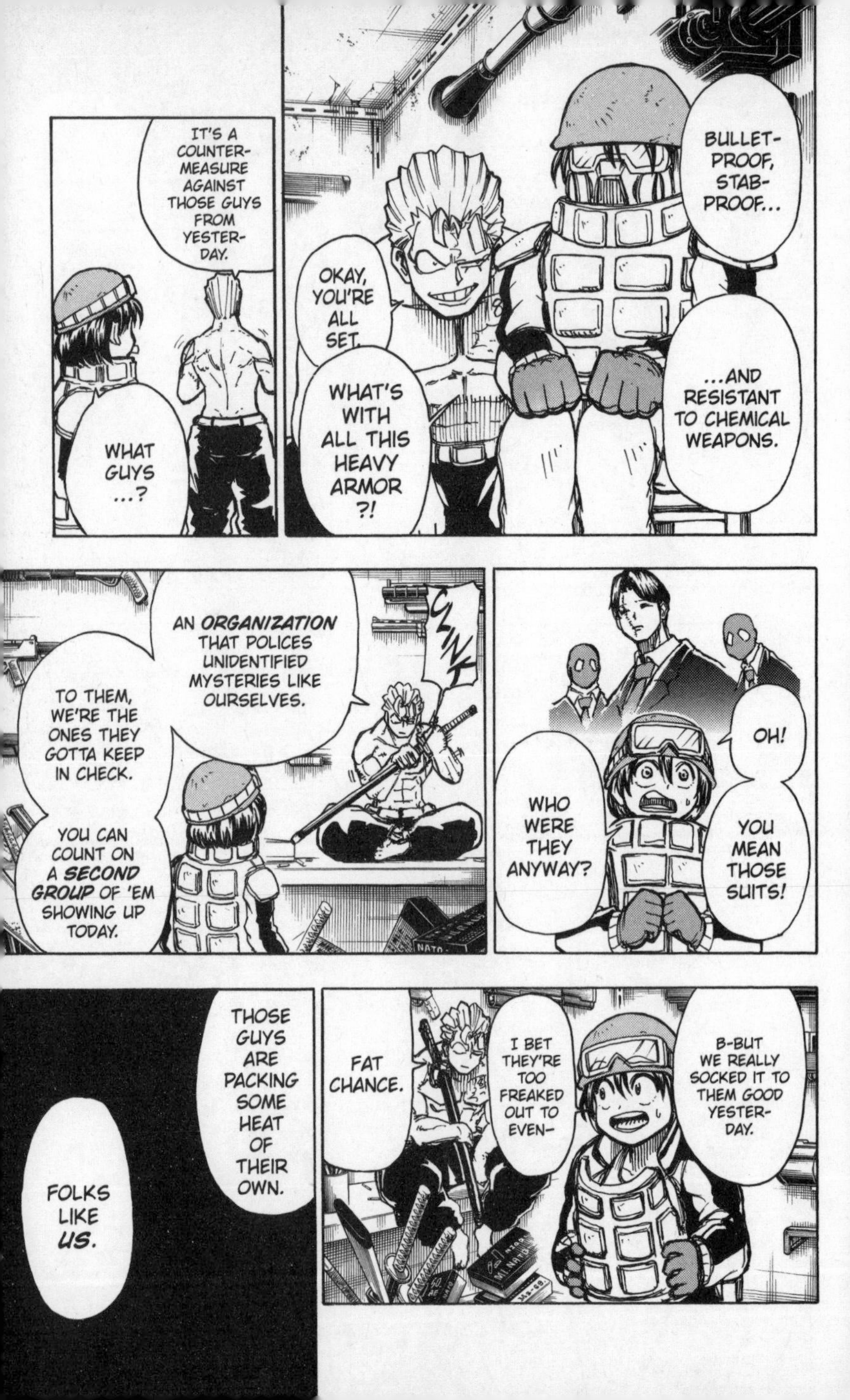
BULLET-PROOF, STAB-PROOF...
...AND RESISTANT TO CHEMICAL WEAPONS.
OKAY, YOU'RE ALL SET.
WHAT'S WITH ALL THIS HEAVY ARMOR?!
IT'S A COUNTER-MEASURE AGAINST THOSE GUYS FROM YESTER-DAY.
WHAT GUYS...?
OH!
YOU MEAN THOSE SUITS!
WHO WERE THEY ANYWAY?
AN *ORGANIZATION* THAT POLICES UNIDENTIFIED MYSTERIES LIKE OURSELVES.
CLINK
TO THEM, WE'RE THE ONES THEY GOTTA KEEP IN CHECK.
YOU CAN COUNT ON A ***SECOND GROUP*** OF 'EM SHOWING UP TODAY.
B-BUT WE REALLY SOCKED IT TO THEM GOOD YESTER-DAY.
I BET THEY'RE TOO FREAKED OUT TO EVEN-
FAT CHANCE.
THOSE GUYS ARE PACKING SOME HEAT OF THEIR OWN.
FOLKS LIKE ***US***.

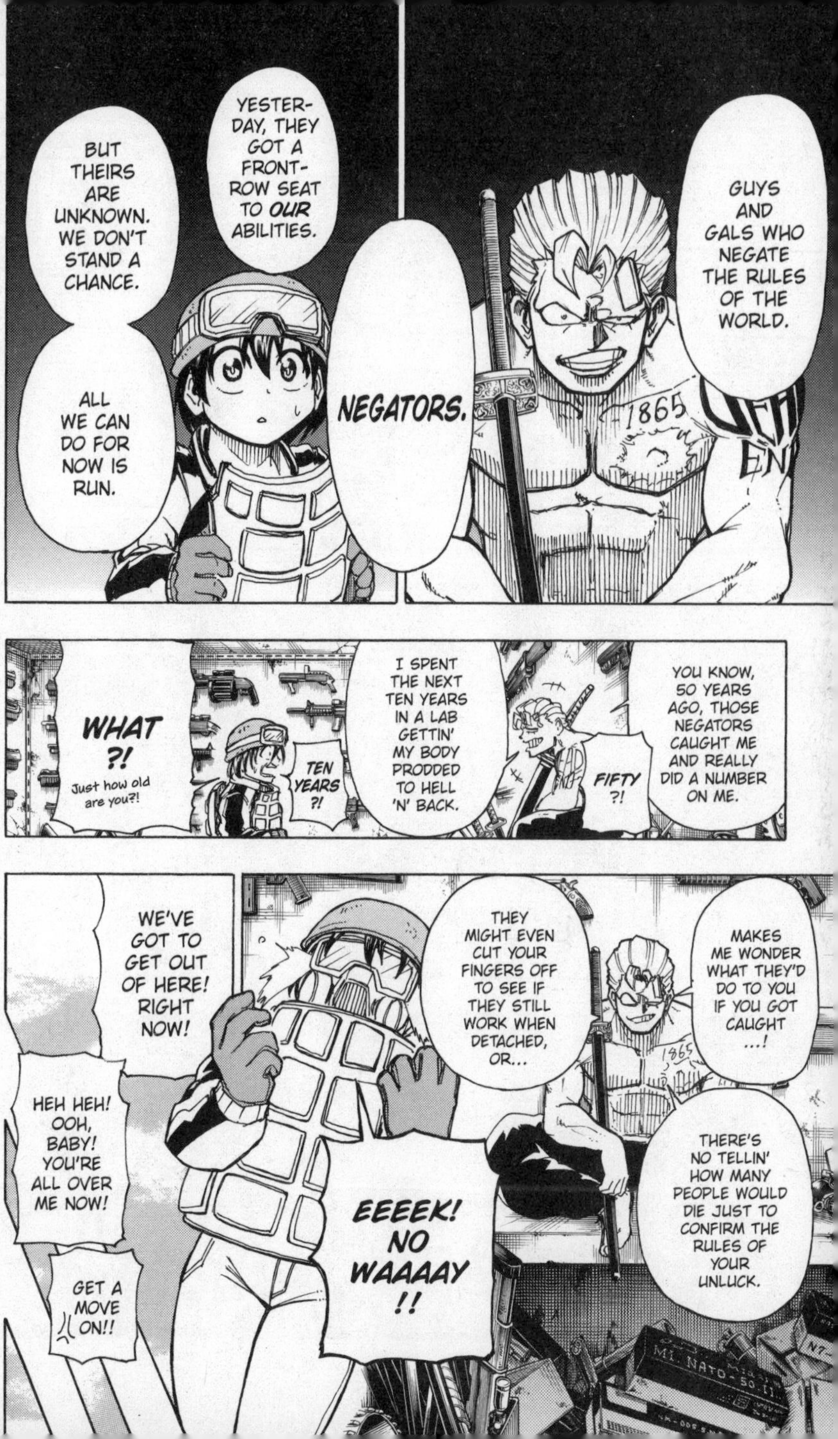
GUYS AND GALS WHO NEGATE THE RULES OF THE WORLD.
NEGATORS.
YESTER-DAY, THEY GOT A FRONT-ROW SEAT TO *OUR* ABILITIES.
BUT THEIRS ARE UNKNOWN. WE DON'T STAND A CHANCE.
ALL WE CAN DO FOR NOW IS RUN.
1865
YOU KNOW, 50 YEARS AGO, THOSE NEGATORS CAUGHT ME AND REALLY DID A NUMBER ON ME.
FIFTY ?!
I SPENT THE NEXT TEN YEARS IN A LAB GETTIN' MY BODY PRODDED TO HELL 'N' BACK.
TEN YEARS ?!
WHAT ?!
Just how old are you?!
MAKES ME WONDER WHAT THEY'D DO TO YOU IF YOU GOT CAUGHT ...!
THEY MIGHT EVEN CUT YOUR FINGERS OFF TO SEE IF THEY STILL WORK WHEN DETACHED, OR...
THERE'S NO TELLIN' HOW MANY PEOPLE WOULD DIE JUST TO CONFIRM THE RULES OF YOUR UNLUCK.
EEEEK! NO WAAAAY !!
WE'VE GOT TO GET OUT OF HERE! RIGHT NOW!
HEH HEH! OOH, BABY! YOU'RE ALL OVER ME NOW!
GET A MOVE ON!!

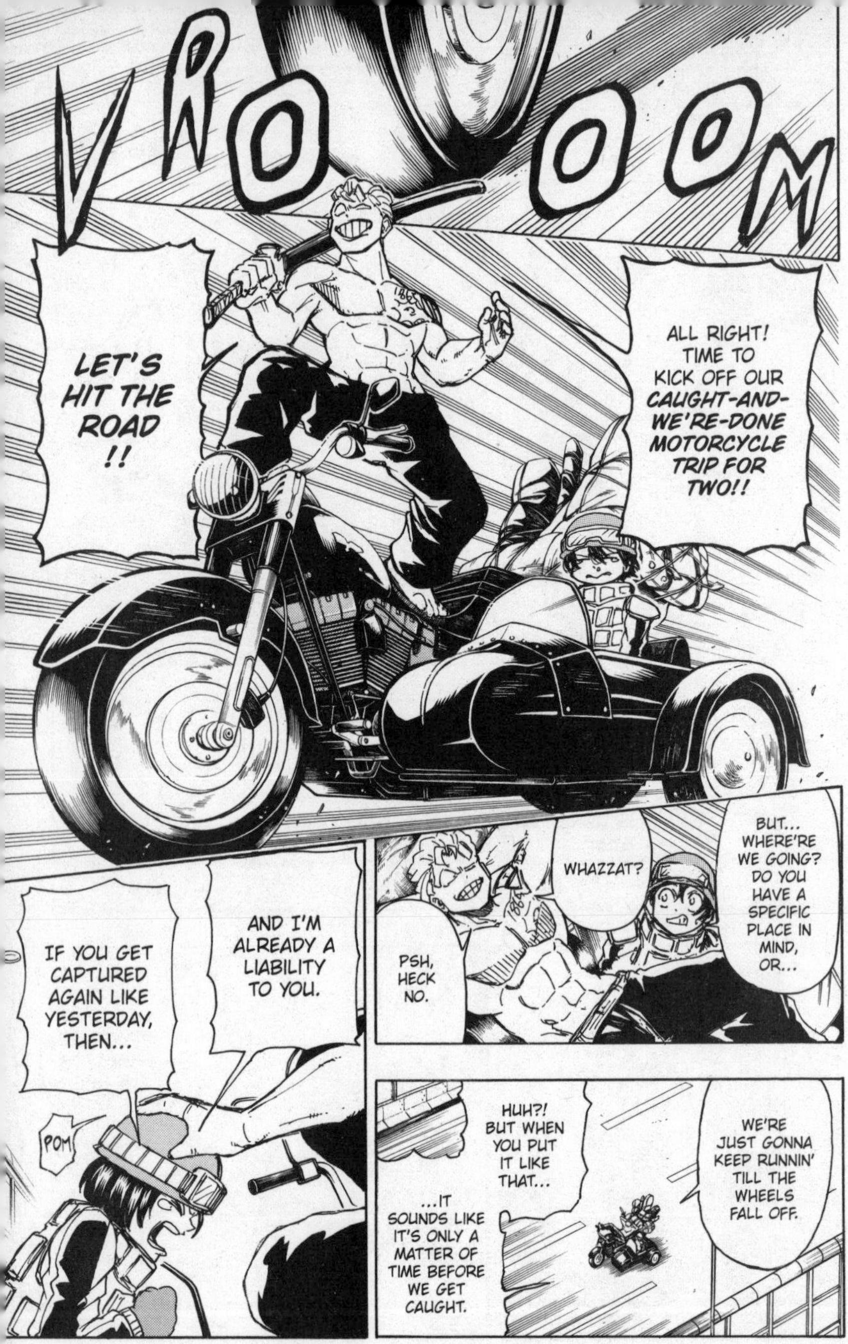
VROOOOM
ALL RIGHT! TIME TO KICK OFF OUR CAUGHT-AND-WE'RE-DONE MOTORCYCLE TRIP FOR TWO!!
LET'S HIT THE ROAD!!
BUT... WHERE'RE WE GOING? DO YOU HAVE A SPECIFIC PLACE IN MIND, OR...
WHAZZAT?
PSH, HECK NO.
WE'RE JUST GONNA KEEP RUNNIN' TILL THE WHEELS FALL OFF.
HUH?! BUT WHEN YOU PUT IT LIKE THAT...
...IT SOUNDS LIKE IT'S ONLY A MATTER OF TIME BEFORE WE GET CAUGHT.
AND I'M ALREADY A LIABILITY TO YOU.
IF YOU GET CAPTURED AGAIN LIKE YESTERDAY, THEN...
POM

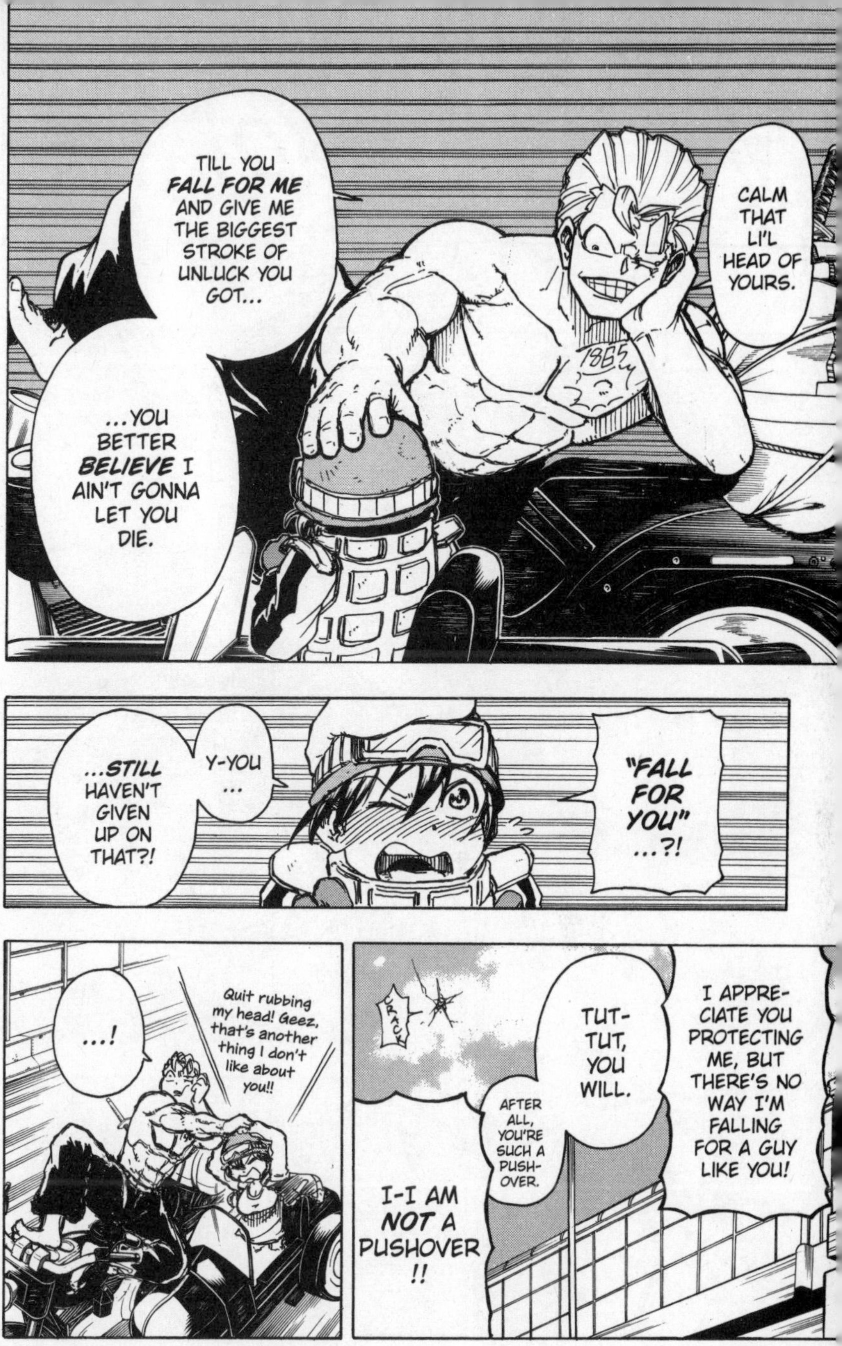
CALM THAT LI'L HEAD OF YOURS.
TILL YOU FALL FOR ME AND GIVE ME THE BIGGEST STROKE OF UNLUCK YOU GOT...
...YOU BETTER BELIEVE I AIN'T GONNA LET YOU DIE.
"FALL FOR YOU" ...?!
Y-YOU ...
...STILL HAVEN'T GIVEN UP ON THAT?!
I APPRE-CIATE YOU PROTECTING ME, BUT THERE'S NO WAY I'M FALLING FOR A GUY LIKE YOU!
TUT-TUT, YOU WILL.
CRACK
AFTER ALL, YOU'RE SUCH A PUSH-OVER.
I-I AM NOT A PUSHOVER!!
Quit rubbing my head! Geez, that's another thing I don't like about you!!
...!

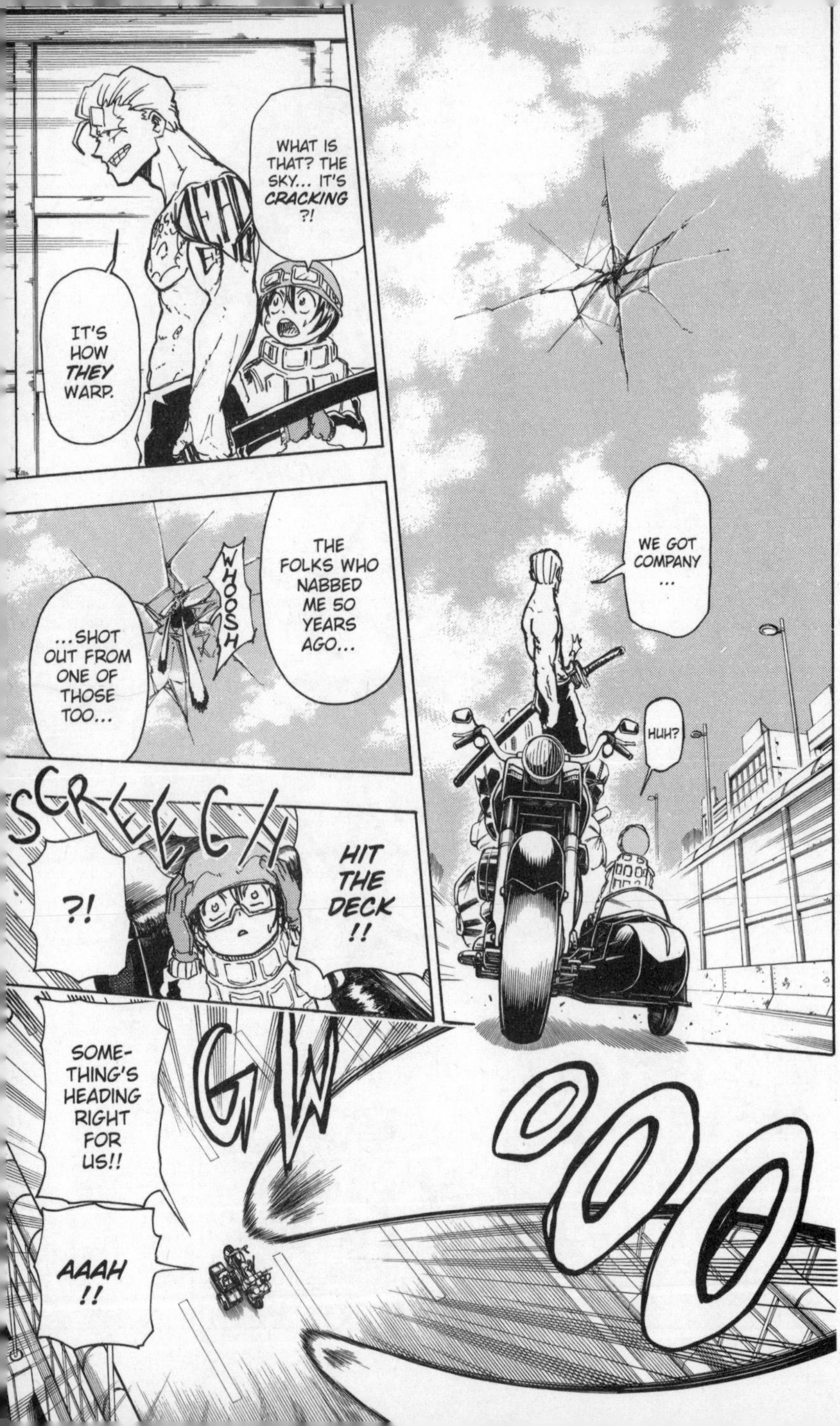
WE GOT COMPANY ...
HUH?
WHAT IS THAT? THE SKY... IT'S CRACKING ?!
IT'S HOW THEY WARP.
THE FOLKS WHO NABBED ME 50 YEARS AGO...
WHOOSH
...SHOT OUT FROM ONE OF THOSE TOO...
SCREECH
HIT THE DECK !!
?!
GWOOO
SOME-THING'S HEADING RIGHT FOR US!!
AAAH !!

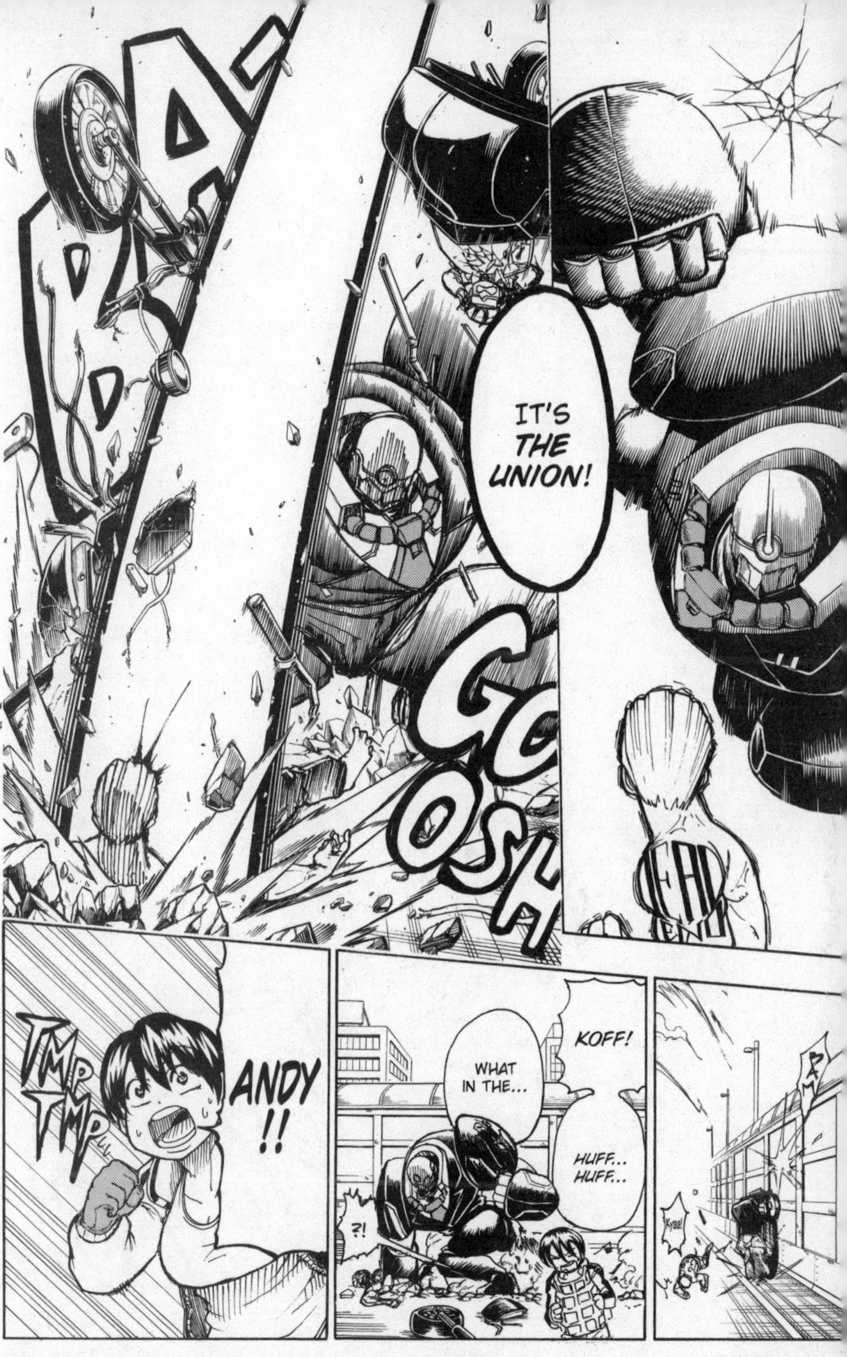
IT'S THE UNION!
GOOSH
ANDY!!
TMP TMP
KOFF!
WHAT IN THE...
HUFF... HUFF...
?!
Kyaa!

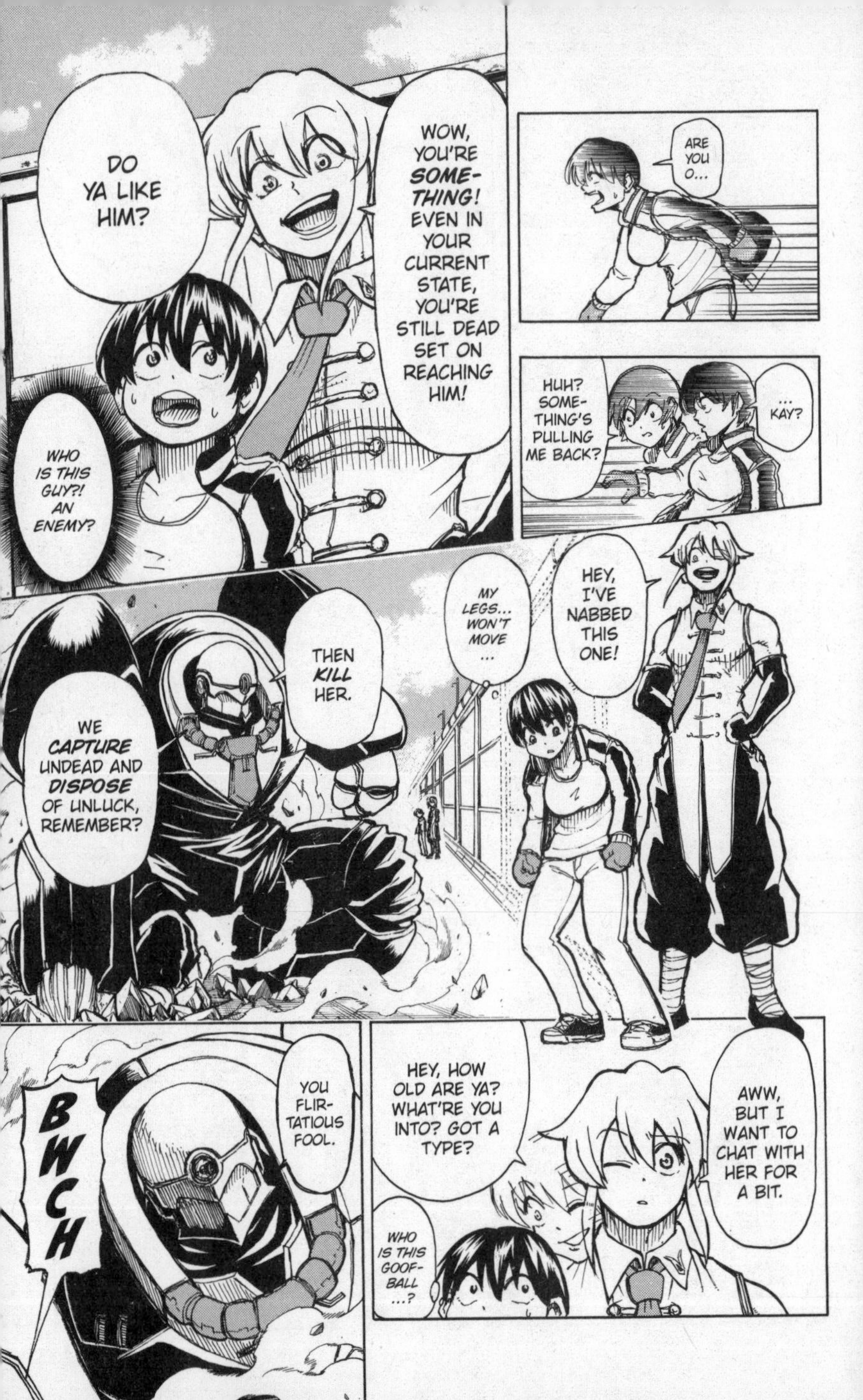
ARE YOU O...
...KAY?
HUH? SOMETHING'S PULLING ME BACK?
WOW, YOU'RE SOMETHING! EVEN IN YOUR CURRENT STATE, YOU'RE STILL DEAD SET ON REACHING HIM!
DO YA LIKE HIM?
WHO IS THIS GUY?! AN ENEMY?
HEY, I'VE NABBED THIS ONE!
MY LEGS... WON'T MOVE...
THEN KILL HER.
WE CAPTURE UNDEAD AND DISPOSE OF UNLUCK, REMEMBER?
AWW, BUT I WANT TO CHAT WITH HER FOR A BIT.
HEY, HOW OLD ARE YA? WHAT'RE YOU INTO? GOT A TYPE?
WHO IS THIS GOOFBALL ...?
YOU FLIRTATIOUS FOOL.
BWCH

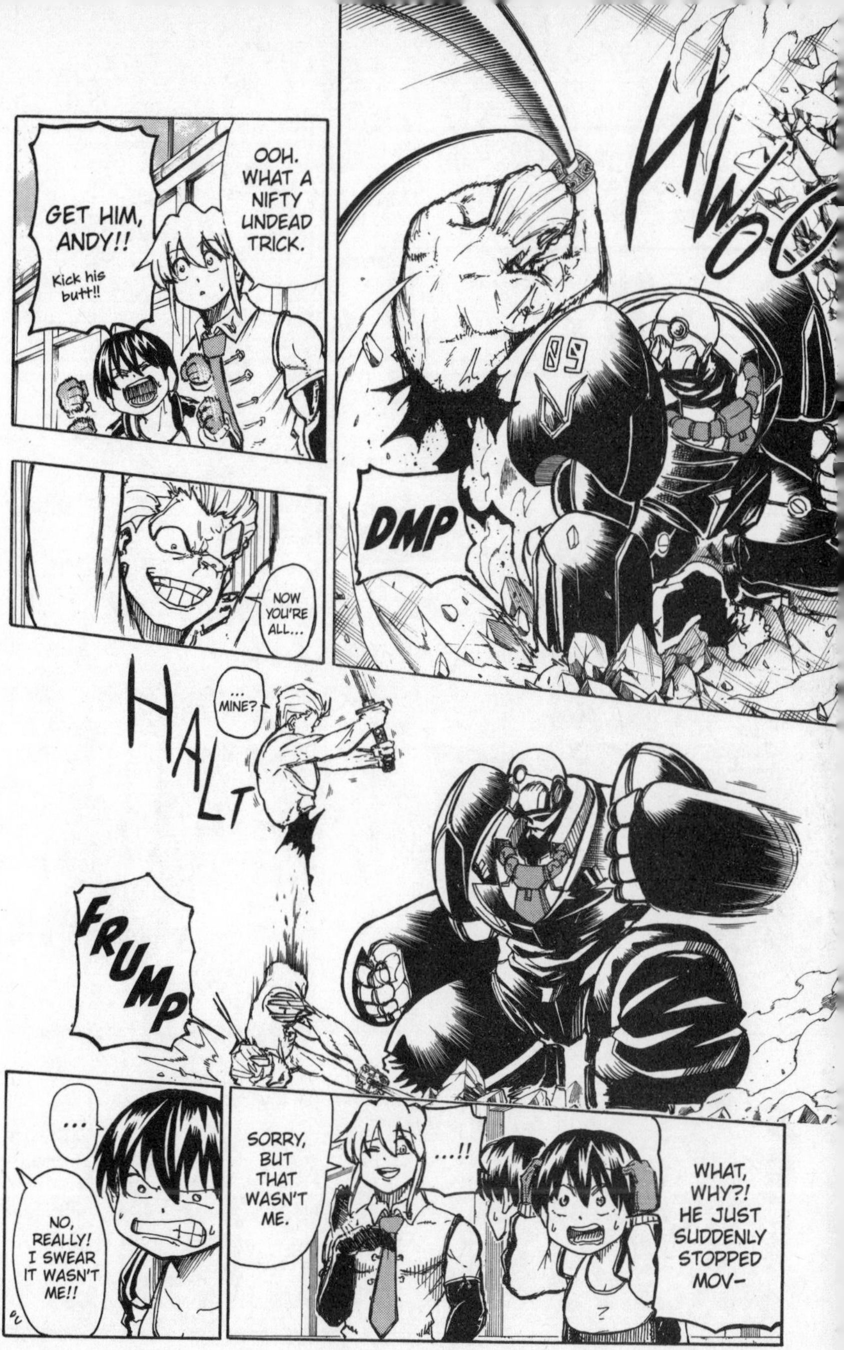
DMP
OOH. WHAT A NIFTY UNDEAD TRICK.
GET HIM, ANDY!!
Kick his butt!!
NOW YOU'RE ALL...
... MINE?
HALT
FRUMP
WHAT, WHY?! HE JUST SUDDENLY STOPPED MOV-
...!!
SORRY, BUT THAT WASN'T ME.
...
NO, REALLY! I SWEAR IT WASN'T ME!!

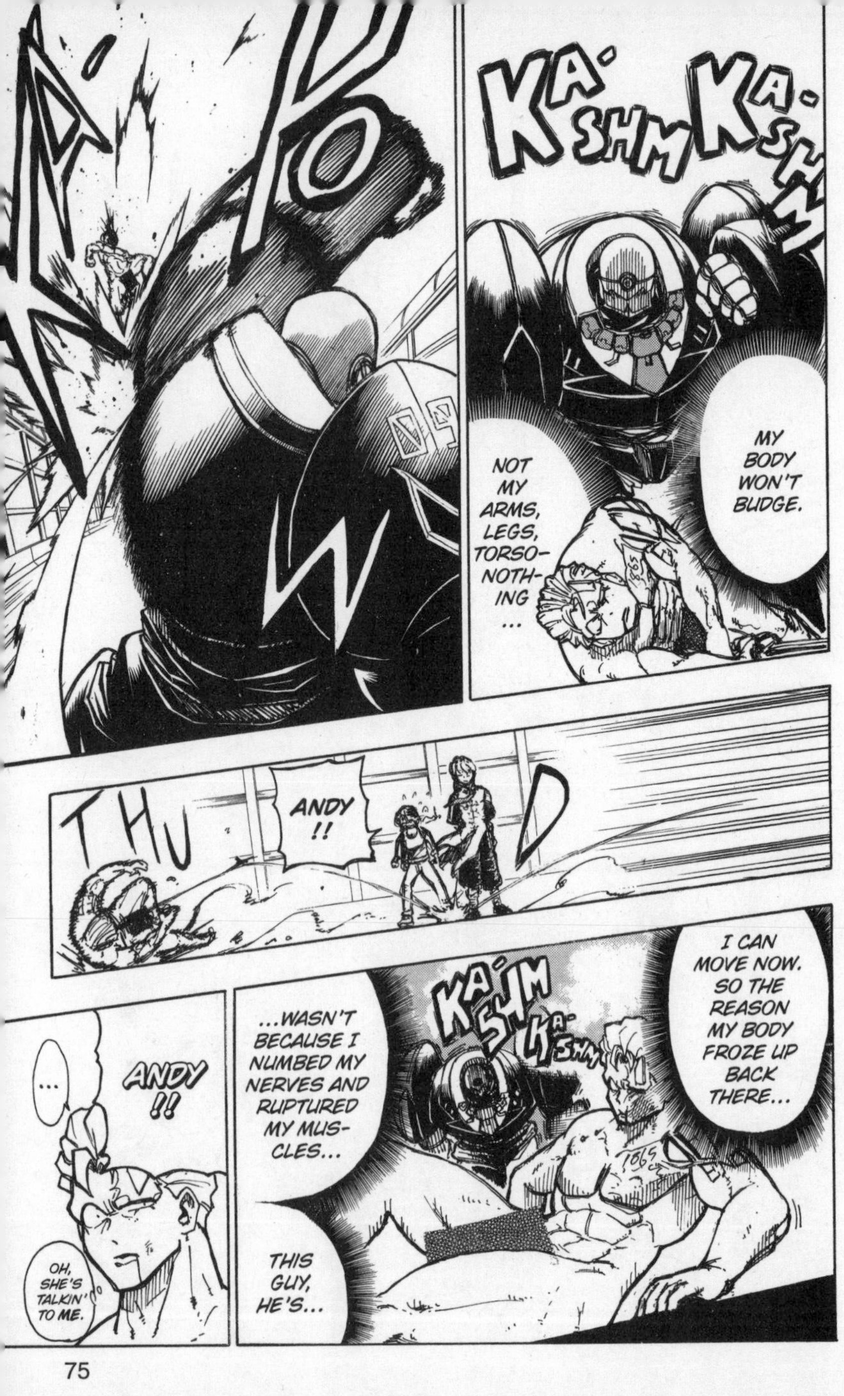
KA-SHM KA-SHM
MY BODY WON'T BUDGE.
NOT MY ARMS, LEGS, TORSO—NOTHING...
THUD
ANDY!!
I CAN MOVE NOW. SO THE REASON MY BODY FROZE UP BACK THERE...
KA-SHM KA-SHM
...WASN'T BECAUSE I NUMBED MY NERVES AND RUPTURED MY MUSCLES...
THIS GUY, HE'S...
...
ANDY!!
OH, SHE'S TALKIN' TO ME.

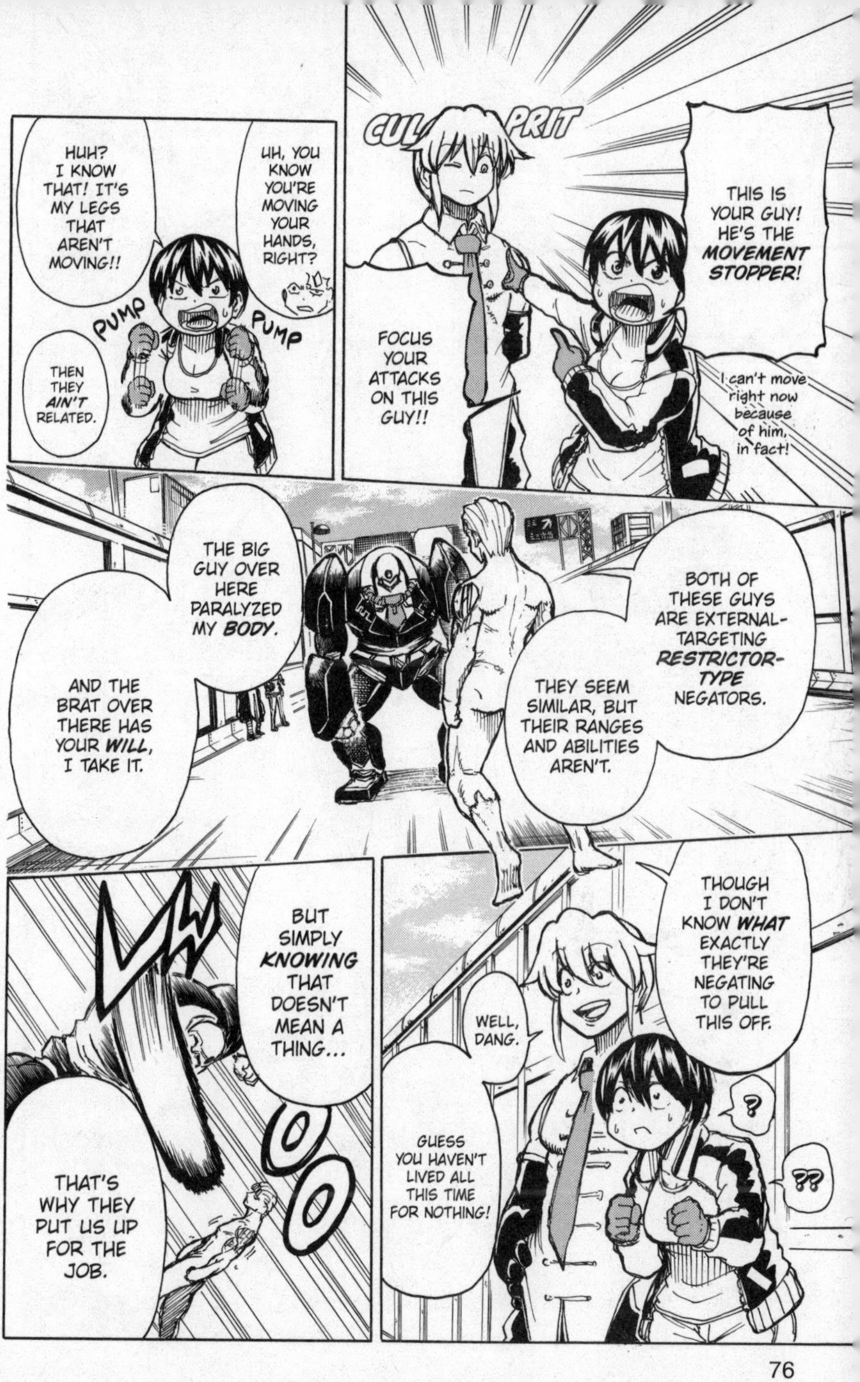
CUL PRIT
THIS IS YOUR GUY! HE'S THE MOVEMENT STOPPER!
FOCUS YOUR ATTACKS ON THIS GUY!!
I can't move right now because of him, in fact!
UH, YOU KNOW YOU'RE MOVING YOUR HANDS, RIGHT?
HUH? I KNOW THAT! IT'S MY LEGS THAT AREN'T MOVING!!
PUMP
PUMP
THEN THEY AIN'T RELATED.
BOTH OF THESE GUYS ARE EXTERNAL-TARGETING RESTRICTOR-TYPE NEGATORS.
THEY SEEM SIMILAR, BUT THEIR RANGES AND ABILITIES AREN'T.
THE BIG GUY OVER HERE PARALYZED MY BODY.
AND THE BRAT OVER THERE HAS YOUR WILL, I TAKE IT.
THOUGH I DON'T KNOW WHAT EXACTLY THEY'RE NEGATING TO PULL THIS OFF.
WELL, DANG.
?
??
GUESS YOU HAVEN'T LIVED ALL THIS TIME FOR NOTHING!
BUT SIMPLY KNOWING THAT DOESN'T MEAN A THING...
THAT'S WHY THEY PUT US UP FOR THE JOB.

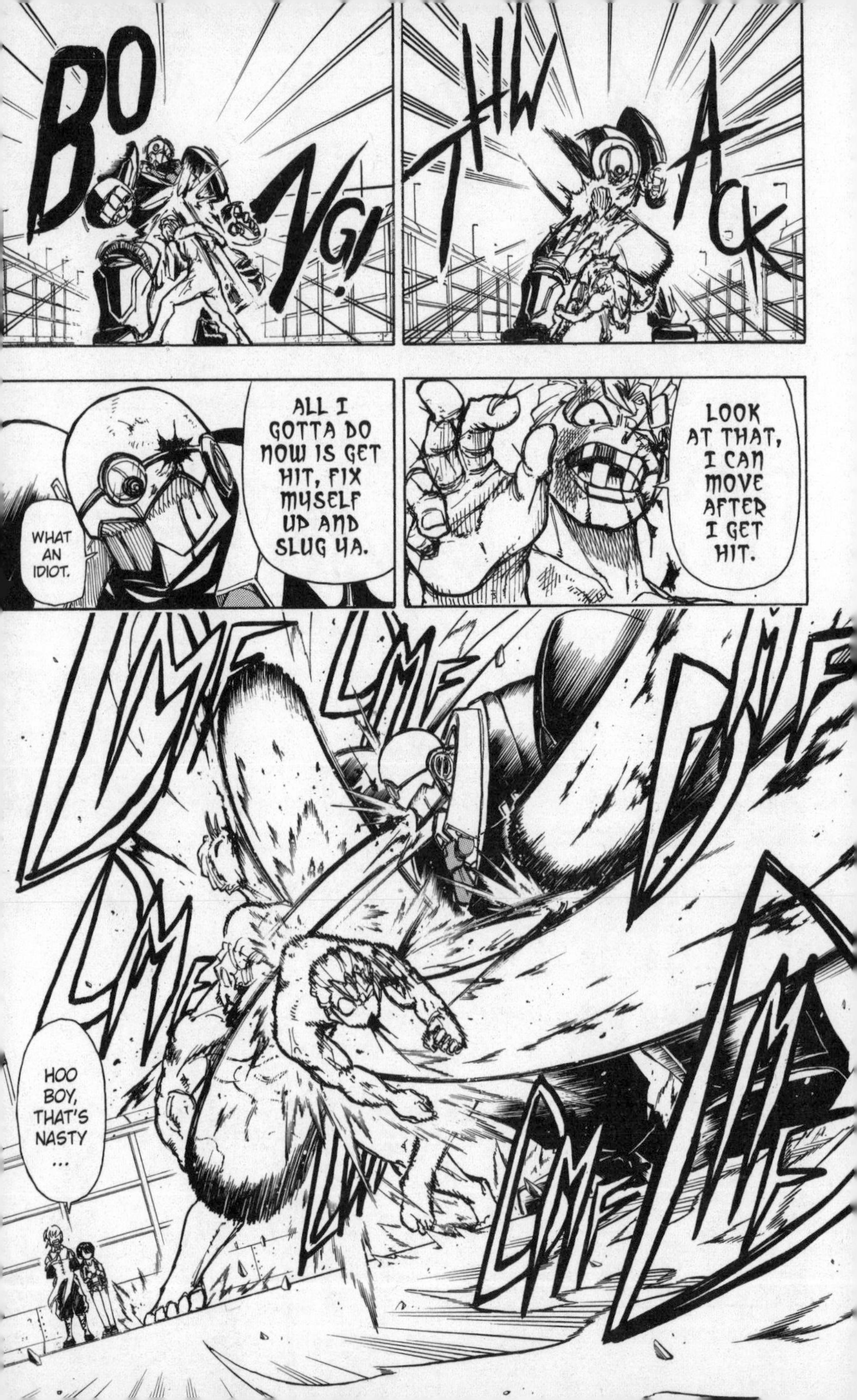
THWACK
BONG!
LOOK AT THAT, I CAN MOVE AFTER I GET HIT.
ALL I GOTTA DO NOW IS GET HIT, FIX MYSELF UP AND SLUG YA.
WHAT AN IDIOT.
HOO BOY, THAT'S NASTY ...

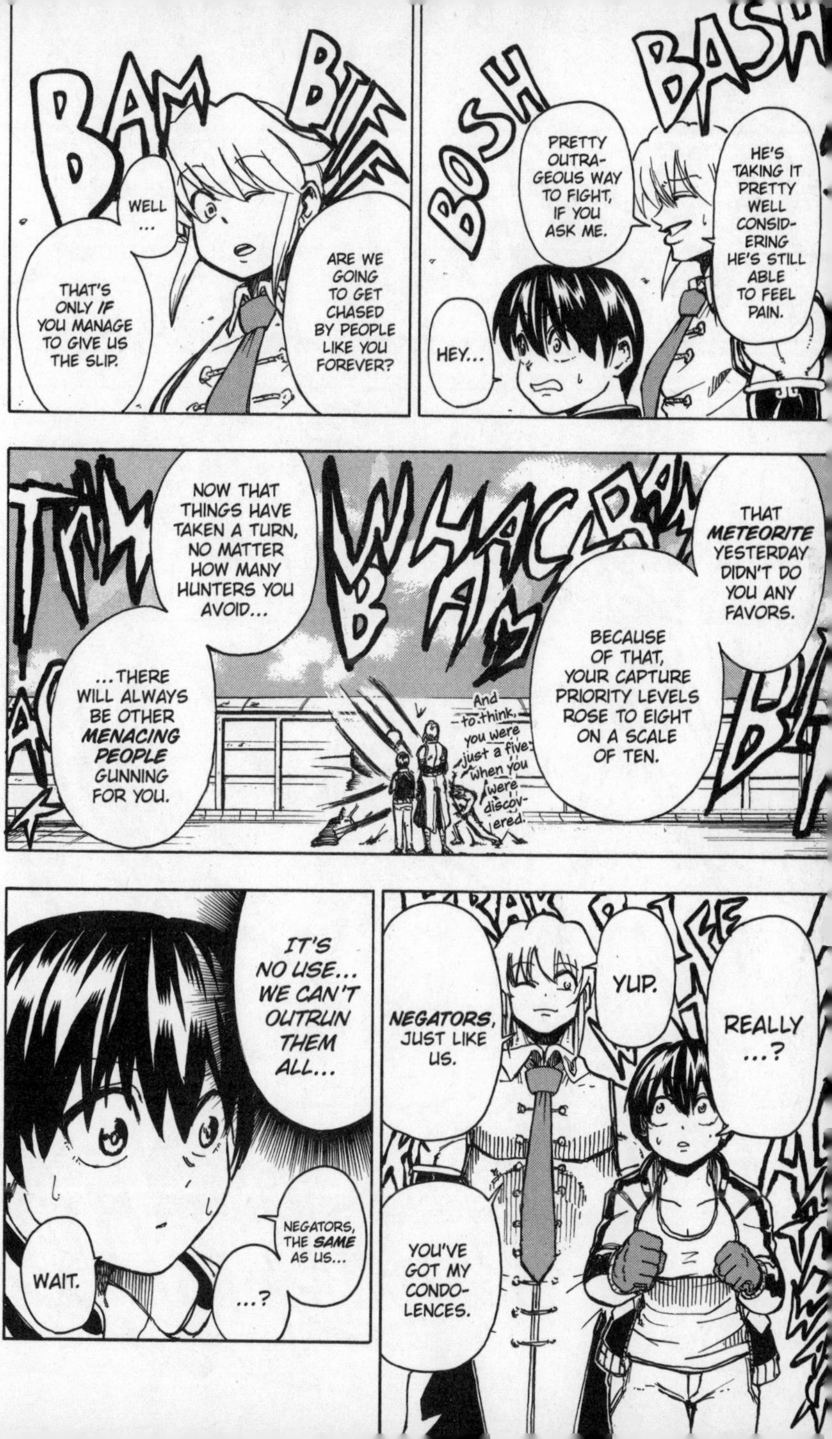
BASH
BOSH
HE'S TAKING IT PRETTY WELL CONSIDERING HE'S STILL ABLE TO FEEL PAIN.
PRETTY OUTRAGEOUS WAY TO FIGHT, IF YOU ASK ME.
HEY...
BIFF
BAM
ARE WE GOING TO GET CHASED BY PEOPLE LIKE YOU FOREVER?
WELL...
THAT'S ONLY *IF* YOU MANAGE TO GIVE US THE SLIP.
THAT *METEORITE* YESTERDAY DIDN'T DO YOU ANY FAVORS.
BECAUSE OF THAT, YOUR CAPTURE PRIORITY LEVELS ROSE TO EIGHT ON A SCALE OF TEN.
And to think, you were just a five when you were discovered.
WHAC
BAM
NOW THAT THINGS HAVE TAKEN A TURN, NO MATTER HOW MANY HUNTERS YOU AVOID...
...THERE WILL ALWAYS BE OTHER *MENACING PEOPLE* GUNNING FOR YOU.
REALLY ...?
YUP.
NEGATORS, JUST LIKE US.
YOU'VE GOT MY CONDOLENCES.
IT'S NO USE... WE CAN'T OUTRUN THEM ALL...
NEGATORS, THE *SAME* AS US...
...?
WAIT.

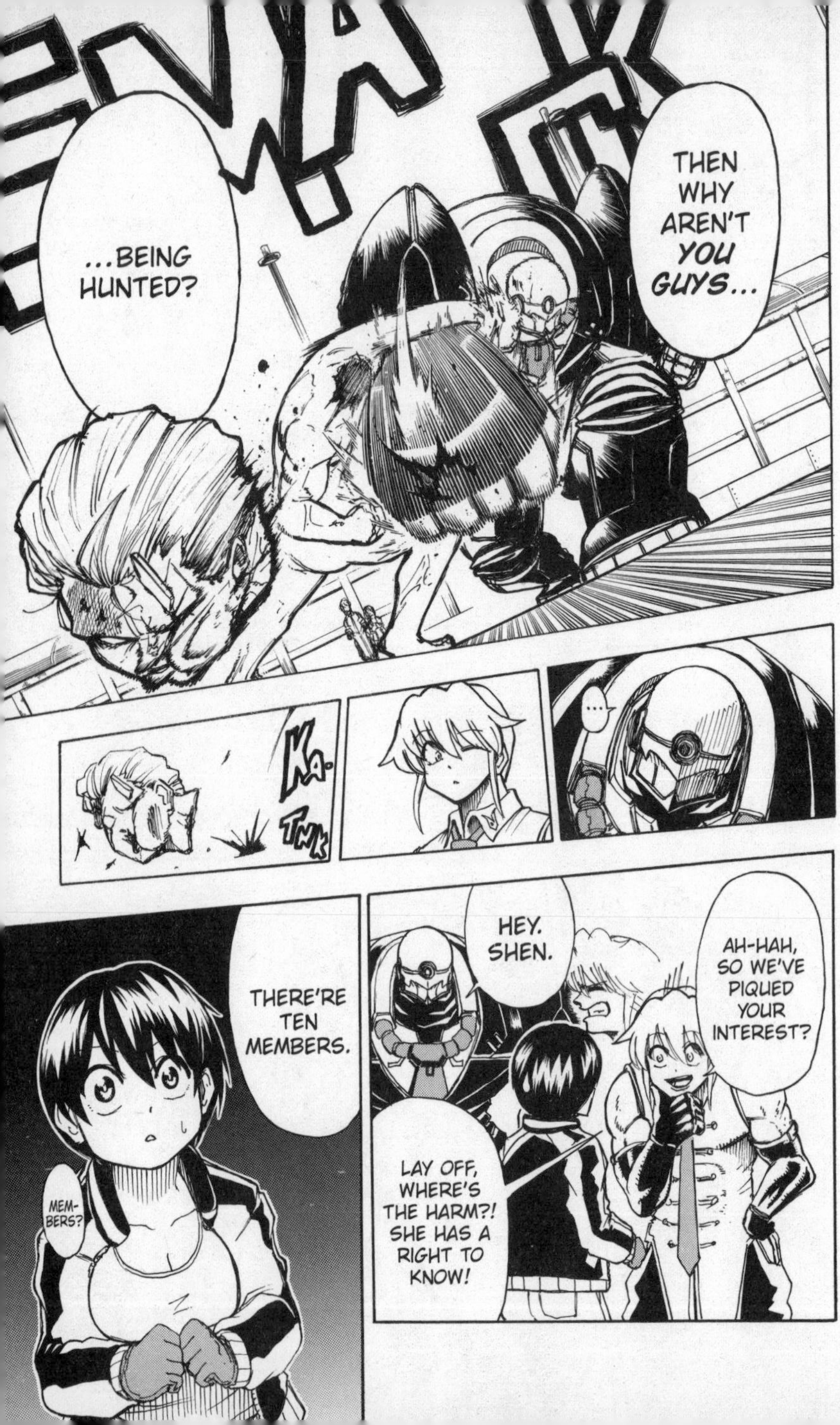
THEN WHY AREN'T YOU GUYS...
...BEING HUNTED?
...
KA-TNK
AH-HAH, SO WE'VE PIQUED YOUR INTEREST?
HEY. SHEN.
LAY OFF, WHERE'S THE HARM?! SHE HAS A RIGHT TO KNOW!
THERE'RE TEN MEMBERS.
MEM-BERS?

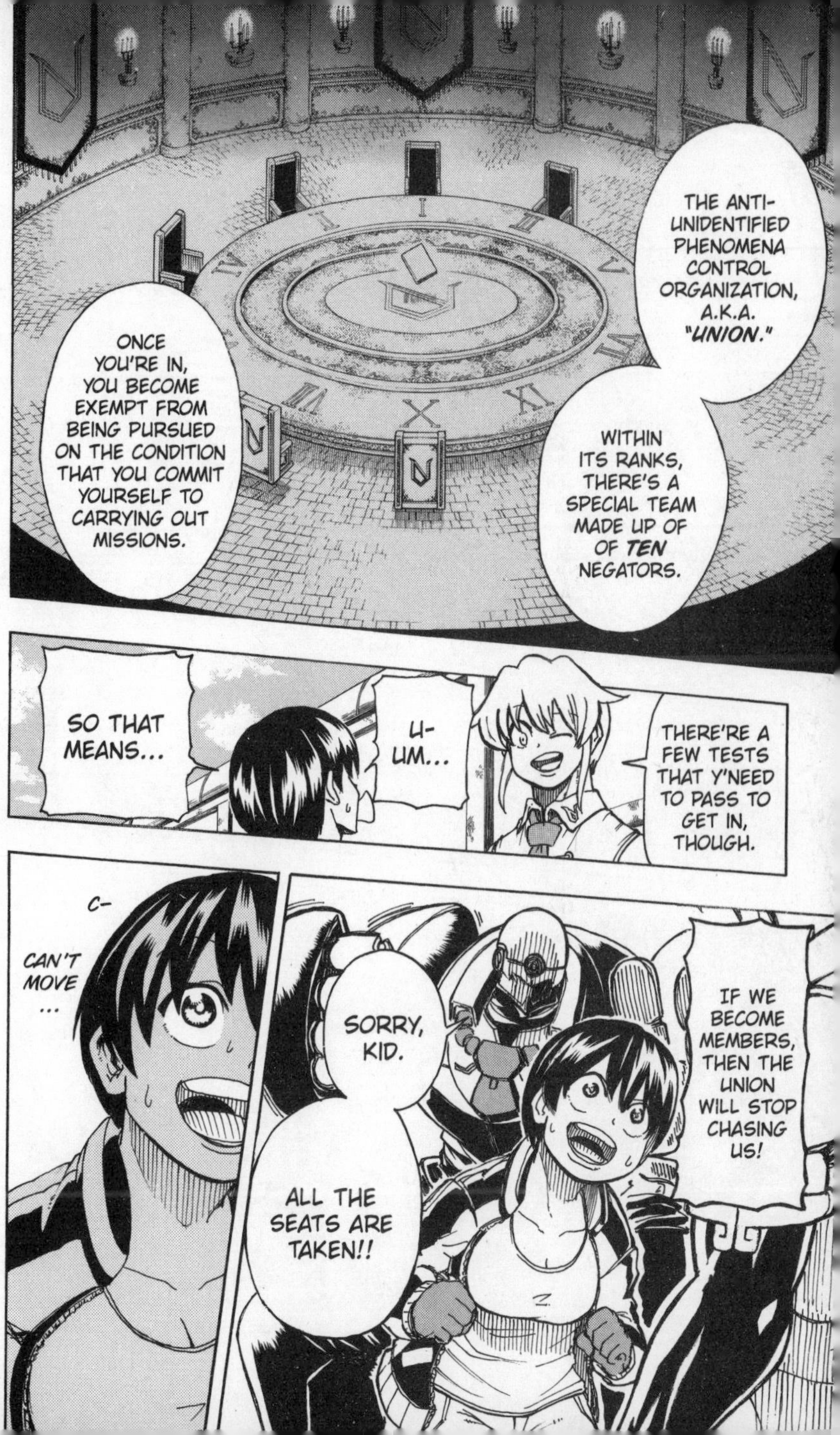
THE ANTI-UNIDENTIFIED PHENOMENA CONTROL ORGANIZATION, A.K.A. "UNION."
WITHIN ITS RANKS, THERE'S A SPECIAL TEAM MADE UP OF OF TEN NEGATORS.
ONCE YOU'RE IN, YOU BECOME EXEMPT FROM BEING PURSUED ON THE CONDITION THAT YOU COMMIT YOURSELF TO CARRYING OUT MISSIONS.
THERE'RE A FEW TESTS THAT Y'NEED TO PASS TO GET IN, THOUGH.
U-UM...
SO THAT MEANS...
IF WE BECOME MEMBERS, THEN THE UNION WILL STOP CHASING US!
SORRY, KID.
ALL THE SEATS ARE TAKEN!!
C-
CAN'T MOVE
...

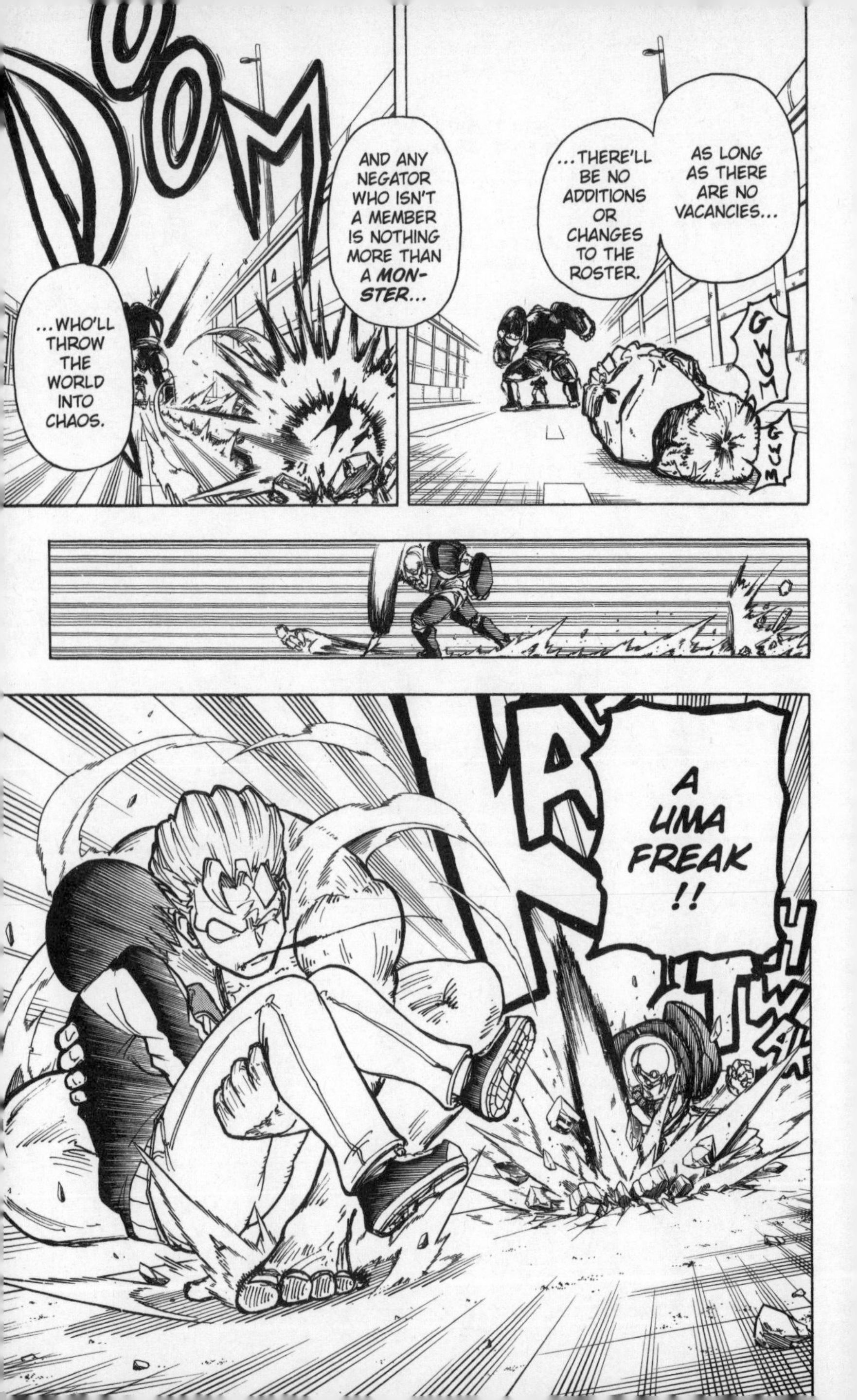
AS LONG AS THERE ARE NO VACANCIES...
...THERE'LL BE NO ADDITIONS OR CHANGES TO THE ROSTER.
GWUM
GWUM
DOOM
AND ANY NEGATOR WHO ISN'T A MEMBER IS NOTHING MORE THAN A *MONSTER*...
...WHO'LL THROW THE WORLD INTO CHAOS.
A UMA FREAK!!

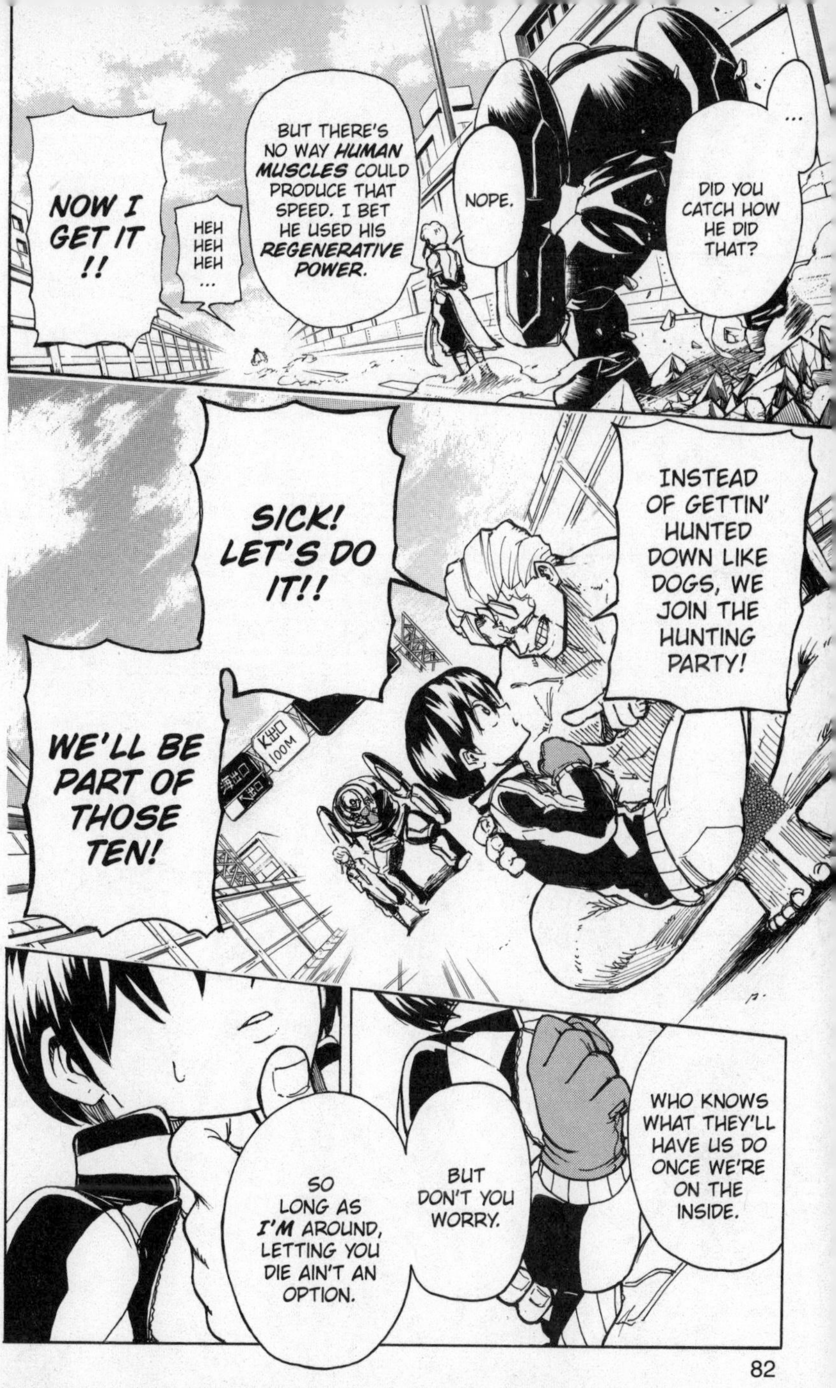
...
DID YOU CATCH HOW HE DID THAT?
NOPE.
BUT THERE'S NO WAY HUMAN MUSCLES COULD PRODUCE THAT SPEED. I BET HE USED HIS REGENERATIVE POWER.
HEH HEH HEH ...
NOW I GET IT !!
INSTEAD OF GETTIN' HUNTED DOWN LIKE DOGS, WE JOIN THE HUNTING PARTY!
SICK! LET'S DO IT!!
WE'LL BE PART OF THOSE TEN!
WHO KNOWS WHAT THEY'LL HAVE US DO ONCE WE'RE ON THE INSIDE.
BUT DON'T YOU WORRY.
SO LONG AS I'M AROUND, LETTING YOU DIE AIN'T AN OPTION.

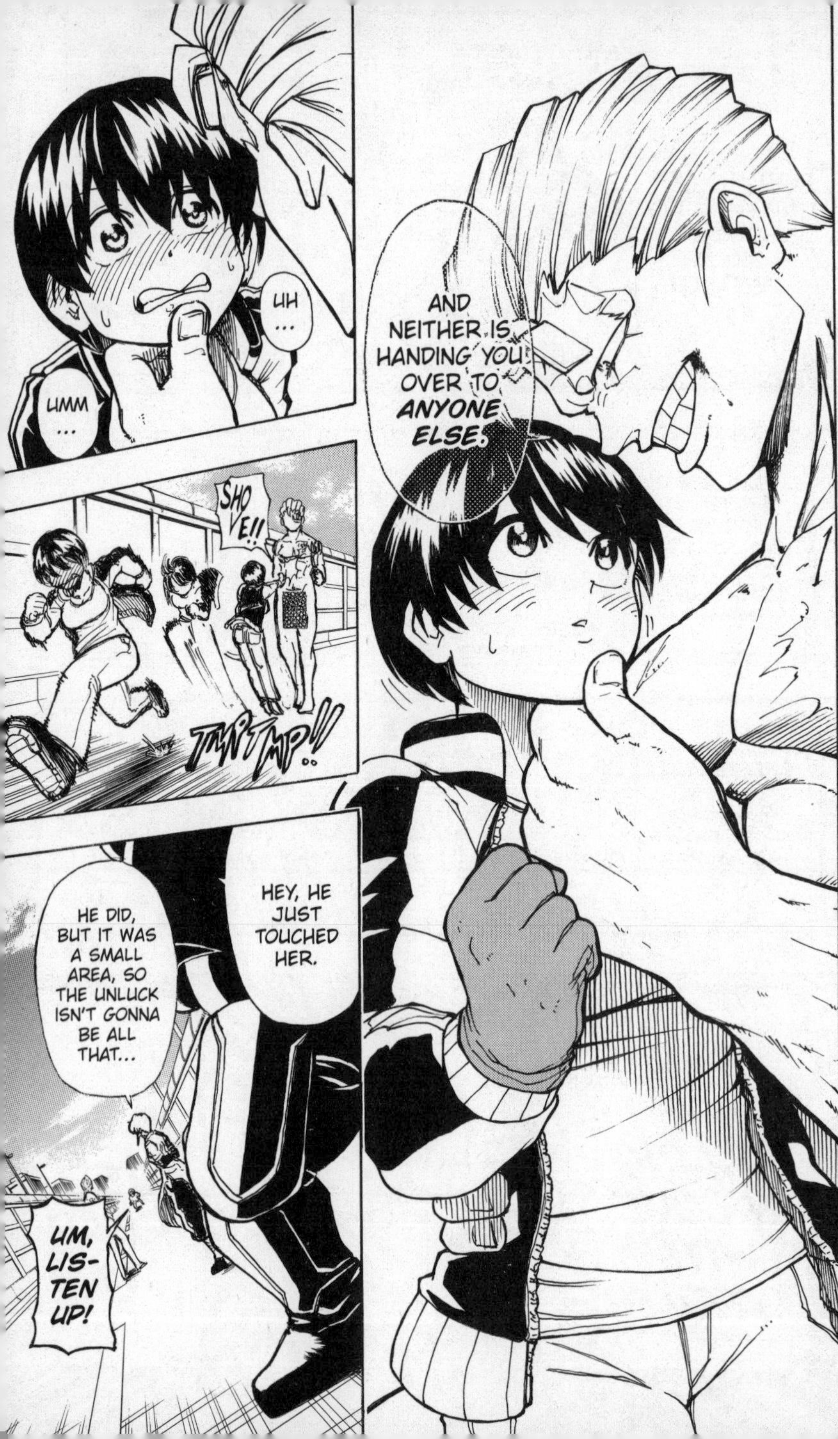
AND NEITHER IS HANDING YOU OVER TO *ANYONE ELSE.*
UH ...
UMM ...
SHOVE!!
HEY, HE JUST TOUCHED HER.
HE DID, BUT IT WAS A SMALL AREA, SO THE UNLUCK ISN'T GONNA BE ALL THAT...
UM, LIS-TEN UP!

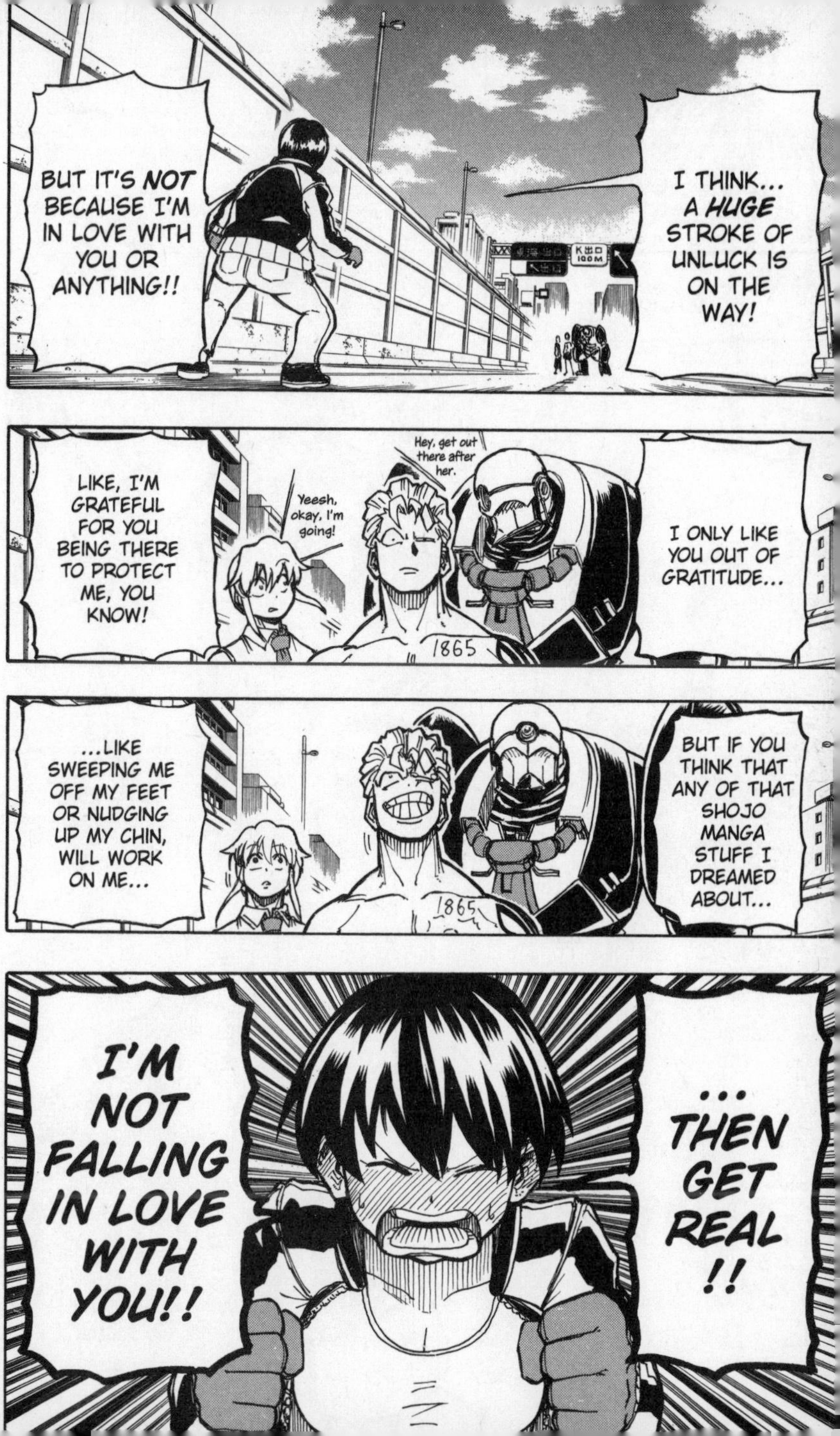
I THINK... A HUGE STROKE OF UNLUCK IS ON THE WAY!
BUT IT'S NOT BECAUSE I'M IN LOVE WITH YOU OR ANYTHING!!
I ONLY LIKE YOU OUT OF GRATITUDE...
Hey, get out there after her.
Yeesh, okay, I'm going!
LIKE, I'M GRATEFUL FOR YOU BEING THERE TO PROTECT ME, YOU KNOW!
1865
BUT IF YOU THINK THAT ANY OF THAT SHOJO MANGA STUFF I DREAMED ABOUT...
...LIKE SWEEPING ME OFF MY FEET OR NUDGING UP MY CHIN, WILL WORK ON ME...
1865
...THEN GET REAL!!
I'M NOT FALLING IN LOVE WITH YOU!!

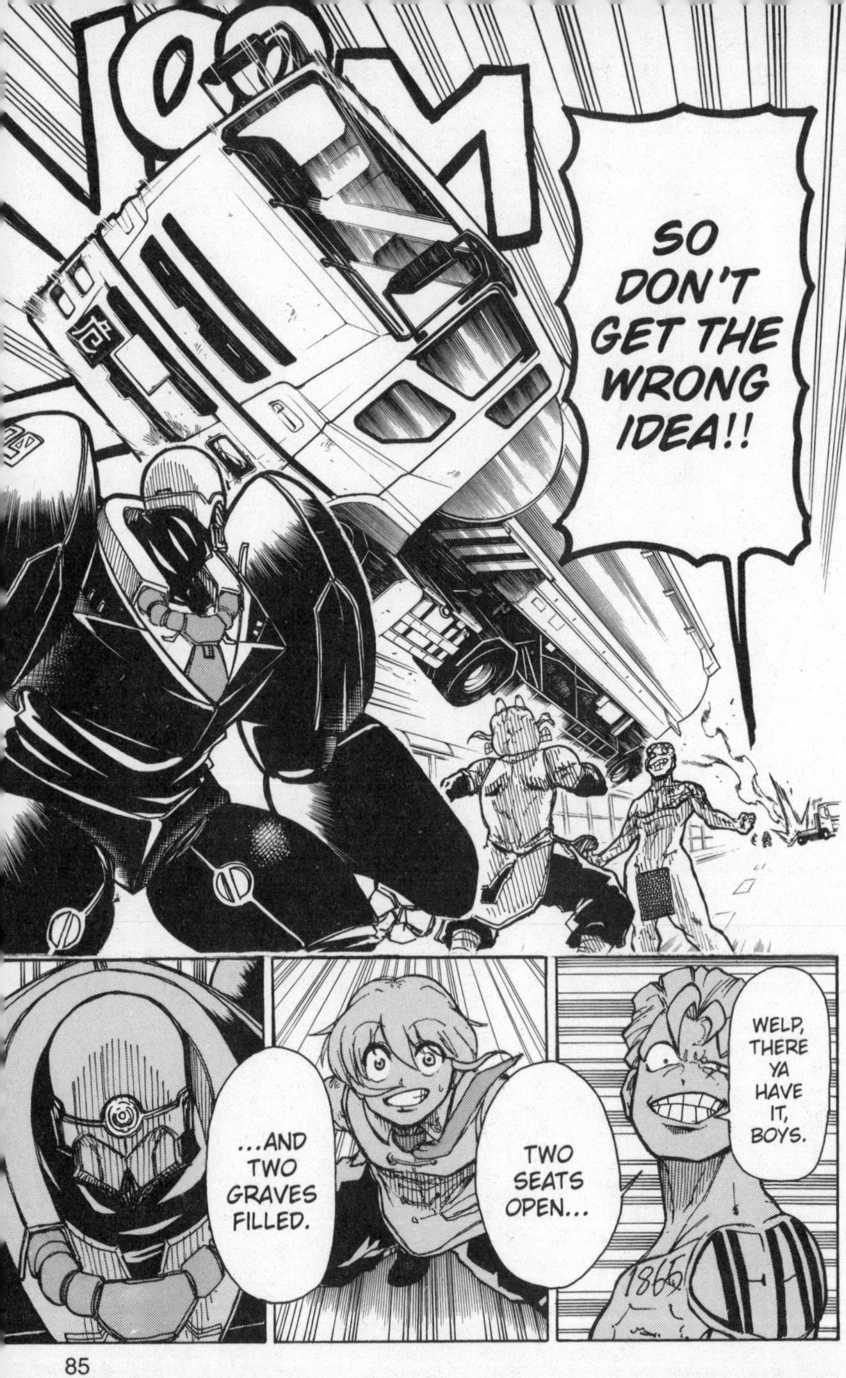
SO DON'T GET THE WRONG IDEA!!
WELP, THERE YA HAVE IT, BOYS.
TWO SEATS OPEN...
...AND TWO GRAVES FILLED.

Safety of the Person Inside

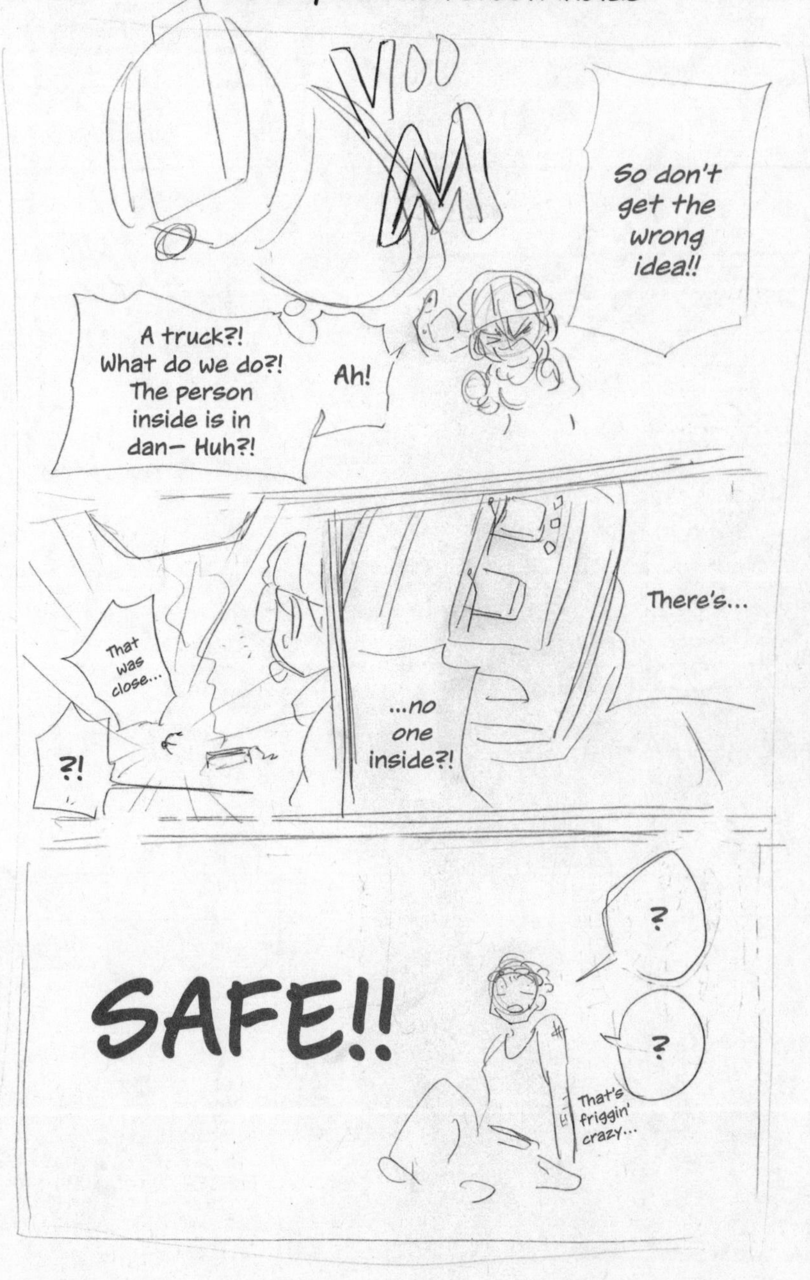

So don't get the wrong idea!!
VROOM
Ah!
A truck?! What do we do?! The person inside is in dan— Huh?!
There's...
...no one inside?!
That was close...
?!
?
?
That's friggin' crazy...
SAFE!!

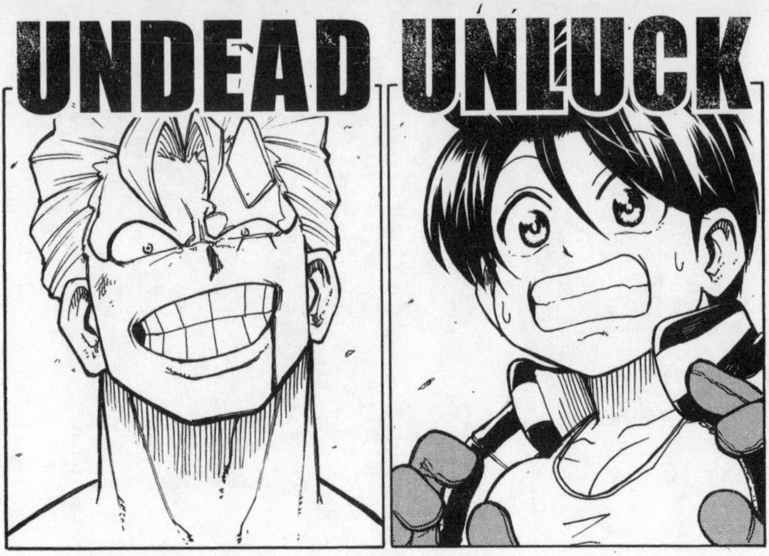
UNDEAD UNLUCK

No. 003
What Do You Negate?

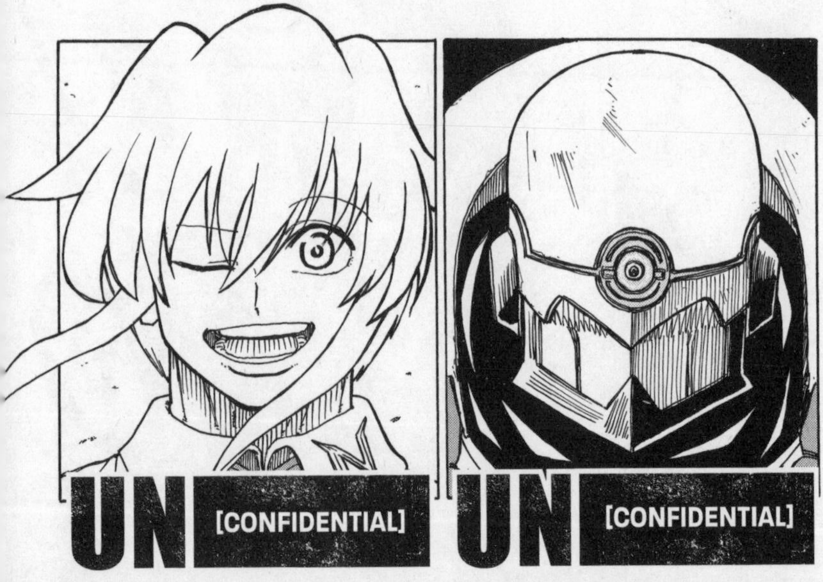
UN [CONFIDENTIAL]
UN [CONFIDENTIAL]

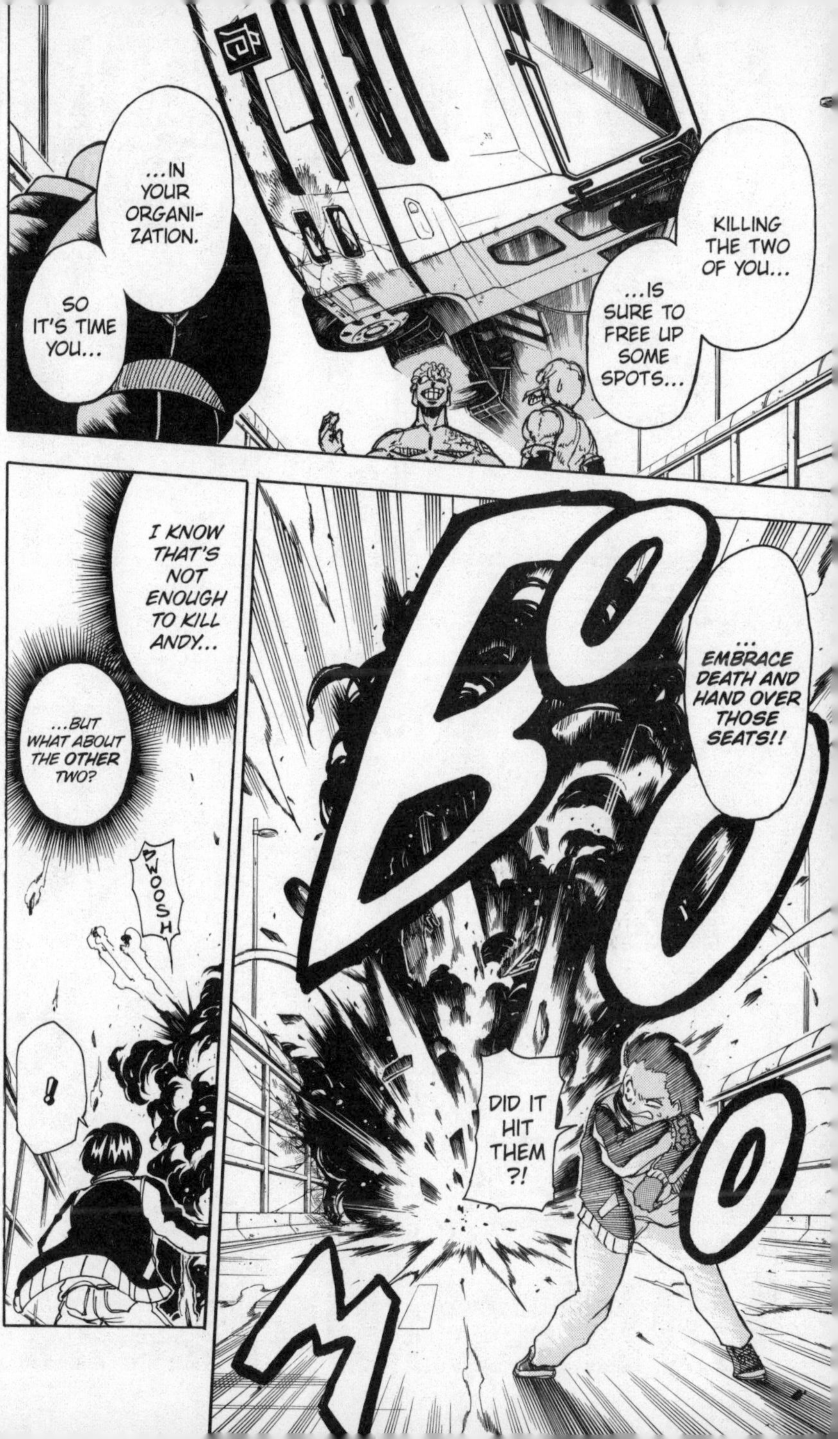
KILLING THE TWO OF YOU...
...IS SURE TO FREE UP SOME SPOTS...
...IN YOUR ORGANIZATION.
SO IT'S TIME YOU...
...EMBRACE DEATH AND HAND OVER THOSE SEATS!!
BOOOOM
DID IT HIT THEM?!
I KNOW THAT'S NOT ENOUGH TO KILL ANDY...
...BUT WHAT ABOUT THE OTHER TWO?
SWOOSH
!

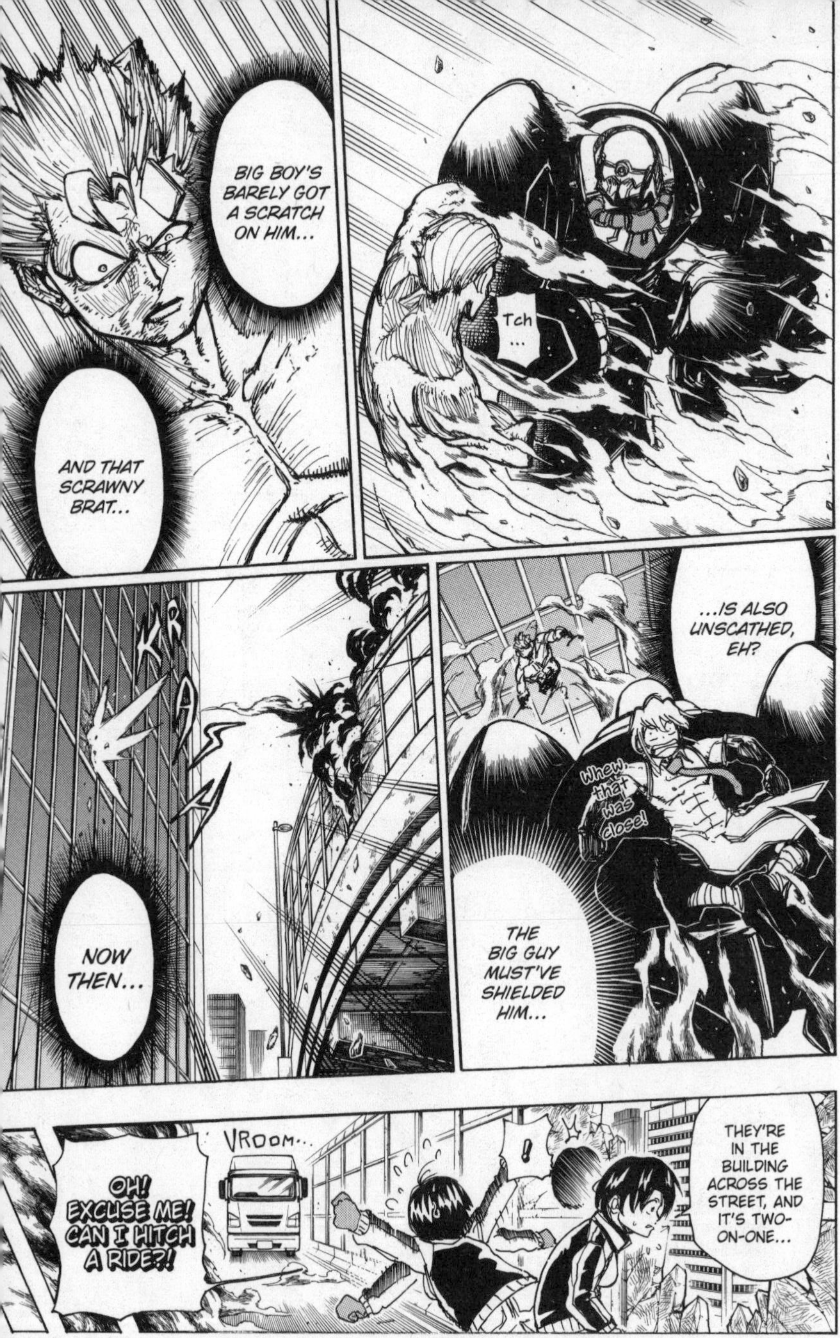
Tch
...
BIG BOY'S BARELY GOT A SCRATCH ON HIM...
AND THAT SCRAWNY BRAT...
...IS ALSO UNSCATHED, EH?
Whew that was close!
THE BIG GUY MUST'VE SHIELDED HIM...
NOW THEN...
THEY'RE IN THE BUILDING ACROSS THE STREET, AND IT'S TWO-ON-ONE...
!
VROOM...
OH! EXCUSE ME! CAN I HITCH A RIDE?!

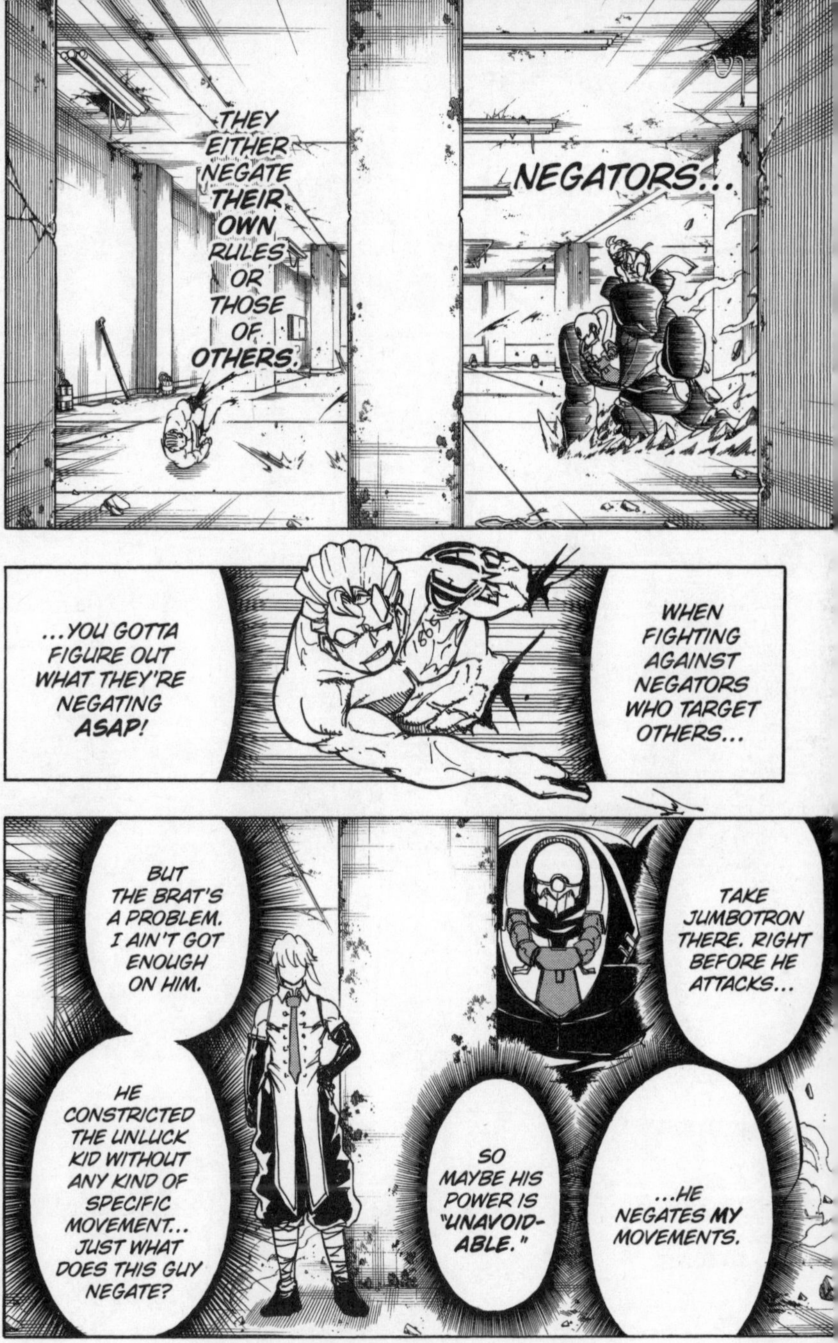
NEGATORS...
THEY EITHER NEGATE THEIR OWN RULES OR THOSE OF OTHERS.
WHEN FIGHTING AGAINST NEGATORS WHO TARGET OTHERS...
...YOU GOTTA FIGURE OUT WHAT THEY'RE NEGATING ASAP!
TAKE JUMBOTRON THERE. RIGHT BEFORE HE ATTACKS...
...HE NEGATES MY MOVEMENTS.
SO MAYBE HIS POWER IS "UNAVOID-ABLE."
BUT THE BRAT'S A PROBLEM. I AIN'T GOT ENOUGH ON HIM.
HE CONSTRICTED THE UNLUCK KID WITHOUT ANY KIND OF SPECIFIC MOVEMENT... JUST WHAT DOES THIS GUY NEGATE?

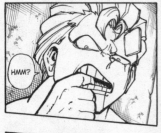

HMM?

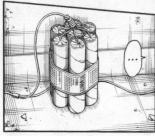

....

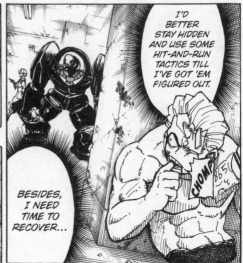

I'D BETTER STAY HIDDEN AND USE SOME HIT-AND-RUN TACTICS TILL I'VE GOT 'EM FIGURED OUT.

BESIDES, I NEED TIME TO RECOVER...

CHOMP

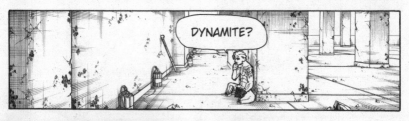

DYNAMITE?

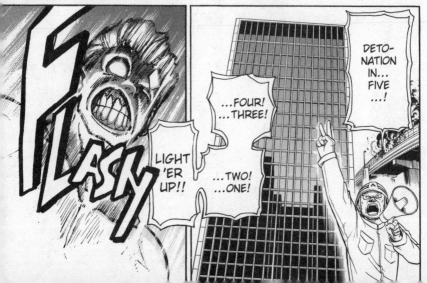

LIGHT 'ER UP!!

...FOUR! ...THREE!

...TWO! ...ONE!

DETO-NATION IN... FIVE ...!

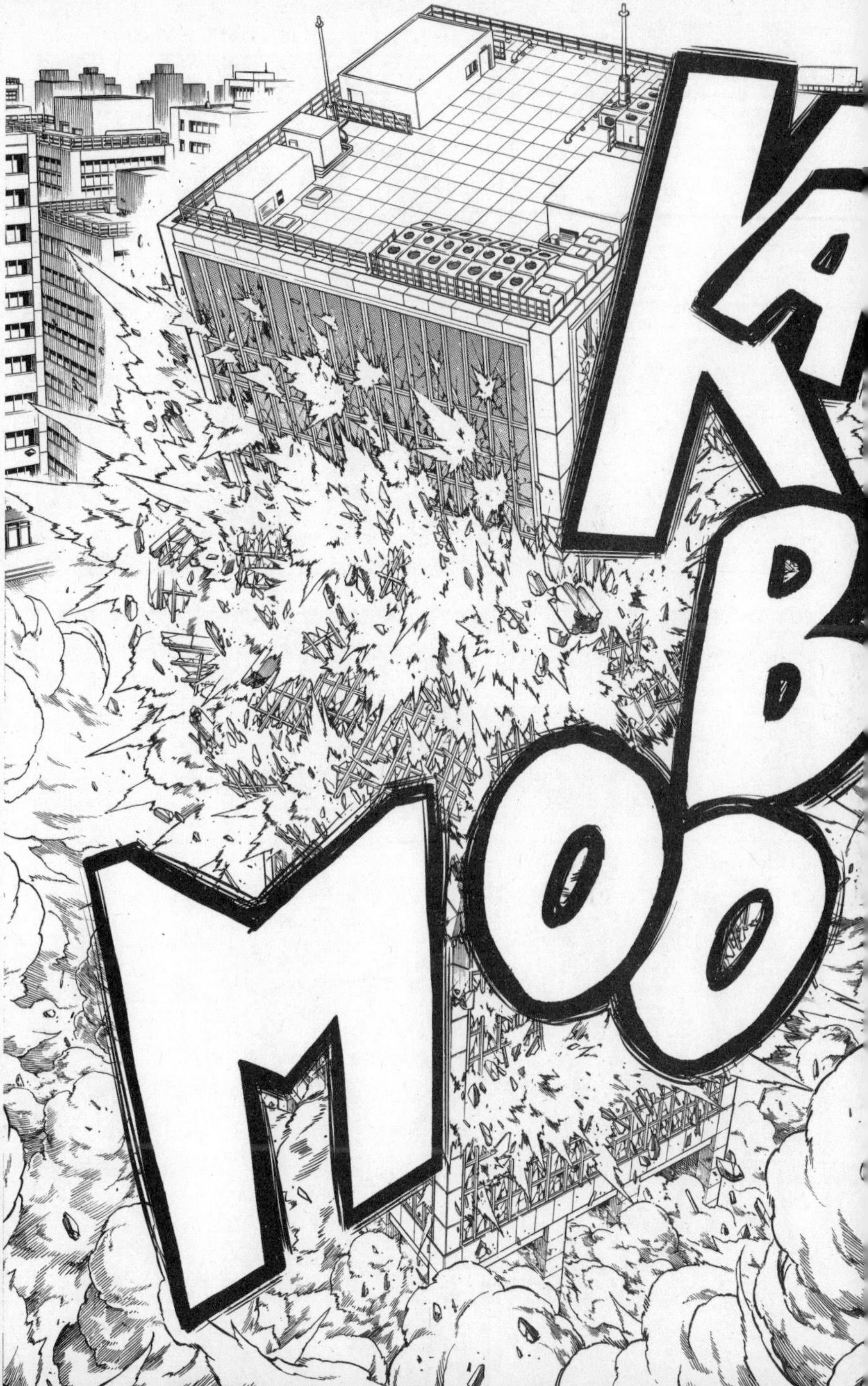
KABOOM

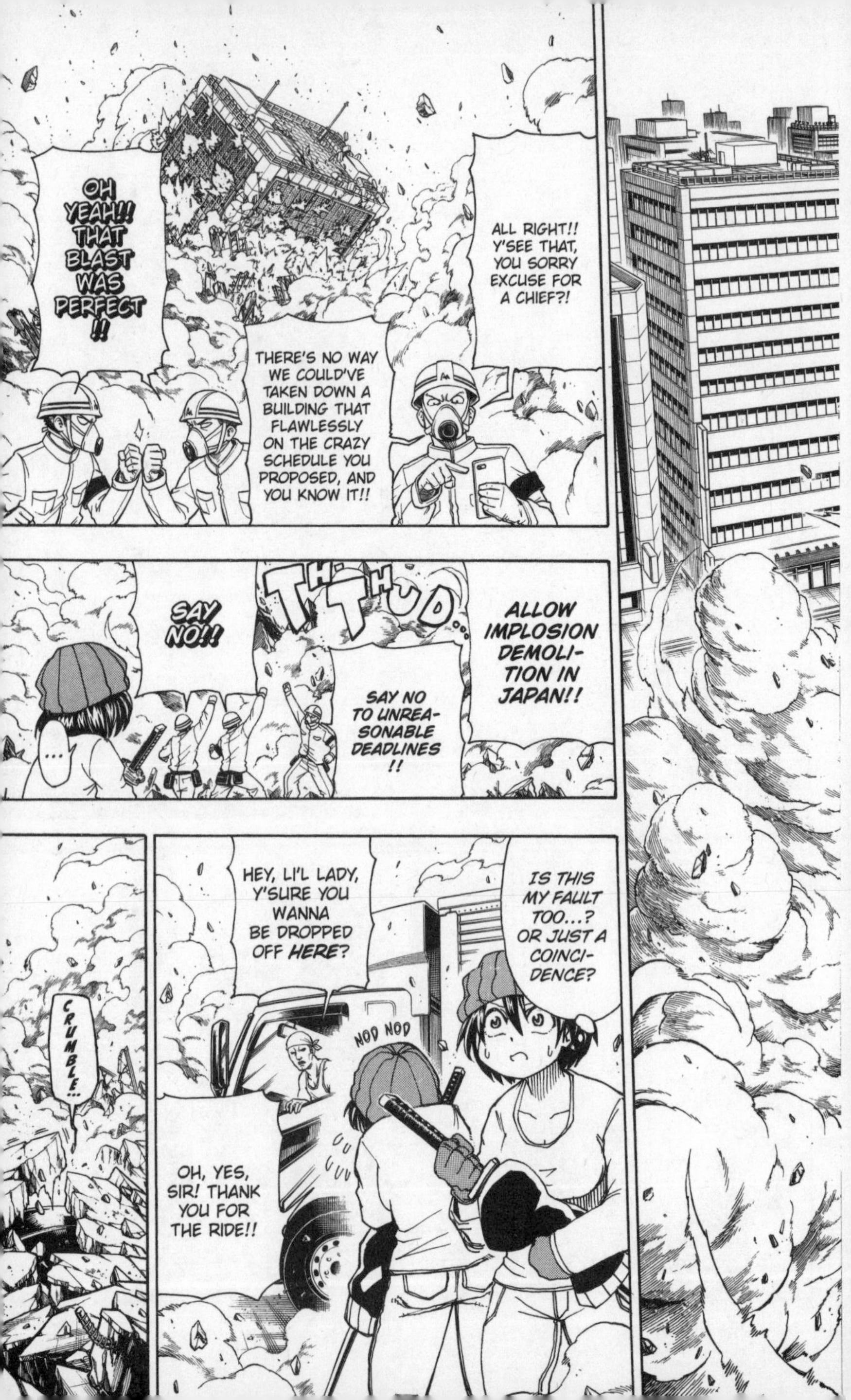
ALL RIGHT!! Y'SEE THAT, YOU SORRY EXCUSE FOR A CHIEF?!
THERE'S NO WAY WE COULD'VE TAKEN DOWN A BUILDING THAT FLAWLESSLY ON THE CRAZY SCHEDULE YOU PROPOSED, AND YOU KNOW IT!!
OH YEAH!! THAT BLAST WAS PERFECT!!
ALLOW IMPLOSION DEMOLITION IN JAPAN!!
TH-THUD...
SAY NO TO UNREASONABLE DEADLINES!!
SAY NO!!
...
IS THIS MY FAULT TOO...? OR JUST A COINCIDENCE?
HEY, LI'L LADY, Y'SURE YOU WANNA BE DROPPED OFF *HERE*?
NOD NOD
OH, YES, SIR! THANK YOU FOR THE RIDE!!
CRUMBLE...

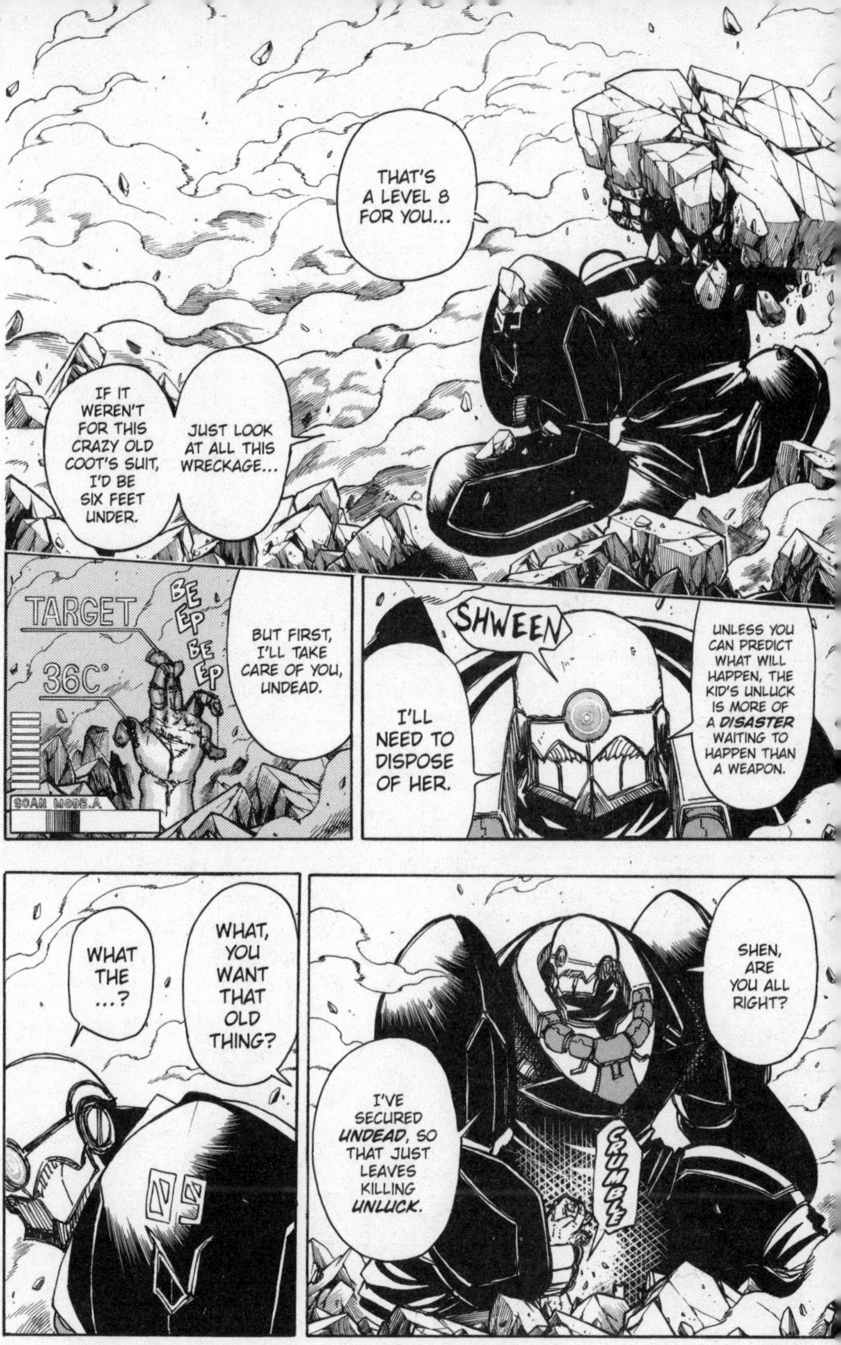
THAT'S A LEVEL 8 FOR YOU...
JUST LOOK AT ALL THIS WRECKAGE...
IF IT WEREN'T FOR THIS CRAZY OLD COOT'S SUIT, I'D BE SIX FEET UNDER.
UNLESS YOU CAN PREDICT WHAT WILL HAPPEN, THE KID'S UNLUCK IS MORE OF A ***DISASTER*** WAITING TO HAPPEN THAN A WEAPON.
SHWEEN
I'LL NEED TO DISPOSE OF HER.
BUT FIRST, I'LL TAKE CARE OF YOU, UNDEAD.
BEEP BEEP
TARGET
36C°
SOAN MODE.A
SHEN, ARE YOU ALL RIGHT?
I'VE SECURED ***UNDEAD***, SO THAT JUST LEAVES KILLING ***UNLUCK***.
CRUMBLE
WHAT, YOU WANT THAT OLD THING?
WHAT THE ...?

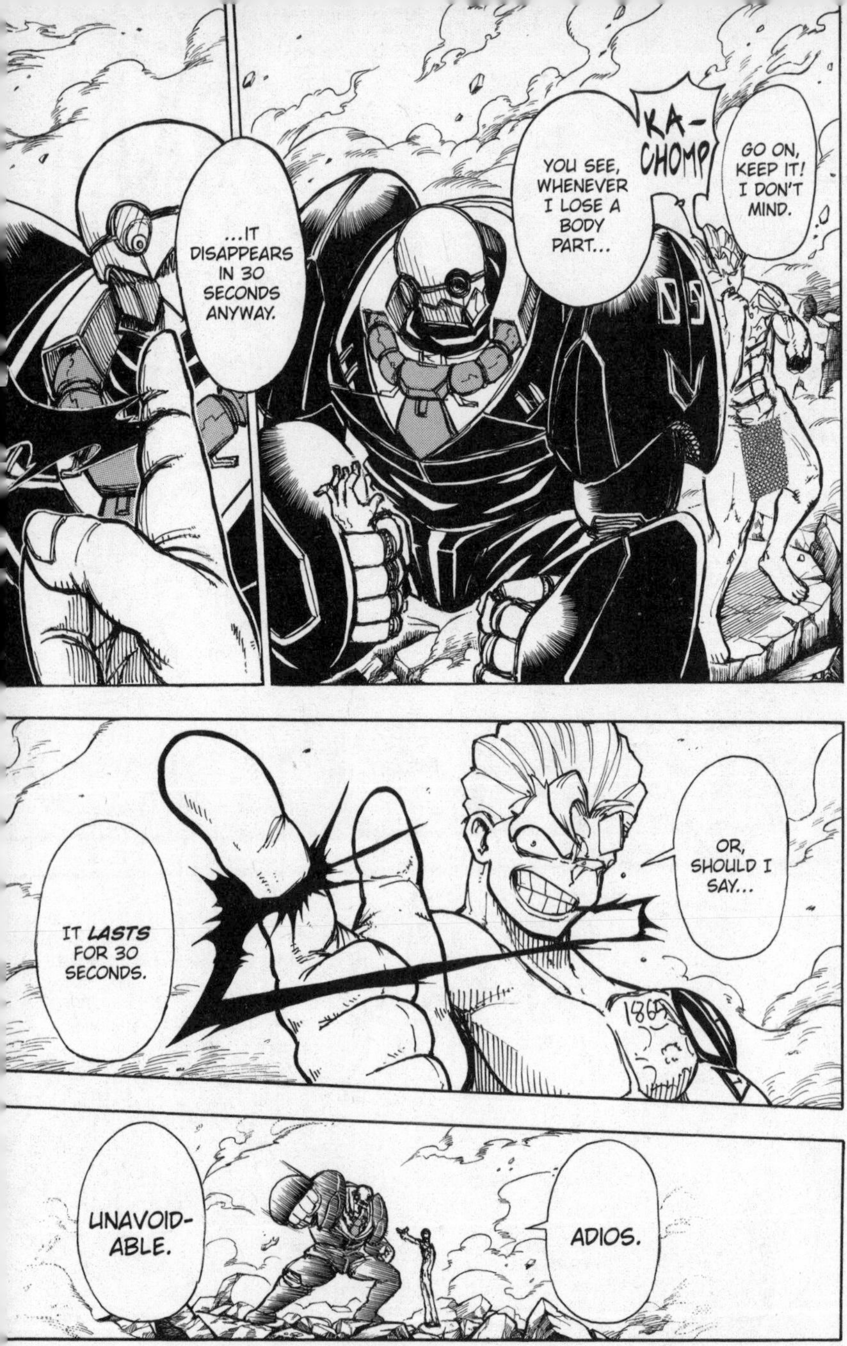
GO ON, KEEP IT! I DON'T MIND.
KA-CHOMP
YOU SEE, WHENEVER I LOSE A BODY PART...
...IT DISAPPEARS IN 30 SECONDS ANYWAY.
OR, SHOULD I SAY...
1865
IT *LASTS* FOR 30 SECONDS.
ADIOS.
UNAVOID-ABLE.

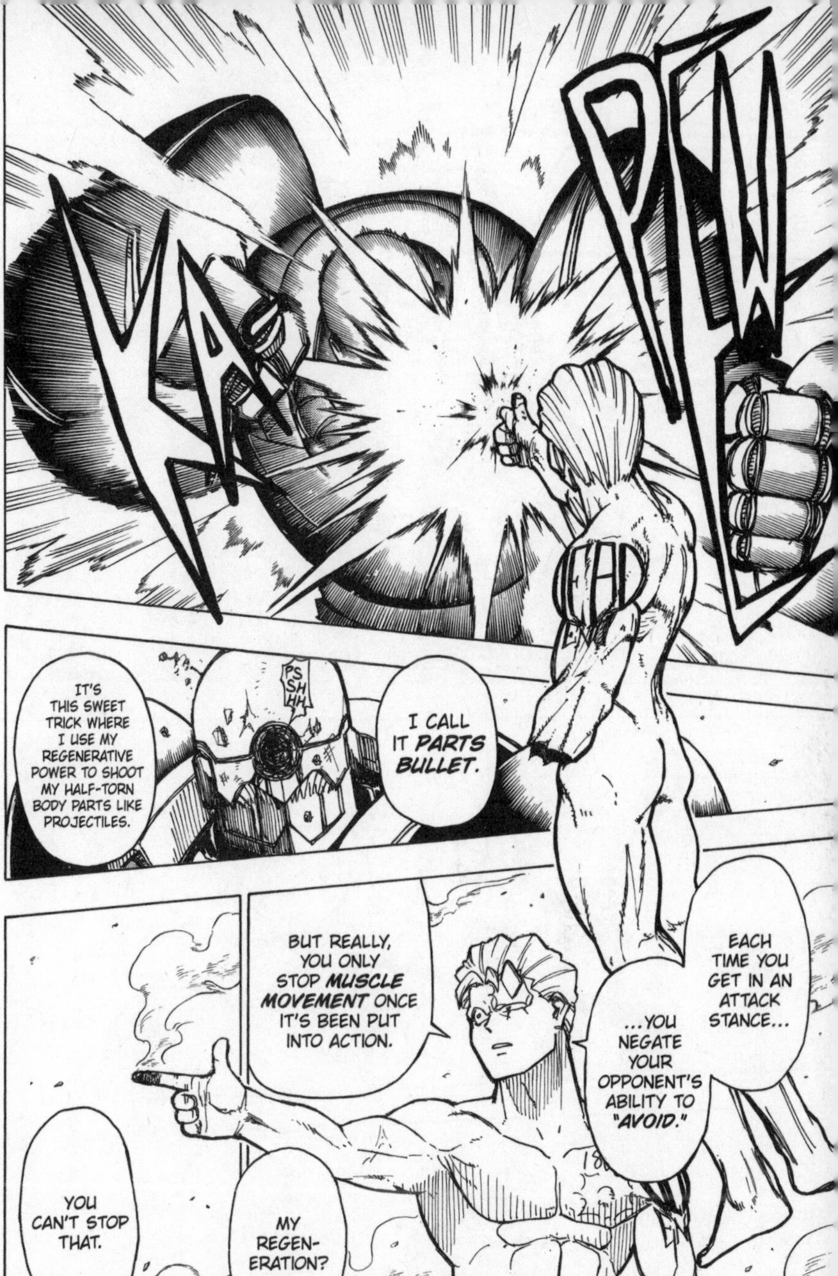
PSSHHH
I CALL IT PARTS BULLET.
IT'S THIS SWEET TRICK WHERE I USE MY REGENERATIVE POWER TO SHOOT MY HALF-TORN BODY PARTS LIKE PROJECTILES.
EACH TIME YOU GET IN AN ATTACK STANCE...
...YOU NEGATE YOUR OPPONENT'S ABILITY TO "AVOID."
BUT REALLY, YOU ONLY STOP MUSCLE MOVEMENT ONCE IT'S BEEN PUT INTO ACTION.
MY REGEN-ERATION?
YOU CAN'T STOP THAT.

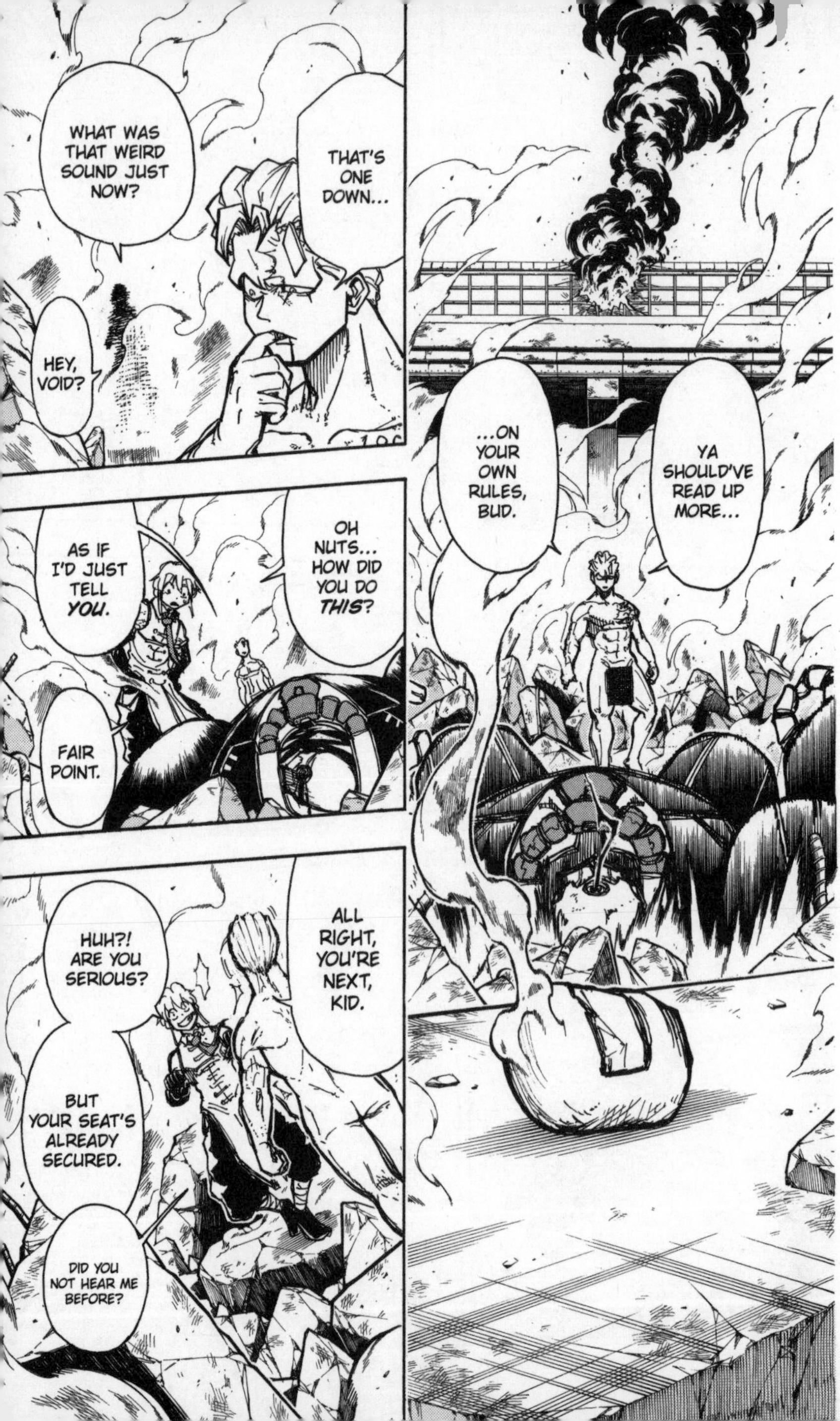
YA SHOULD'VE READ UP MORE...
...ON YOUR OWN RULES, BUD.
THAT'S ONE DOWN...
WHAT WAS THAT WEIRD SOUND JUST NOW?
HEY, VOID?
OH NUTS... HOW DID YOU DO *THIS*?
AS IF I'D JUST TELL *YOU*.
FAIR POINT.
ALL RIGHT, YOU'RE NEXT, KID.
HUH?! ARE YOU SERIOUS?
BUT YOUR SEAT'S ALREADY SECURED.
DID YOU NOT HEAR ME BEFORE?

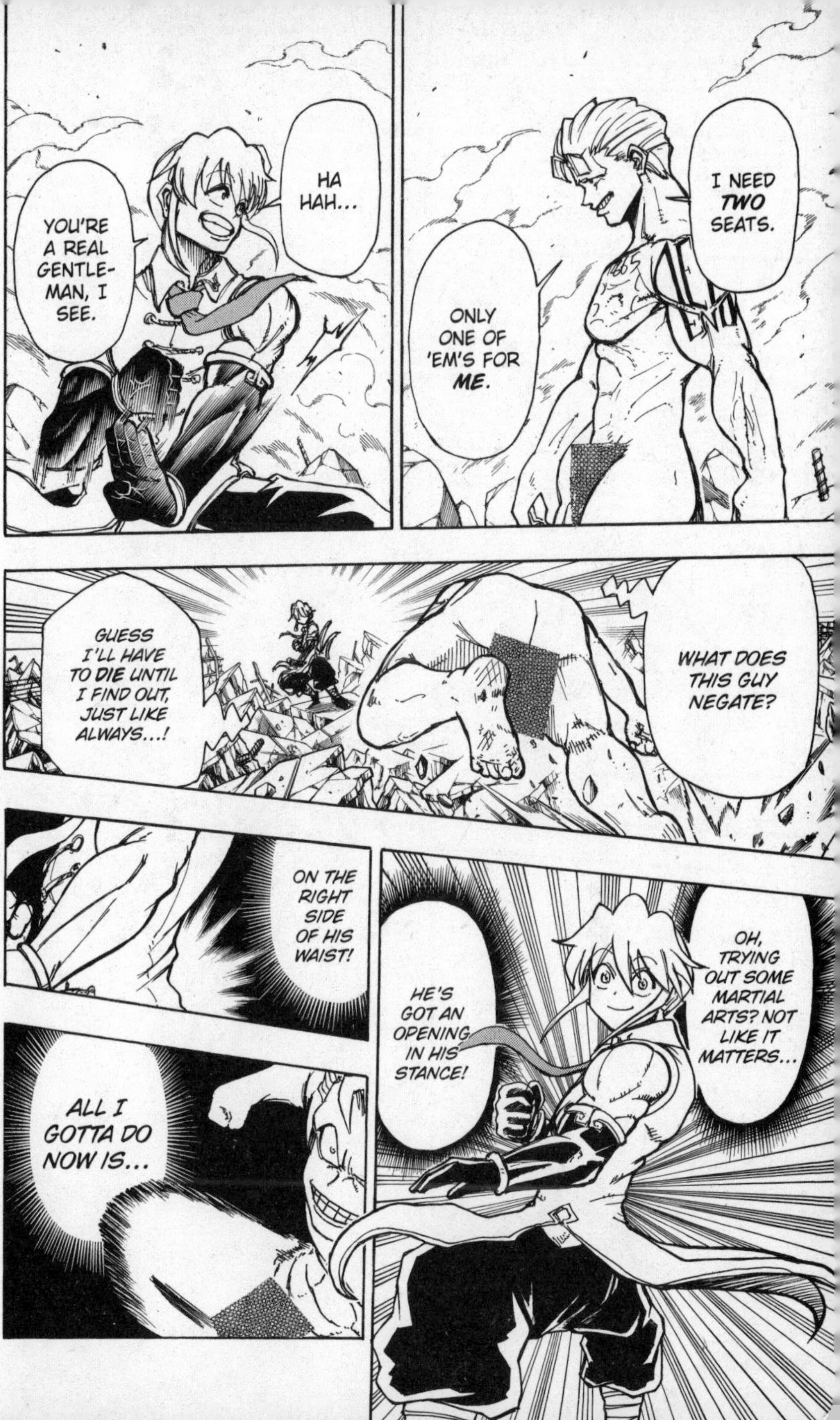
I NEED **TWO** SEATS.
ONLY ONE OF 'EM'S FOR **ME**.
HA HAH...
YOU'RE A REAL GENTLE-MAN, I SEE.
WHAT DOES THIS GUY NEGATE?
GUESS I'LL HAVE TO **DIE** UNTIL I FIND OUT, JUST LIKE ALWAYS...!
OH, TRYING OUT SOME MARTIAL ARTS? NOT LIKE IT MATTERS...
HE'S GOT AN OPENING IN HIS STANCE!
ON THE RIGHT SIDE OF HIS WAIST!
ALL I GOTTA DO NOW IS...

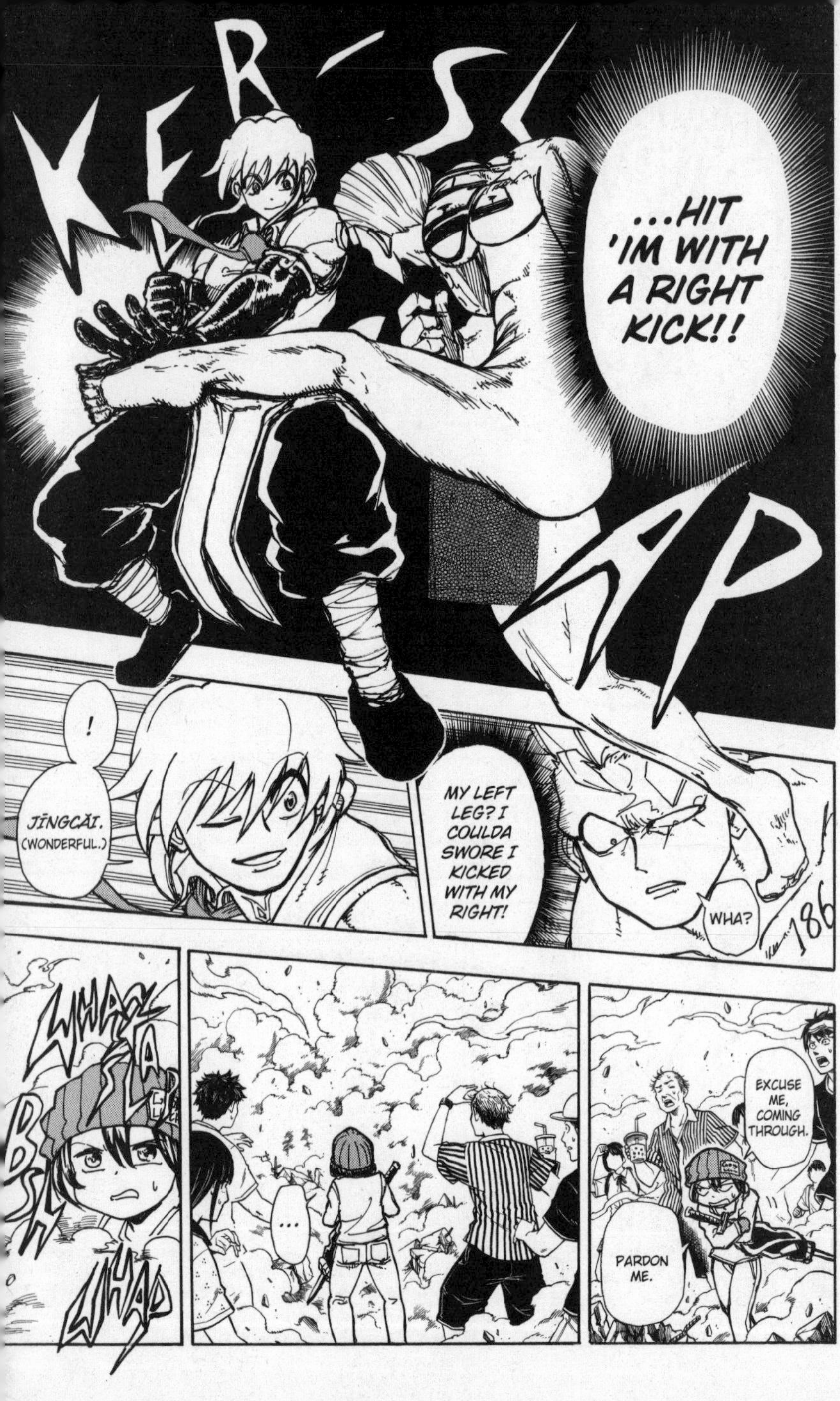
...HIT 'IM WITH A RIGHT KICK!!
WHA?
MY LEFT LEG? I COULDA SWORE I KICKED WITH MY RIGHT!
!
JĪNGCĀI. (WONDERFUL.)
EXCUSE ME, COMING THROUGH.
PARDON ME.
...

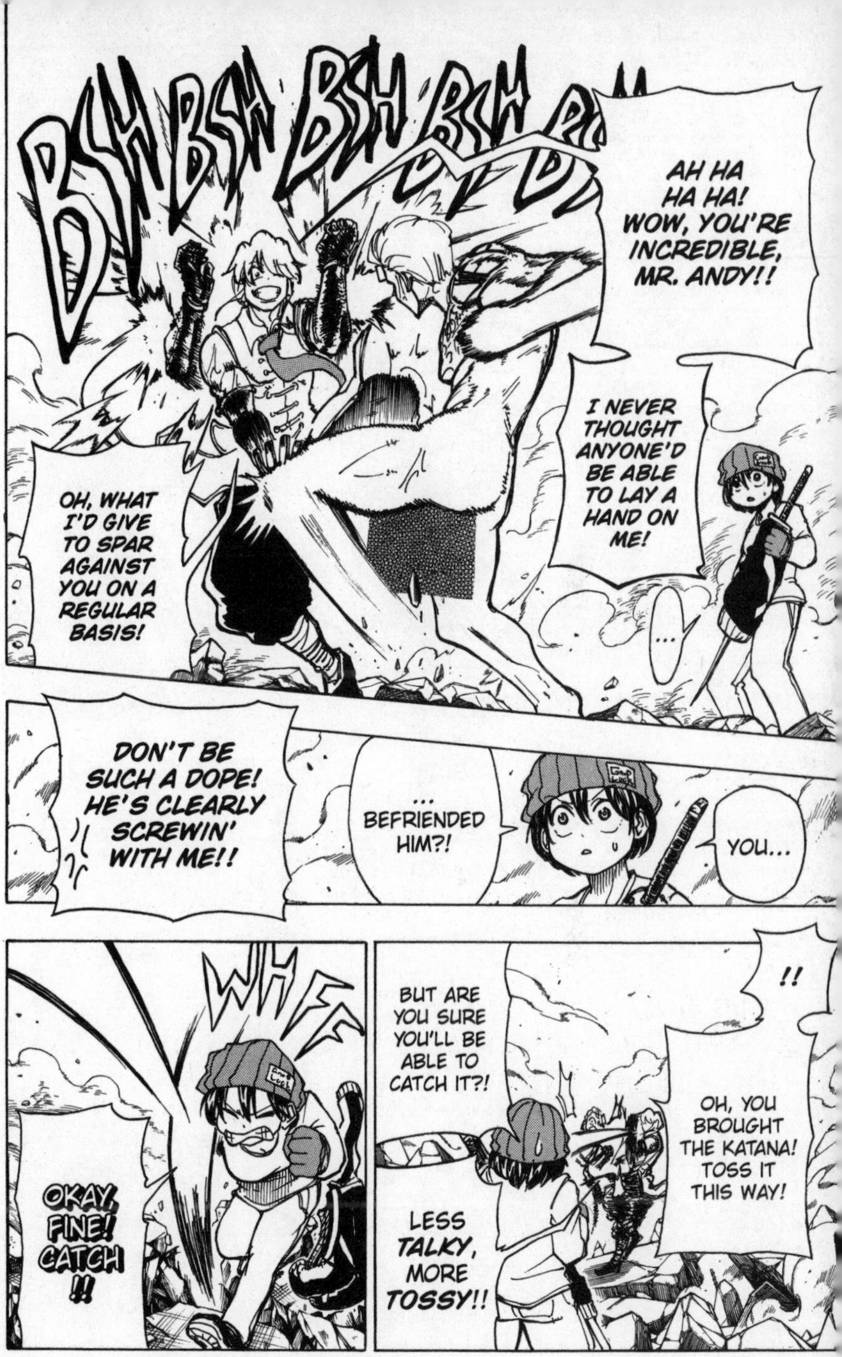
BSH BSH BSH BSH
AH HA HA HA! WOW, YOU'RE INCREDIBLE, MR. ANDY!!
I NEVER THOUGHT ANYONE'D BE ABLE TO LAY A HAND ON ME!
OH, WHAT I'D GIVE TO SPAR AGAINST YOU ON A REGULAR BASIS!
...
YOU...
...BEFRIENDED HIM?!
DON'T BE SUCH A DOPE! HE'S CLEARLY SCREWIN' WITH ME!!
!!
OH, YOU BROUGHT THE KATANA! TOSS IT THIS WAY!
BUT ARE YOU SURE YOU'LL BE ABLE TO CATCH IT?!
LESS TALKY, MORE TOSSY!!
WHF
OKAY, FINE! CATCH!!

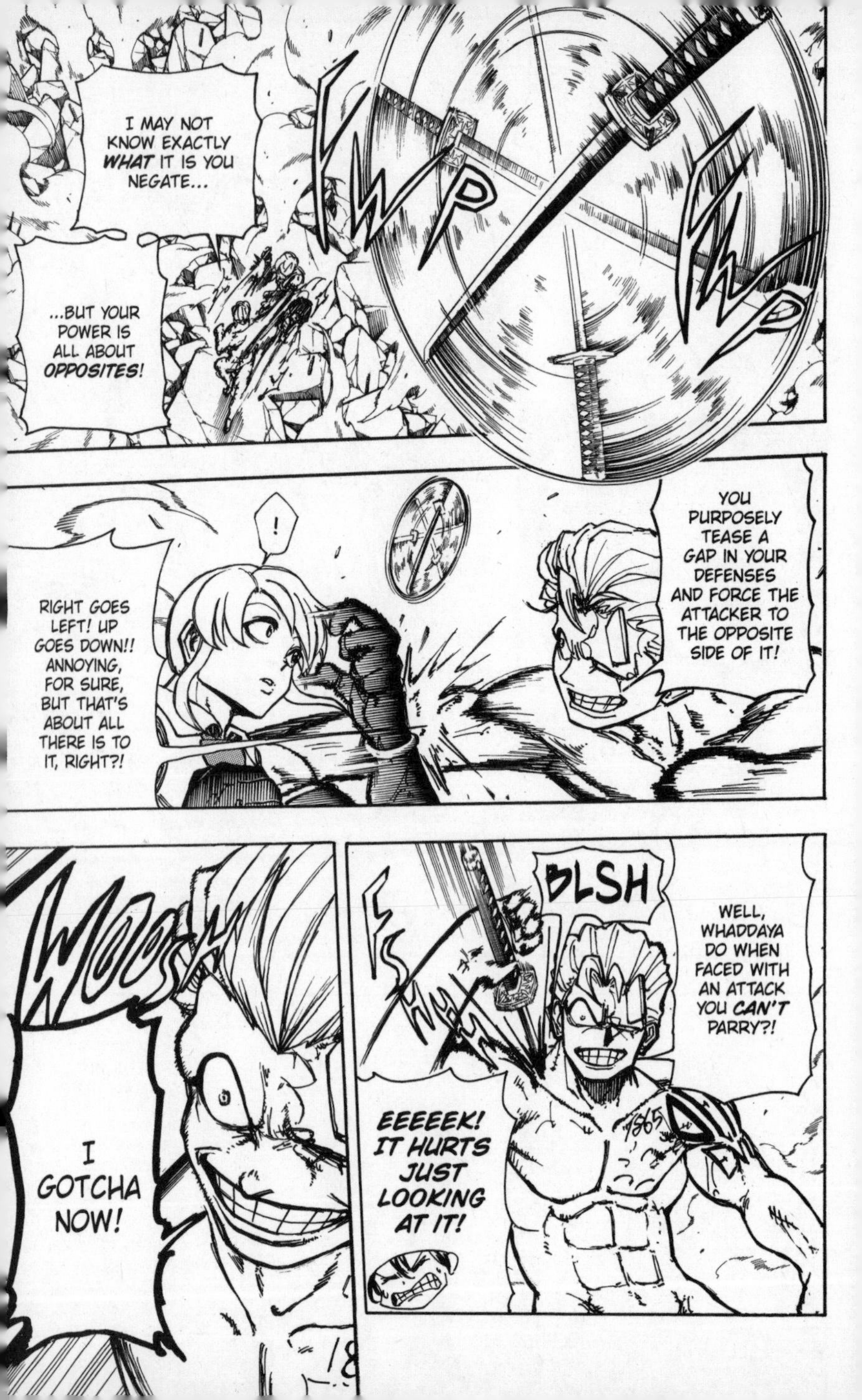
I MAY NOT KNOW EXACTLY *WHAT* IT IS YOU NEGATE...
...BUT YOUR POWER IS ALL ABOUT *OPPOSITES*!
FWP
YOU PURPOSELY TEASE A GAP IN YOUR DEFENSES AND FORCE THE ATTACKER TO THE OPPOSITE SIDE OF IT!
!
RIGHT GOES LEFT! UP GOES DOWN!! ANNOYING, FOR SURE, BUT THAT'S ABOUT ALL THERE IS TO IT, RIGHT?!
BLSH
WELL, WHADDAYA DO WHEN FACED WITH AN ATTACK YOU *CAN'T* PARRY?!
EEEEEK! IT HURTS JUST LOOKING AT IT!
I GOTCHA NOW!

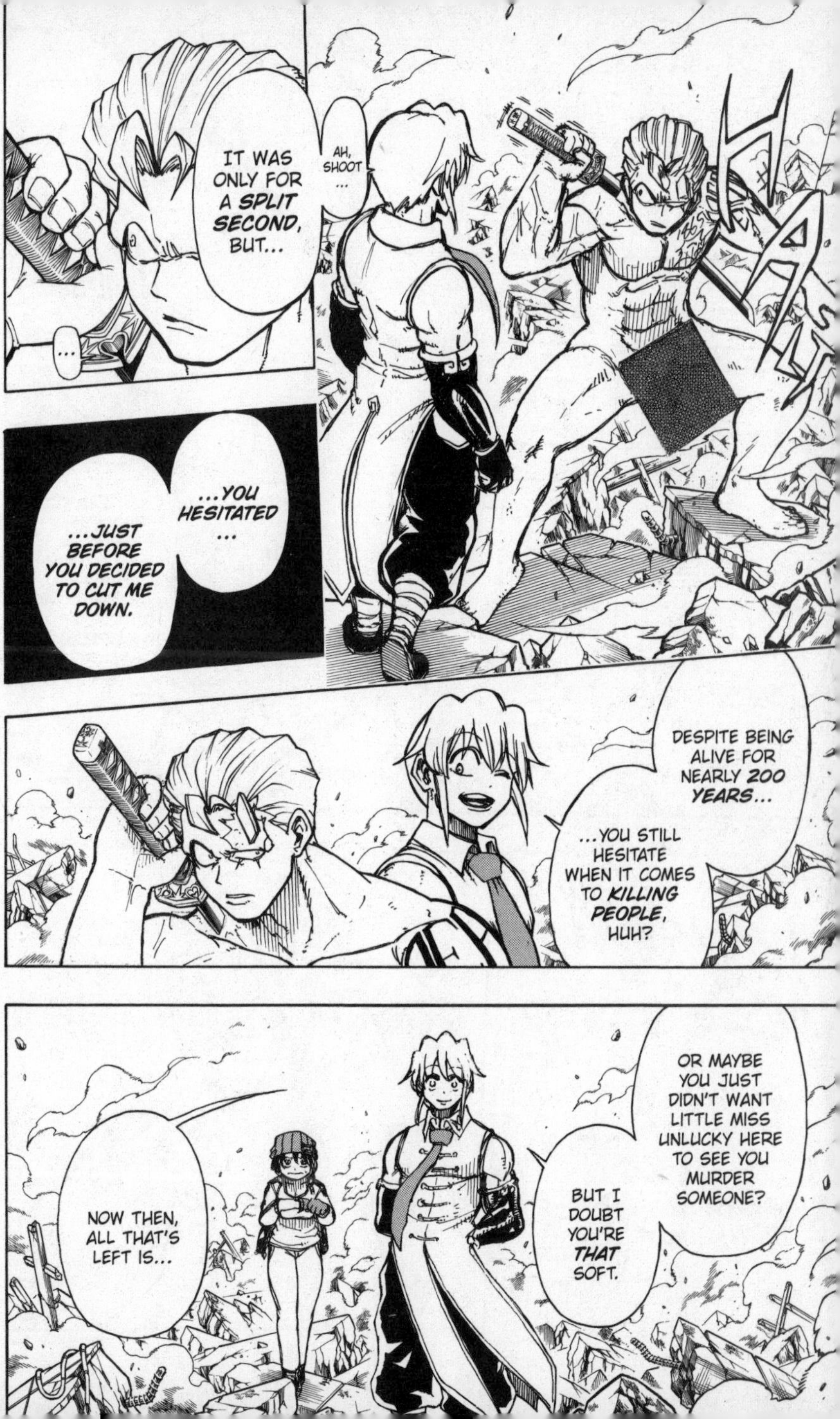
AH, SHOOT ...
IT WAS ONLY FOR A SPLIT SECOND, BUT...
...
...YOU HESITATED ...
...JUST BEFORE YOU DECIDED TO CUT ME DOWN.
DESPITE BEING ALIVE FOR NEARLY 200 YEARS...
...YOU STILL HESITATE WHEN IT COMES TO KILLING PEOPLE, HUH?
OR MAYBE YOU JUST DIDN'T WANT LITTLE MISS UNLUCKY HERE TO SEE YOU MURDER SOMEONE?
BUT I DOUBT YOU'RE THAT SOFT.
NOW THEN, ALL THAT'S LEFT IS...

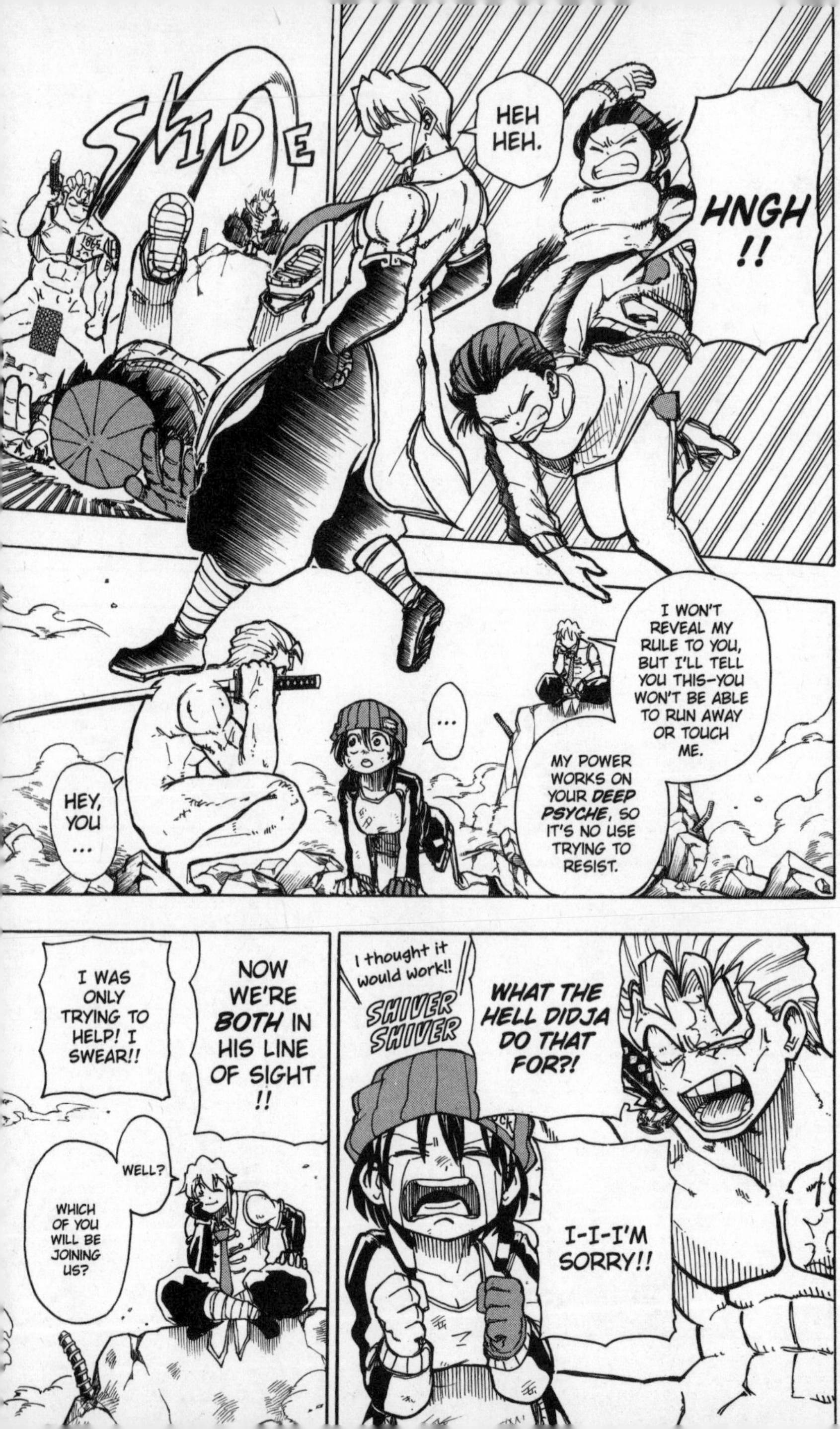
HNGH!!
HEH HEH.
SLIDE
I WON'T REVEAL MY RULE TO YOU, BUT I'LL TELL YOU THIS—YOU WON'T BE ABLE TO RUN AWAY OR TOUCH ME.
MY POWER WORKS ON YOUR DEEP PSYCHE, SO IT'S NO USE TRYING TO RESIST.
...
HEY, YOU ...
WHAT THE HELL DIDJA DO THAT FOR?!
I thought it would work!!
SHIVER SHIVER
I-I-I'M SORRY!!
NOW WE'RE BOTH IN HIS LINE OF SIGHT!!
I WAS ONLY TRYING TO HELP! I SWEAR!!
WELL?
WHICH OF YOU WILL BE JOINING US?

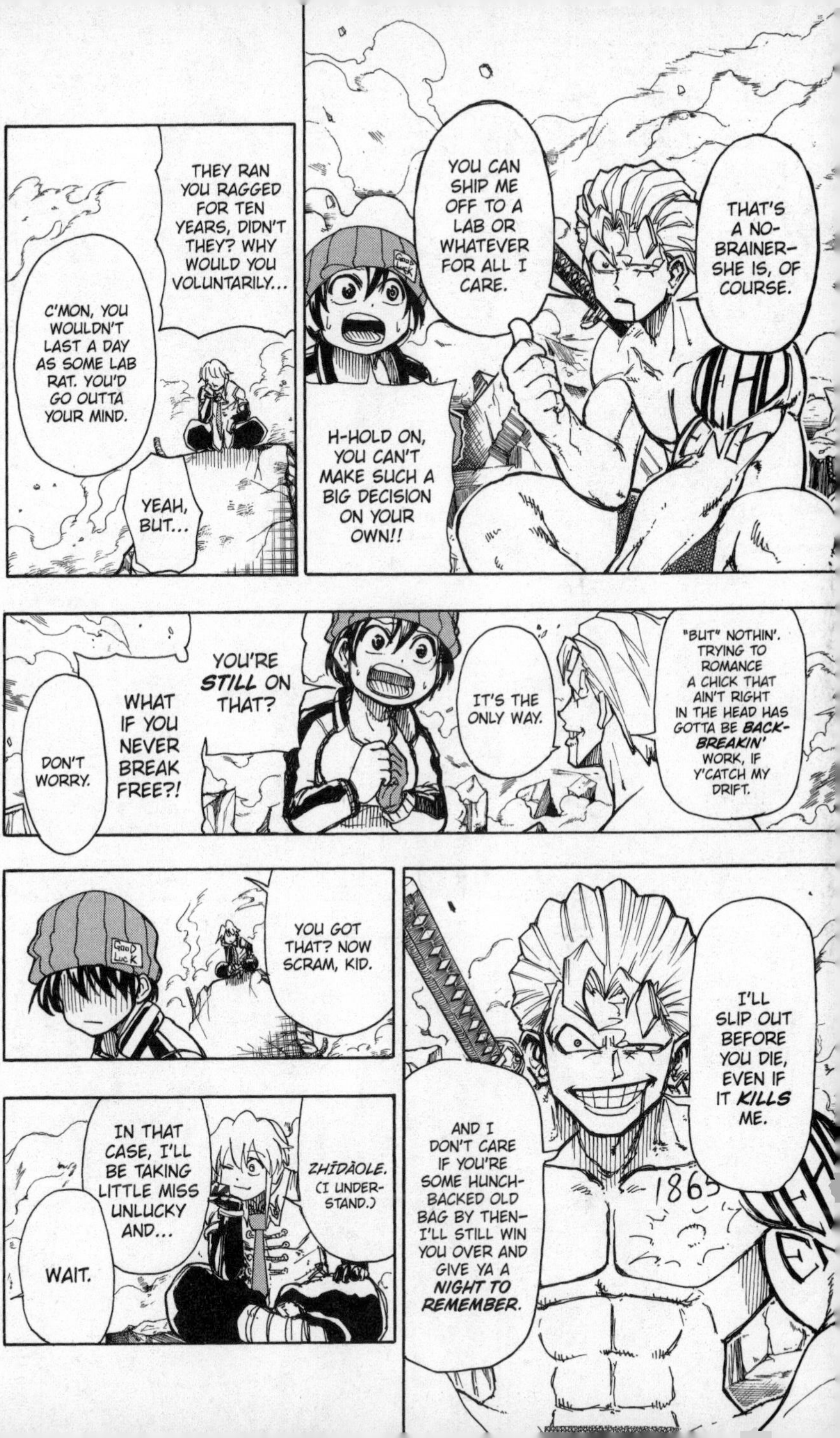
THAT'S A NO-BRAINER—SHE IS, OF COURSE.
YOU CAN SHIP ME OFF TO A LAB OR WHATEVER FOR ALL I CARE.
H-HOLD ON, YOU CAN'T MAKE SUCH A BIG DECISION ON YOUR OWN!!
THEY RAN YOU RAGGED FOR TEN YEARS, DIDN'T THEY? WHY WOULD YOU VOLUNTARILY...
C'MON, YOU WOULDN'T LAST A DAY AS SOME LAB RAT. YOU'D GO OUTTA YOUR MIND.
YEAH, BUT...
"BUT" NOTHIN'. TRYING TO ROMANCE A CHICK THAT AIN'T RIGHT IN THE HEAD HAS GOTTA BE ***BACK-BREAKIN'*** WORK, IF Y'CATCH MY DRIFT.
IT'S THE ONLY WAY.
YOU'RE ***STILL*** ON THAT?
WHAT IF YOU NEVER BREAK FREE?!
DON'T WORRY.
I'LL SLIP OUT BEFORE YOU DIE, EVEN IF IT ***KILLS*** ME.
AND I DON'T CARE IF YOU'RE SOME HUNCH-BACKED OLD BAG BY THEN—I'LL STILL WIN YOU OVER AND GIVE YA A ***NIGHT TO REMEMBER***.
1865
YOU GOT THAT? NOW SCRAM, KID.
ZHĪDÀOLE. (I UNDER-STAND.)
IN THAT CASE, I'LL BE TAKING LITTLE MISS UNLUCKY AND...
WAIT.

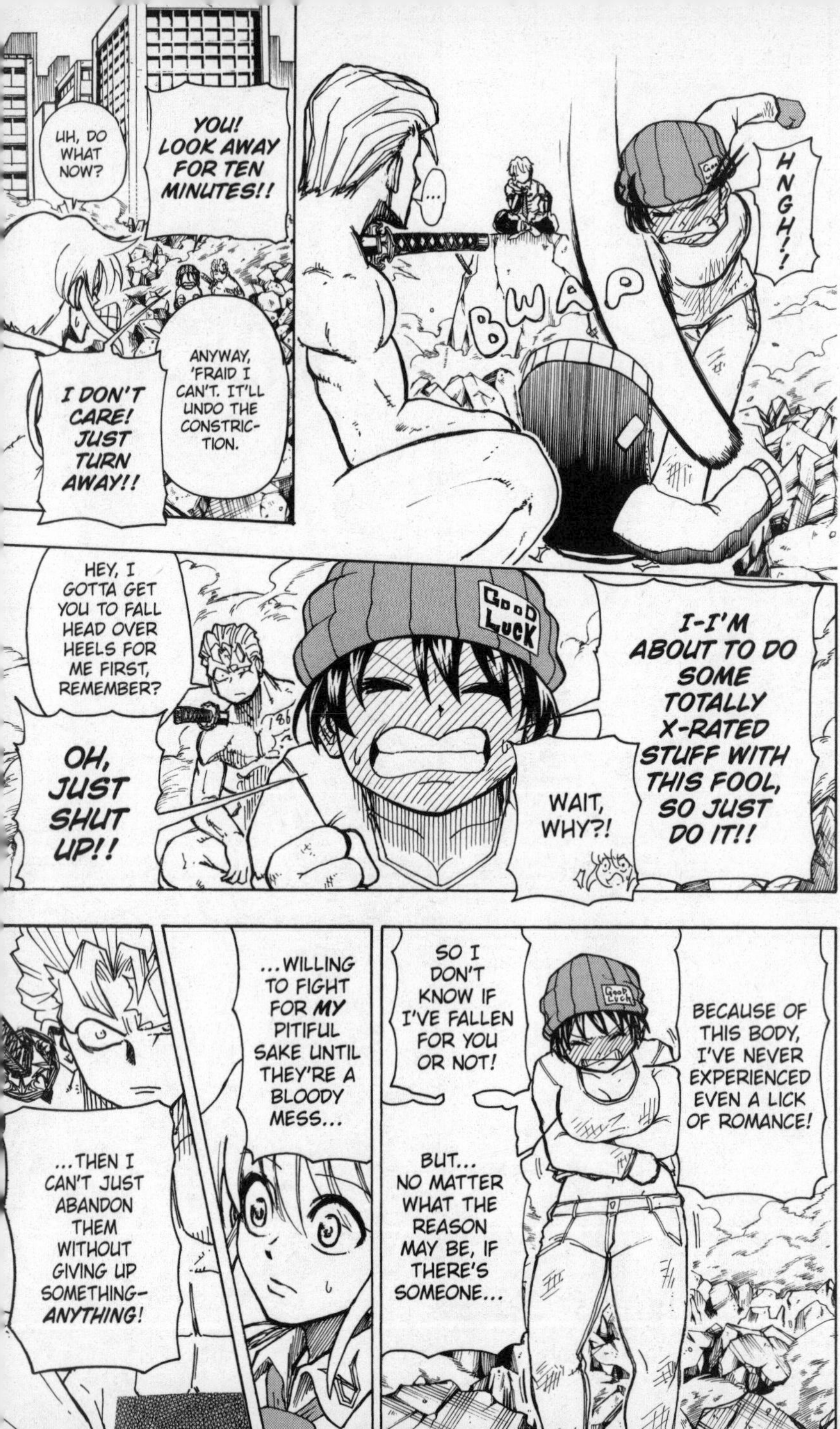
HNGH!!
...
BWAP
YOU! LOOK AWAY FOR TEN MINUTES!!
UH, DO WHAT NOW?
ANYWAY, 'FRAID I CAN'T. IT'LL UNDO THE CONSTRICTION.
I DON'T CARE! JUST TURN AWAY!!
I-I'M ABOUT TO DO SOME TOTALLY X-RATED STUFF WITH THIS FOOL, SO JUST DO IT!!
WAIT, WHY?!
HEY, I GOTTA GET YOU TO FALL HEAD OVER HEELS FOR ME FIRST, REMEMBER?
OH, JUST SHUT UP!!
BECAUSE OF THIS BODY, I'VE NEVER EXPERIENCED EVEN A LICK OF ROMANCE!
SO I DON'T KNOW IF I'VE FALLEN FOR YOU OR NOT!
BUT... NO MATTER WHAT THE REASON MAY BE, IF THERE'S SOMEONE...
...WILLING TO FIGHT FOR MY PITIFUL SAKE UNTIL THEY'RE A BLOODY MESS...
...THEN I CAN'T JUST ABANDON THEM WITHOUT GIVING UP SOMETHING-ANYTHING!

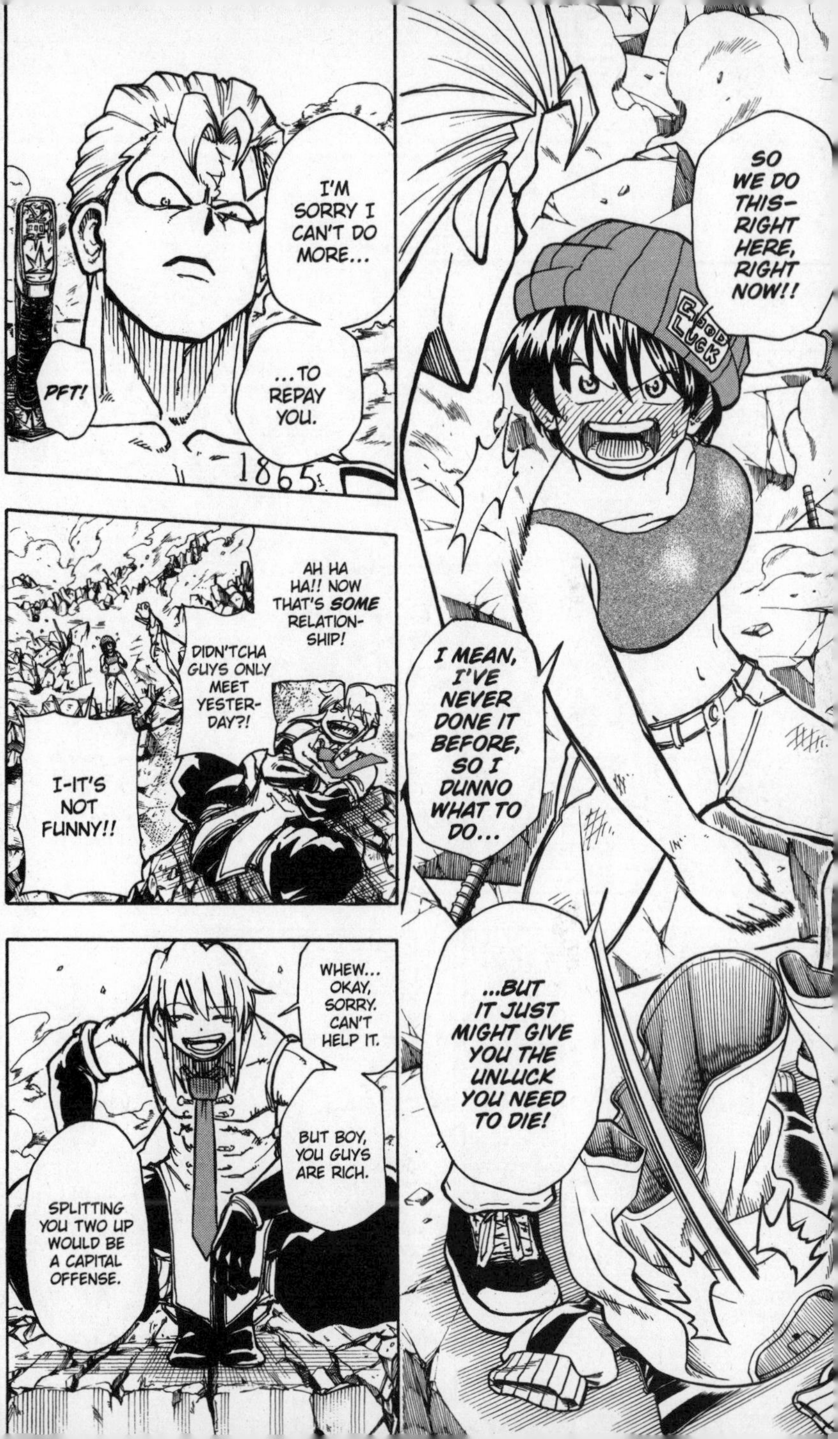
SO WE DO THIS- RIGHT HERE, RIGHT NOW!!
GOOD LUCK
I MEAN, I'VE NEVER DONE IT BEFORE, SO I DUNNO WHAT TO DO...
...BUT IT JUST MIGHT GIVE YOU THE UNLUCK YOU NEED TO DIE!
I'M SORRY I CAN'T DO MORE...
...TO REPAY YOU.
PFT!
1865
AH HA HA!! NOW THAT'S *SOME* RELATIONSHIP!
DIDN'TCHA GUYS ONLY MEET YESTERDAY?!
I-IT'S NOT FUNNY!!
WHEW... OKAY, SORRY. CAN'T HELP IT.
BUT BOY, YOU GUYS ARE RICH.
SPLITTING YOU TWO UP WOULD BE A CAPITAL OFFENSE.

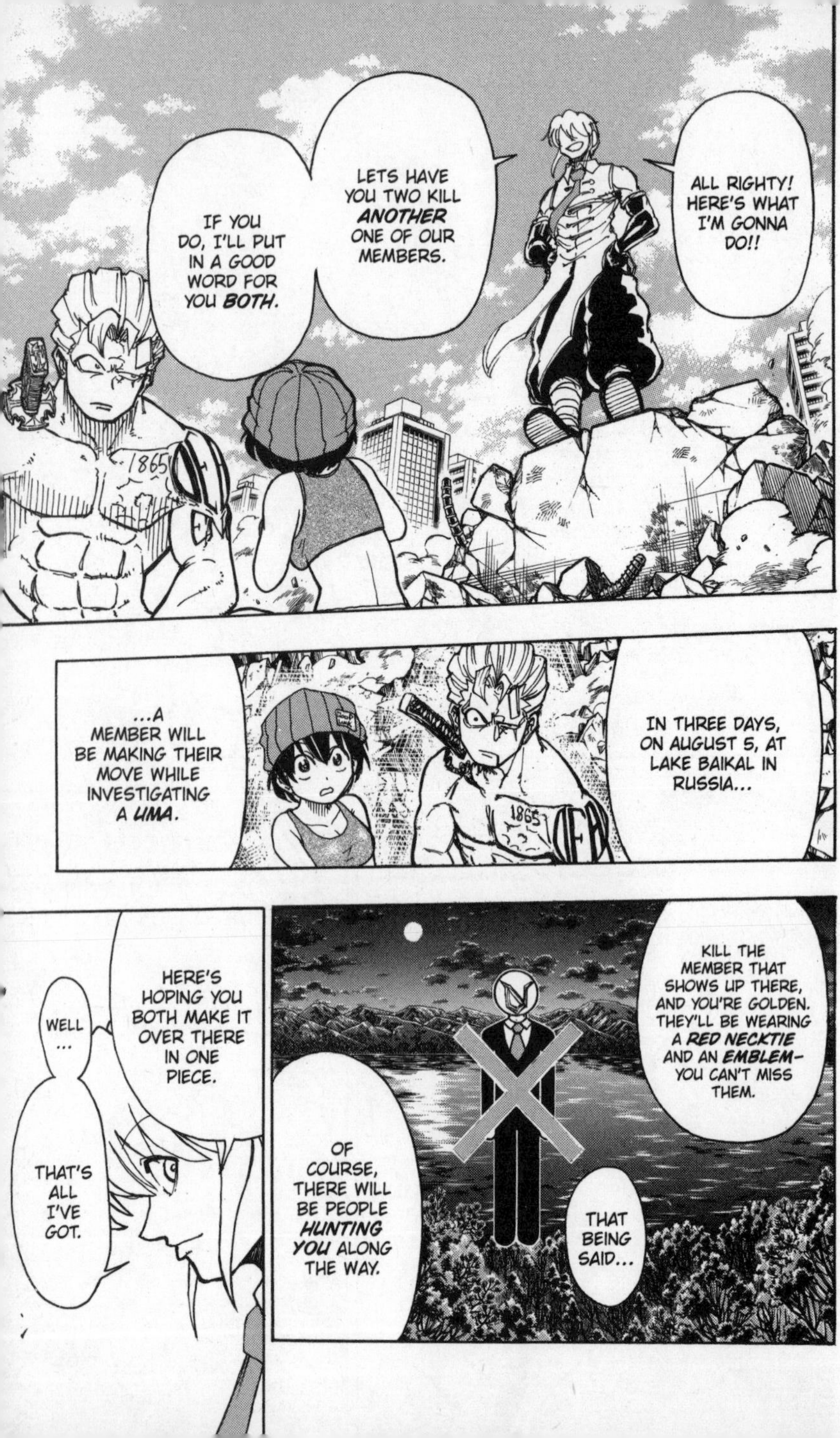
ALL RIGHTY! HERE'S WHAT I'M GONNA DO!!
LETS HAVE YOU TWO KILL ANOTHER ONE OF OUR MEMBERS.
IF YOU DO, I'LL PUT IN A GOOD WORD FOR YOU BOTH.
IN THREE DAYS, ON AUGUST 5, AT LAKE BAIKAL IN RUSSIA...
...A MEMBER WILL BE MAKING THEIR MOVE WHILE INVESTIGATING A UMA.
KILL THE MEMBER THAT SHOWS UP THERE, AND YOU'RE GOLDEN. THEY'LL BE WEARING A RED NECKTIE AND AN EMBLEM- YOU CAN'T MISS THEM.
THAT BEING SAID...
OF COURSE, THERE WILL BE PEOPLE HUNTING YOU ALONG THE WAY.
HERE'S HOPING YOU BOTH MAKE IT OVER THERE IN ONE PIECE.
WELL...
THAT'S ALL I'VE GOT.

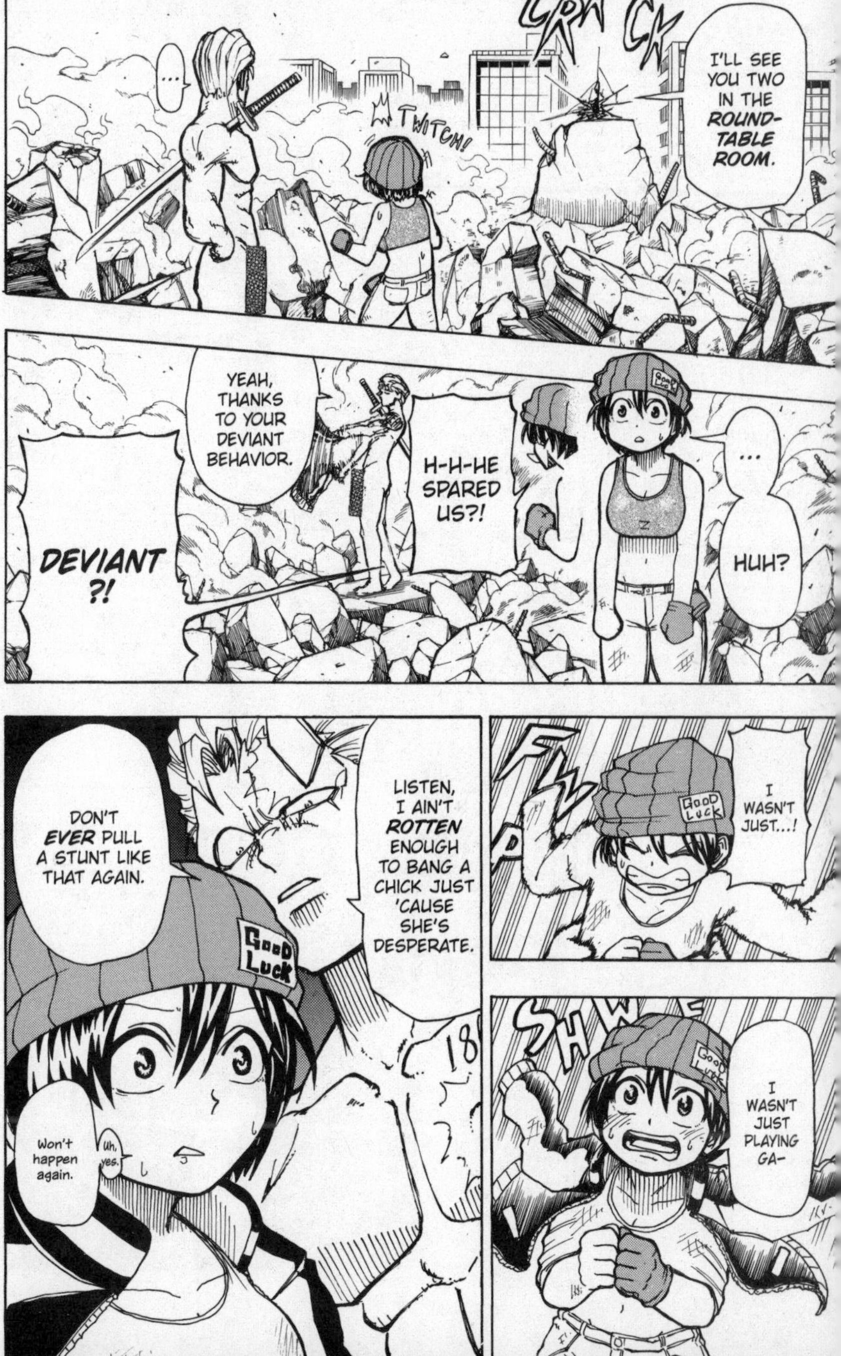
I'LL SEE YOU TWO IN THE ROUND-TABLE ROOM.
CRACK
TWITCH!
...
...
HUH?
H-H-HE SPARED US?!
YEAH, THANKS TO YOUR DEVIANT BEHAVIOR.
DEVIANT?!
I WASN'T JUST...!
I WASN'T JUST PLAYING GA-
LISTEN, I AIN'T ROTTEN ENOUGH TO BANG A CHICK JUST 'CAUSE SHE'S DESPERATE.
DON'T EVER PULL A STUNT LIKE THAT AGAIN.
Uh, yes.
Won't happen again.

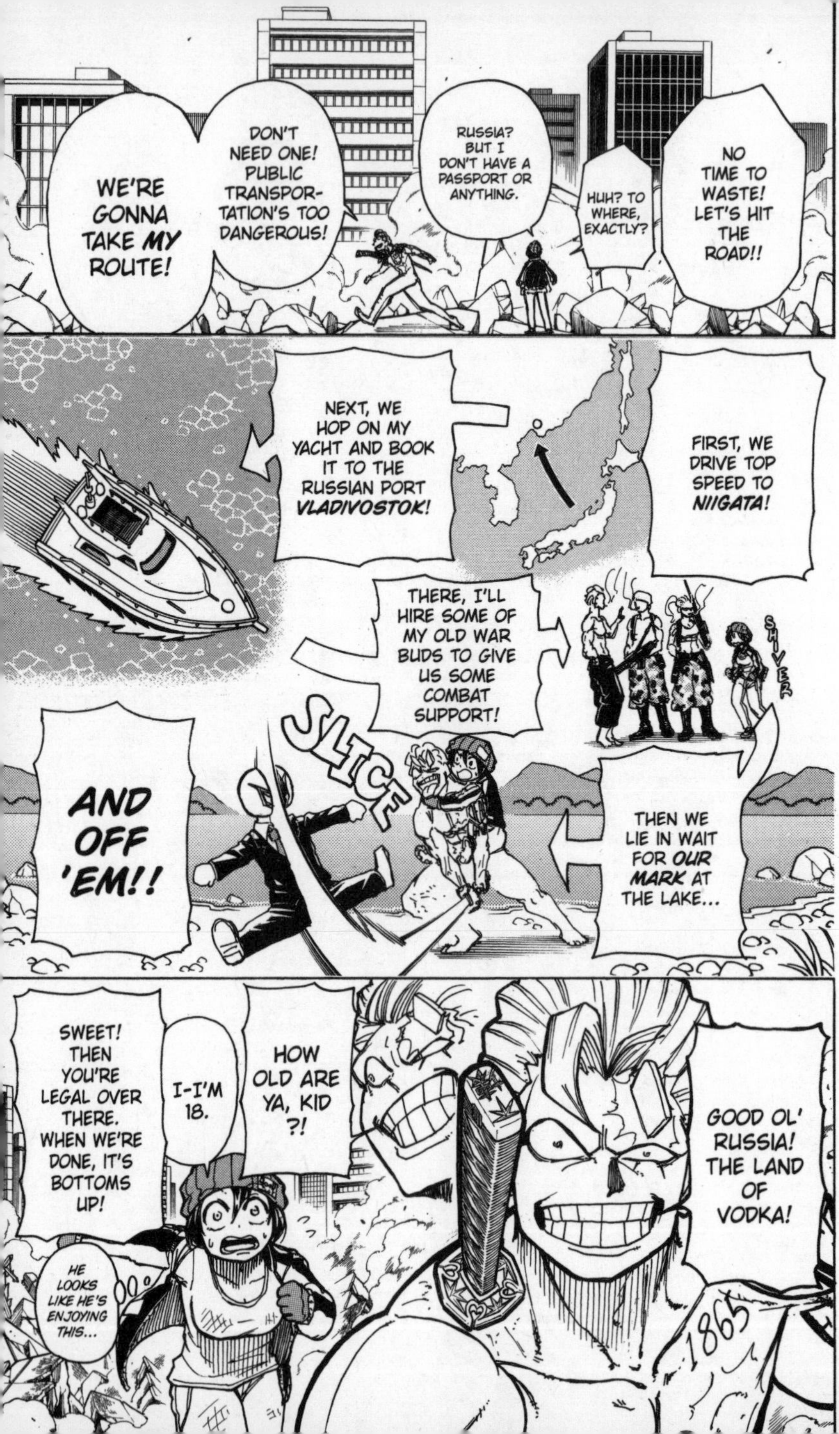
NO TIME TO WASTE! LET'S HIT THE ROAD!!
HUH? TO WHERE, EXACTLY?
RUSSIA? BUT I DON'T HAVE A PASSPORT OR ANYTHING.
DON'T NEED ONE! PUBLIC TRANSPORTATION'S TOO DANGEROUS!
WE'RE GONNA TAKE MY ROUTE!
FIRST, WE DRIVE TOP SPEED TO NIIGATA!
NEXT, WE HOP ON MY YACHT AND BOOK IT TO THE RUSSIAN PORT VLADIVOSTOK!
THERE, I'LL HIRE SOME OF MY OLD WAR BUDS TO GIVE US SOME COMBAT SUPPORT!
SHIVER
THEN WE LIE IN WAIT FOR OUR MARK AT THE LAKE...
SLICE
AND OFF 'EM!!
GOOD OL' RUSSIA! THE LAND OF VODKA!
1865
HOW OLD ARE YA, KID?!
I-I'M 18.
SWEET! THEN YOU'RE LEGAL OVER THERE. WHEN WE'RE DONE, IT'S BOTTOMS UP!
HE LOOKS LIKE HE'S ENJOYING THIS...

Unavoidable "Void"

A lot of you tweeted at the official Twitter account wanting to know his background, so here it is! My handwriting sucks!!
Sorry, guys!!

Former World Heavyweight Boxing Champion. He was well-known for his brute force-driven wild style and specialized in one-hit KOs. While defending his third title, when he was down on points and it seemed the judges would hand his opponent the win, his ability manifested. The right uppercut he landed on his defenseless opponent shattered his skull, killing him. Due to his ability, he was forced to leave the professional boxing scene behind.

By the time the Union scouted and recruited him he had already fallen into alcoholism. Upon joining the Union, he found his life worth living again, as his missions allowed him to use his ability to its full potential. But as time went on, he grew more and more violent.

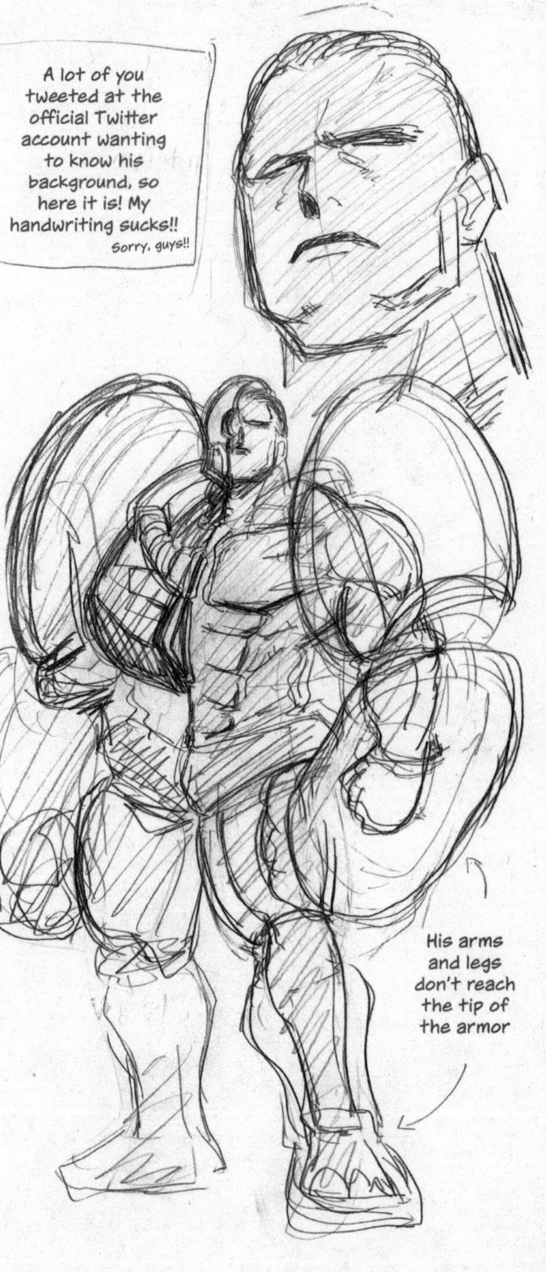
His arms and legs don't reach the tip of the armor

No. 004 How to Use My Unluck

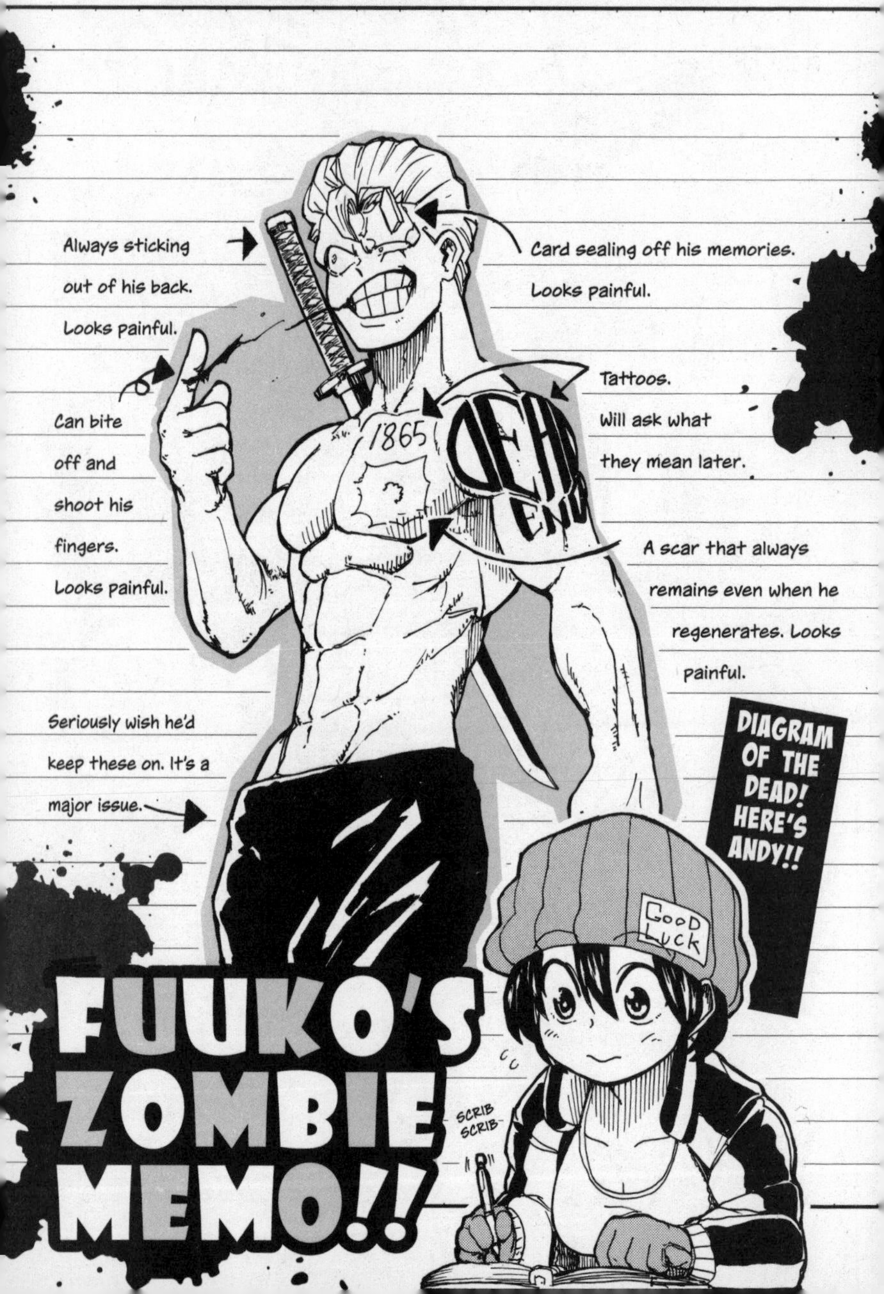
Card sealing off his memories. Looks painful.
Always sticking out of his back. Looks painful.
Tattoos. Will ask what they mean later.
Can bite off and shoot his fingers. Looks painful.
1865
A scar that always remains even when he regenerates. Looks painful.
Seriously wish he'd keep these on. It's a major issue.
DIAGRAM OF THE DEAD! HERE'S ANDY!!
GOOD LUCK
FUUKO'S ZOMBIE MEMO!!
SCRIB SCRIB

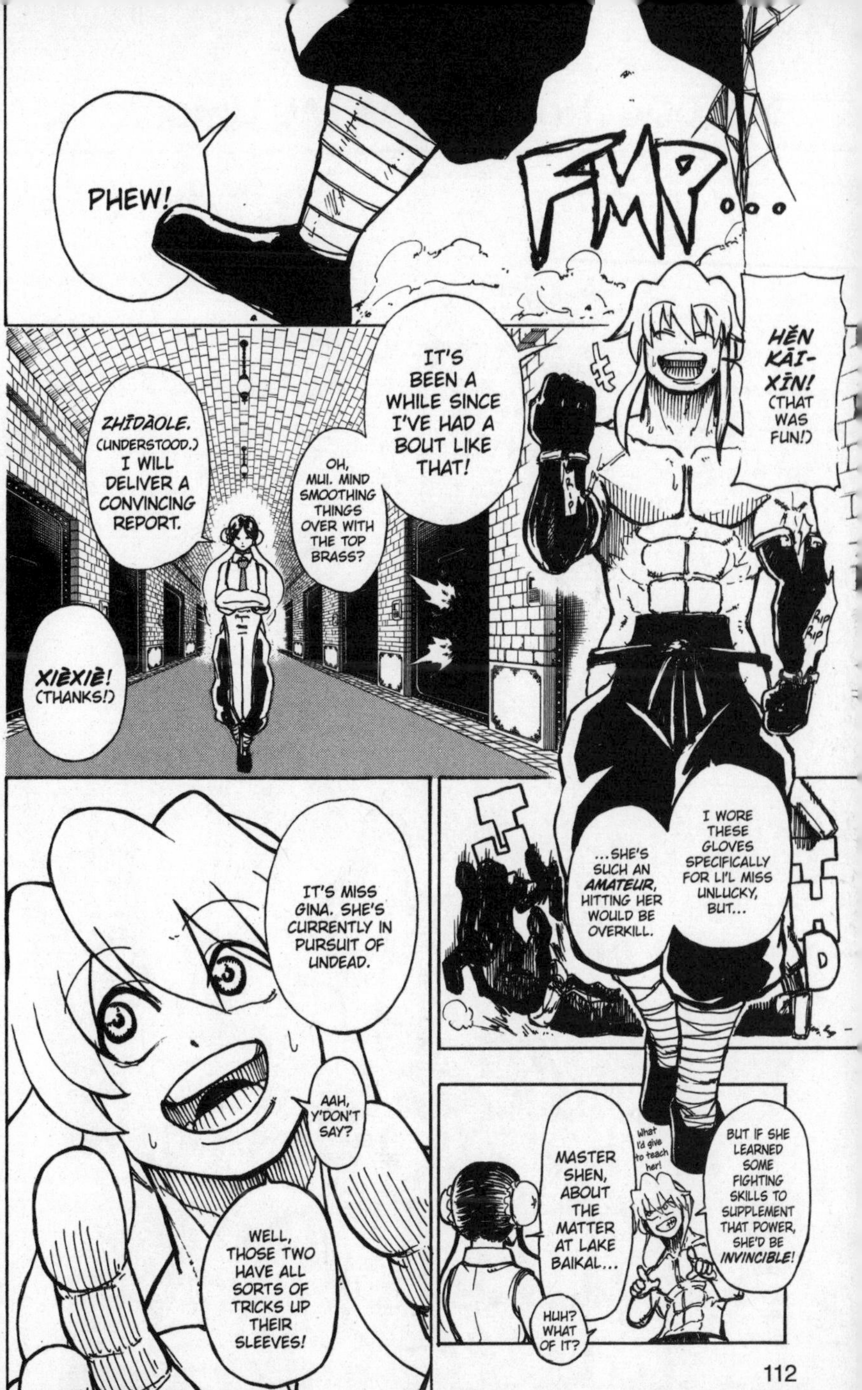
FMP...
PHEW!
HĚN KĀI-XĪN! (THAT WAS FUN!)
IT'S BEEN A WHILE SINCE I'VE HAD A BOUT LIKE THAT!
OH, MUI. MIND SMOOTHING THINGS OVER WITH THE TOP BRASS?
ZHĪDÀOLE. (UNDERSTOOD.) I WILL DELIVER A CONVINCING REPORT.
XIÈXIÈ! (THANKS!)
I WORE THESE GLOVES SPECIFICALLY FOR LI'L MISS UNLUCKY, BUT...
...SHE'S SUCH AN *AMATEUR*, HITTING HER WOULD BE OVERKILL.
BUT IF SHE LEARNED SOME FIGHTING SKILLS TO SUPPLEMENT THAT POWER, SHE'D BE *INVINCIBLE*!
What I'd give to teach her!
MASTER SHEN, ABOUT THE MATTER AT LAKE BAIKAL...
HUH? WHAT OF IT?
IT'S MISS GINA. SHE'S CURRENTLY IN PURSUIT OF UNDEAD.
AAH, Y'DON'T SAY?
WELL, THOSE TWO HAVE ALL SORTS OF TRICKS UP THEIR SLEEVES!

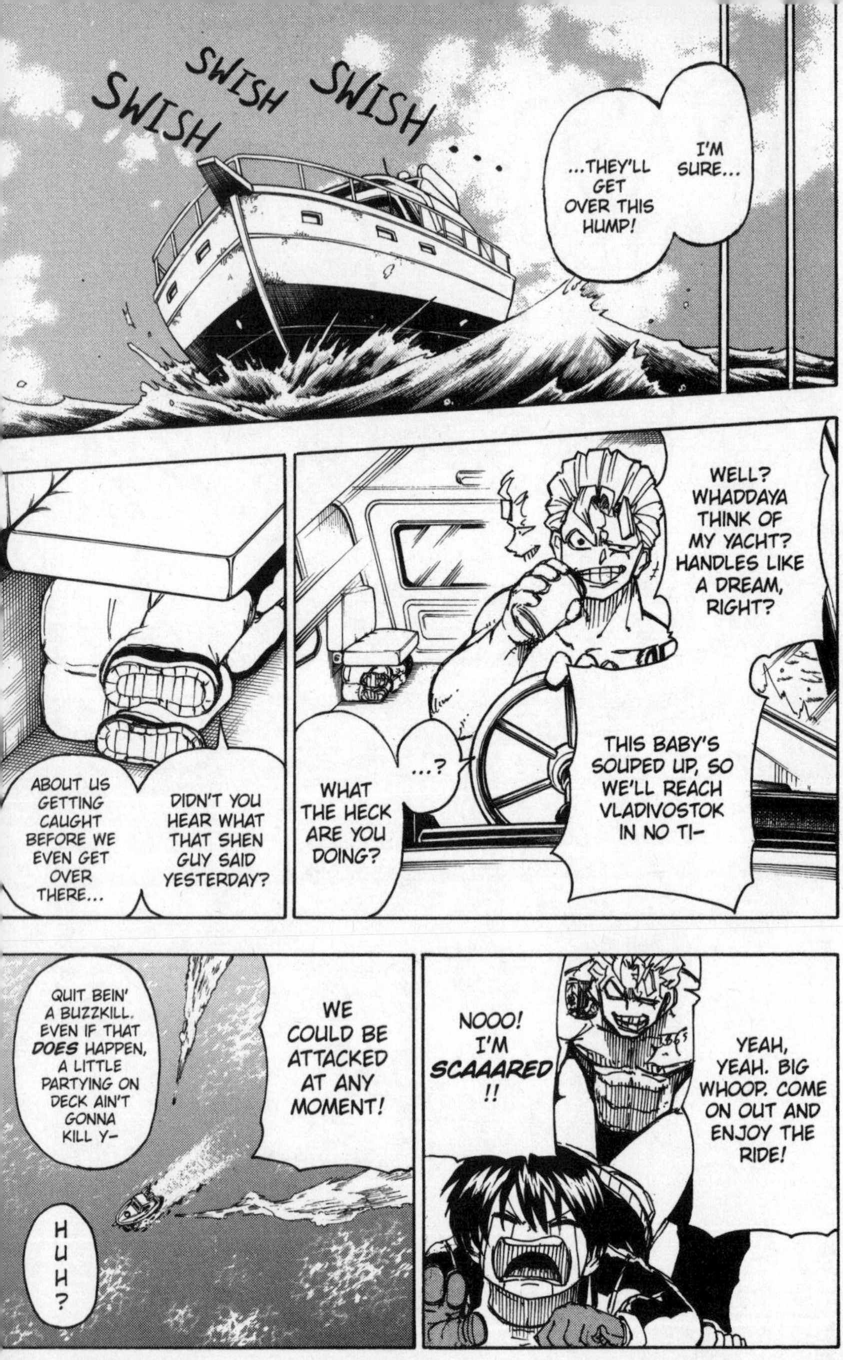
SWISH SWISH SWISH
I'M SURE... ...THEY'LL GET OVER THIS HUMP!
WELL? WHADDAYA THINK OF MY YACHT? HANDLES LIKE A DREAM, RIGHT?
THIS BABY'S SOUPED UP, SO WE'LL REACH VLADIVOSTOK IN NO TI-
...?
WHAT THE HECK ARE YOU DOING?
DIDN'T YOU HEAR WHAT THAT SHEN GUY SAID YESTERDAY?
ABOUT US GETTING CAUGHT BEFORE WE EVEN GET OVER THERE...
YEAH, YEAH. BIG WHOOP. COME ON OUT AND ENJOY THE RIDE!
NOOO! I'M SCAAARED!!
WE COULD BE ATTACKED AT ANY MOMENT!
QUIT BEIN' A BUZZKILL. EVEN IF THAT DOES HAPPEN, A LITTLE PARTYING ON DECK AIN'T GONNA KILL Y-
HUH?

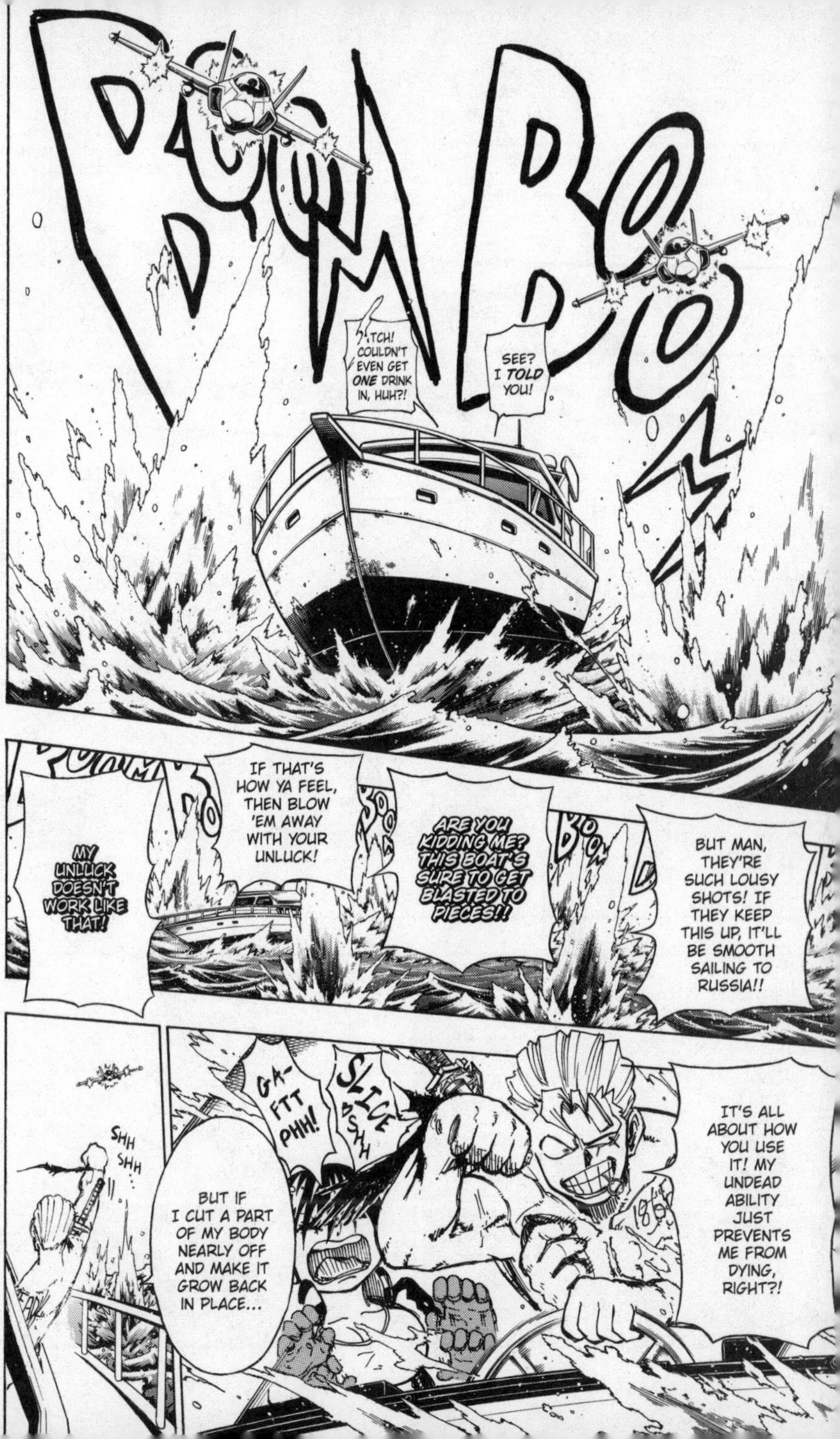
BOOM
SEE? I TOLD YOU!
TCH! COULDN'T EVEN GET ONE DRINK IN, HUH?!
BUT MAN, THEY'RE SUCH LOUSY SHOTS! IF THEY KEEP THIS UP, IT'LL BE SMOOTH SAILING TO RUSSIA!!
ARE YOU KIDDING ME? THIS BOAT'S SURE TO GET BLASTED TO PIECES!!
IF THAT'S HOW YA FEEL, THEN BLOW 'EM AWAY WITH YOUR UNLUCK!
MY UNLUCK DOESN'T WORK LIKE THAT!
IT'S ALL ABOUT HOW YOU USE IT! MY UNDEAD ABILITY JUST PREVENTS ME FROM DYING, RIGHT?!
SLICE
GA-FTT PHH!
BUT IF I CUT A PART OF MY BODY NEARLY OFF AND MAKE IT GROW BACK IN PLACE...
SHH SHH

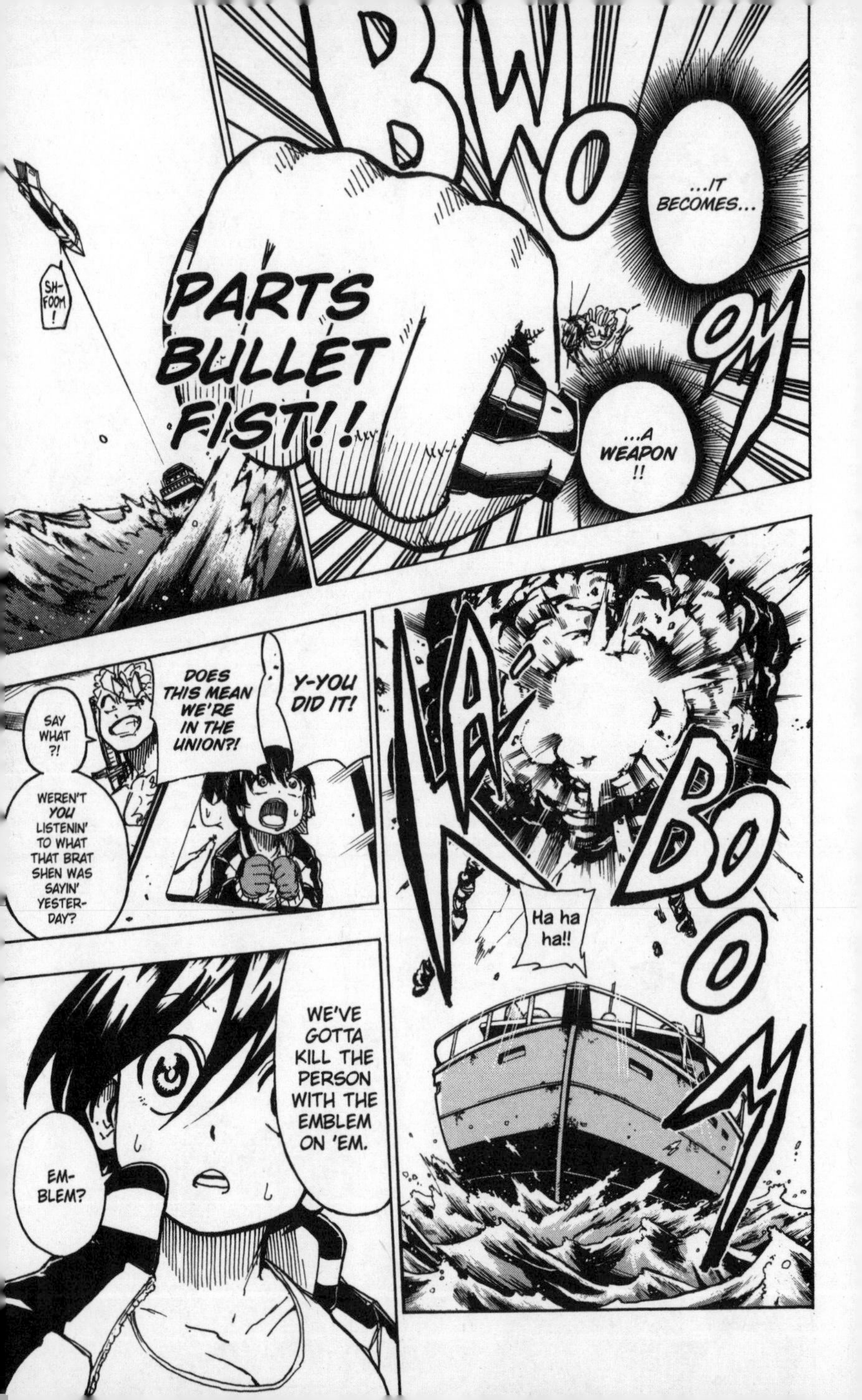

BWOOOOM
...IT BECOMES...
...A WEAPON!!
PARTS BULLET FIST!!
SH-FOOM!
KA-BOOOOM
Ha ha ha!!
Y-YOU DID IT!
DOES THIS MEAN WE'RE IN THE UNION?!
SAY WHAT?!
WEREN'T *YOU* LISTENIN' TO WHAT THAT BRAT SHEN WAS SAYIN' YESTER-DAY?
WE'VE GOTTA KILL THE PERSON WITH THE EMBLEM ON 'EM.
EM-BLEM?

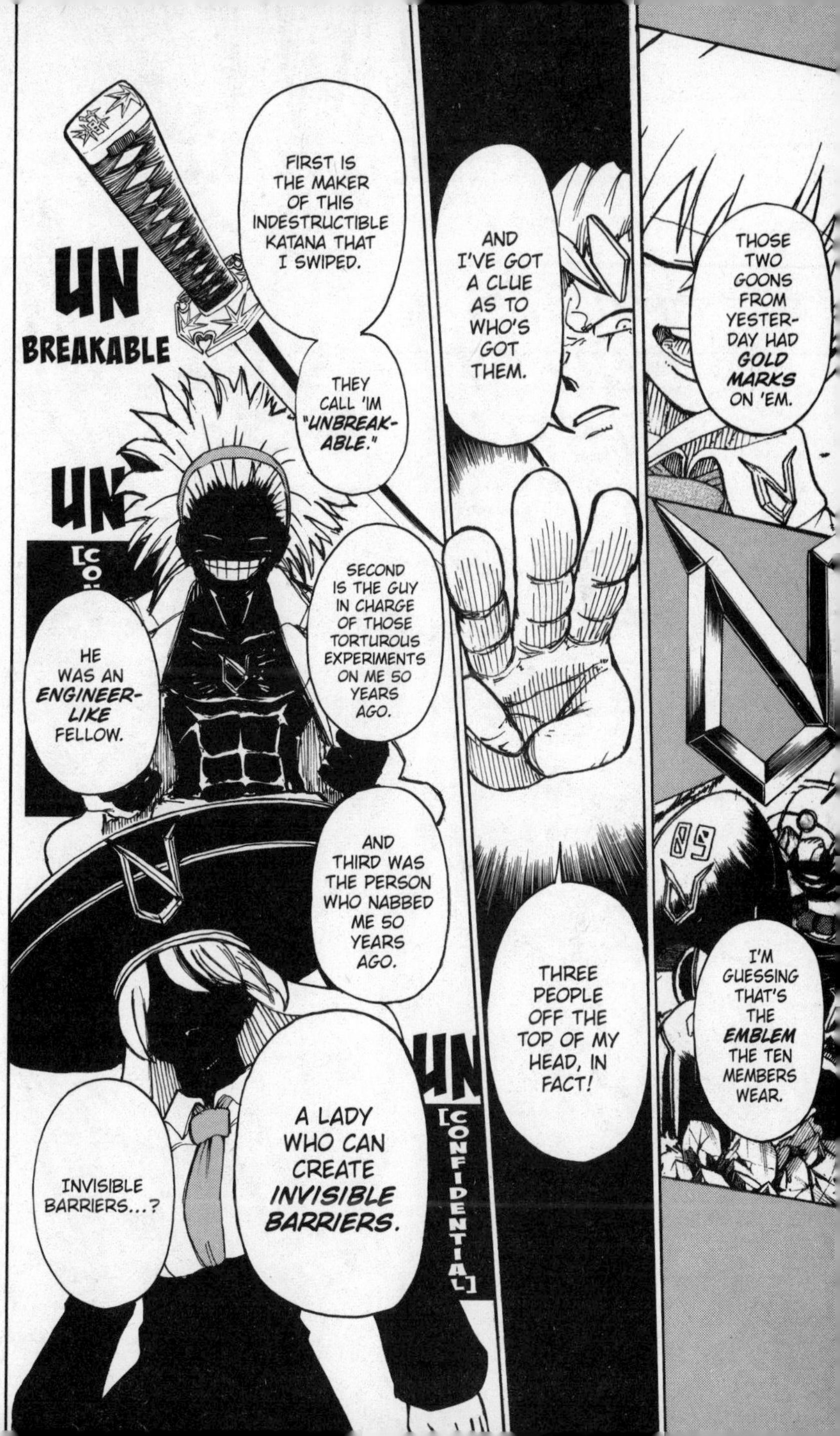
THOSE TWO GOONS FROM YESTERDAY HAD GOLD MARKS ON 'EM.
I'M GUESSING THAT'S THE EMBLEM THE TEN MEMBERS WEAR.
AND I'VE GOT A CLUE AS TO WHO'S GOT THEM.
THREE PEOPLE OFF THE TOP OF MY HEAD, IN FACT!
UN BREAKABLE
FIRST IS THE MAKER OF THIS INDESTRUCTIBLE KATANA THAT I SWIPED.
THEY CALL 'IM "UNBREAKABLE."
UN
SECOND IS THE GUY IN CHARGE OF THOSE TORTUROUS EXPERIMENTS ON ME 50 YEARS AGO.
HE WAS AN ENGINEER-LIKE FELLOW.
AND THIRD WAS THE PERSON WHO NABBED ME 50 YEARS AGO.
UN [CONFIDENTIAL]
A LADY WHO CAN CREATE INVISIBLE BARRIERS.
INVISIBLE BARRIERS...?

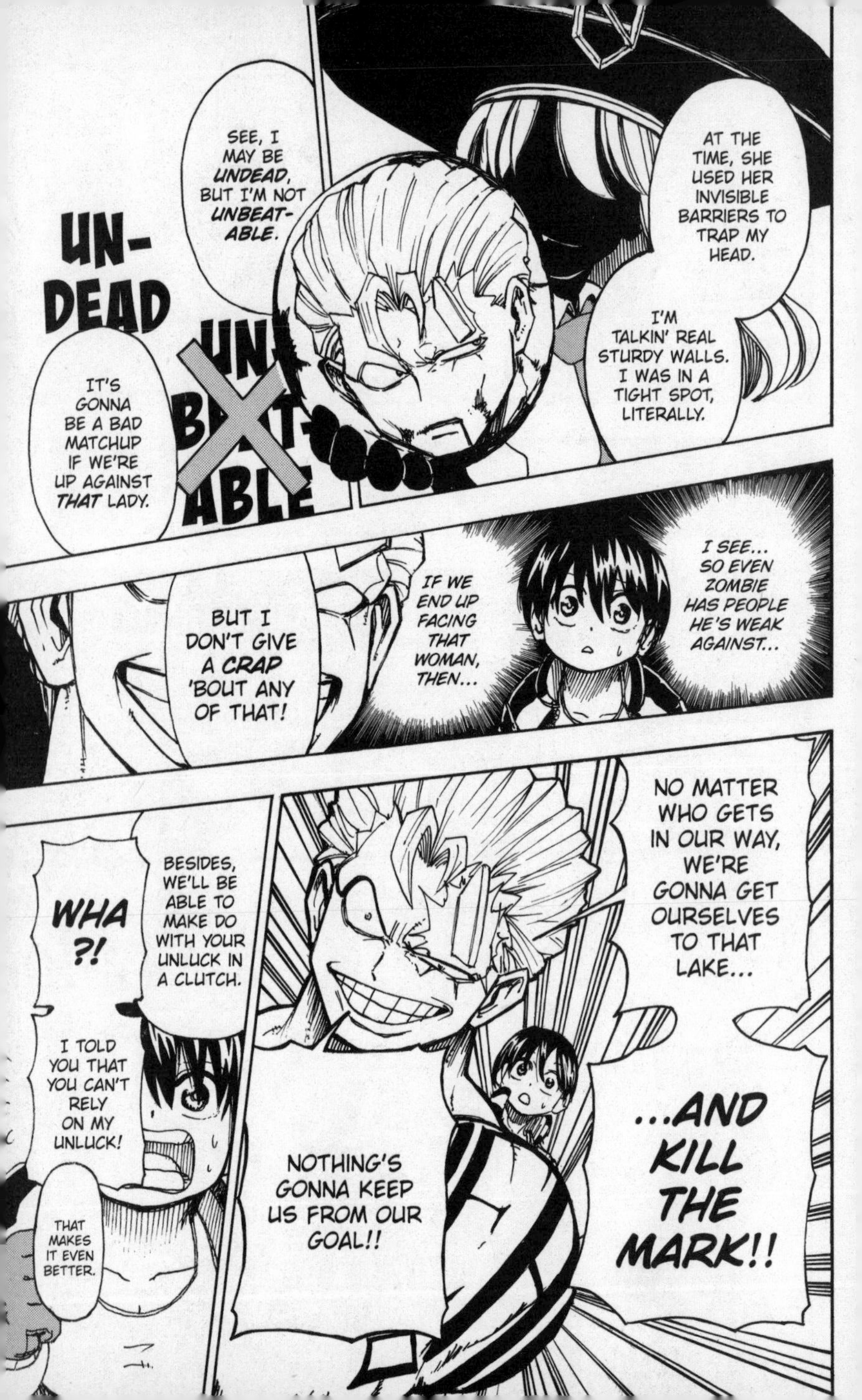
AT THE TIME, SHE USED HER INVISIBLE BARRIERS TO TRAP MY HEAD.
I'M TALKIN' REAL STURDY WALLS. I WAS IN A TIGHT SPOT, LITERALLY.
SEE, I MAY BE UNDEAD, BUT I'M NOT UNBEAT-ABLE.
UN-DEAD
UN-BEAT-ABLE
IT'S GONNA BE A BAD MATCHUP IF WE'RE UP AGAINST THAT LADY.
I SEE... SO EVEN ZOMBIE HAS PEOPLE HE'S WEAK AGAINST...
IF WE END UP FACING THAT WOMAN, THEN...
BUT I DON'T GIVE A CRAP 'BOUT ANY OF THAT!
NO MATTER WHO GETS IN OUR WAY, WE'RE GONNA GET OURSELVES TO THAT LAKE...
...AND KILL THE MARK!!
NOTHING'S GONNA KEEP US FROM OUR GOAL!!
BESIDES, WE'LL BE ABLE TO MAKE DO WITH YOUR UNLUCK IN A CLUTCH.
WHA ?!
I TOLD YOU THAT YOU CAN'T RELY ON MY UNLUCK!
THAT MAKES IT EVEN BETTER.

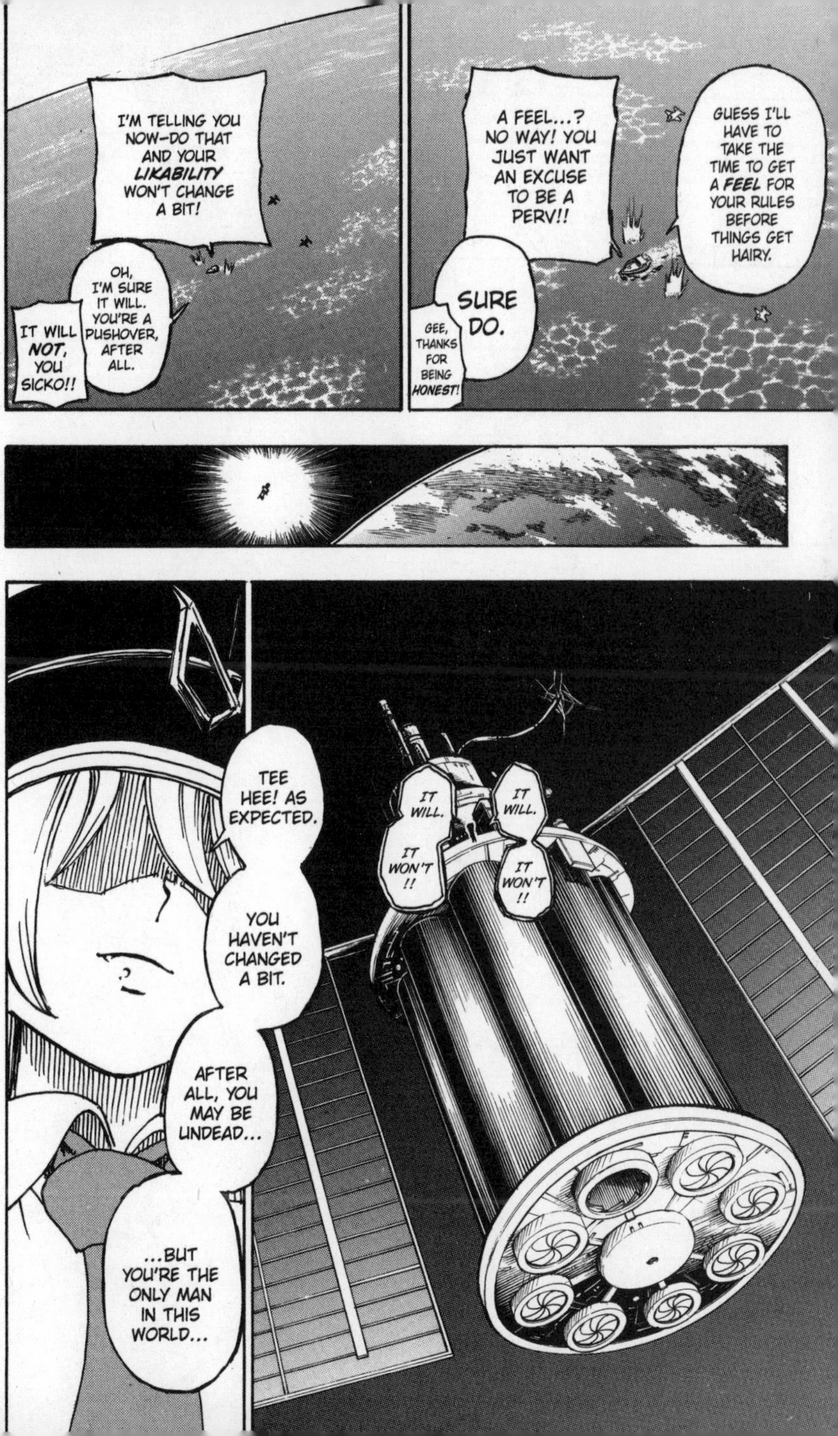
GUESS I'LL HAVE TO TAKE THE TIME TO GET A **FEEL** FOR YOUR RULES BEFORE THINGS GET HAIRY.
A FEEL...? NO WAY! YOU JUST WANT AN EXCUSE TO BE A PERV!!
SURE DO.
GEE, THANKS FOR BEING **HONEST!**
I'M TELLING YOU NOW—DO THAT AND YOUR **LIKABILITY** WON'T CHANGE A BIT!
OH, I'M SURE IT WILL. YOU'RE A PUSHOVER, AFTER ALL.
IT WILL **NOT**, YOU SICKO!!
IT WILL.
IT WON'T!!
IT WILL.
IT WON'T!!
TEE HEE! AS EXPECTED.
YOU HAVEN'T CHANGED A BIT.
AFTER ALL, YOU MAY BE UNDEAD...
...BUT YOU'RE THE ONLY MAN IN THIS WORLD...

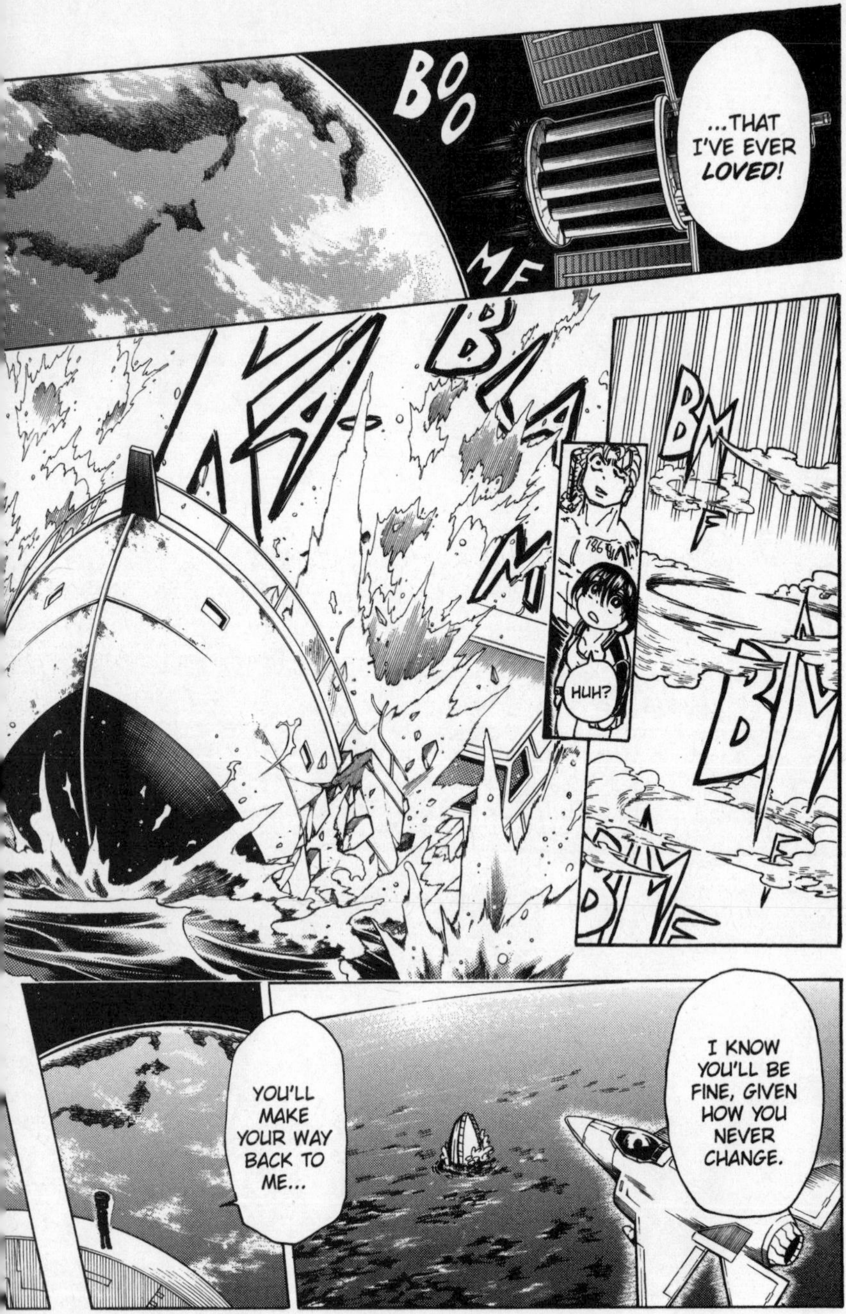
...THAT I'VE EVER LOVED!
BOOMF
BMF
HUH?
KABLAM
I KNOW YOU'LL BE FINE, GIVEN HOW YOU NEVER CHANGE.
YOU'LL MAKE YOUR WAY BACK TO ME...

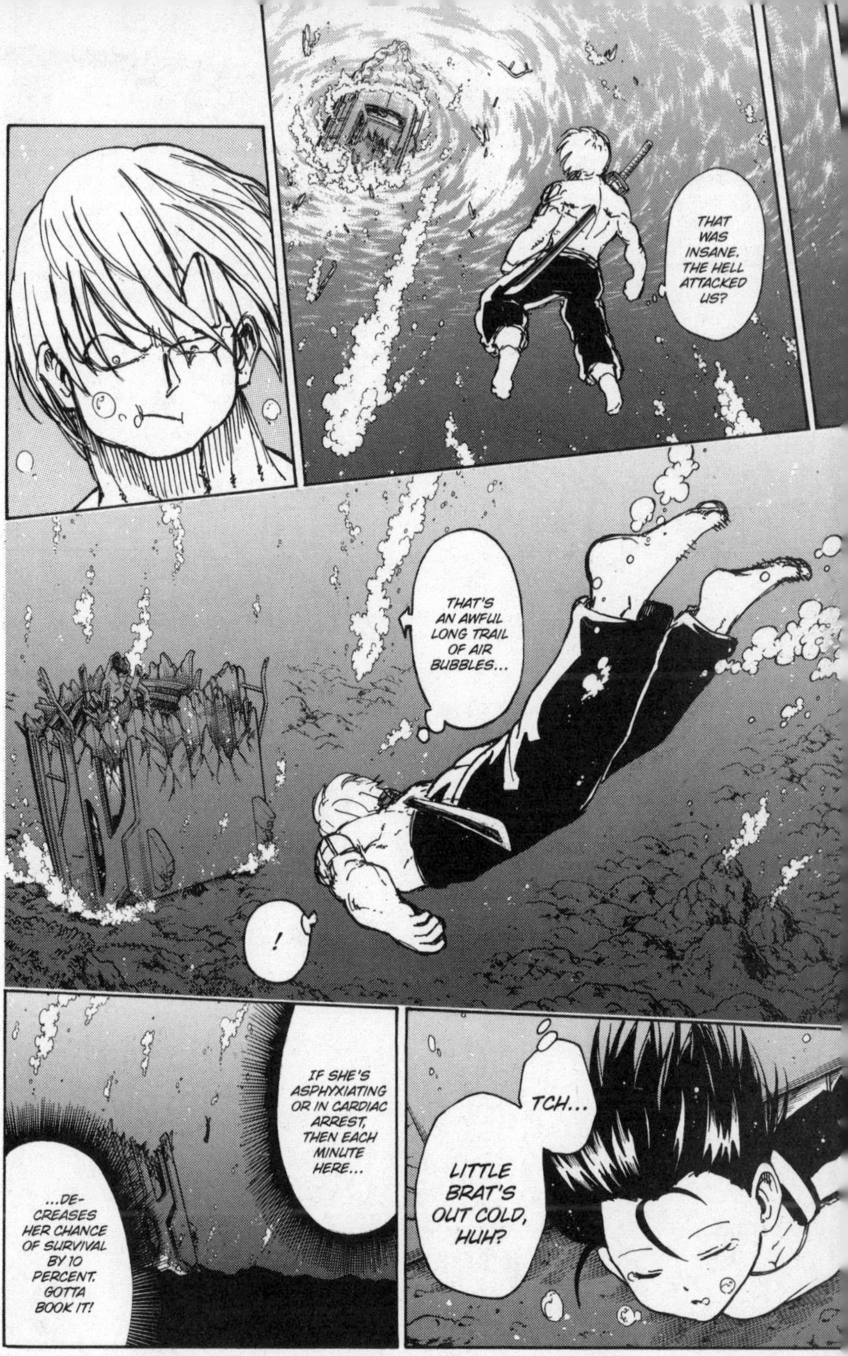
THAT WAS INSANE. THE HELL ATTACKED US?
THAT'S AN AWFUL LONG TRAIL OF AIR BUBBLES...
!
TCH...
LITTLE BRAT'S OUT COLD, HUH?
IF SHE'S ASPHYXIATING OR IN CARDIAC ARREST, THEN EACH MINUTE HERE...
...DE-CREASES HER CHANCE OF SURVIVAL BY 10 PERCENT. GOTTA BOOK IT!

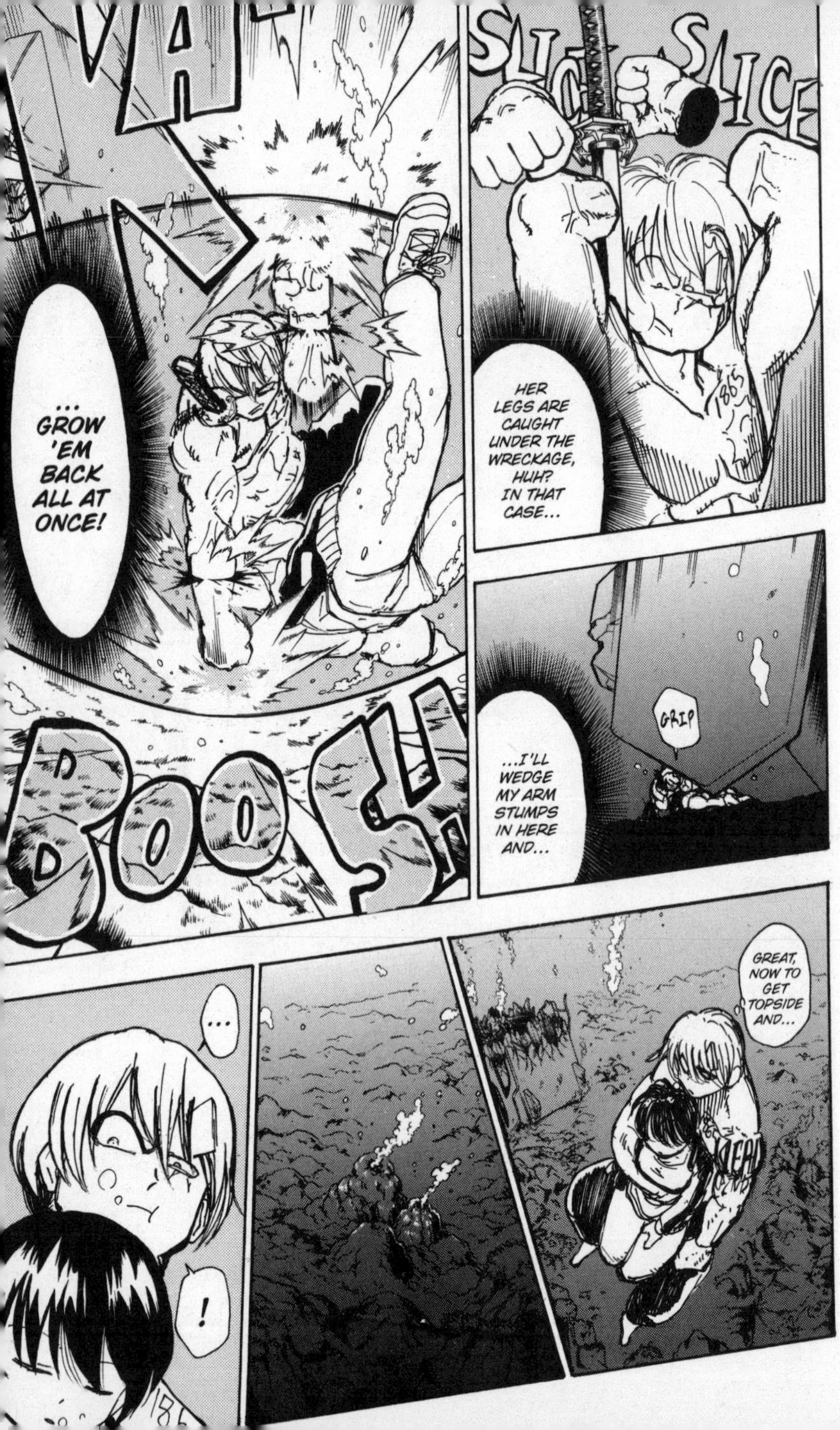
SLIC
SLICE
HER LEGS ARE CAUGHT UNDER THE WRECKAGE, HUH? IN THAT CASE...
GRIP
...I'LL WEDGE MY ARM STUMPS IN HERE AND...
...GROW 'EM BACK ALL AT ONCE!
DOOSH
GREAT, NOW TO GET TOPSIDE AND...
...
!

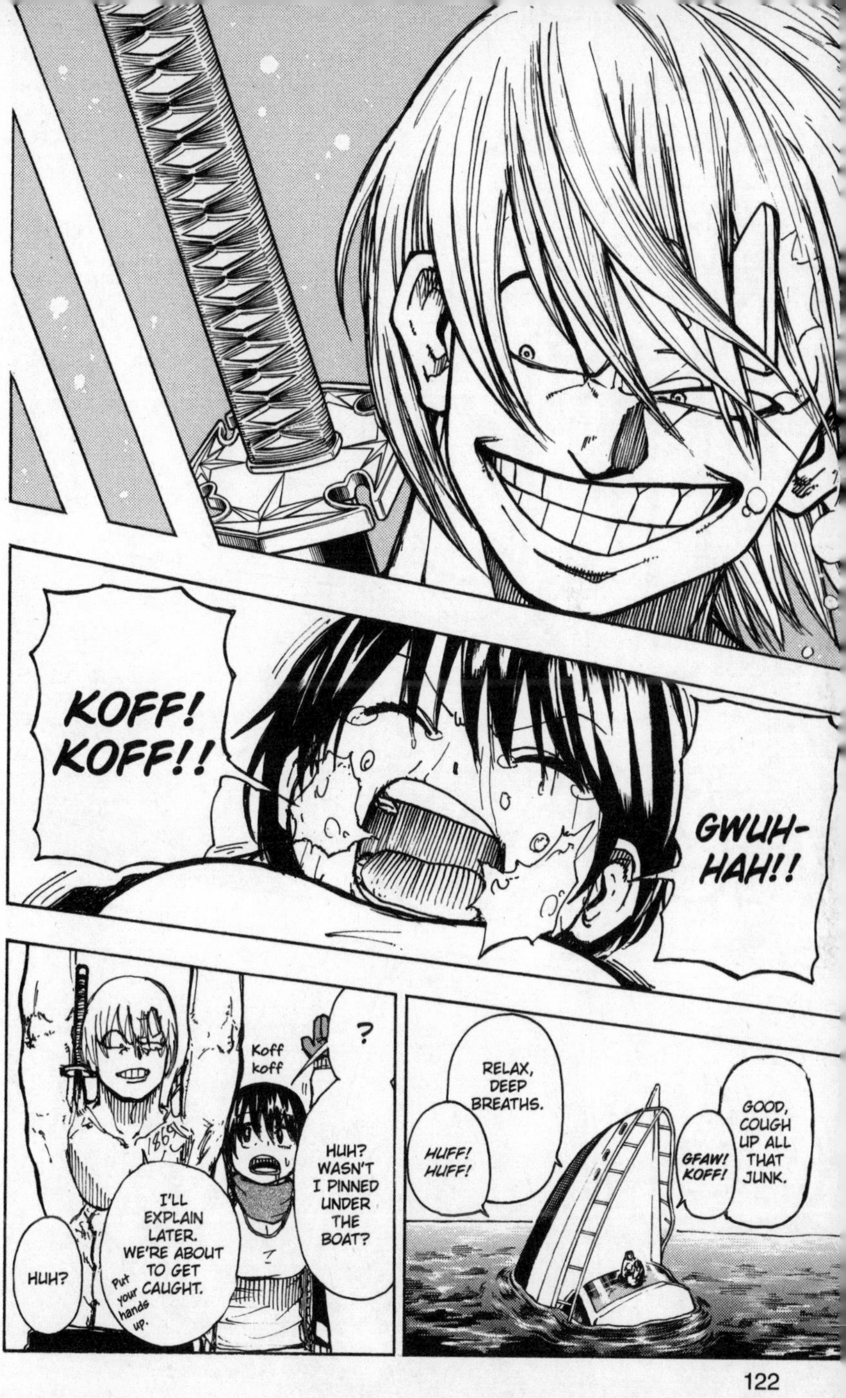
GWUH-HAH!!
KOFF! KOFF!!
GOOD, COUGH UP ALL THAT JUNK.
GFAW! KOFF!
RELAX, DEEP BREATHS.
HUFF! HUFF!
?
Koff koff
HUH? WASN'T I PINNED UNDER THE BOAT?
I'LL EXPLAIN LATER. WE'RE ABOUT TO GET CAUGHT.
Put your hands up.
HUH?

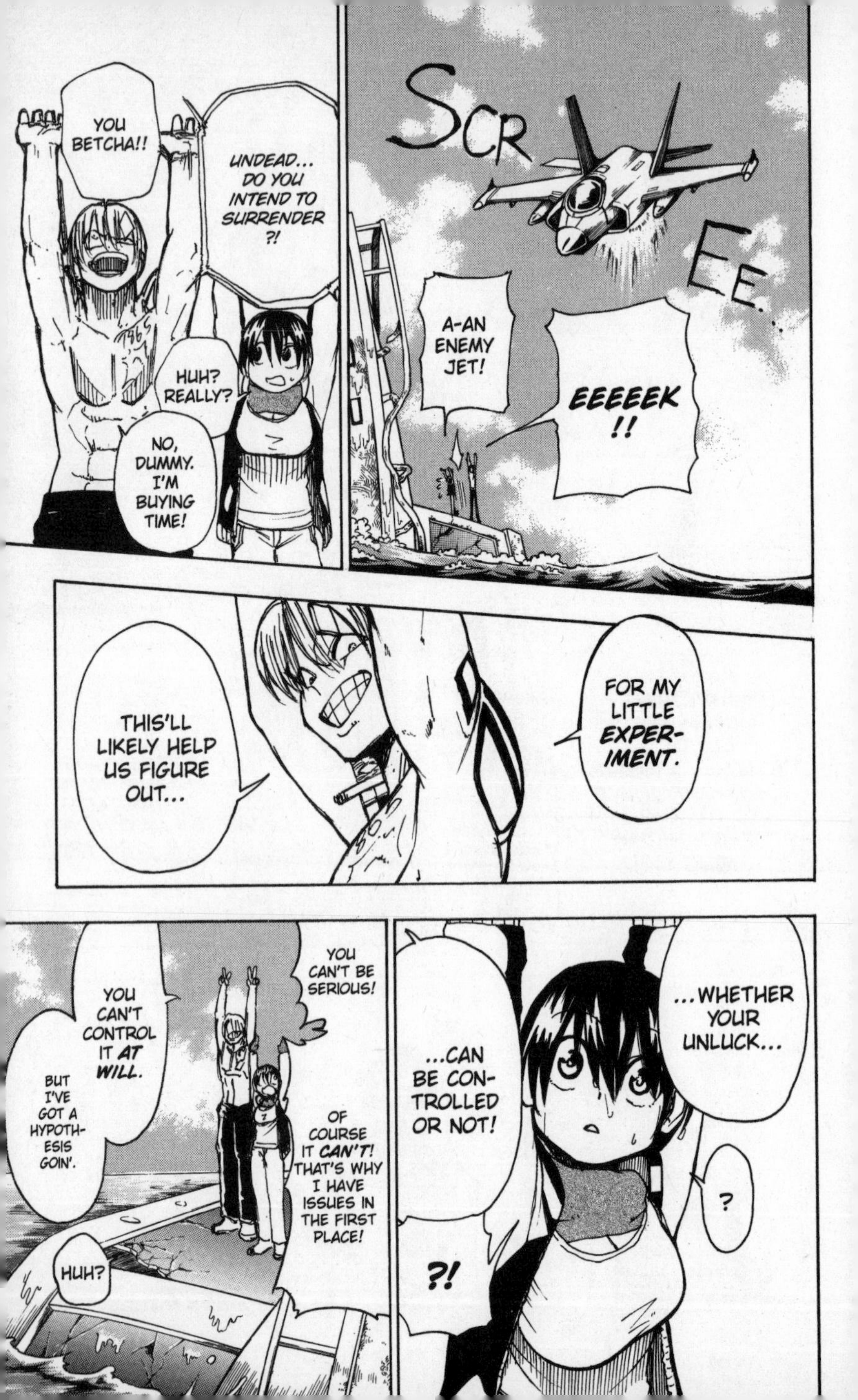
SCR
EE...
A-AN ENEMY JET!
EEEEEK!!
UNDEAD... DO YOU INTEND TO SURRENDER?!
YOU BETCHA!!
HUH? REALLY?
NO, DUMMY. I'M BUYING TIME!
FOR MY LITTLE EXPERIMENT.
THIS'LL LIKELY HELP US FIGURE OUT...
...WHETHER YOUR UNLUCK...
...CAN BE CONTROLLED OR NOT!
?
?!
YOU CAN'T BE SERIOUS!
YOU CAN'T CONTROL IT AT WILL.
OF COURSE IT CAN'T! THAT'S WHY I HAVE ISSUES IN THE FIRST PLACE!
BUT I'VE GOT A HYPOTHESIS GOIN'.
HUH?

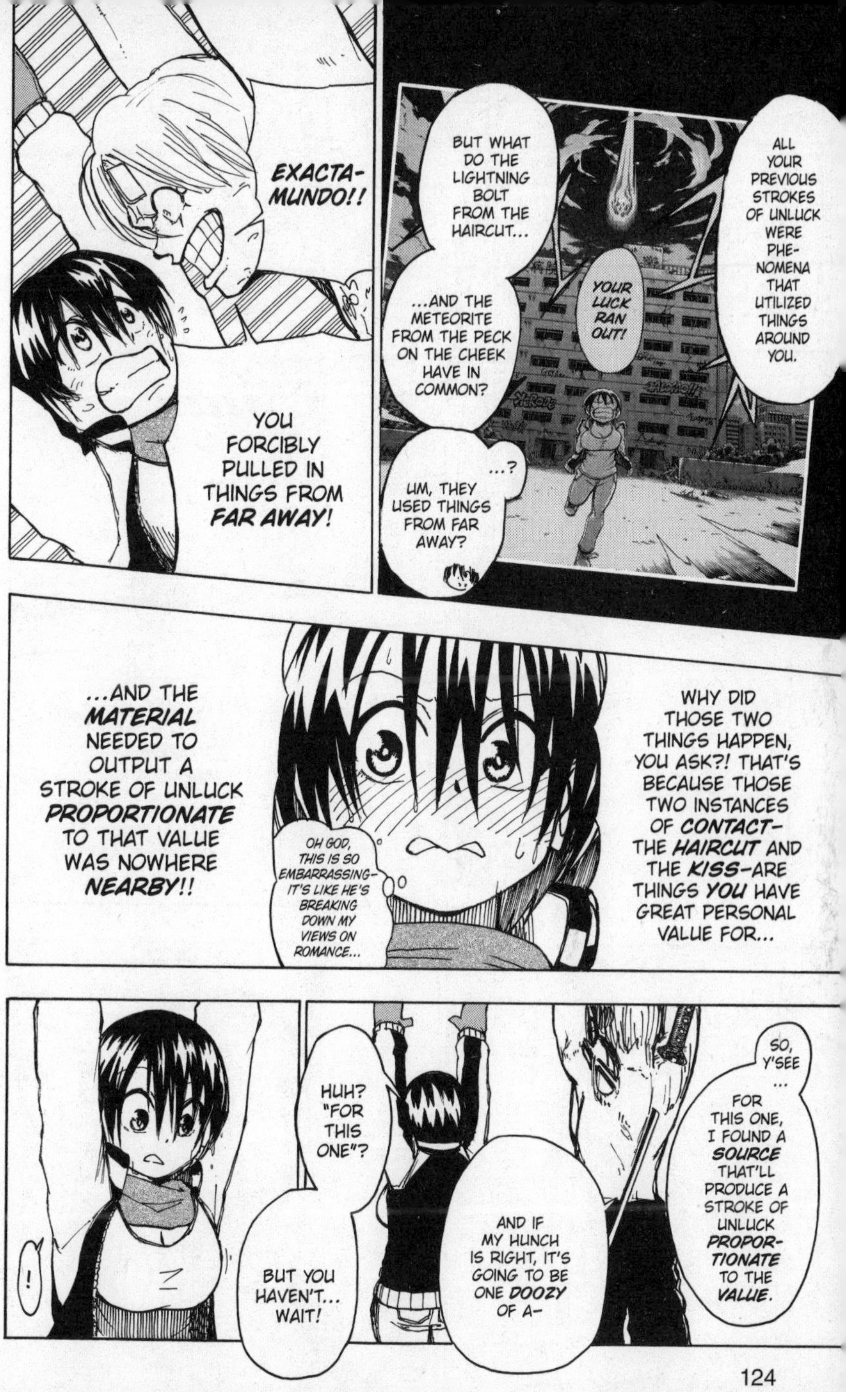
ALL YOUR PREVIOUS STROKES OF UNLUCK WERE PHENOMENA THAT UTILIZED THINGS AROUND YOU.
YOUR LUCK RAN OUT!
BUT WHAT DO THE LIGHTNING BOLT FROM THE HAIRCUT...
...AND THE METEORITE FROM THE PECK ON THE CHEEK HAVE IN COMMON?
...?
UM, THEY USED THINGS FROM FAR AWAY?
EXACTA-MUNDO!!
YOU FORCIBLY PULLED IN THINGS FROM FAR AWAY!
WHY DID THOSE TWO THINGS HAPPEN, YOU ASK?! THAT'S BECAUSE THOSE TWO INSTANCES OF CONTACT-THE HAIRCUT AND THE KISS-ARE THINGS YOU HAVE GREAT PERSONAL VALUE FOR...
OH GOD, THIS IS SO EMBARRASSING-IT'S LIKE HE'S BREAKING DOWN MY VIEWS ON ROMANCE...
...AND THE MATERIAL NEEDED TO OUTPUT A STROKE OF UNLUCK PROPORTIONATE TO THAT VALUE WAS NOWHERE NEARBY!!
SO, Y'SEE ...
FOR THIS ONE, I FOUND A SOURCE THAT'LL PRODUCE A STROKE OF UNLUCK PROPORTIONATE TO THE VALUE.
HUH? "FOR THIS ONE"?
AND IF MY HUNCH IS RIGHT, IT'S GOING TO BE ONE DOOZY OF A-
BUT YOU HAVEN'T... WAIT!
!

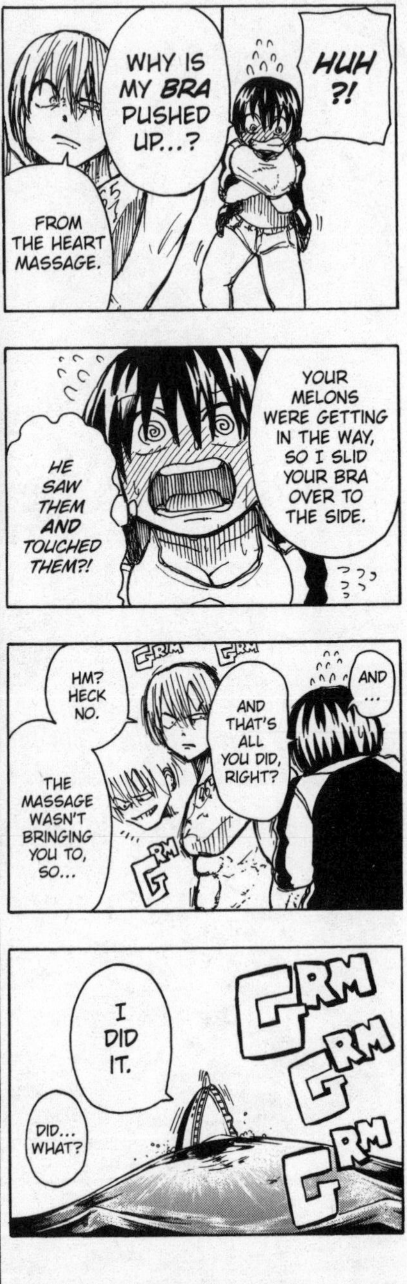
HUH ?!
WHY IS MY BRA PUSHED UP...?
FROM THE HEART MASSAGE.
YOUR MELONS WERE GETTING IN THE WAY, SO I SLID YOUR BRA OVER TO THE SIDE.
HE SAW THEM AND TOUCHED THEM?!
AND ...
AND THAT'S ALL YOU DID, RIGHT?
GRM
GRM
HM? HECK NO.
THE MASSAGE WASN'T BRINGING YOU TO, SO...
GRM
GRM
GRM
GRM
I DID IT.
DID... WHAT?
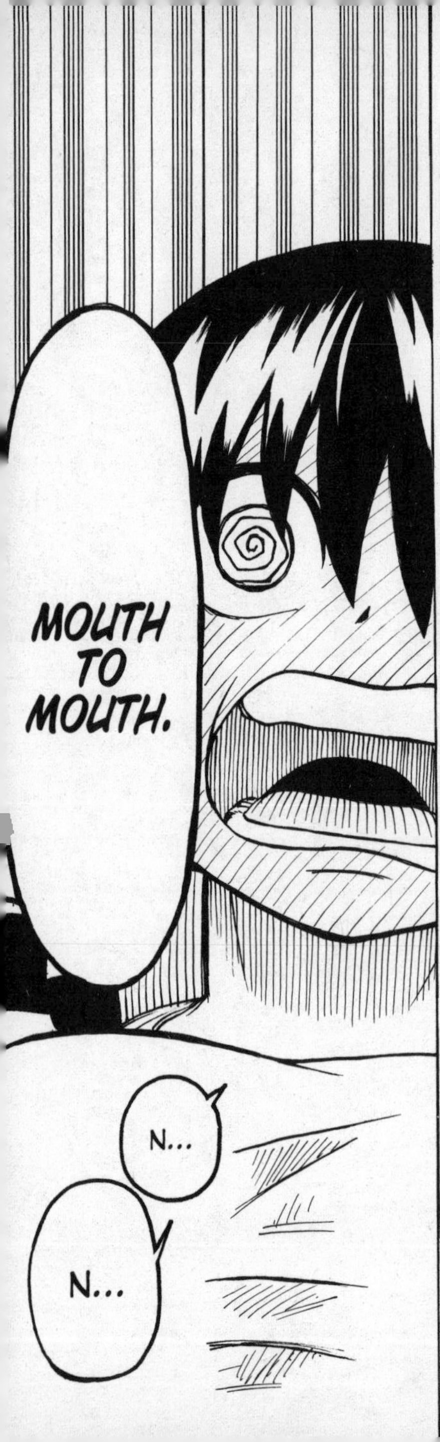
MOUTH TO MOUTH.
N...
N...

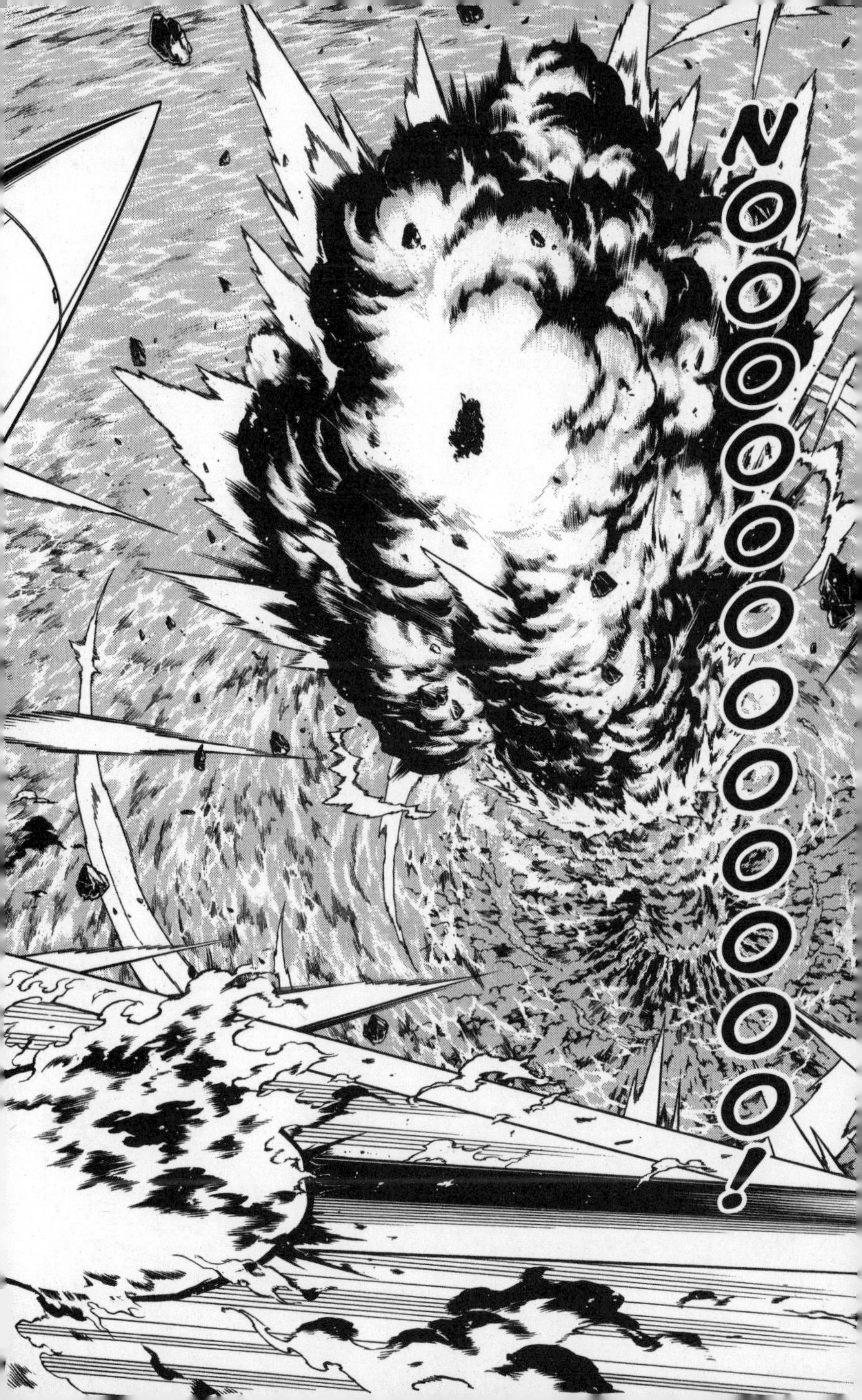
NOOOOOOOOOOOOOO!

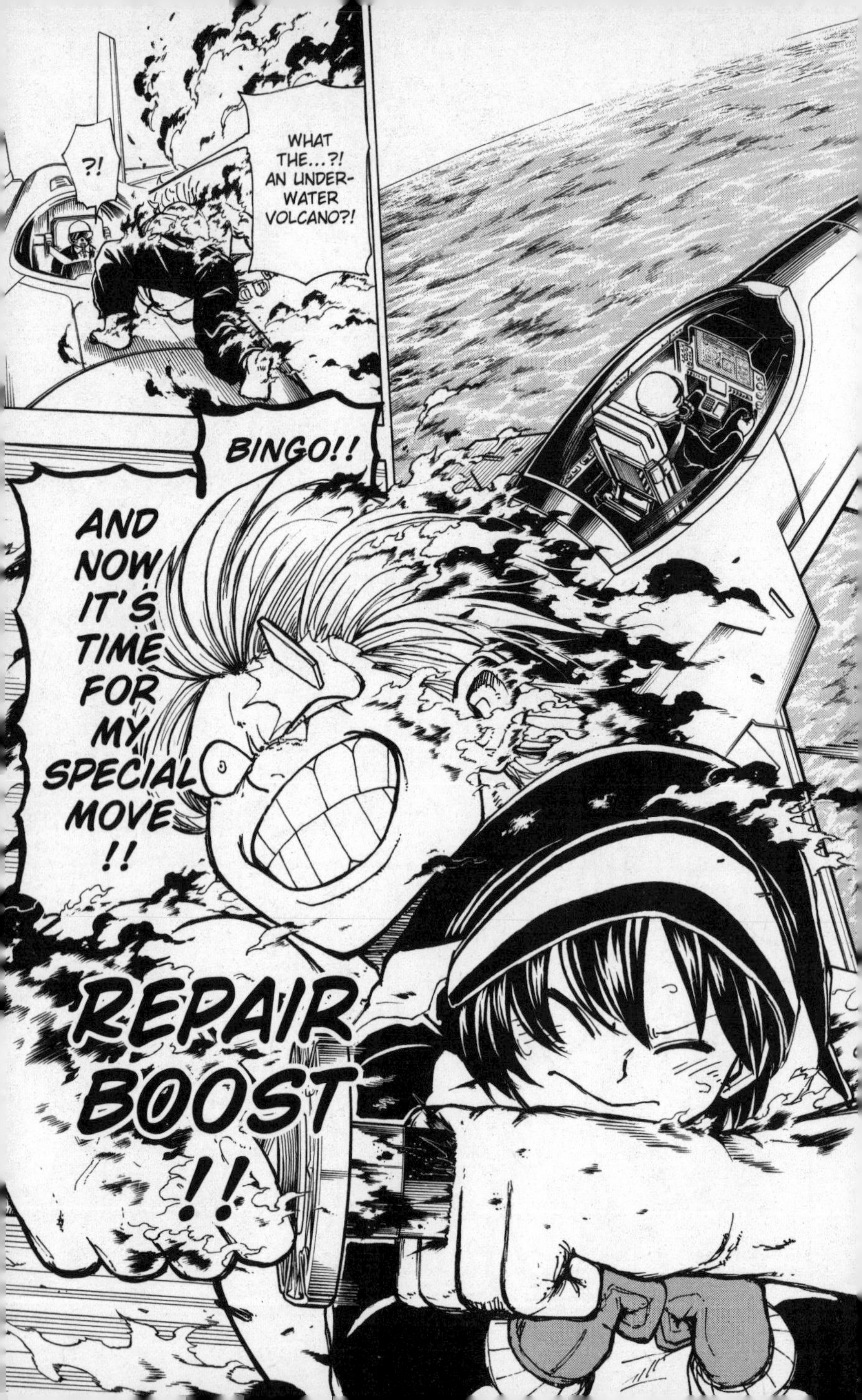
WHAT THE...?! AN UNDER-WATER VOLCANO?!
?!
BINGO!!
AND NOW IT'S TIME FOR MY SPECIAL MOVE!!
REPAIR BOOST!!

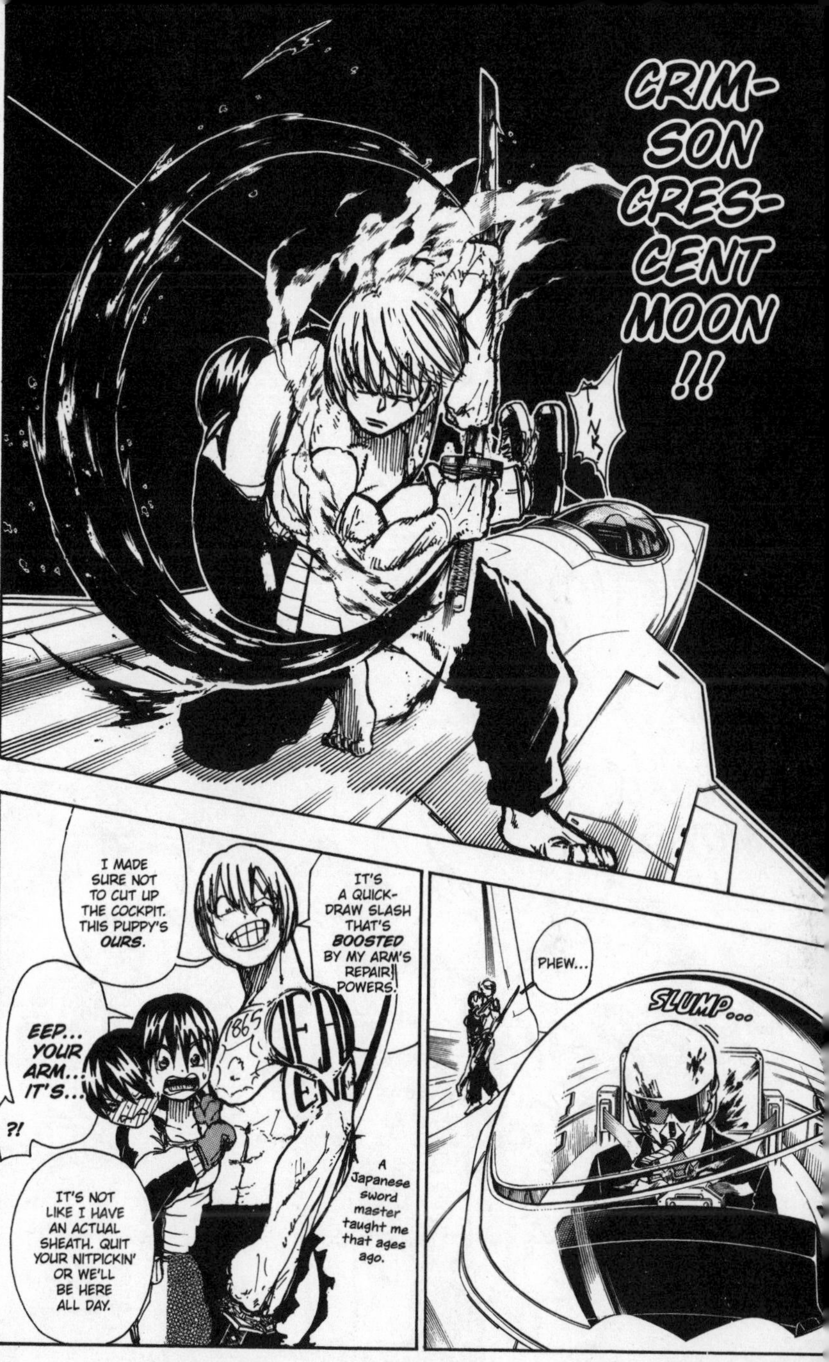
CRIM-SON CRES-CENT MOON!!
TINK
PHEW...
SLUMP...
IT'S A QUICK-DRAW SLASH THAT'S **BOOSTED** BY MY ARM'S REPAIR POWERS.
I MADE SURE NOT TO CUT UP THE COCKPIT. THIS PUPPY'S **OURS**.
A Japanese sword master taught me that ages ago.
EEP... YOUR ARM... IT'S...
?!
IT'S NOT LIKE I HAVE AN ACTUAL SHEATH. QUIT YOUR NITPICKIN' OR WE'LL BE HERE ALL DAY.

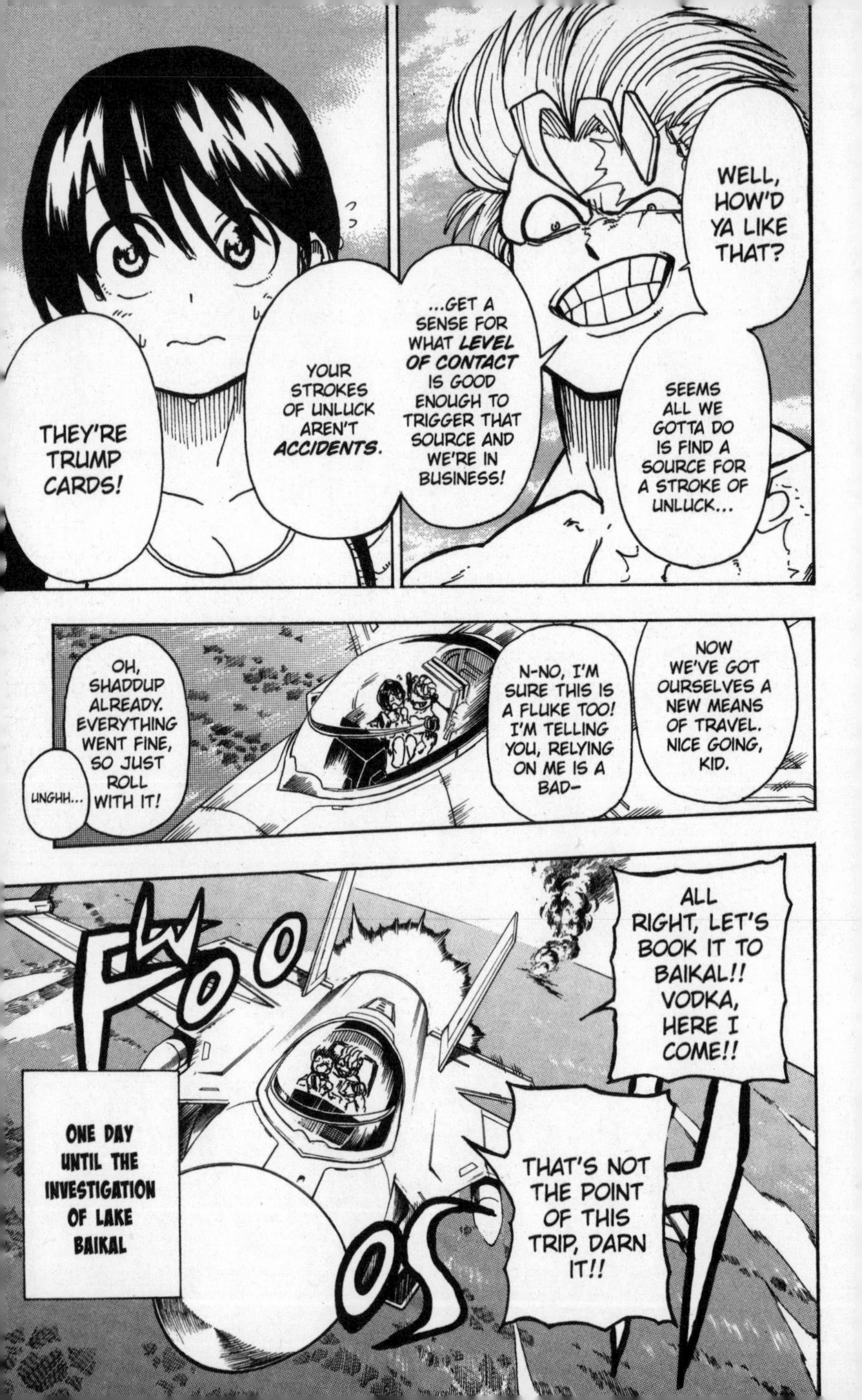
WELL, HOW'D YA LIKE THAT?
SEEMS ALL WE GOTTA DO IS FIND A SOURCE FOR A STROKE OF UNLUCK...
...GET A SENSE FOR WHAT *LEVEL OF CONTACT* IS GOOD ENOUGH TO TRIGGER THAT SOURCE AND WE'RE IN BUSINESS!
YOUR STROKES OF UNLUCK AREN'T *ACCIDENTS*.
THEY'RE TRUMP CARDS!
NOW WE'VE GOT OURSELVES A NEW MEANS OF TRAVEL. NICE GOING, KID.
N-NO, I'M SURE THIS IS A FLUKE TOO! I'M TELLING YOU, RELYING ON ME IS A BAD-
OH, SHADDUP ALREADY. EVERYTHING WENT FINE, SO JUST ROLL WITH IT!
UNGHH...
ALL RIGHT, LET'S BOOK IT TO BAIKAL!! VODKA, HERE I COME!!
THAT'S NOT THE POINT OF THIS TRIP, DARN IT!!
ONE DAY UNTIL THE INVESTIGATION OF LAKE BAIKAL

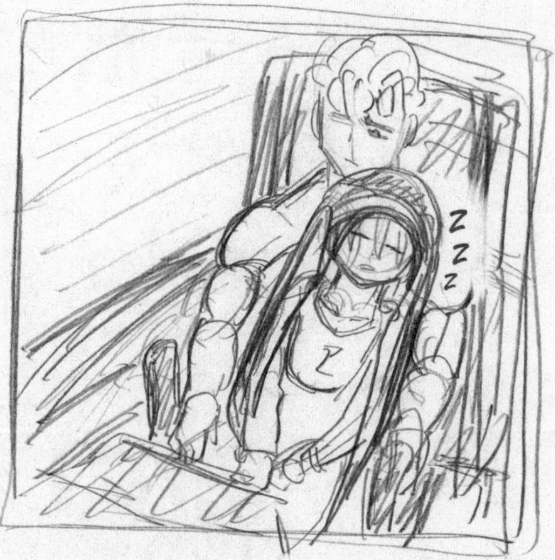
Z
Z
Z

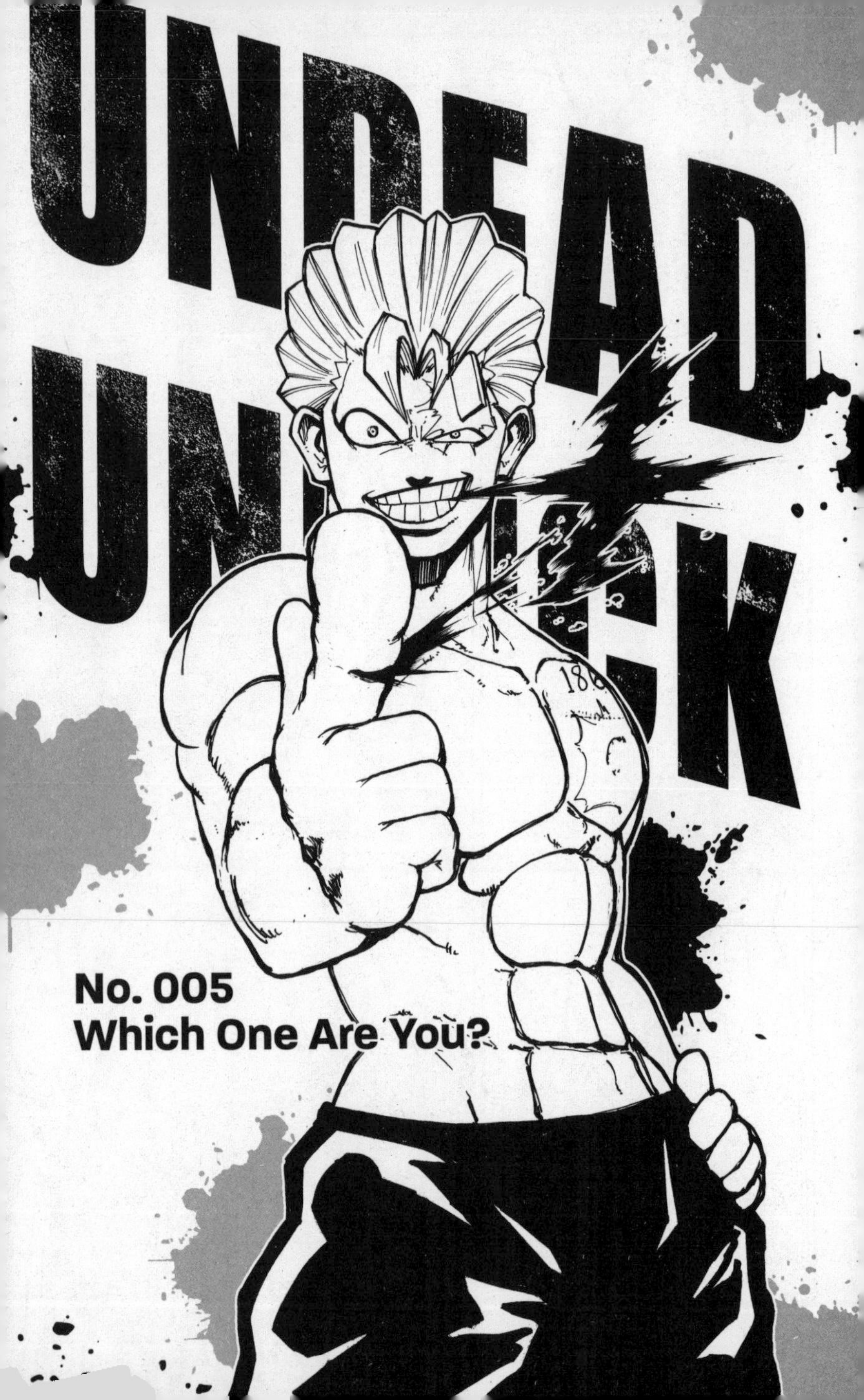
UNDEAD
No. 005
Which One Are You?

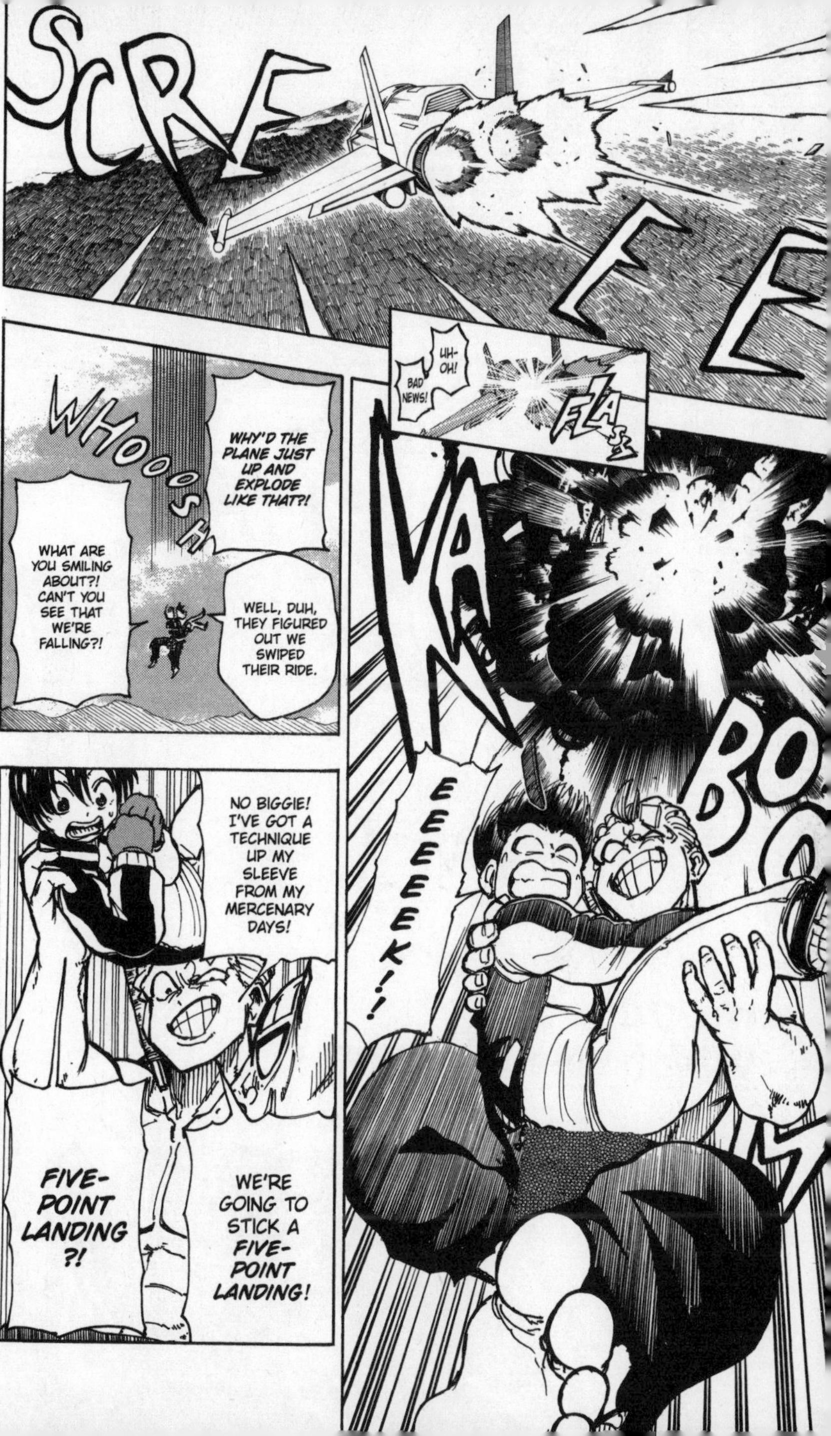
SCREE
UH-OH!
BAD NEWS!
FLAS
VA
BOO
EEEEEEK!!
WHOOOSH
WHY'D THE PLANE JUST UP AND EXPLODE LIKE THAT?!
WELL, DUH, THEY FIGURED OUT WE SWIPED THEIR RIDE.
WHAT ARE YOU SMILING ABOUT?! CAN'T YOU SEE THAT WE'RE FALLING?!
NO BIGGIE! I'VE GOT A TECHNIQUE UP MY SLEEVE FROM MY MERCENARY DAYS!
WE'RE GOING TO STICK A FIVE-POINT LANDING!
FIVE-POINT LANDING?!

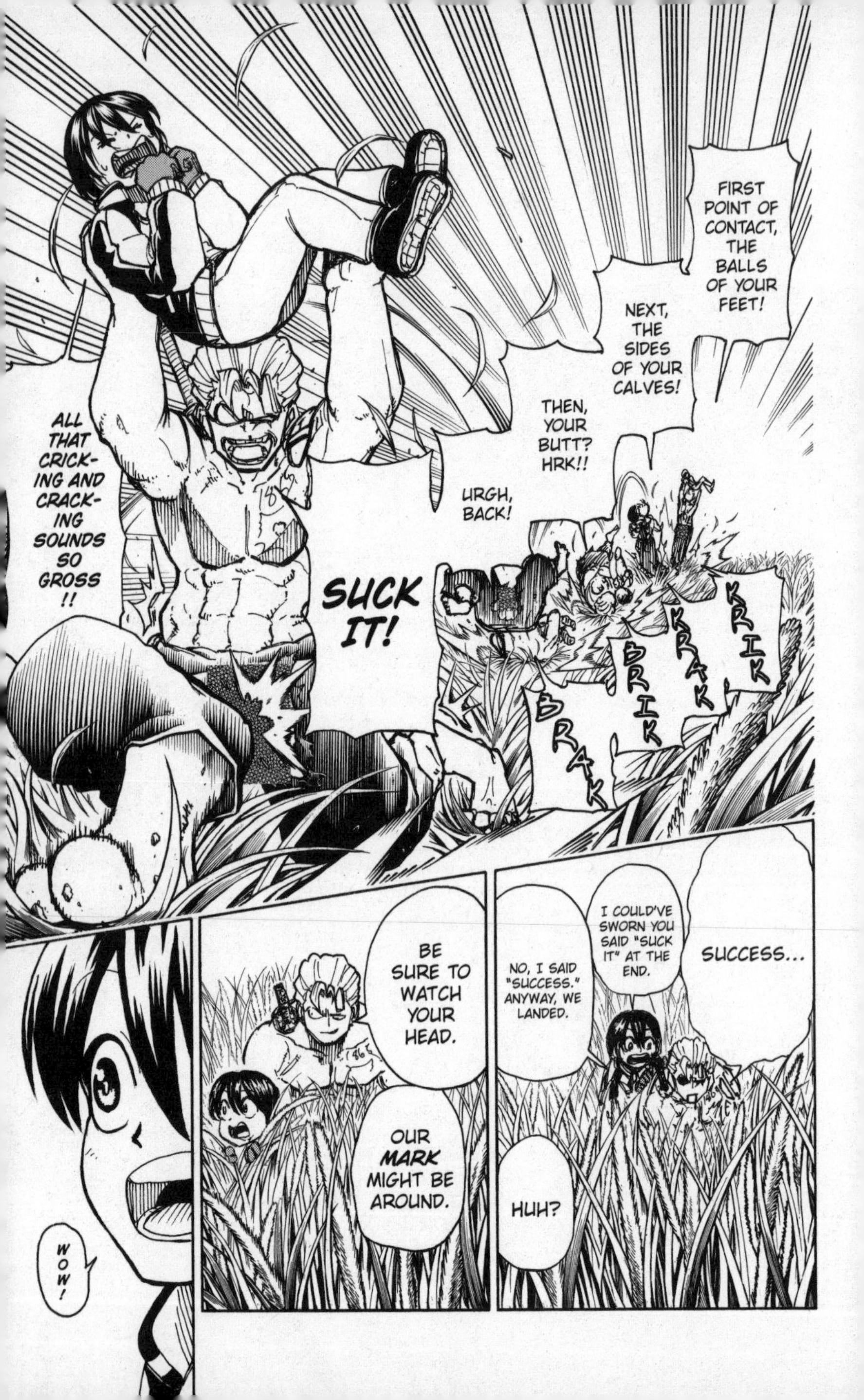
FIRST POINT OF CONTACT, THE BALLS OF YOUR FEET!
NEXT, THE SIDES OF YOUR CALVES!
THEN, YOUR BUTT? HRK!!
URGH, BACK!
KRIK
KRAK
BRIK
BRAK
SUCK IT!
ALL THAT CRICKING AND CRACKING SOUNDS SO GROSS!!
SUCCESS...
I COULD'VE SWORN YOU SAID "SUCK IT" AT THE END.
NO, I SAID "SUCCESS." ANYWAY, WE LANDED.
HUH?
BE SURE TO WATCH YOUR HEAD.
OUR *MARK* MIGHT BE AROUND.
WOW!

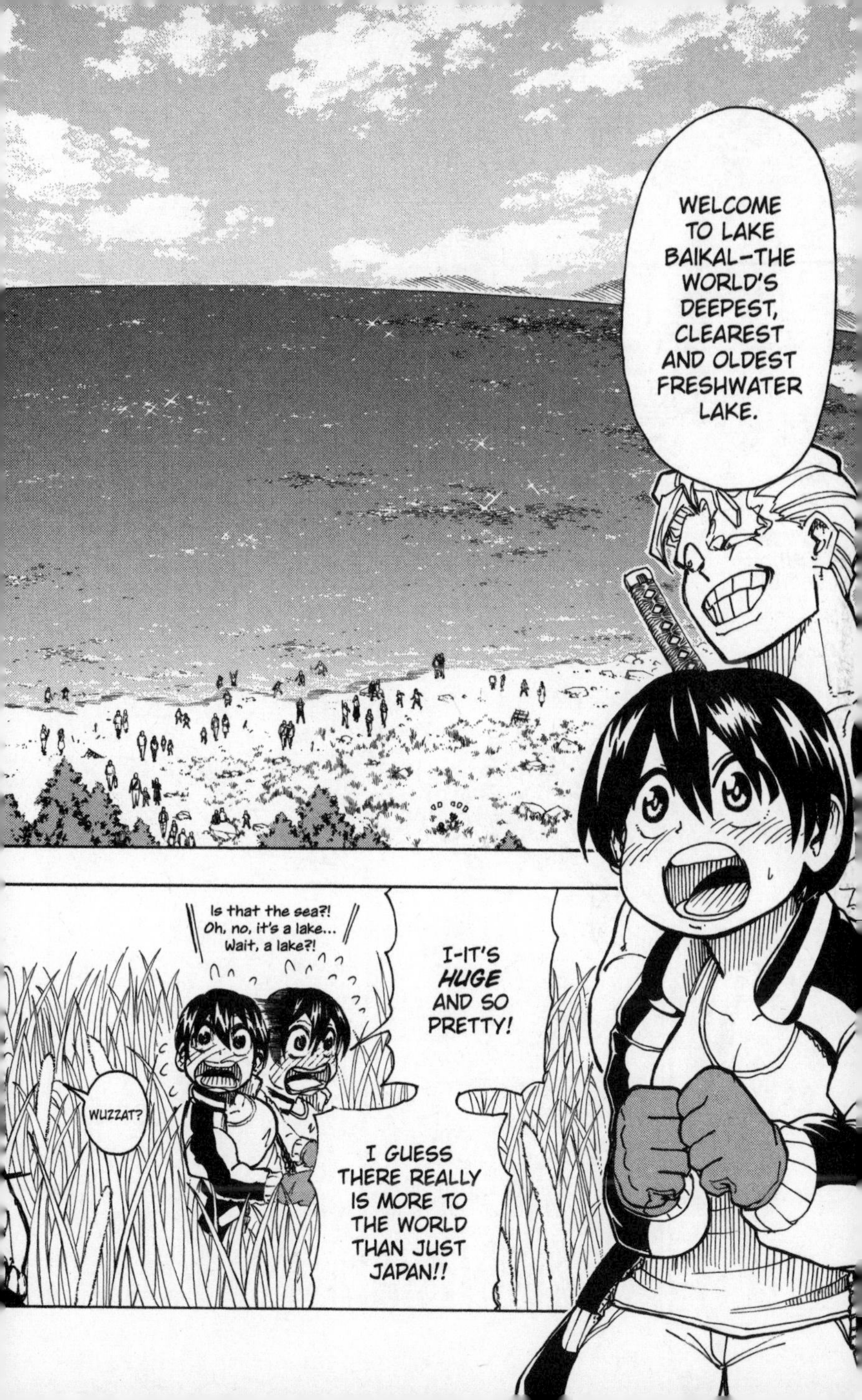
WELCOME TO LAKE BAIKAL—THE WORLD'S DEEPEST, CLEAREST AND OLDEST FRESHWATER LAKE.
I-IT'S *HUGE* AND SO PRETTY!
I GUESS THERE REALLY IS MORE TO THE WORLD THAN JUST JAPAN!!
Is that the sea?! Oh, no, it's a lake... Wait, a lake?!
WUZZAT?

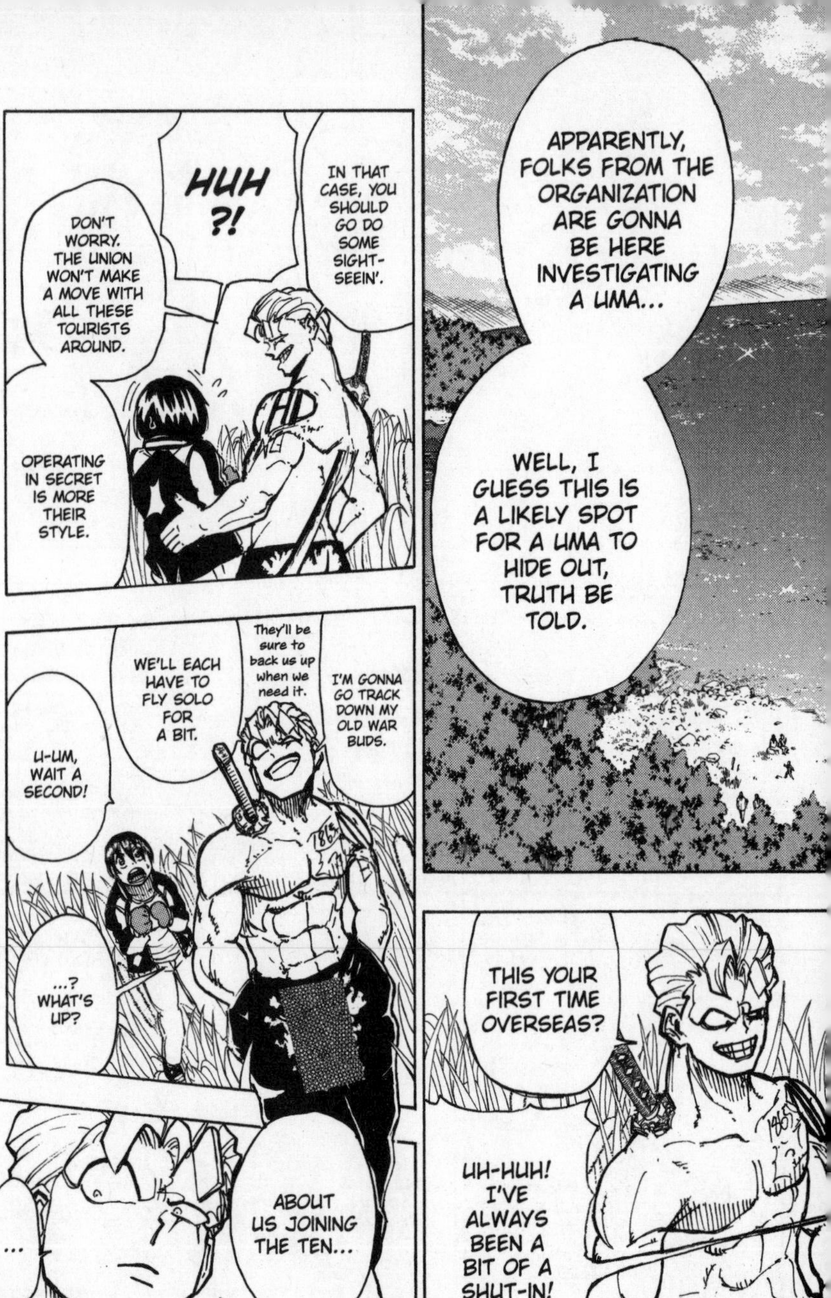
APPARENTLY, FOLKS FROM THE ORGANIZATION ARE GONNA BE HERE INVESTIGATING A UMA...
WELL, I GUESS THIS IS A LIKELY SPOT FOR A UMA TO HIDE OUT, TRUTH BE TOLD.
THIS YOUR FIRST TIME OVERSEAS?
UH-HUH! I'VE ALWAYS BEEN A BIT OF A SHUT-IN!
IN THAT CASE, YOU SHOULD GO DO SOME SIGHT-SEEIN'.
HUH ?!
DON'T WORRY. THE UNION WON'T MAKE A MOVE WITH ALL THESE TOURISTS AROUND.
OPERATING IN SECRET IS MORE THEIR STYLE.
I'M GONNA GO TRACK DOWN MY OLD WAR BUDS.
They'll be sure to back us up when we need it.
WE'LL EACH HAVE TO FLY SOLO FOR A BIT.
U-UM, WAIT A SECOND!
...? WHAT'S UP?
ABOUT US JOINING THE TEN...
...

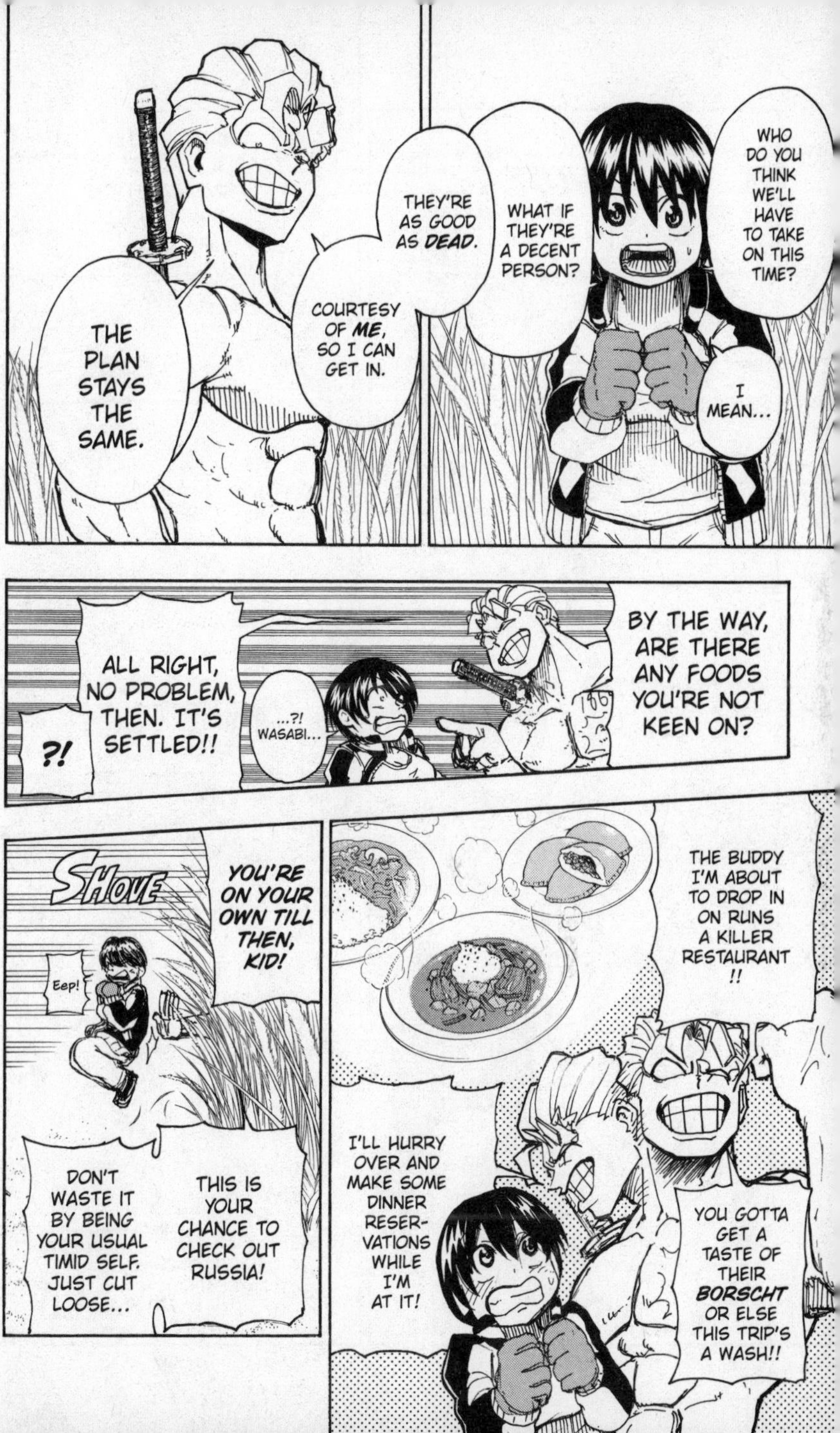
WHO DO YOU THINK WE'LL HAVE TO TAKE ON THIS TIME?
I MEAN...
WHAT IF THEY'RE A DECENT PERSON?
THEY'RE AS GOOD AS *DEAD*.
COURTESY OF *ME*, SO I CAN GET IN.
THE PLAN STAYS THE SAME.
BY THE WAY, ARE THERE ANY FOODS YOU'RE NOT KEEN ON?
...?! WASABI...
ALL RIGHT, NO PROBLEM, THEN. IT'S SETTLED!!
?!
THE BUDDY I'M ABOUT TO DROP IN ON RUNS A KILLER RESTAURANT!!
YOU GOTTA GET A TASTE OF THEIR *BORSCHT* OR ELSE THIS TRIP'S A WASH!!
I'LL HURRY OVER AND MAKE SOME DINNER RESER-VATIONS WHILE I'M AT IT!
YOU'RE ON YOUR OWN TILL THEN, KID!
SHOVE
Eep!
THIS IS YOUR CHANCE TO CHECK OUT RUSSIA!
DON'T WASTE IT BY BEING YOUR USUAL TIMID SELF. JUST CUT LOOSE...

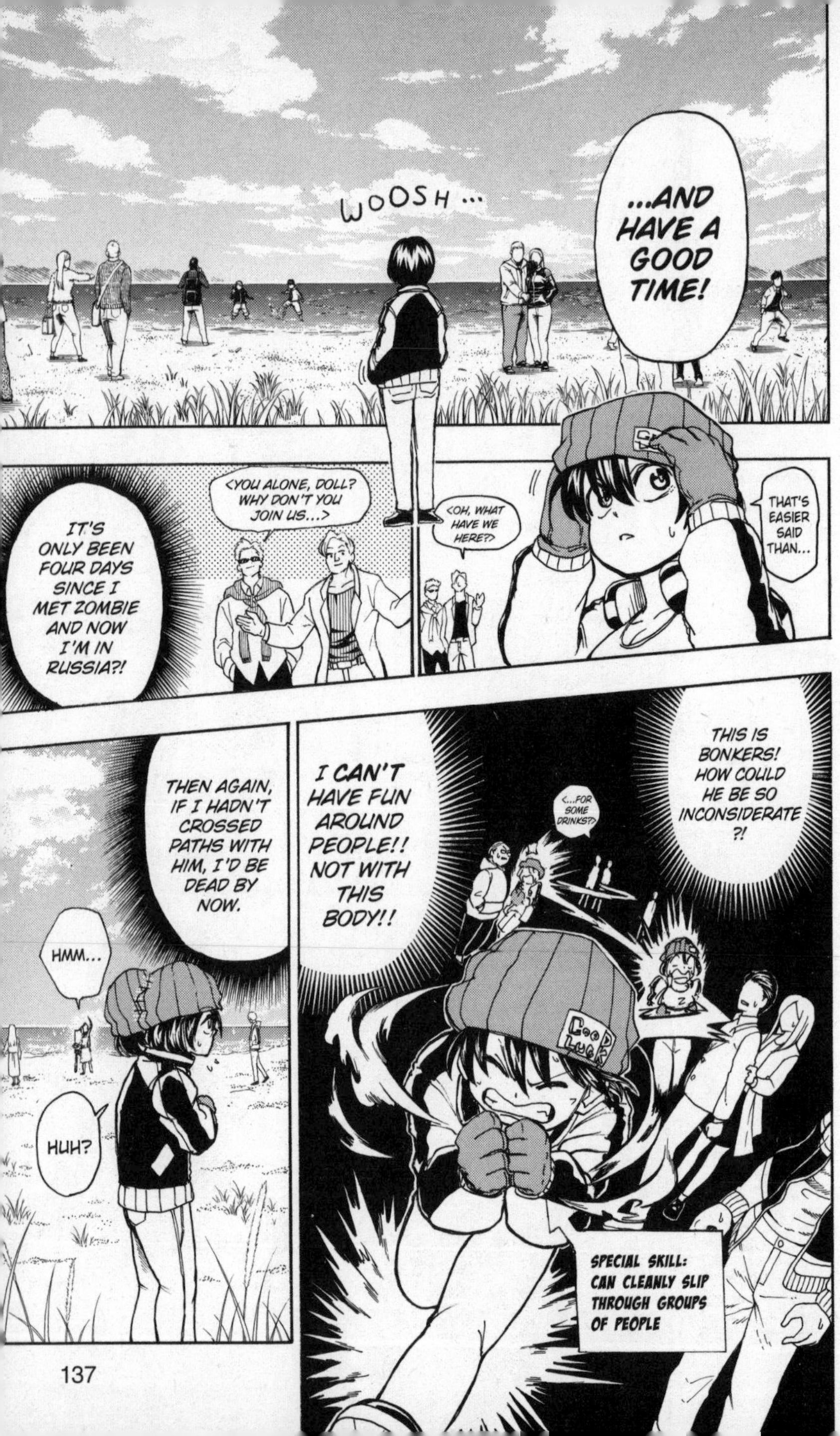
...AND HAVE A GOOD TIME!
WOOSH...
THAT'S EASIER SAID THAN...
<OH, WHAT HAVE WE HERE?>
<YOU ALONE, DOLL? WHY DON'T YOU JOIN US...>
IT'S ONLY BEEN FOUR DAYS SINCE I MET ZOMBIE AND NOW I'M IN RUSSIA?!
THIS IS BONKERS! HOW COULD HE BE SO INCONSIDERATE?!
I CAN'T HAVE FUN AROUND PEOPLE!! NOT WITH THIS BODY!!
<...FOR SOME DRINKS?>
GOOD LUCK
SPECIAL SKILL: CAN CLEANLY SLIP THROUGH GROUPS OF PEOPLE
THEN AGAIN, IF I HADN'T CROSSED PATHS WITH HIM, I'D BE DEAD BY NOW.
HMM...
HUH?

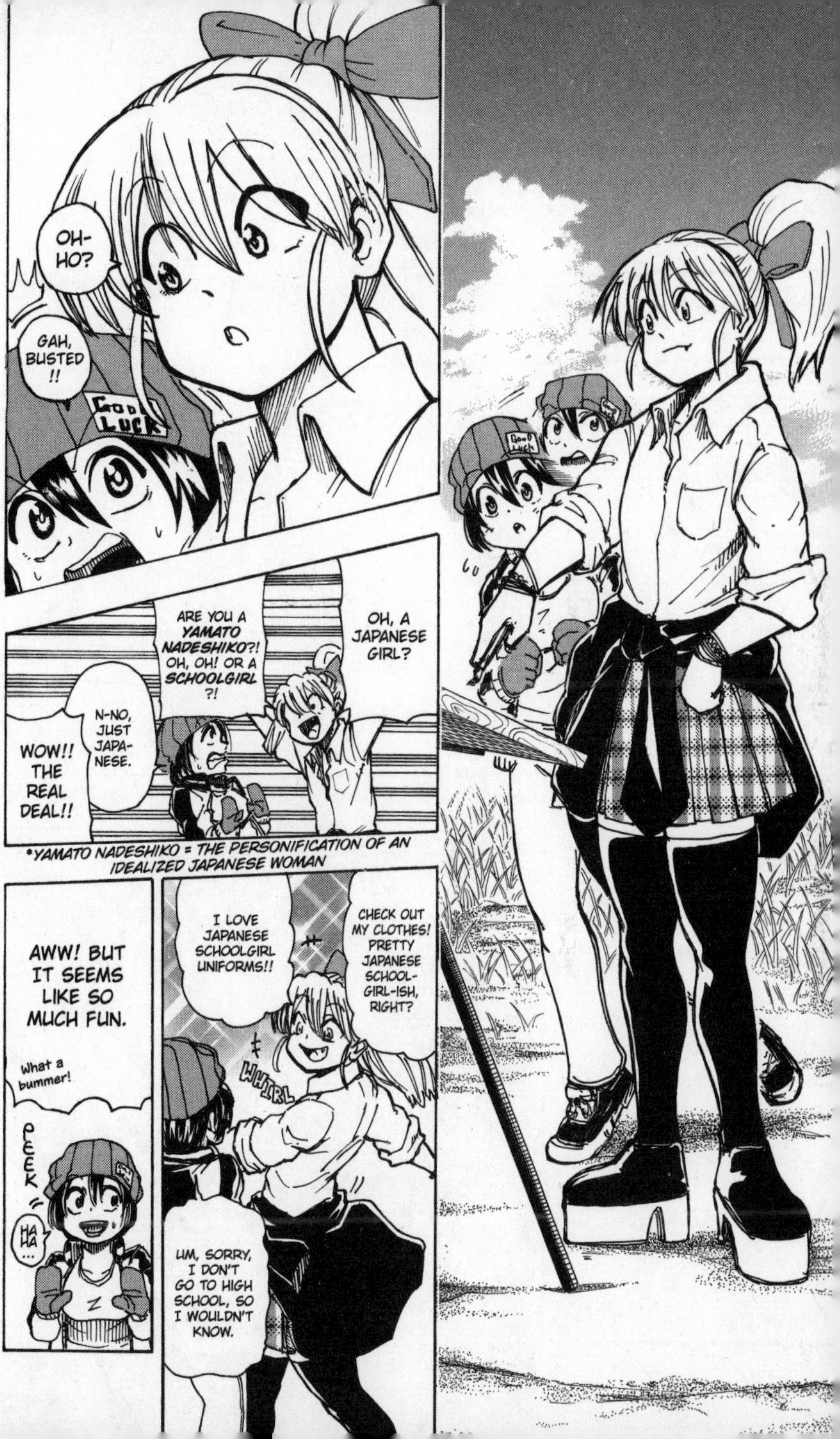
OH-HO?
GAH, BUSTED!!
GOOD LUCK
OH, A JAPANESE GIRL?
ARE YOU A *YAMATO NADESHIKO*?! OH, OH! OR A *SCHOOLGIRL*?!
N-NO, JUST JAPANESE.
WOW!! THE REAL DEAL!!
*YAMATO NADESHIKO = THE PERSONIFICATION OF AN IDEALIZED JAPANESE WOMAN
CHECK OUT MY CLOTHES! PRETTY JAPANESE SCHOOL-GIRL-ISH, RIGHT?
I LOVE JAPANESE SCHOOLGIRL UNIFORMS!!
WHIRL
UM, SORRY, I DON'T GO TO HIGH SCHOOL, SO I WOULDN'T KNOW.
AWW! BUT IT SEEMS LIKE SO MUCH FUN.
What a bummer!
PEEK
HA HA ...

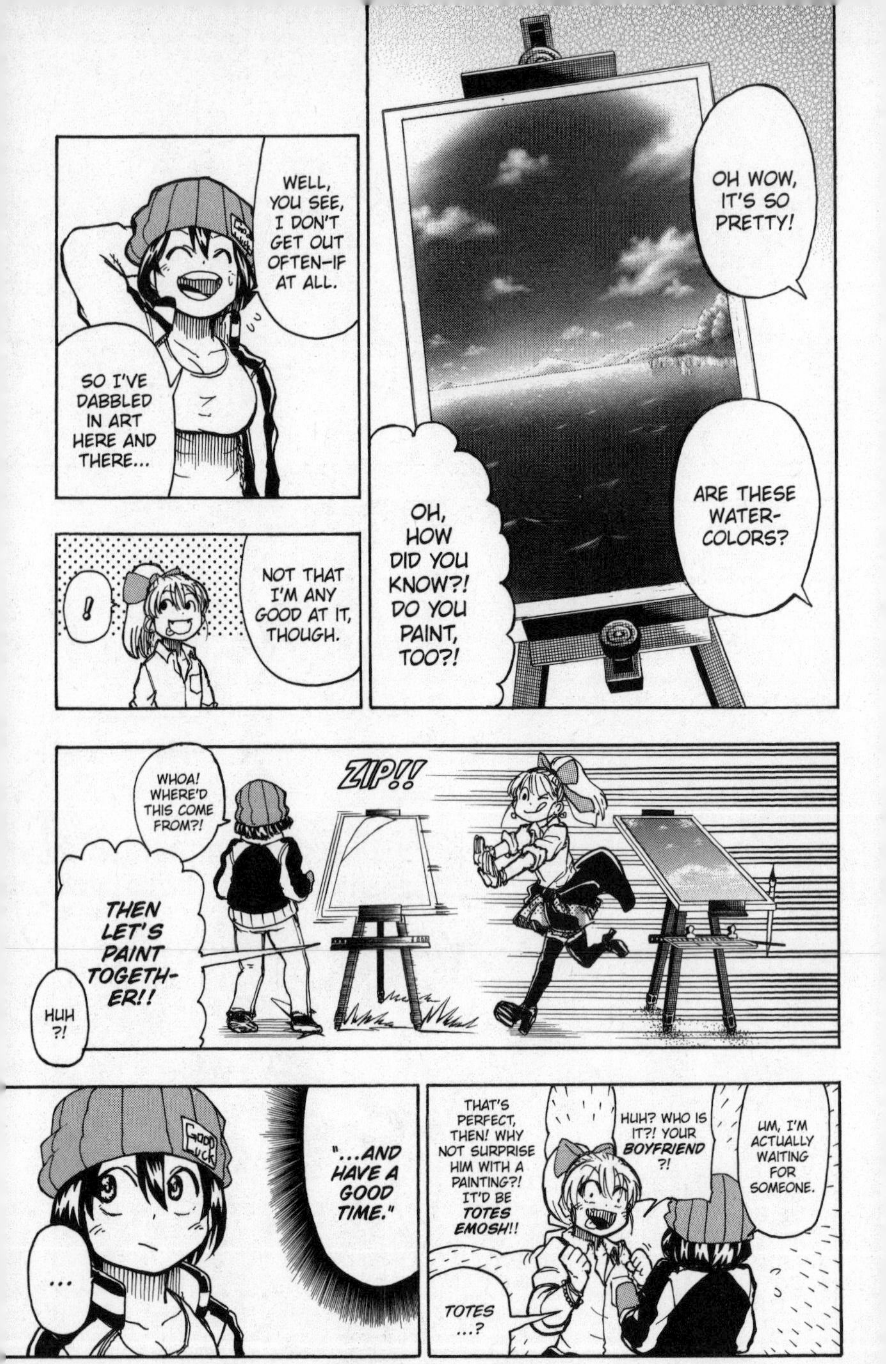

OH WOW, IT'S SO PRETTY!
ARE THESE WATER-COLORS?
OH, HOW DID YOU KNOW?! DO YOU PAINT, TOO?!
WELL, YOU SEE, I DON'T GET OUT OFTEN—IF AT ALL.
SO I'VE DABBLED IN ART HERE AND THERE...
NOT THAT I'M ANY GOOD AT IT, THOUGH.
!
ZIP!!
WHOA! WHERE'D THIS COME FROM?!
THEN LET'S PAINT TOGETHER!!
HUH?!
UM, I'M ACTUALLY WAITING FOR SOMEONE.
HUH? WHO IS IT?! YOUR BOYFRIEND?!
THAT'S PERFECT, THEN! WHY NOT SURPRISE HIM WITH A PAINTING?! IT'D BE TOTES EMOSH!!
TOTES ...?
"...AND HAVE A GOOD TIME."
...

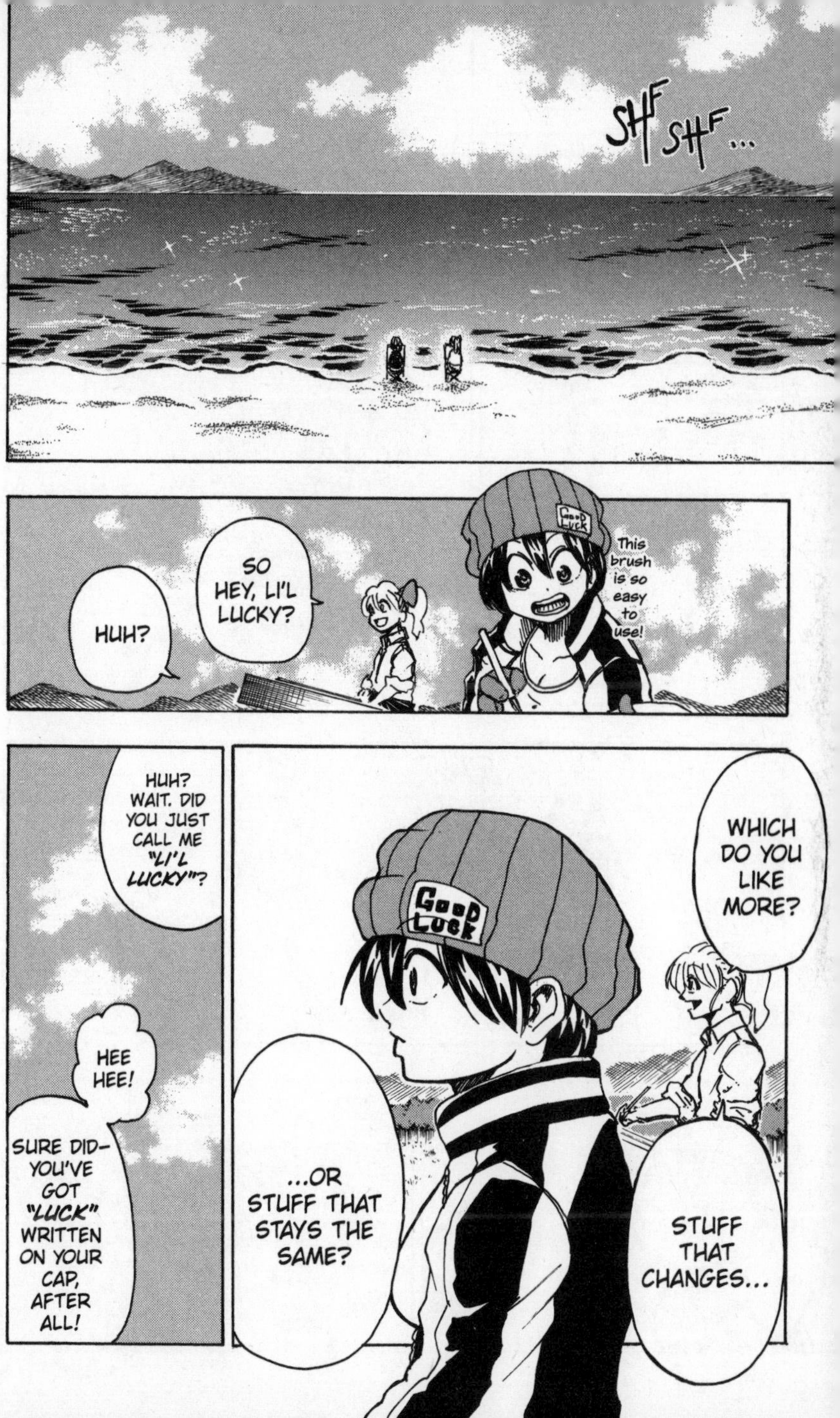
SHF SHF...
This brush is so easy to use!
GOOD LUCK
SO HEY, LI'L LUCKY?
HUH?
WHICH DO YOU LIKE MORE?
STUFF THAT CHANGES...
...OR STUFF THAT STAYS THE SAME?
HUH? WAIT. DID YOU JUST CALL ME *"LI'L LUCKY"*?
HEE HEE!
SURE DID— YOU'VE GOT *"LUCK"* WRITTEN ON YOUR CAP, AFTER ALL!

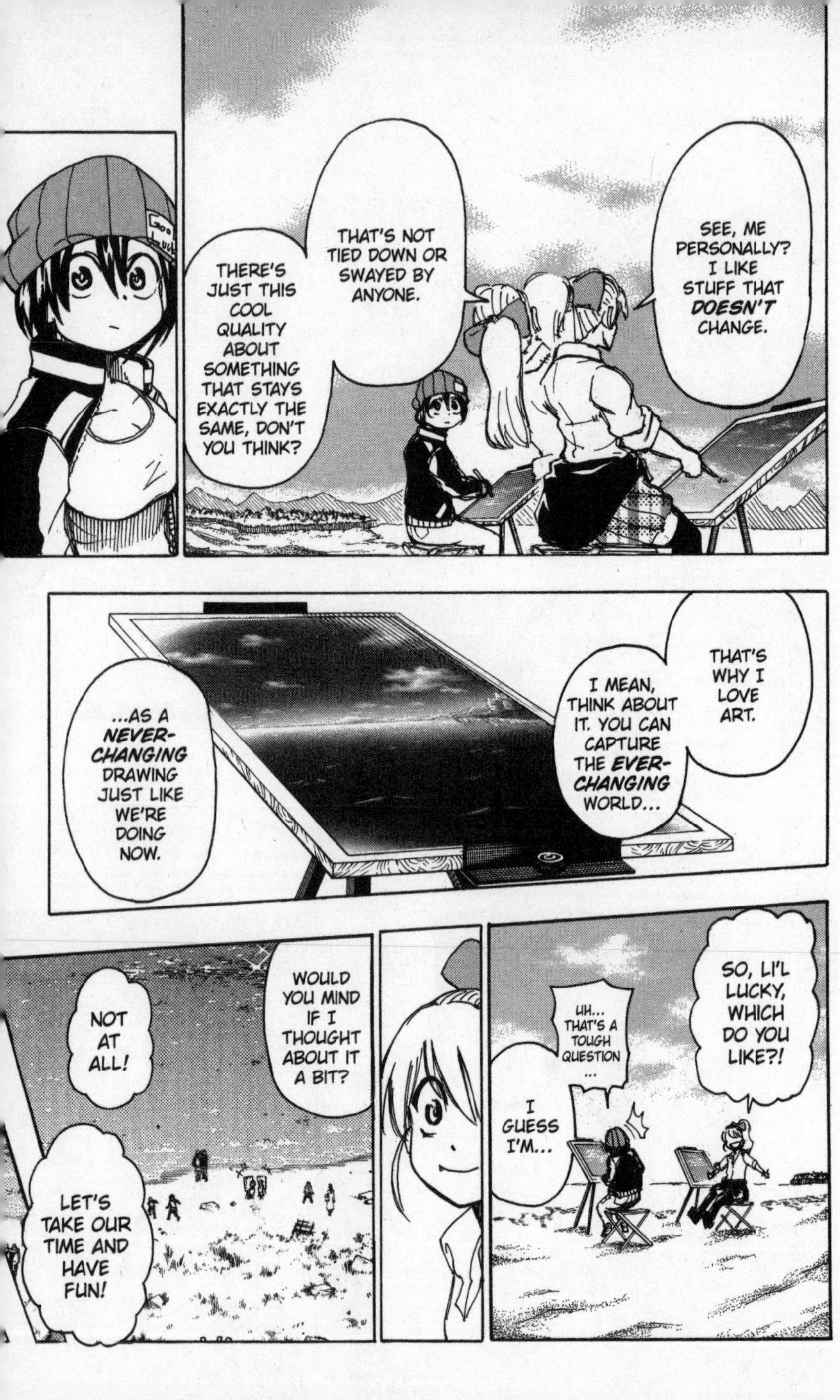
SEE, ME PERSONALLY? I LIKE STUFF THAT **DOESN'T** CHANGE.
THAT'S NOT TIED DOWN OR SWAYED BY ANYONE.
THERE'S JUST THIS COOL QUALITY ABOUT SOMETHING THAT STAYS EXACTLY THE SAME, DON'T YOU THINK?
THAT'S WHY I LOVE ART.
I MEAN, THINK ABOUT IT. YOU CAN CAPTURE THE ***EVER-CHANGING*** WORLD...
...AS A ***NEVER-CHANGING*** DRAWING JUST LIKE WE'RE DOING NOW.
SO, LI'L LUCKY, WHICH DO YOU LIKE?!
UH... THAT'S A TOUGH QUESTION...
I GUESS I'M...
WOULD YOU MIND IF I THOUGHT ABOUT IT A BIT?
NOT AT ALL!
LET'S TAKE OUR TIME AND HAVE FUN!

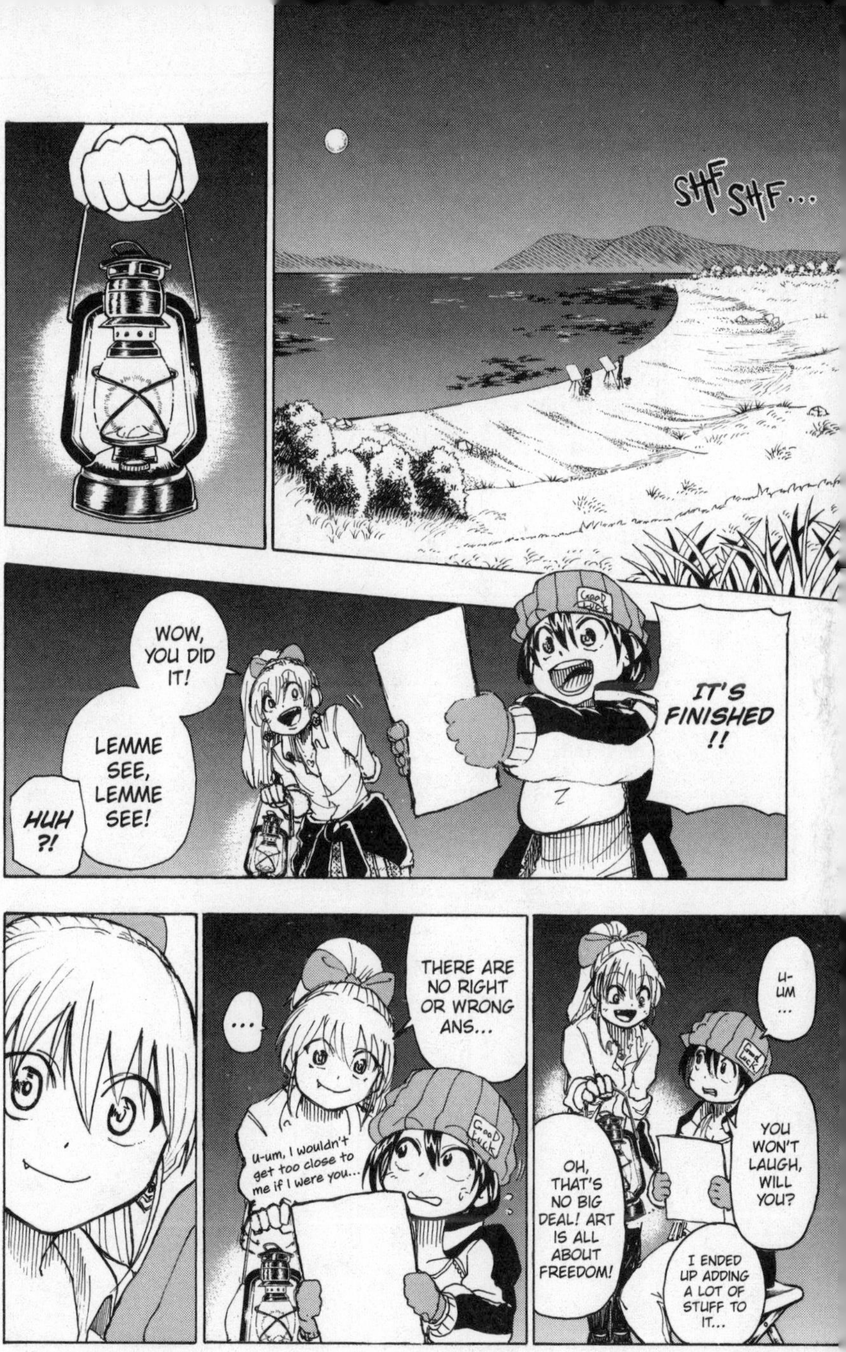
SHF SHF...
IT'S FINISHED!!
WOW, YOU DID IT!
LEMME SEE, LEMME SEE!
HUH?!
U-UM...
YOU WON'T LAUGH, WILL YOU?
I ENDED UP ADDING A LOT OF STUFF TO IT...
OH, THAT'S NO BIG DEAL! ART IS ALL ABOUT FREEDOM!
THERE ARE NO RIGHT OR WRONG ANS...
...
U-um, I wouldn't get too close to me if I were you...

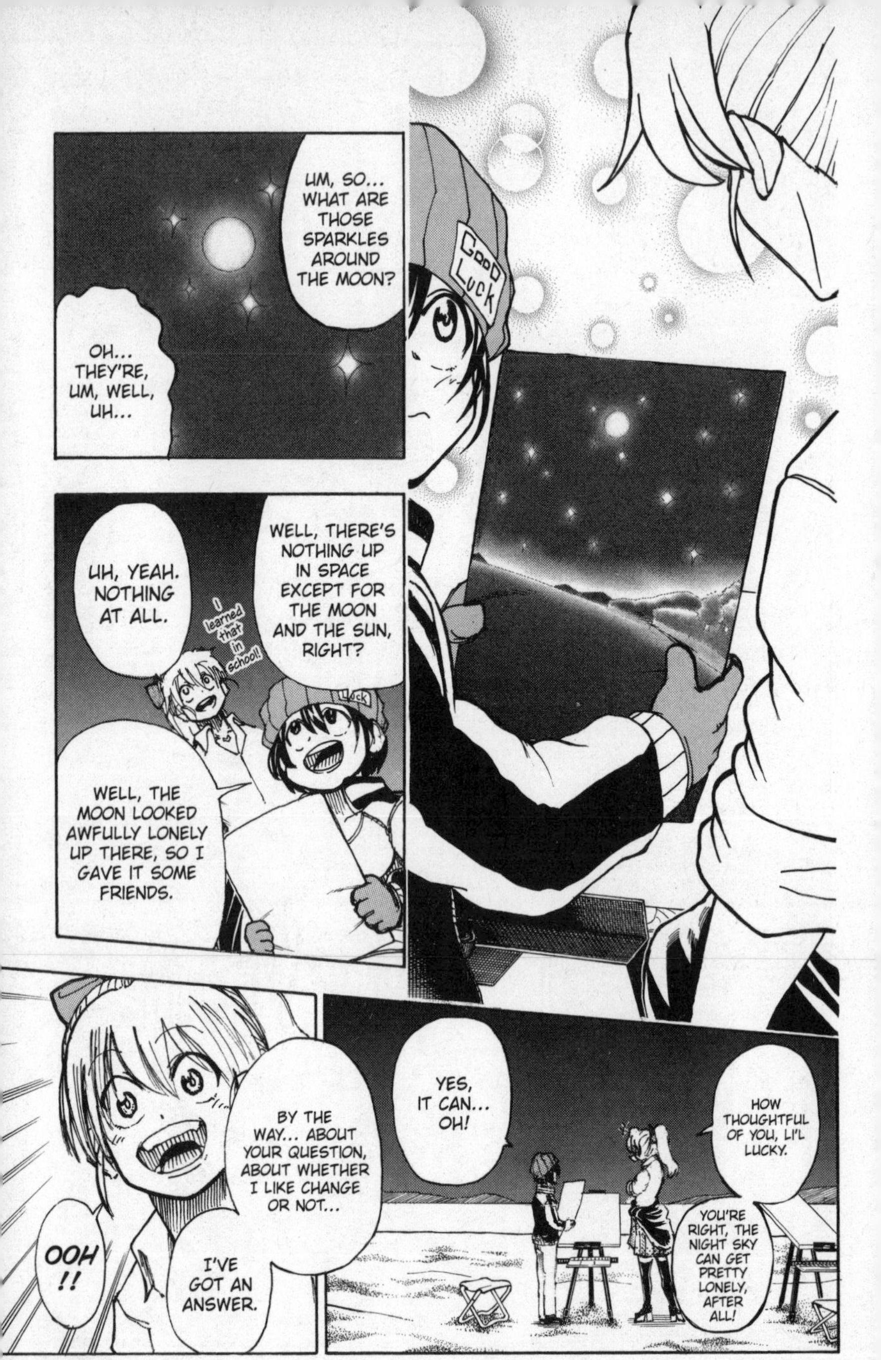
UM, SO... WHAT ARE THOSE SPARKLES AROUND THE MOON?
OH... THEY'RE, UM, WELL, UH...
WELL, THERE'S NOTHING UP IN SPACE EXCEPT FOR THE MOON AND THE SUN, RIGHT?
UH, YEAH. NOTHING AT ALL.
I learned that in school!
WELL, THE MOON LOOKED AWFULLY LONELY UP THERE, SO I GAVE IT SOME FRIENDS.
HOW THOUGHTFUL OF YOU, LI'L LUCKY.
YOU'RE RIGHT, THE NIGHT SKY CAN GET PRETTY LONELY, AFTER ALL!
YES, IT CAN... OH!
BY THE WAY... ABOUT YOUR QUESTION, ABOUT WHETHER I LIKE CHANGE OR NOT...
I'VE GOT AN ANSWER.
OOH!!

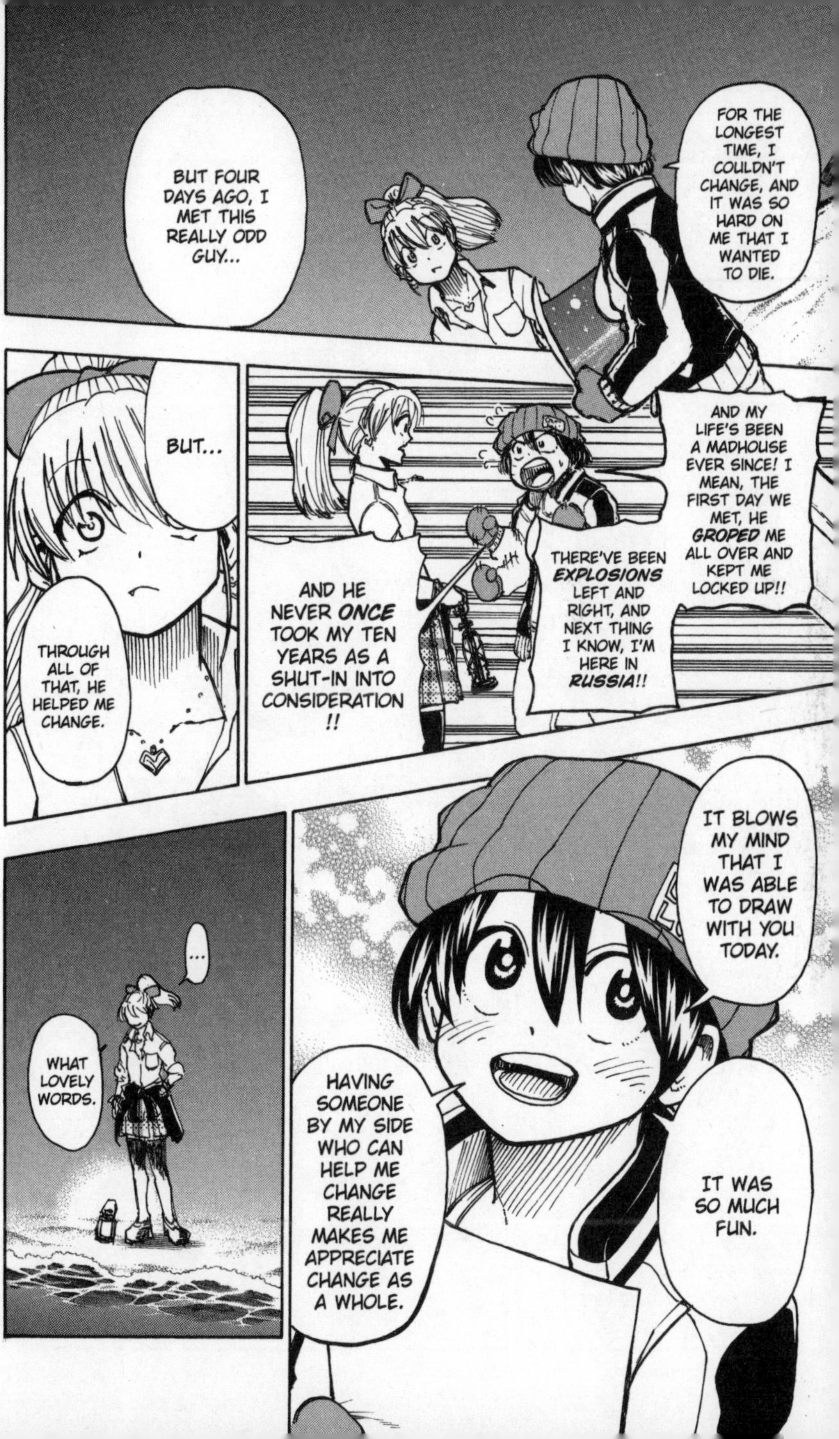
FOR THE LONGEST TIME, I COULDN'T CHANGE, AND IT WAS SO HARD ON ME THAT I WANTED TO DIE.
BUT FOUR DAYS AGO, I MET THIS REALLY ODD GUY...
AND MY LIFE'S BEEN A MADHOUSE EVER SINCE! I MEAN, THE FIRST DAY WE MET, HE **GROPED** ME ALL OVER AND KEPT ME LOCKED UP!!
THERE'VE BEEN **EXPLOSIONS** LEFT AND RIGHT, AND NEXT THING I KNOW, I'M HERE IN **RUSSIA**!!
AND HE NEVER **ONCE** TOOK MY TEN YEARS AS A SHUT-IN INTO CONSIDERATION !!
BUT...
THROUGH ALL OF THAT, HE HELPED ME CHANGE.
IT BLOWS MY MIND THAT I WAS ABLE TO DRAW WITH YOU TODAY.
IT WAS SO MUCH FUN.
HAVING SOMEONE BY MY SIDE WHO CAN HELP ME CHANGE REALLY MAKES ME APPRECIATE CHANGE AS A WHOLE.
...
WHAT LOVELY WORDS.

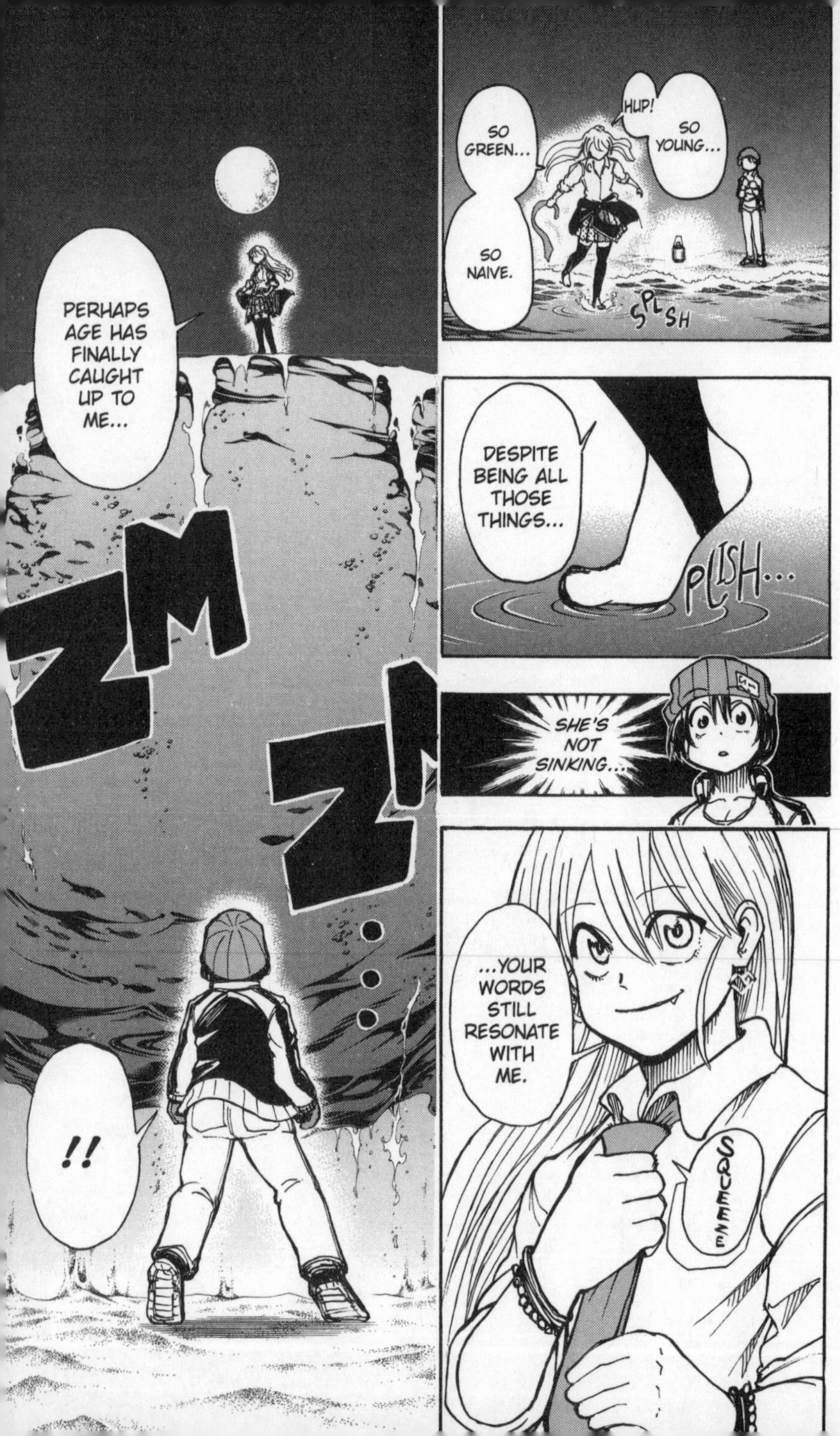
HUP!
SO YOUNG...
SO GREEN...
SO NAIVE.
SPLSH
DESPITE BEING ALL THOSE THINGS...
PLISH...
SHE'S NOT SINKING...
...YOUR WORDS STILL RESONATE WITH ME.
SQUEEZE
PERHAPS AGE HAS FINALLY CAUGHT UP TO ME...
ZM
ZM
!!

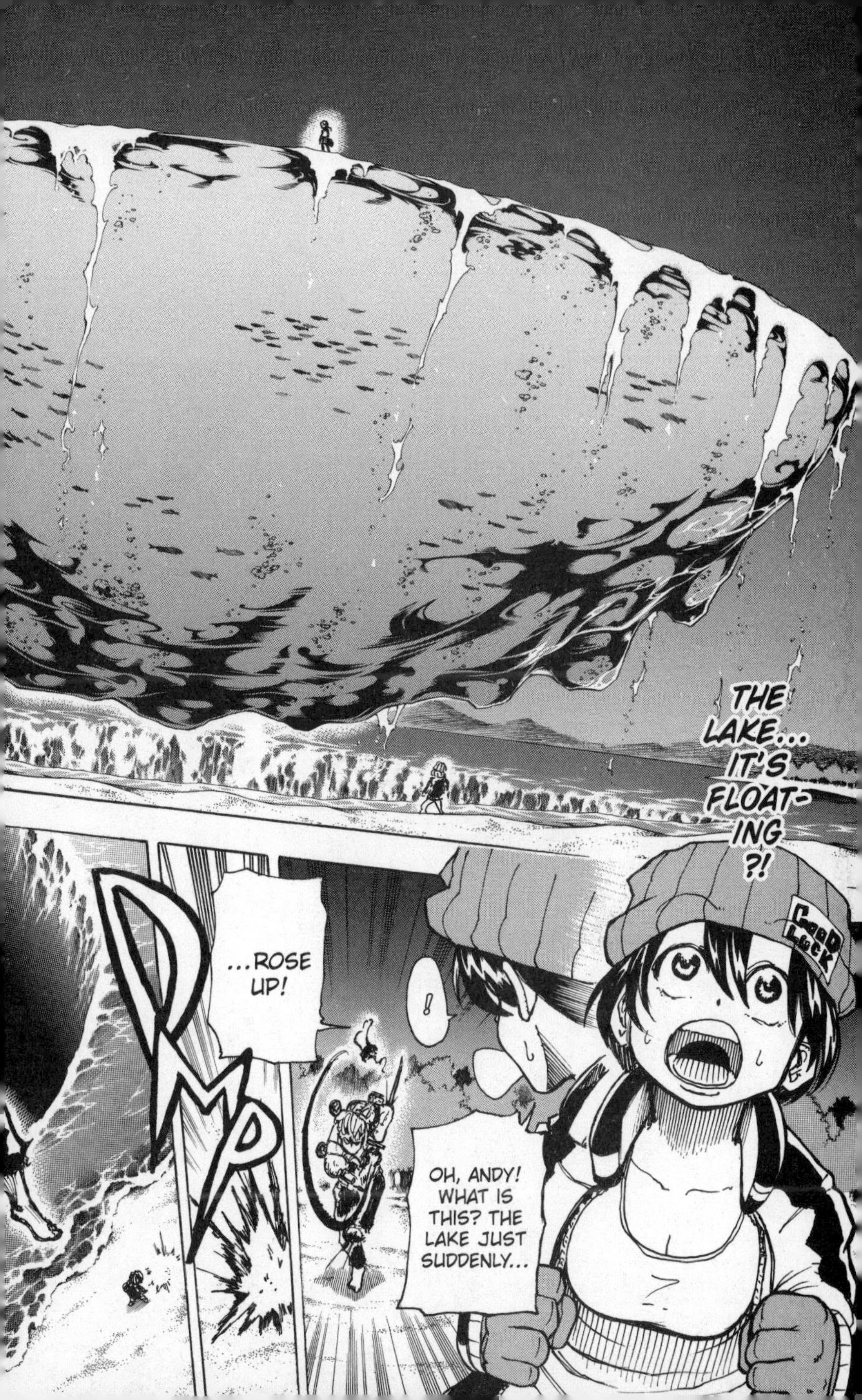
THE LAKE... IT'S FLOAT-ING ?!
OH, ANDY! WHAT IS THIS? THE LAKE JUST SUDDENLY...
!
...ROSE UP!
DMP

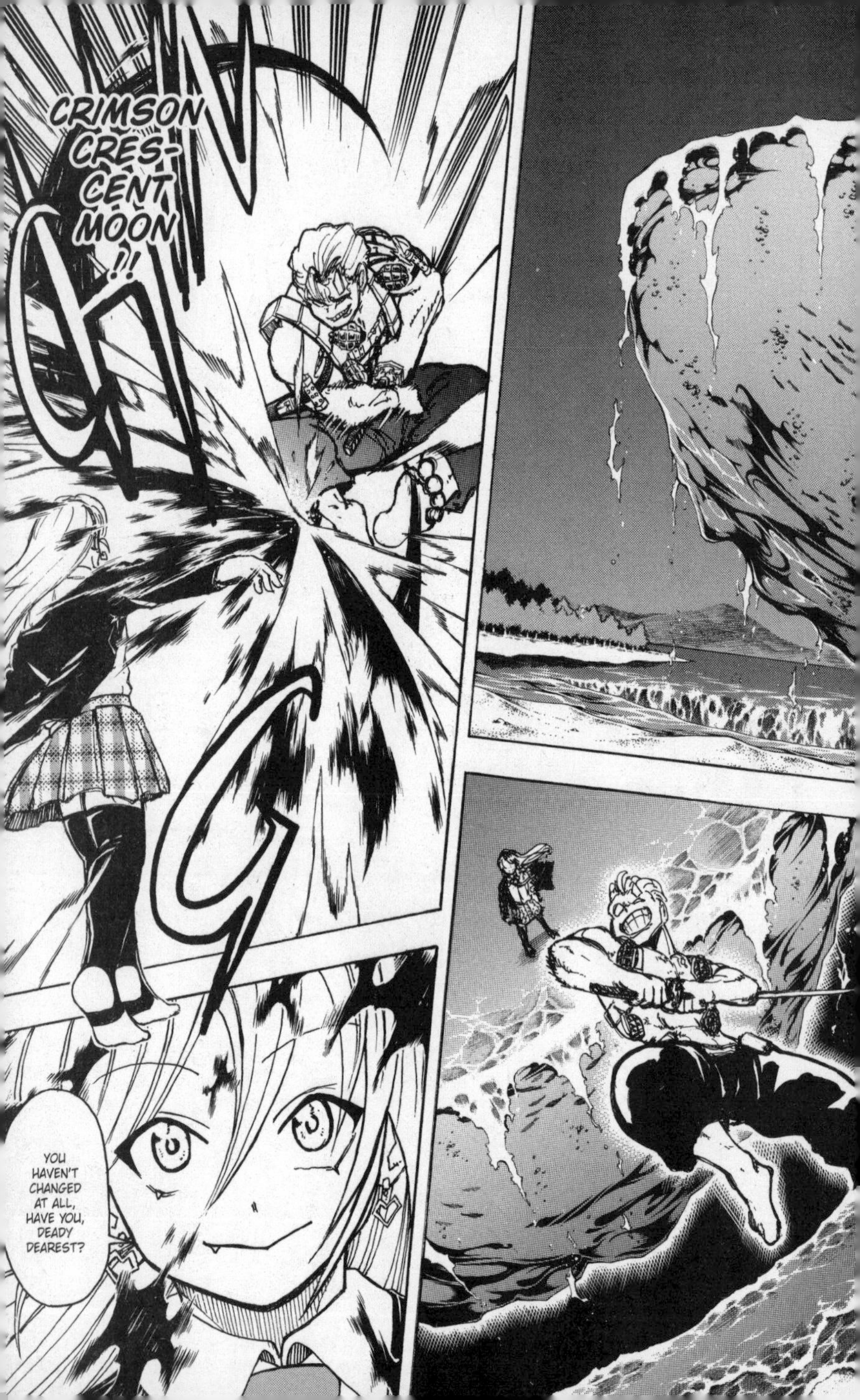
CRIMSON CRES-CENT MOON!!
YOU HAVEN'T CHANGED AT ALL, HAVE YOU, DEADY DEAREST?

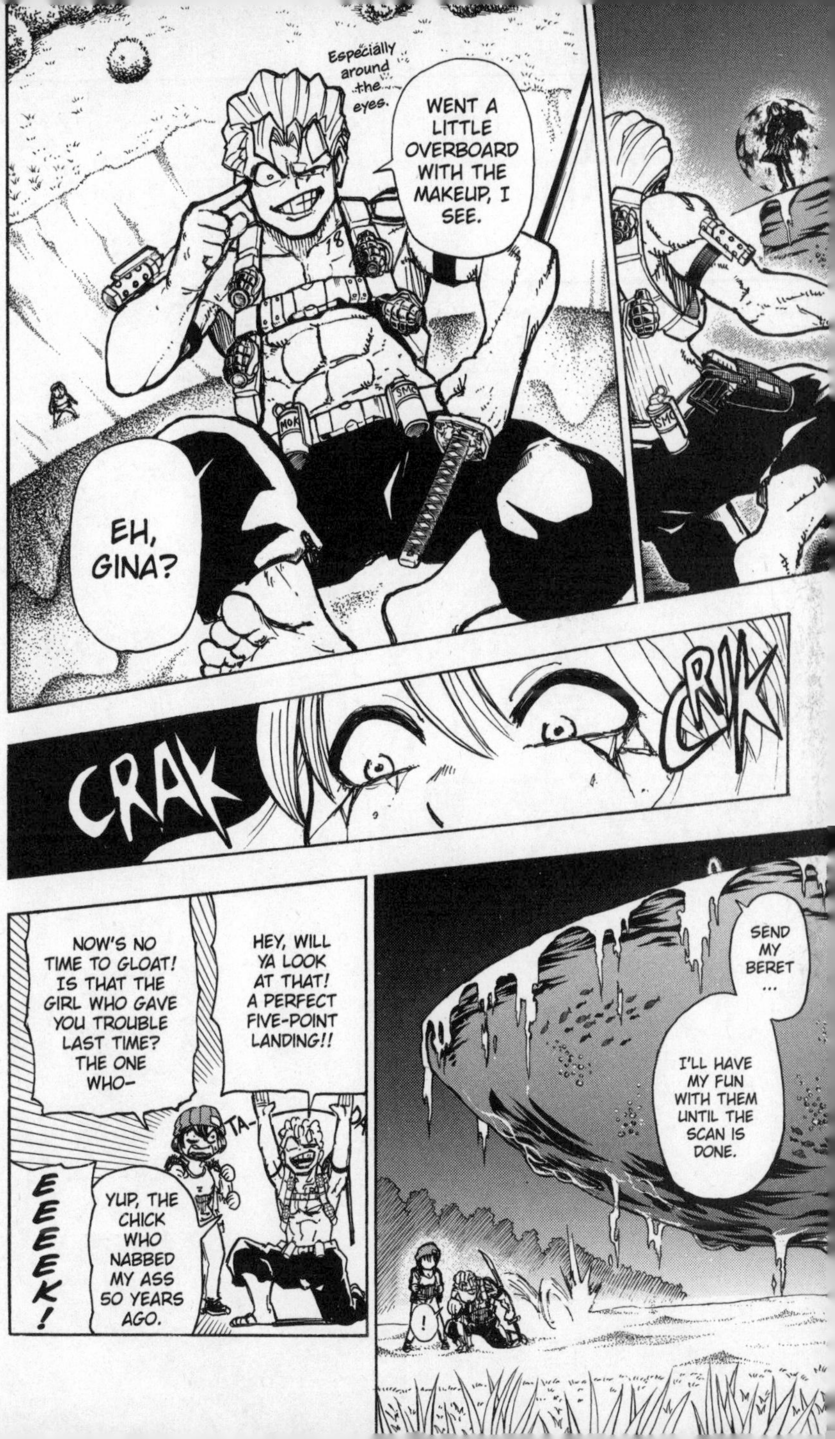
WENT A LITTLE OVERBOARD WITH THE MAKEUP, I SEE.
Especially around the eyes.
EH, GINA?
CRK
CRAK
SEND MY BERET ...
I'LL HAVE MY FUN WITH THEM UNTIL THE SCAN IS DONE.
!
HEY, WILL YA LOOK AT THAT! A PERFECT FIVE-POINT LANDING!!
TA-DA
NOW'S NO TIME TO GLOAT! IS THAT THE GIRL WHO GAVE YOU TROUBLE LAST TIME? THE ONE WHO–
EEEEEK!
YUP, THE CHICK WHO NABBED MY ASS 50 YEARS AGO.

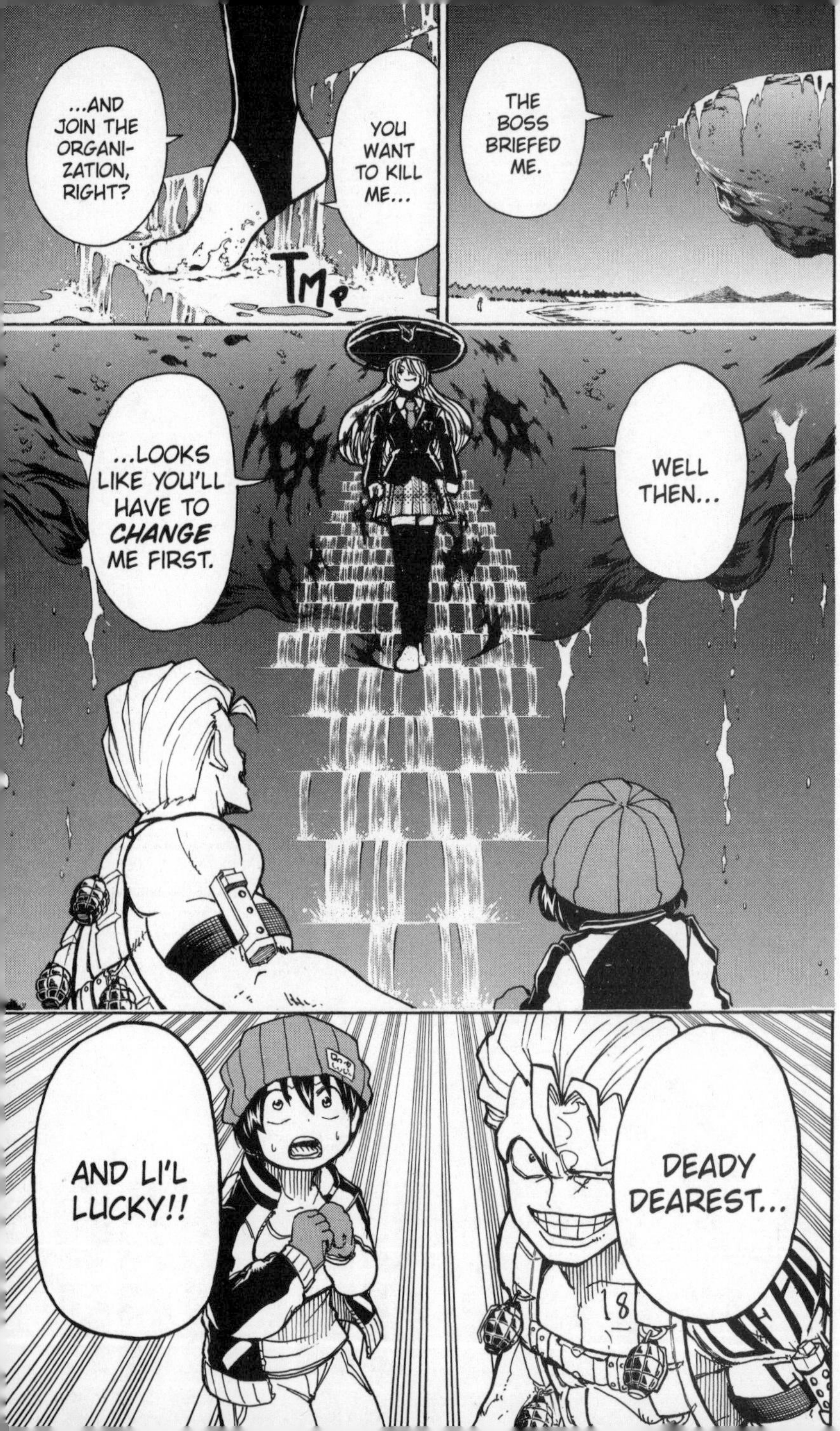
THE BOSS BRIEFED ME.
YOU WANT TO KILL ME...
...AND JOIN THE ORGANI-ZATION, RIGHT?
TMP
WELL THEN...
...LOOKS LIKE YOU'LL HAVE TO *CHANGE* ME FIRST.
DEADY DEAREST...
AND LI'L LUCKY!!

UNDEAD
UNLUCK

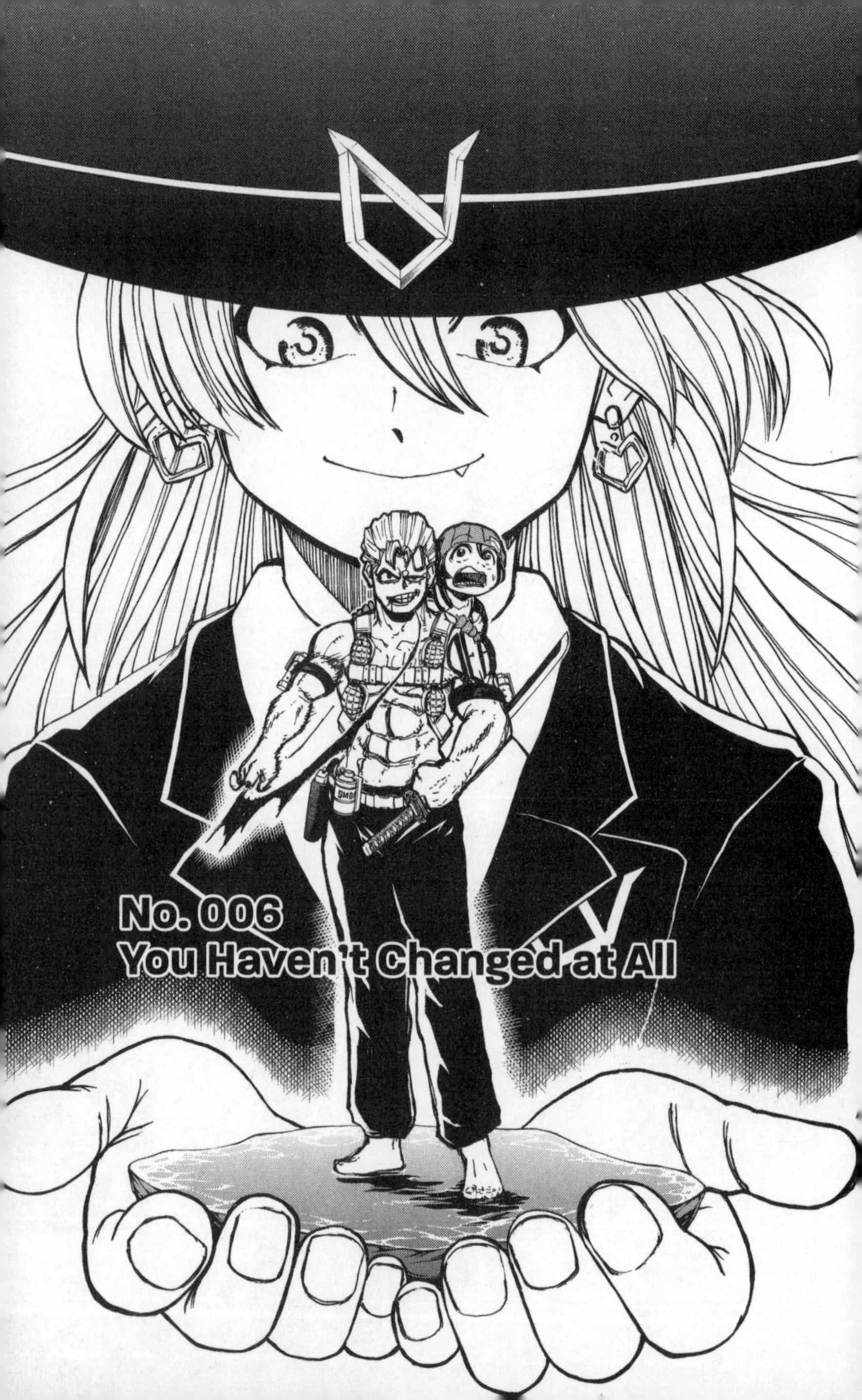

No. 006
You Haven't Changed at All

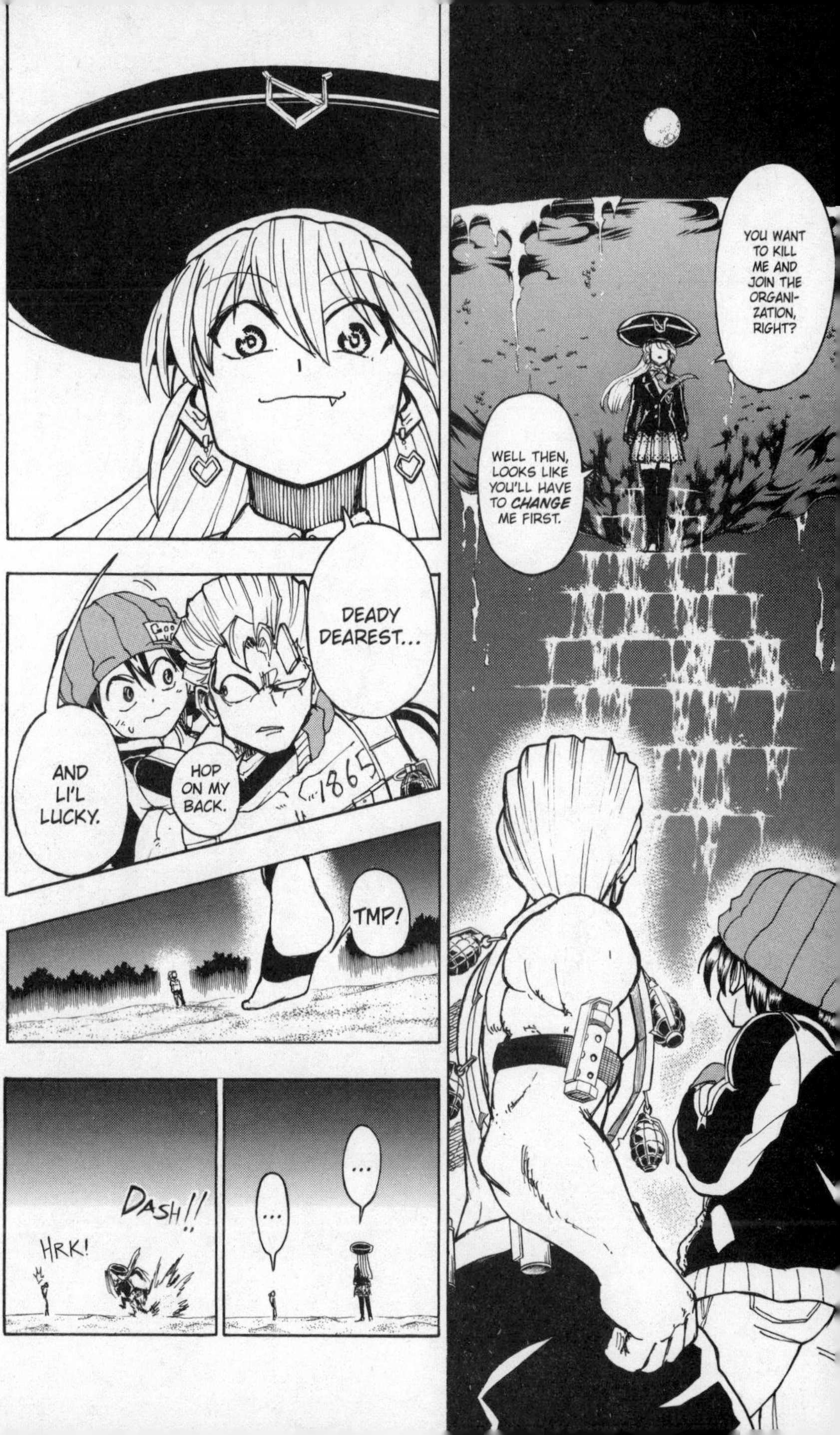
YOU WANT TO KILL ME AND JOIN THE ORGANIZATION, RIGHT?
WELL THEN, LOOKS LIKE YOU'LL HAVE TO *CHANGE* ME FIRST.
DEADY DEAREST...
HOP ON MY BACK.
AND LI'L LUCKY.
TMP!
...
...
DASH!!
HRK!

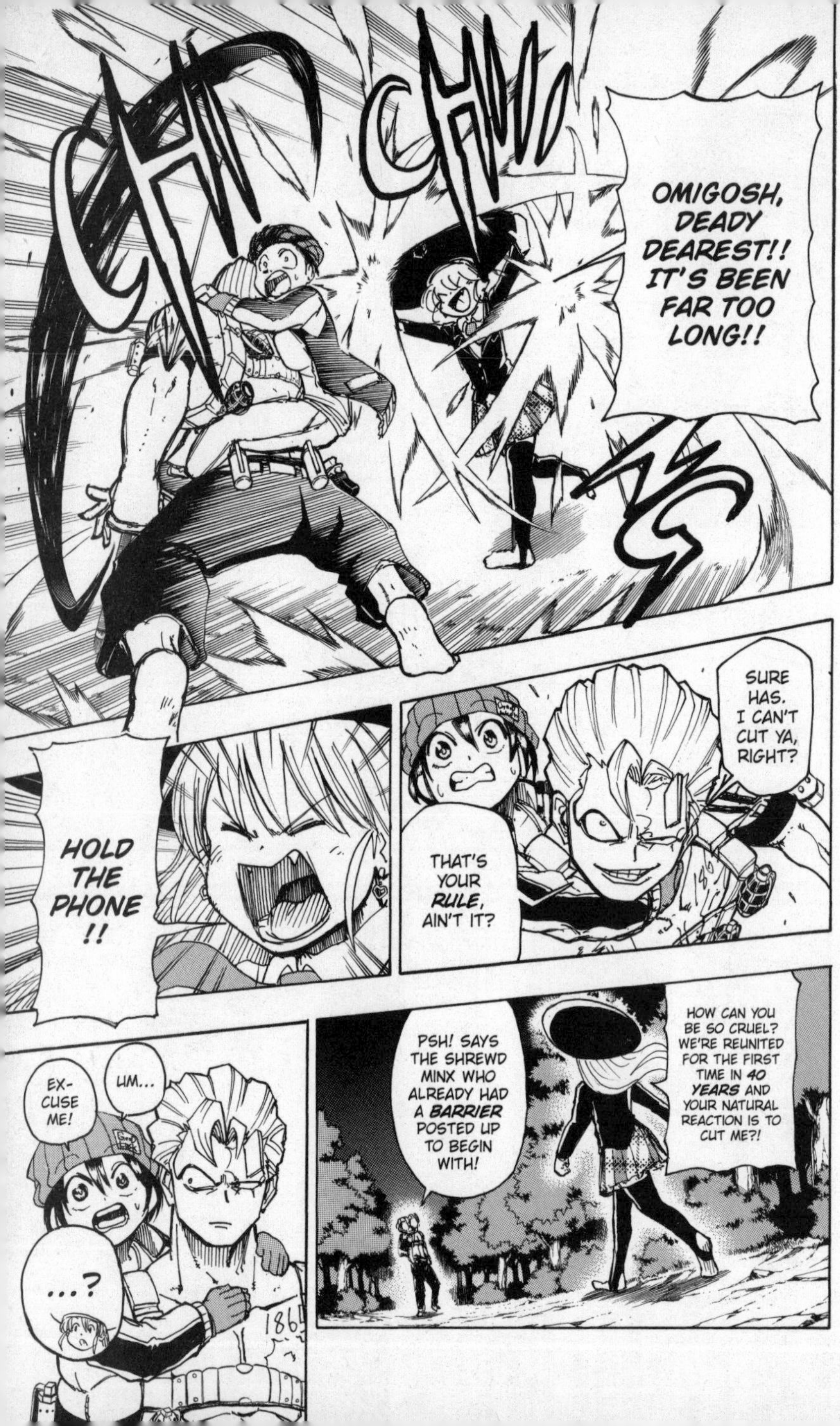
OMIGOSH, DEADY DEAREST!! IT'S BEEN FAR TOO LONG!!
SURE HAS. I CAN'T CUT YA, RIGHT?
THAT'S YOUR RULE, AIN'T IT?
HOLD THE PHONE!!
HOW CAN YOU BE SO CRUEL? WE'RE REUNITED FOR THE FIRST TIME IN 40 YEARS AND YOUR NATURAL REACTION IS TO CUT ME?!
PSH! SAYS THE SHREWD MINX WHO ALREADY HAD A BARRIER POSTED UP TO BEGIN WITH!
UM...
EX-CUSE ME!
...?

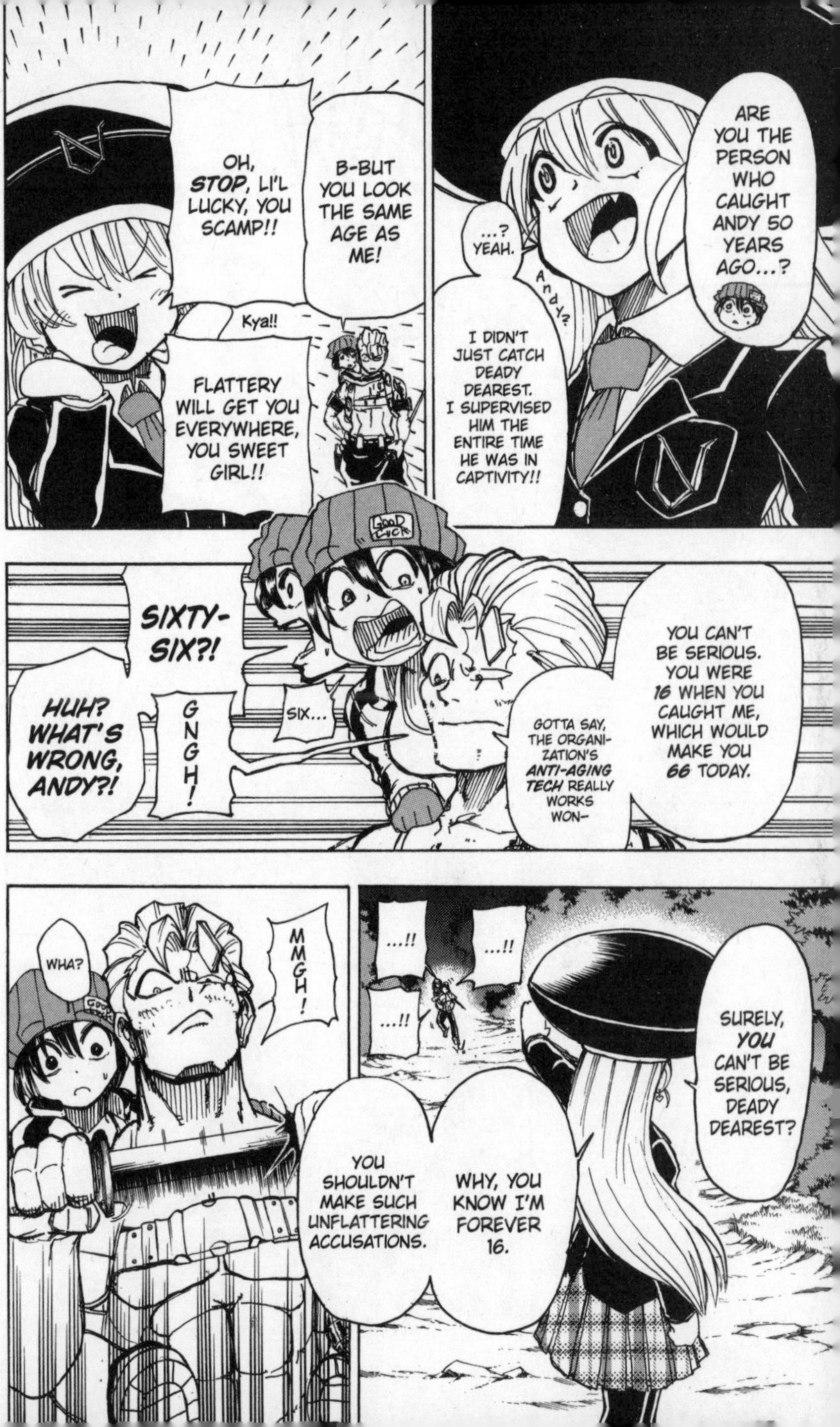
ARE YOU THE PERSON WHO CAUGHT ANDY 50 YEARS AGO...?
...? YEAH.
Andy?
I DIDN'T JUST CATCH DEADY DEAREST. I SUPERVISED HIM THE ENTIRE TIME HE WAS IN CAPTIVITY!!
B-BUT YOU LOOK THE SAME AGE AS ME!
OH, STOP, LI'L LUCKY, YOU SCAMP!!
Kya!!
FLATTERY WILL GET YOU EVERYWHERE, YOU SWEET GIRL!!
YOU CAN'T BE SERIOUS. YOU WERE 16 WHEN YOU CAUGHT ME, WHICH WOULD MAKE YOU 66 TODAY.
GOTTA SAY, THE ORGANIZATION'S ANTI-AGING TECH REALLY WORKS WON-
SIX...
GNGH!
SIXTY-SIX?!
HUH? WHAT'S WRONG, ANDY?!
SURELY, YOU CAN'T BE SERIOUS, DEADY DEAREST?
...!!
...!!
...!!
WHY, YOU KNOW I'M FOREVER 16.
YOU SHOULDN'T MAKE SUCH UNFLATTERING ACCUSATIONS.
MMGH!
WHA?

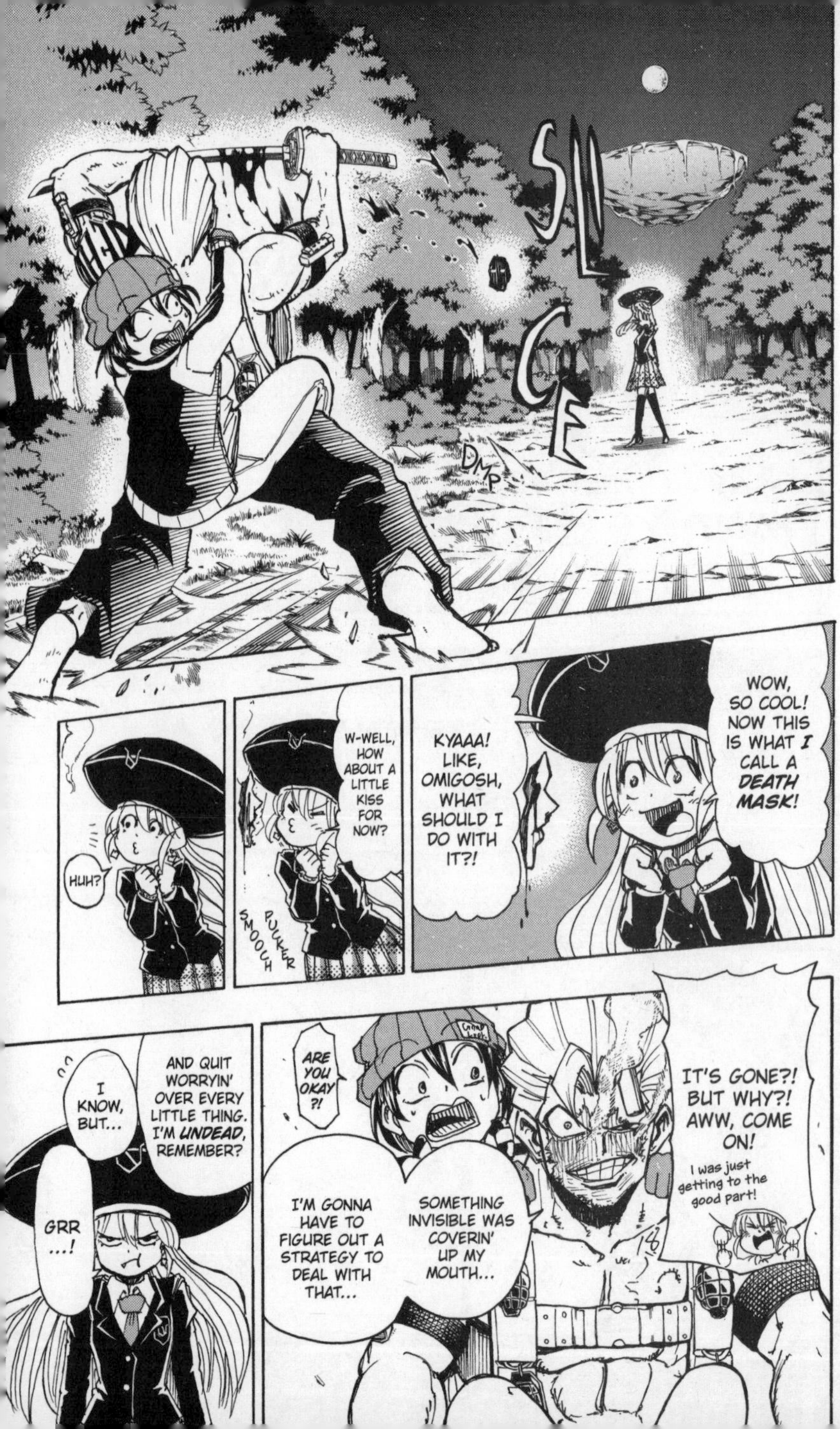
SLICE
DMP
WOW, SO COOL! NOW THIS IS WHAT I CALL A DEATH MASK!
KYAAA! LIKE, OMIGOSH, WHAT SHOULD I DO WITH IT?!
W-WELL, HOW ABOUT A LITTLE KISS FOR NOW?
PUCKER SMOOCH
HUH?
IT'S GONE?! BUT WHY?! AWW, COME ON!
I was just getting to the good part!
ARE YOU OKAY?!
SOMETHING INVISIBLE WAS COVERIN' UP MY MOUTH...
I'M GONNA HAVE TO FIGURE OUT A STRATEGY TO DEAL WITH THAT...
AND QUIT WORRYIN' OVER EVERY LITTLE THING. I'M UNDEAD, REMEMBER?
I KNOW, BUT...
GRR...!

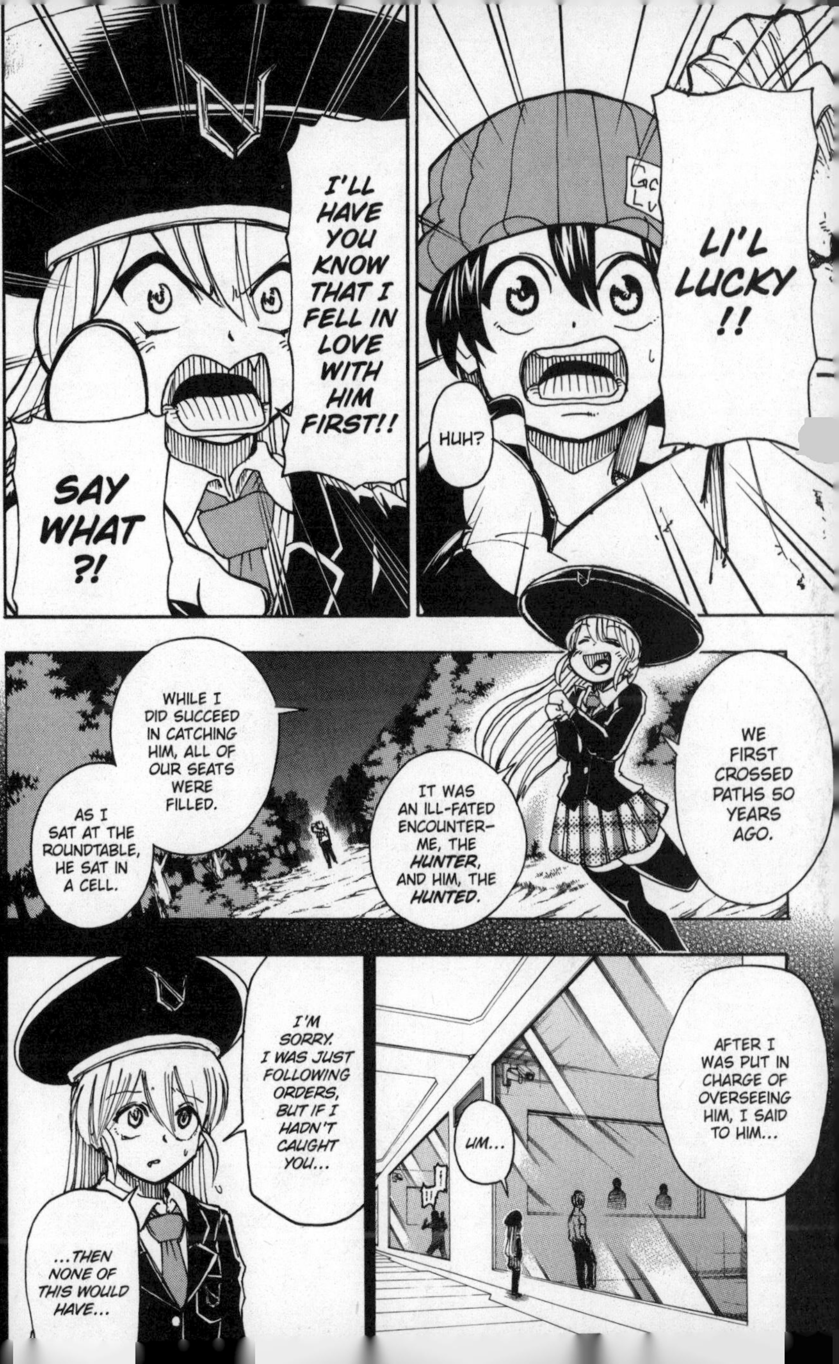
LI'L LUCKY!!
HUH?
I'LL HAVE YOU KNOW THAT I FELL IN LOVE WITH HIM FIRST!!
SAY WHAT?!
WE FIRST CROSSED PATHS 50 YEARS AGO.
IT WAS AN ILL-FATED ENCOUNTER—ME, THE *HUNTER*, AND HIM, THE *HUNTED*.
WHILE I DID SUCCEED IN CATCHING HIM, ALL OF OUR SEATS WERE FILLED.
AS I SAT AT THE ROUNDTABLE, HE SAT IN A CELL.
AFTER I WAS PUT IN CHARGE OF OVERSEEING HIM, I SAID TO HIM...
UM...
I'M SORRY. I WAS JUST FOLLOWING ORDERS, BUT IF I HADN'T CAUGHT YOU...
...THEN NONE OF THIS WOULD HAVE...

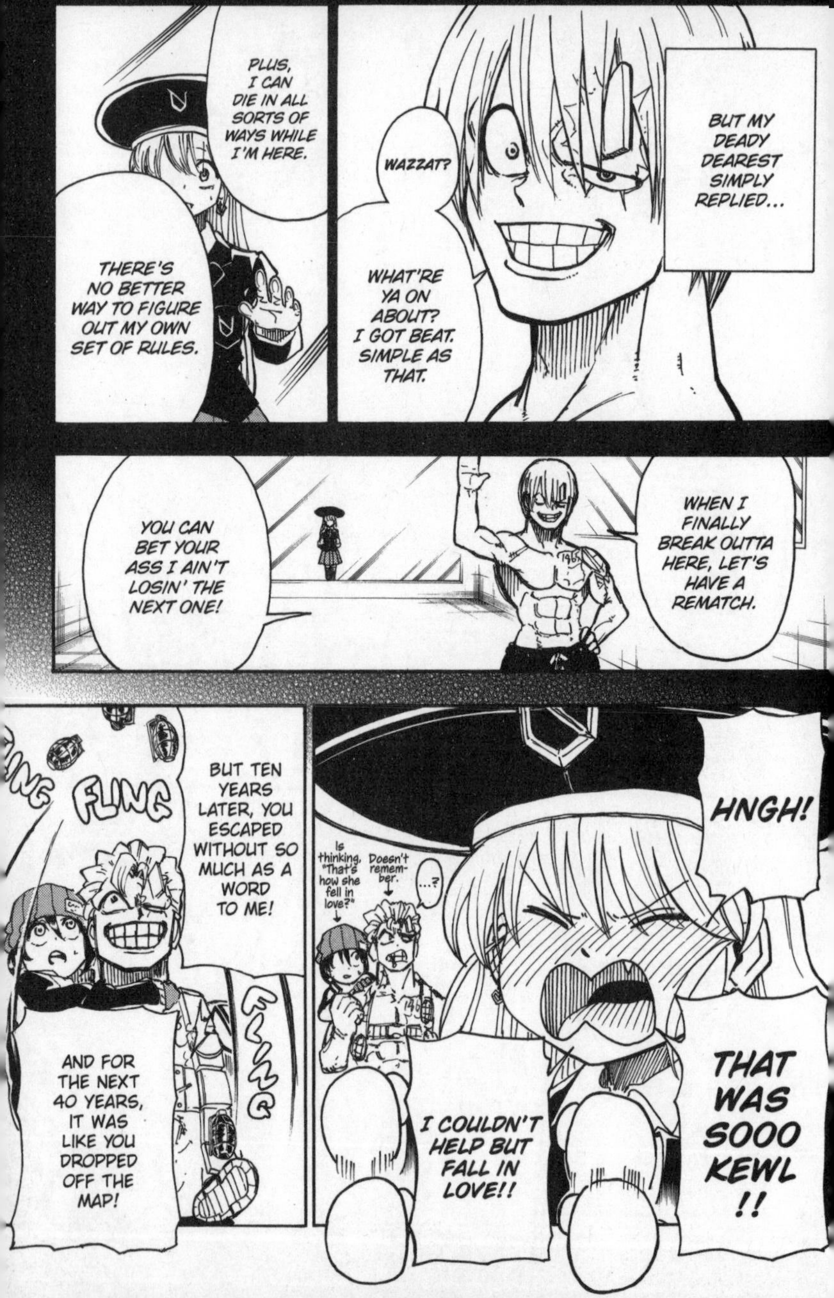
BUT MY DEADY DEAREST SIMPLY REPLIED...
WAZZAT?
WHAT'RE YA ON ABOUT? I GOT BEAT. SIMPLE AS THAT.
PLUS, I CAN DIE IN ALL SORTS OF WAYS WHILE I'M HERE.
THERE'S NO BETTER WAY TO FIGURE OUT MY OWN SET OF RULES.
WHEN I FINALLY BREAK OUTTA HERE, LET'S HAVE A REMATCH.
YOU CAN BET YOUR ASS I AIN'T LOSIN' THE NEXT ONE!
HNGH!
THAT WAS SOOO KEWL!!
...?
Doesn't remember.
Is thinking, "That's how she fell in love?"
I COULDN'T HELP BUT FALL IN LOVE!!
BUT TEN YEARS LATER, YOU ESCAPED WITHOUT SO MUCH AS A WORD TO ME!
FLING
FLING
AND FOR THE NEXT 40 YEARS, IT WAS LIKE YOU DROPPED OFF THE MAP!

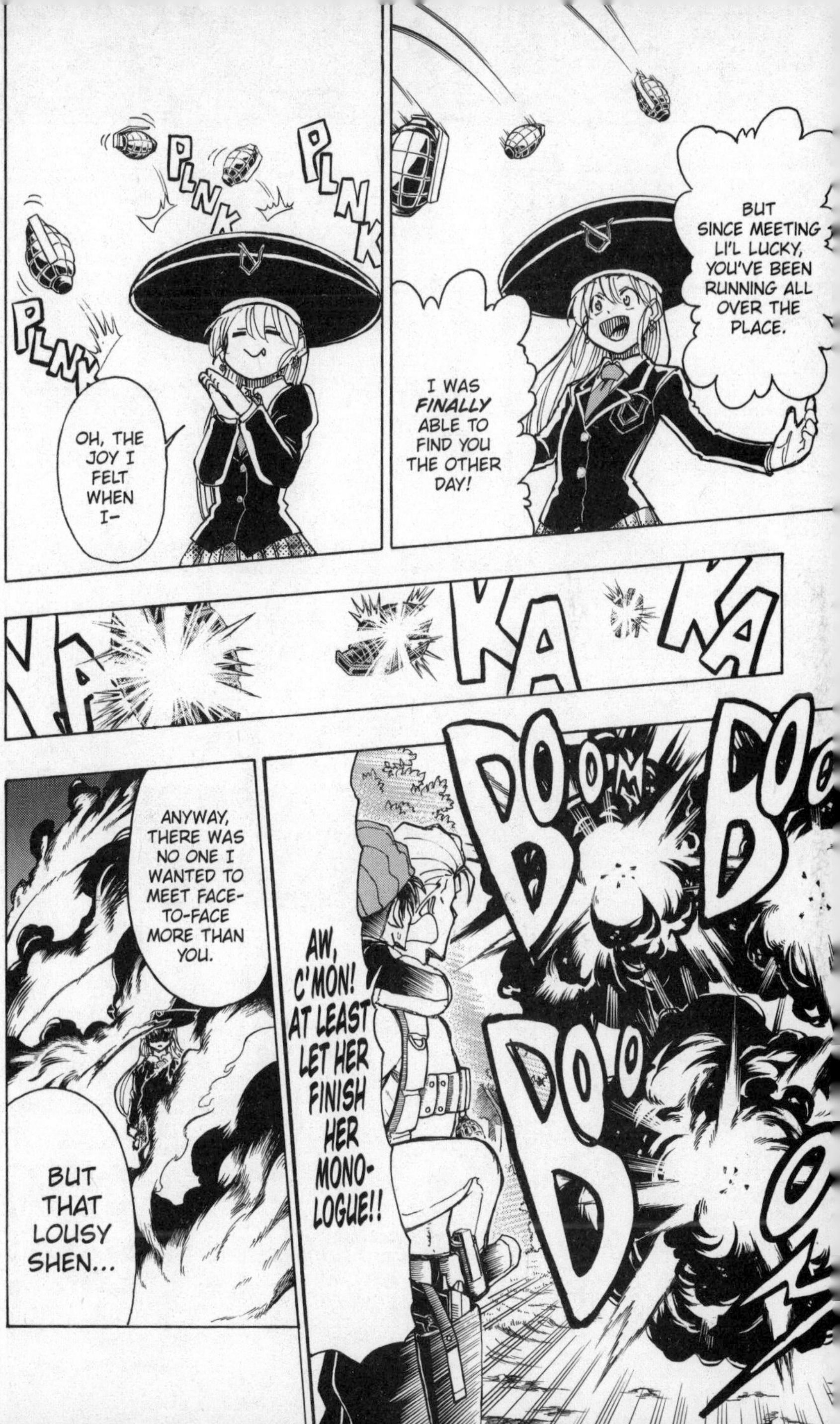
BUT SINCE MEETING LI'L LUCKY, YOU'VE BEEN RUNNING ALL OVER THE PLACE.
I WAS *FINALLY* ABLE TO FIND YOU THE OTHER DAY!
PLNK
PLNK
PLNK
OH, THE JOY I FELT WHEN I-
KA
KA
KA
AW, C'MON! AT LEAST LET HER FINISH HER MONO-LOGUE!!
ANYWAY, THERE WAS NO ONE I WANTED TO MEET FACE-TO-FACE MORE THAN YOU.
BUT THAT LOUSY SHEN...

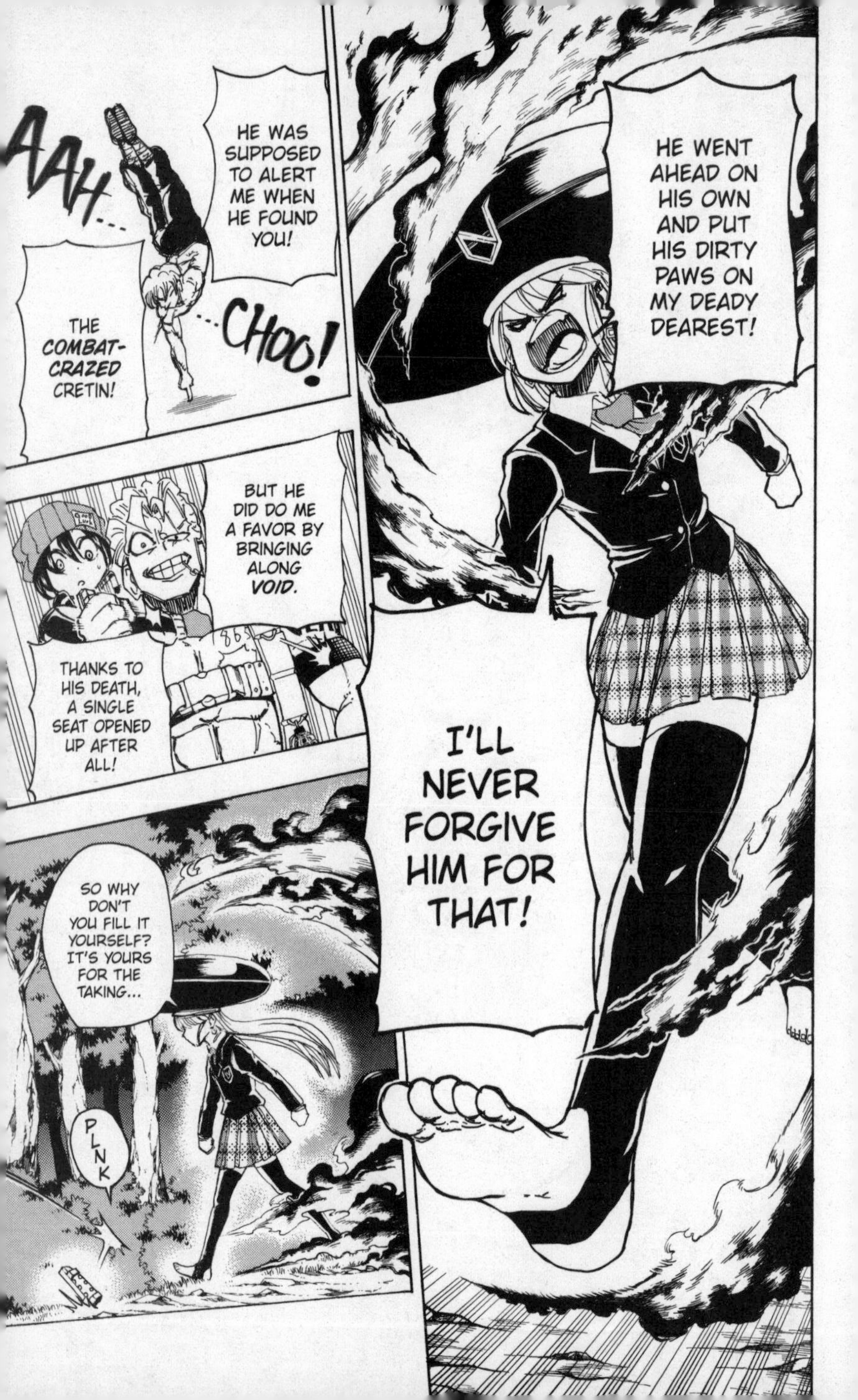
HE WENT AHEAD ON HIS OWN AND PUT HIS DIRTY PAWS ON MY DEADY DEAREST!
I'LL NEVER FORGIVE HIM FOR THAT!
HE WAS SUPPOSED TO ALERT ME WHEN HE FOUND YOU!
AAH...
...CHOO!
THE COMBAT-CRAZED CRETIN!
BUT HE DID DO ME A FAVOR BY BRINGING ALONG VOID.
THANKS TO HIS DEATH, A SINGLE SEAT OPENED UP AFTER ALL!
SO WHY DON'T YOU FILL IT YOURSELF? IT'S YOURS FOR THE TAKING...
PLNK

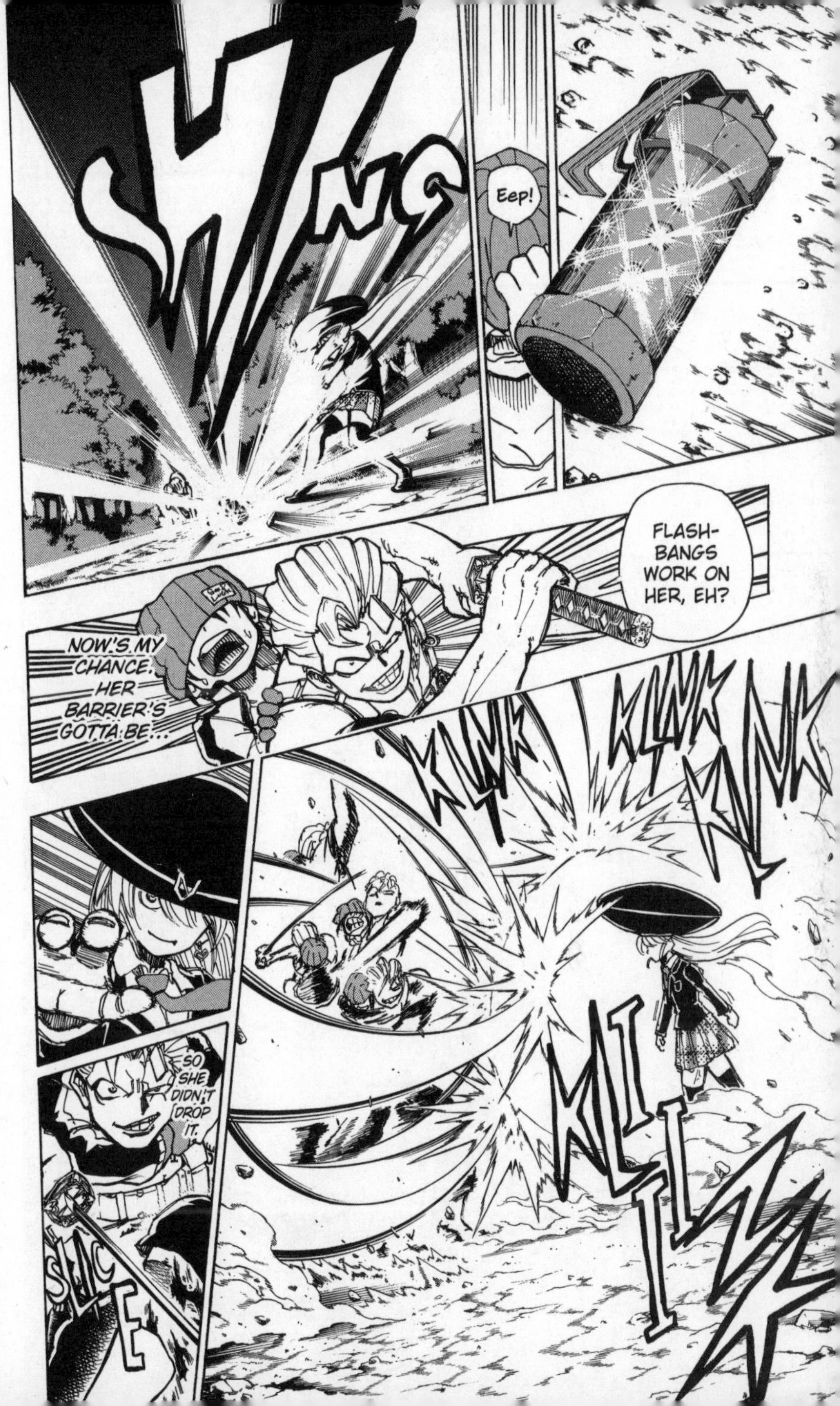
Eep!
SHING
FLASH-BANGS WORK ON HER, EH?
NOW'S MY CHANCE. HER BARRIER'S GOTTA BE...
KLINK
KLINK
KLINK
SO SHE DIDN'T DROP IT.
SLICE

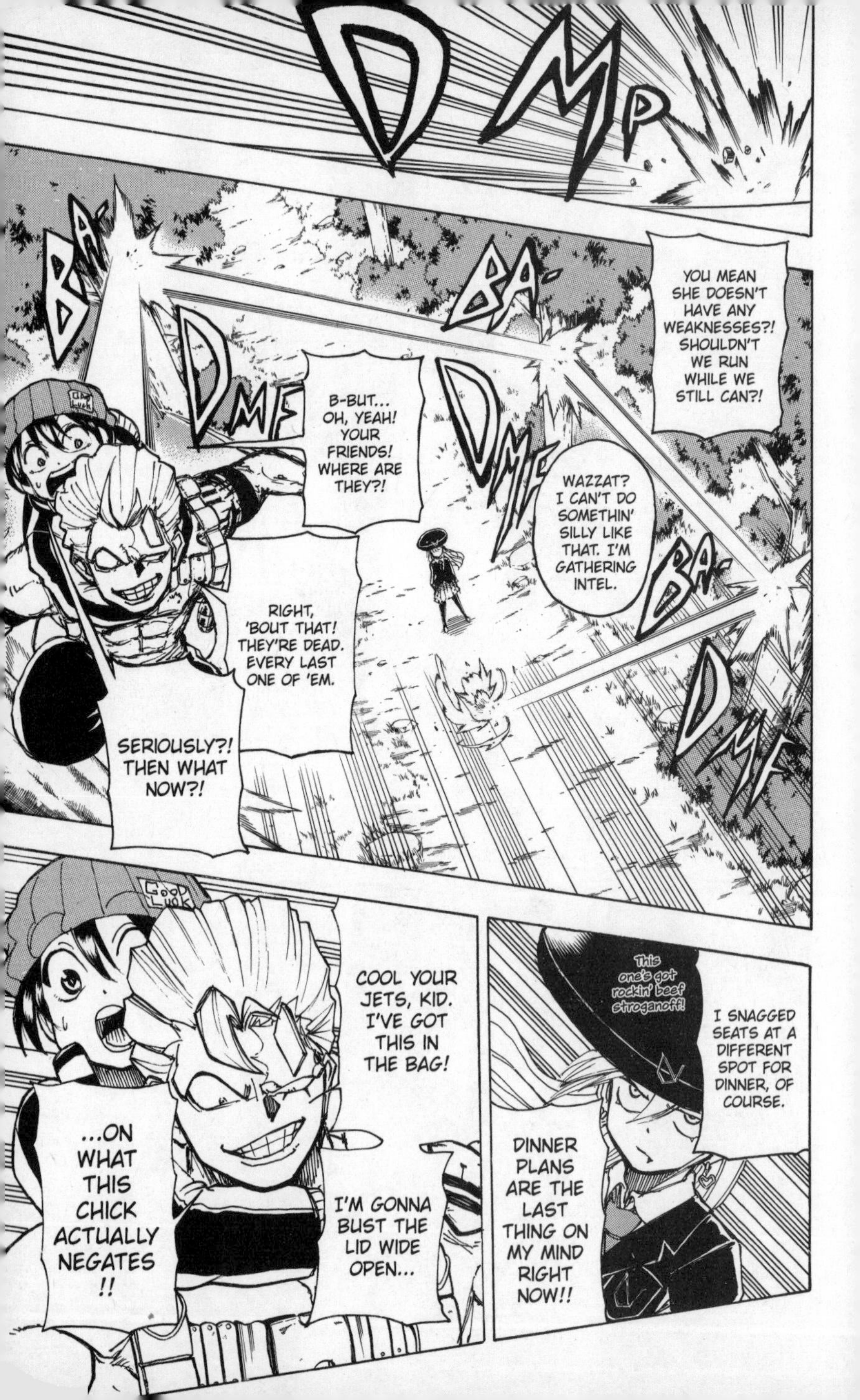
DMP
YOU MEAN SHE DOESN'T HAVE ANY WEAKNESSES?! SHOULDN'T WE RUN WHILE WE STILL CAN?!
BA-
DMF
WAZZAT? I CAN'T DO SOMETHIN' SILLY LIKE THAT. I'M GATHERING INTEL.
BA-
DMF
B-BUT... OH, YEAH! YOUR FRIENDS! WHERE ARE THEY?!
BA-
DMF
RIGHT, 'BOUT THAT! THEY'RE DEAD. EVERY LAST ONE OF 'EM.
SERIOUSLY?! THEN WHAT NOW?!
This one's got rockin' beef stroganoff!
I SNAGGED SEATS AT A DIFFERENT SPOT FOR DINNER, OF COURSE.
DINNER PLANS ARE THE LAST THING ON MY MIND RIGHT NOW!!
COOL YOUR JETS, KID. I'VE GOT THIS IN THE BAG!
I'M GONNA BUST THE LID WIDE OPEN...
...ON WHAT THIS CHICK ACTUALLY NEGATES!!

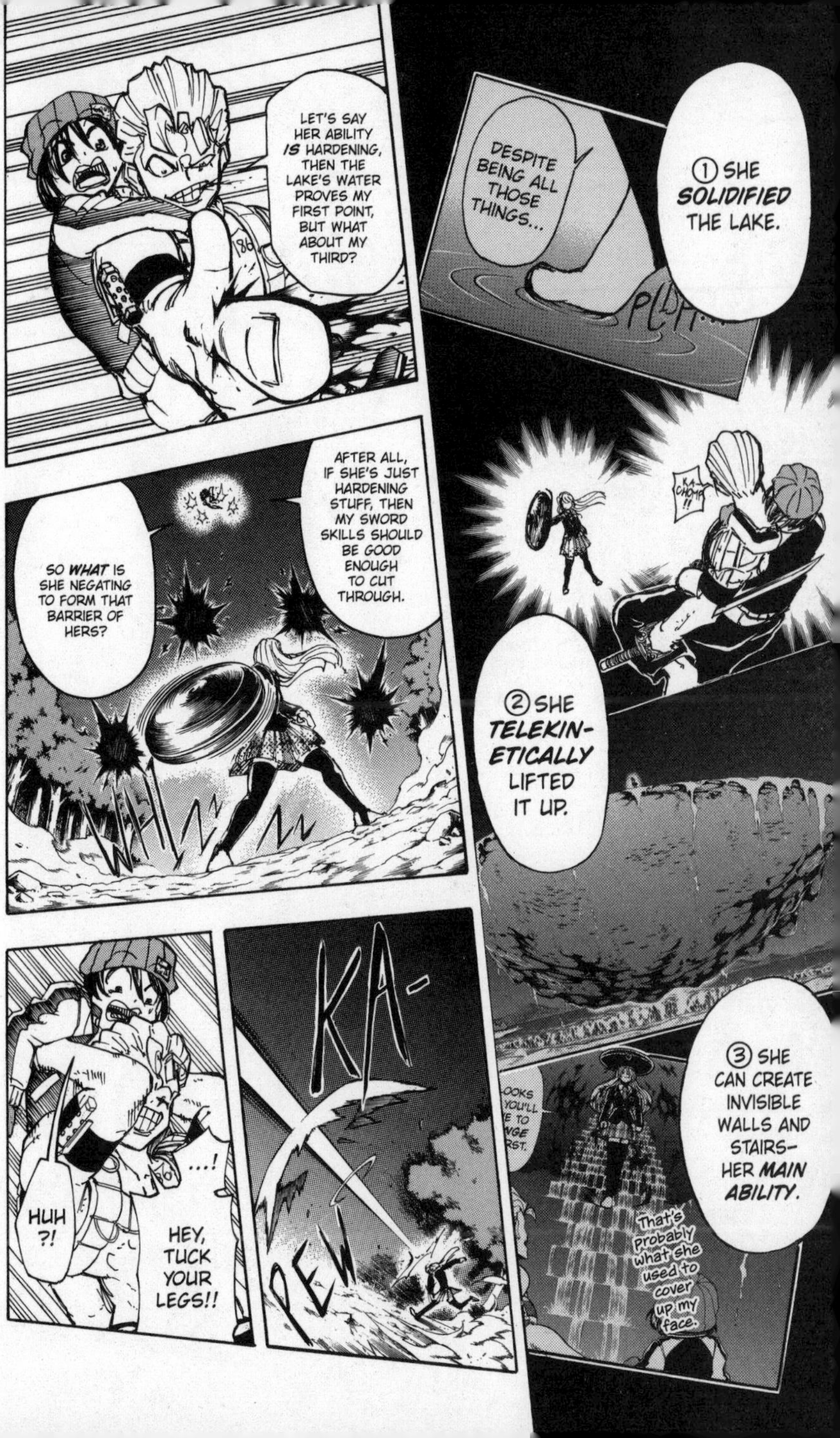

① SHE ***SOLIDIFIED*** THE LAKE.
DESPITE BEING ALL THOSE THINGS...
KA-CHOMP!!
② SHE ***TELEKINETICALLY*** LIFTED IT UP.
③ SHE CAN CREATE INVISIBLE WALLS AND STAIRS— HER ***MAIN ABILITY***.
That's probably what she used to cover up my face.
LET'S SAY HER ABILITY ***IS*** HARDENING, THEN THE LAKE'S WATER PROVES MY FIRST POINT, BUT WHAT ABOUT MY THIRD?
AFTER ALL, IF SHE'S JUST HARDENING STUFF, THEN MY SWORD SKILLS SHOULD BE GOOD ENOUGH TO CUT THROUGH.
SO ***WHAT*** IS SHE NEGATING TO FORM THAT BARRIER OF HERS?
KA-PEW
...!
HEY, TUCK YOUR LEGS!!
HUH?!

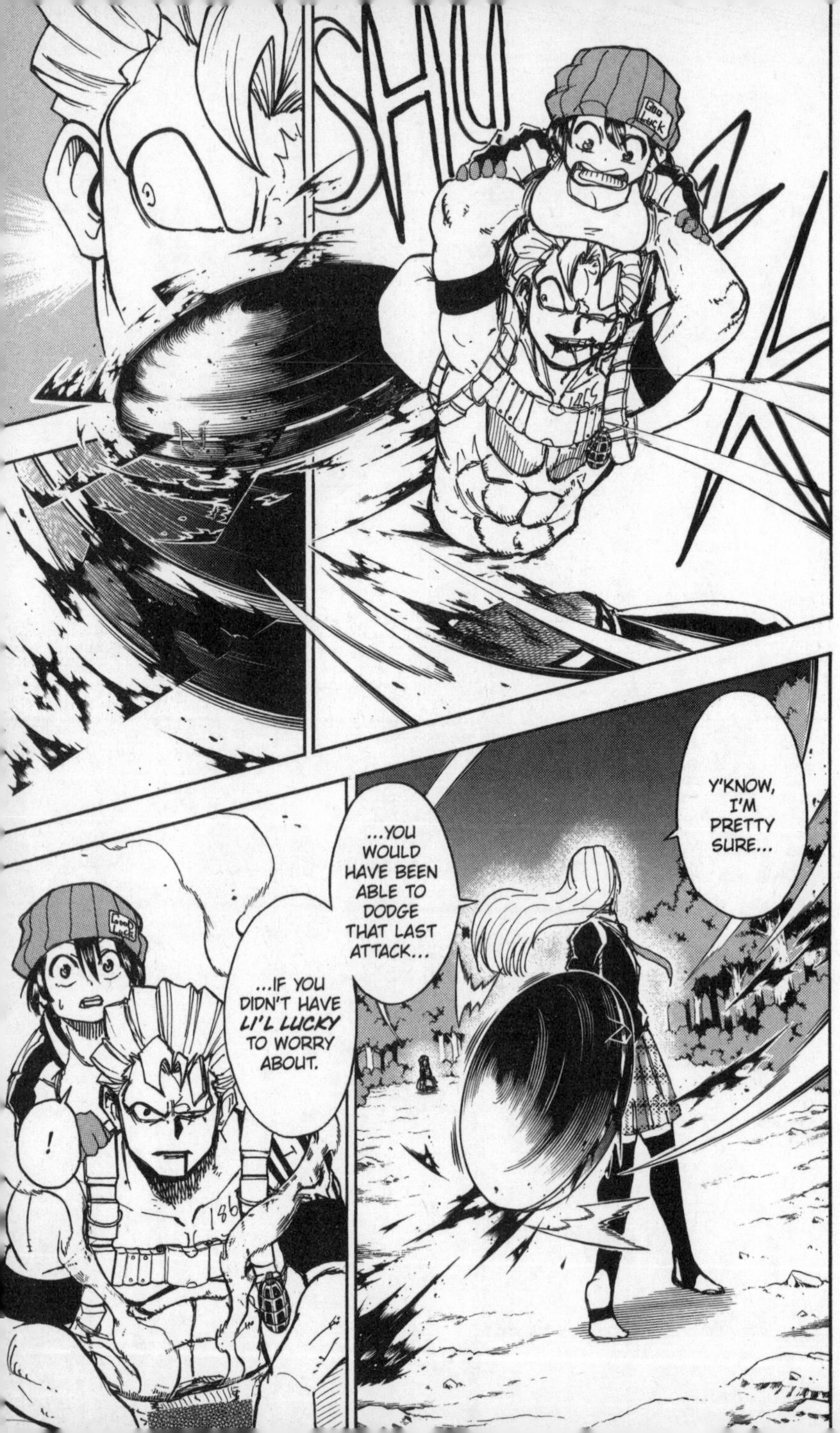
SHU
Good Luck
Y'KNOW, I'M PRETTY SURE...
...YOU WOULD HAVE BEEN ABLE TO DODGE THAT LAST ATTACK...
...IF YOU DIDN'T HAVE *LI'L LUCKY* TO WORRY ABOUT.
Good Luck
!
186

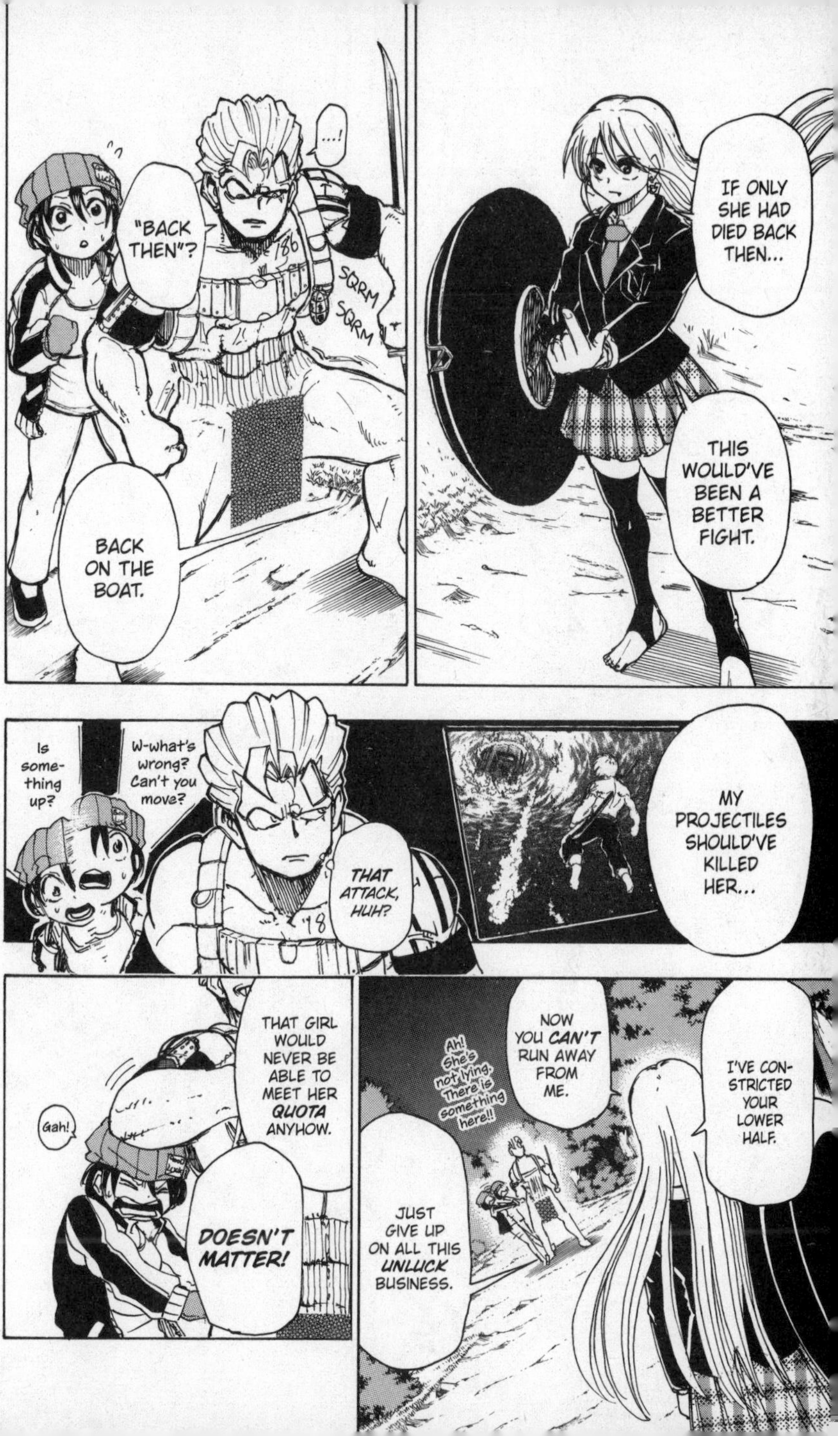
IF ONLY SHE HAD DIED BACK THEN...
THIS WOULD'VE BEEN A BETTER FIGHT.
...!
"BACK THEN"?
SQRM SQRM
BACK ON THE BOAT.
MY PROJECTILES SHOULD'VE KILLED HER...
THAT ATTACK, HUH?
W-what's wrong? Can't you move?
Is something up?
I'VE CONSTRICTED YOUR LOWER HALF.
NOW YOU CAN'T RUN AWAY FROM ME.
Ah! She's not lying. There is something here!!
JUST GIVE UP ON ALL THIS UNLUCK BUSINESS.
THAT GIRL WOULD NEVER BE ABLE TO MEET HER QUOTA ANYHOW.
Gah!
DOESN'T MATTER!

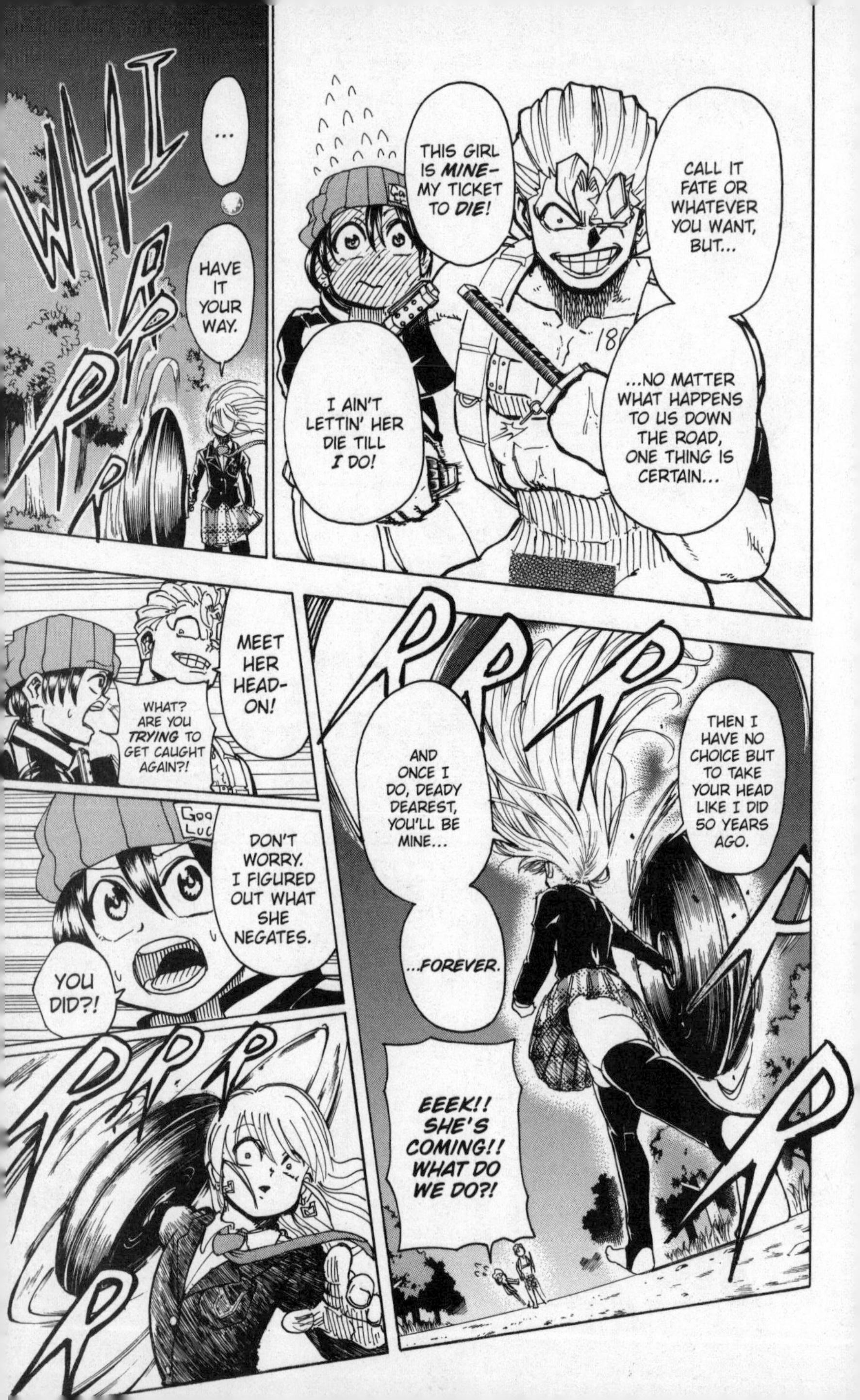
CALL IT FATE OR WHATEVER YOU WANT, BUT...
...NO MATTER WHAT HAPPENS TO US DOWN THE ROAD, ONE THING IS CERTAIN...
THIS GIRL IS *MINE*— MY TICKET TO *DIE*!
I AIN'T LETTIN' HER DIE TILL *I* DO!
...
HAVE IT YOUR WAY.
WHIRRRRR
RRRR
THEN I HAVE NO CHOICE BUT TO TAKE YOUR HEAD LIKE I DID 50 YEARS AGO.
AND ONCE I DO, DEADY DEAREST, YOU'LL BE MINE...
...FOREVER.
EEEK!! SHE'S COMING!! WHAT DO WE DO?!
MEET HER HEAD-ON!
WHAT? ARE YOU *TRYING* TO GET CAUGHT AGAIN?!
DON'T WORRY. I FIGURED OUT WHAT SHE NEGATES.
YOU DID?!
RRRRR

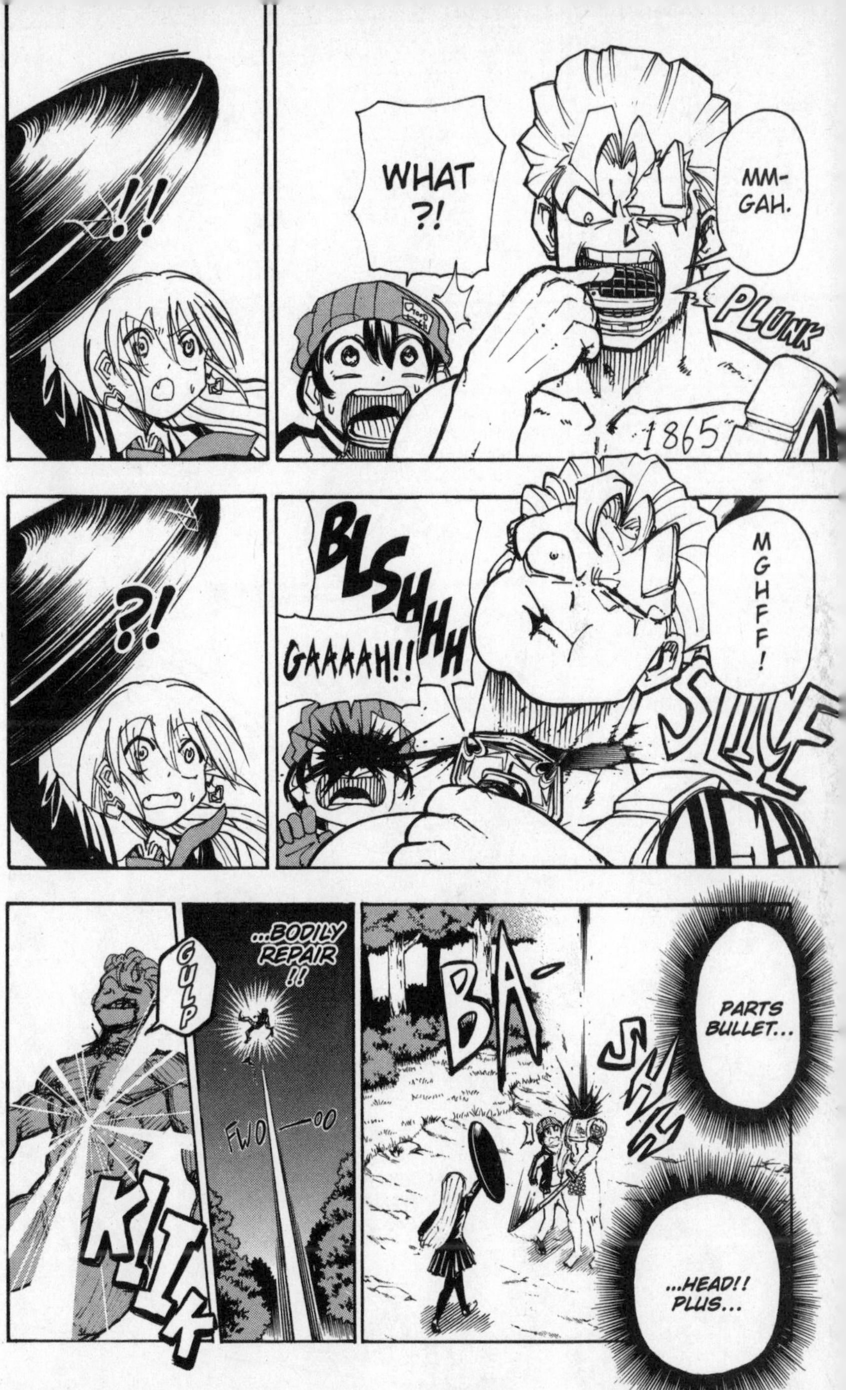
MM-GAH.
PLUNK
WHAT ?!
!!
MGHFF!
SLICE
BLSHHHH
GAAAAH!!
?!
PARTS BULLET...
...HEAD!! PLUS...
SHH
BA-
...BODILY REPAIR !!
FWO—OO
GULP
KLIK

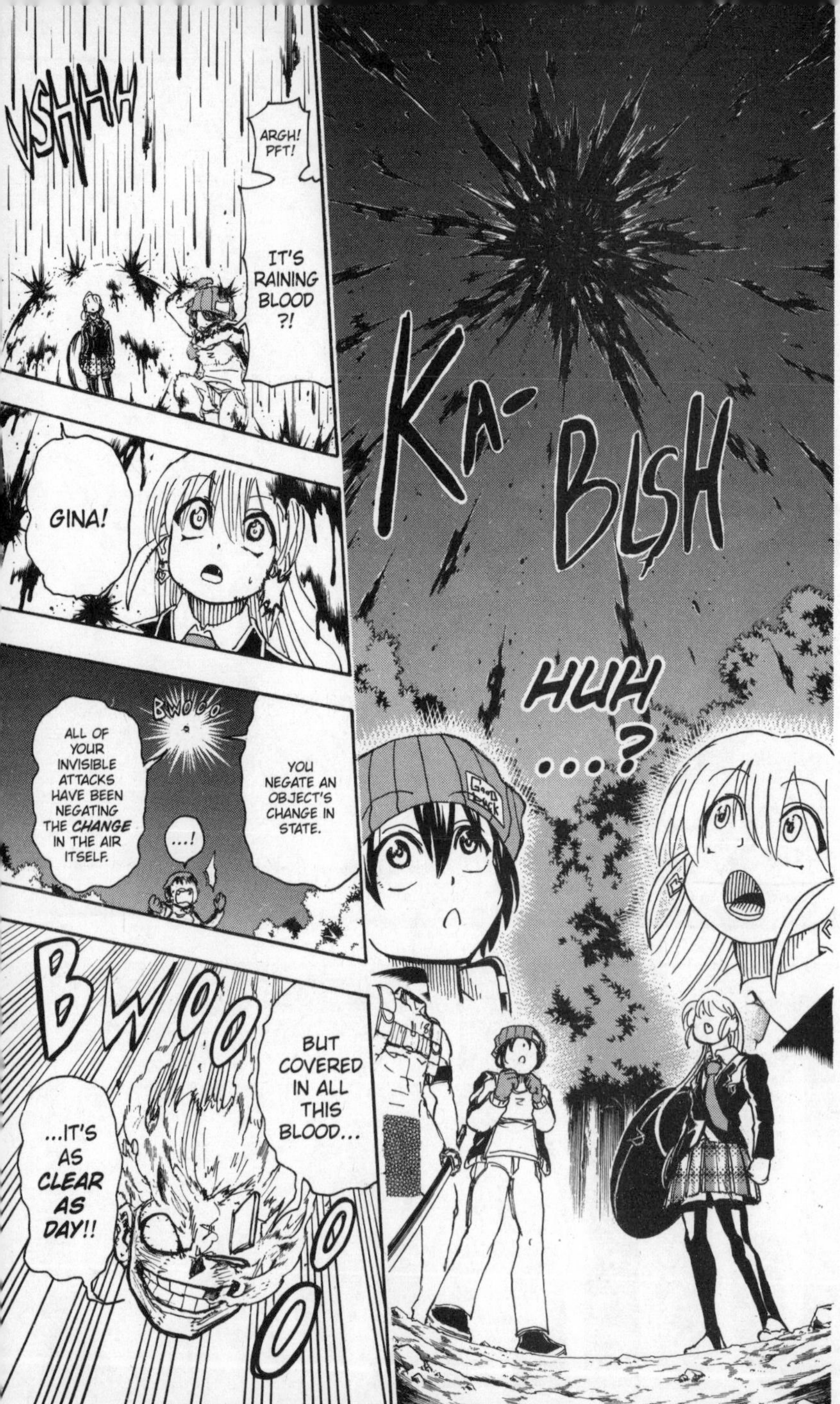
KA-BLSH
HUH ...?
VSHHH
ARGH! PFT!
IT'S RAINING BLOOD ?!
GINA!
BWOOO
YOU NEGATE AN OBJECT'S CHANGE IN STATE.
ALL OF YOUR INVISIBLE ATTACKS HAVE BEEN NEGATING THE *CHANGE* IN THE AIR ITSELF.
...!
BWOOO
BUT COVERED IN ALL THIS BLOOD...
...IT'S AS **CLEAR AS DAY!!**

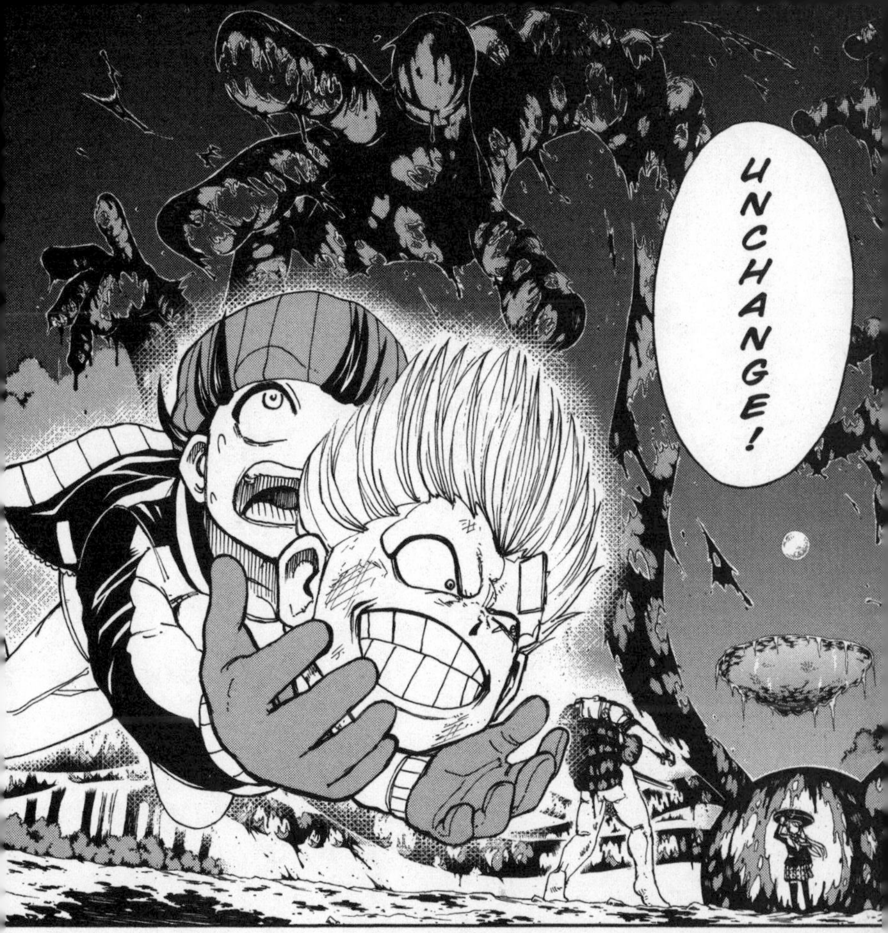
UNCHANGE!
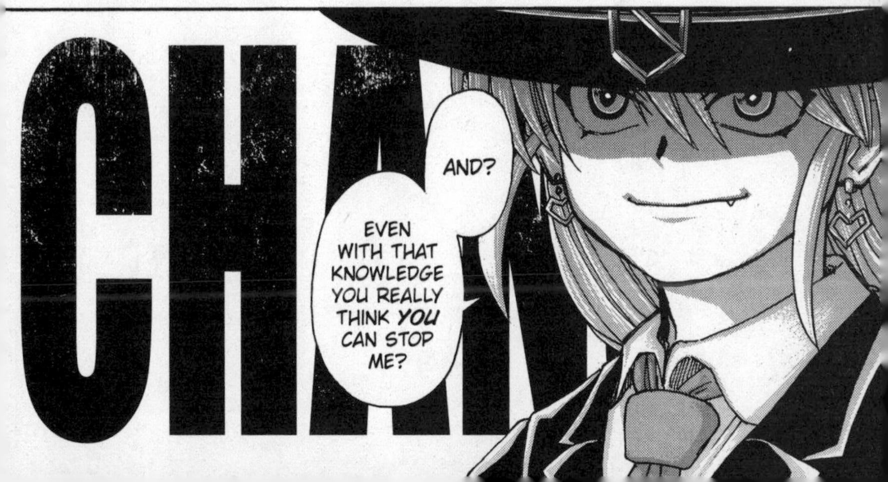
AND?
EVEN WITH THAT KNOWLEDGE YOU REALLY THINK *YOU* CAN STOP ME?

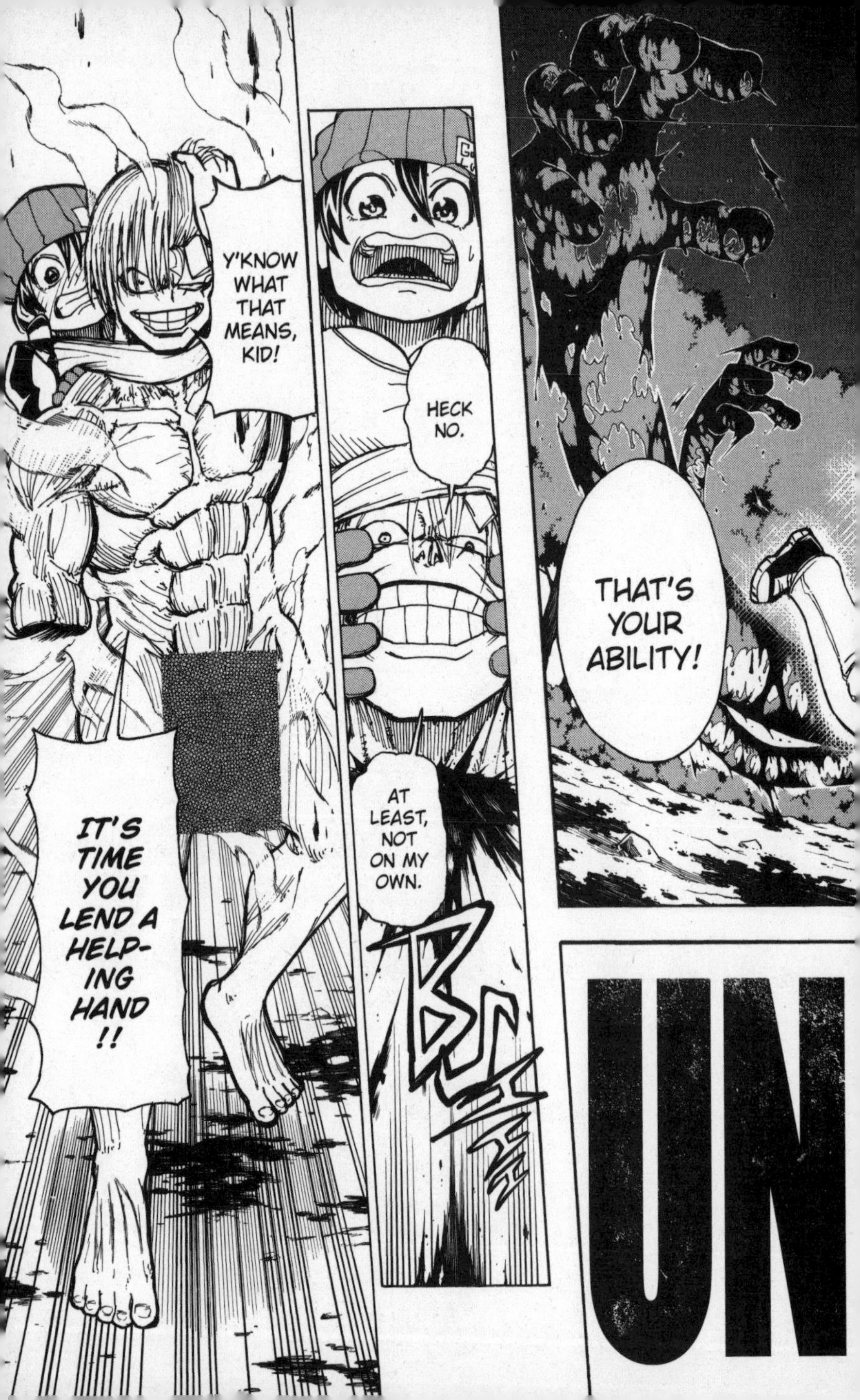
THAT'S YOUR ABILITY!
UN
HECK NO.
AT LEAST, NOT ON MY OWN.
Y'KNOW WHAT THAT MEANS, KID!
IT'S TIME YOU LEND A HELP-ING HAND!!

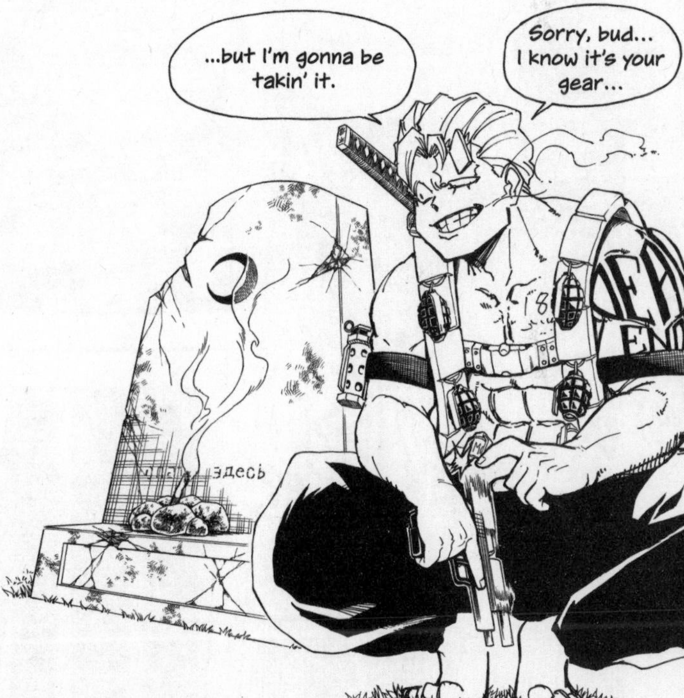
Sorry, bud... I know it's your gear...
...but I'm gonna be takin' it.
здесь

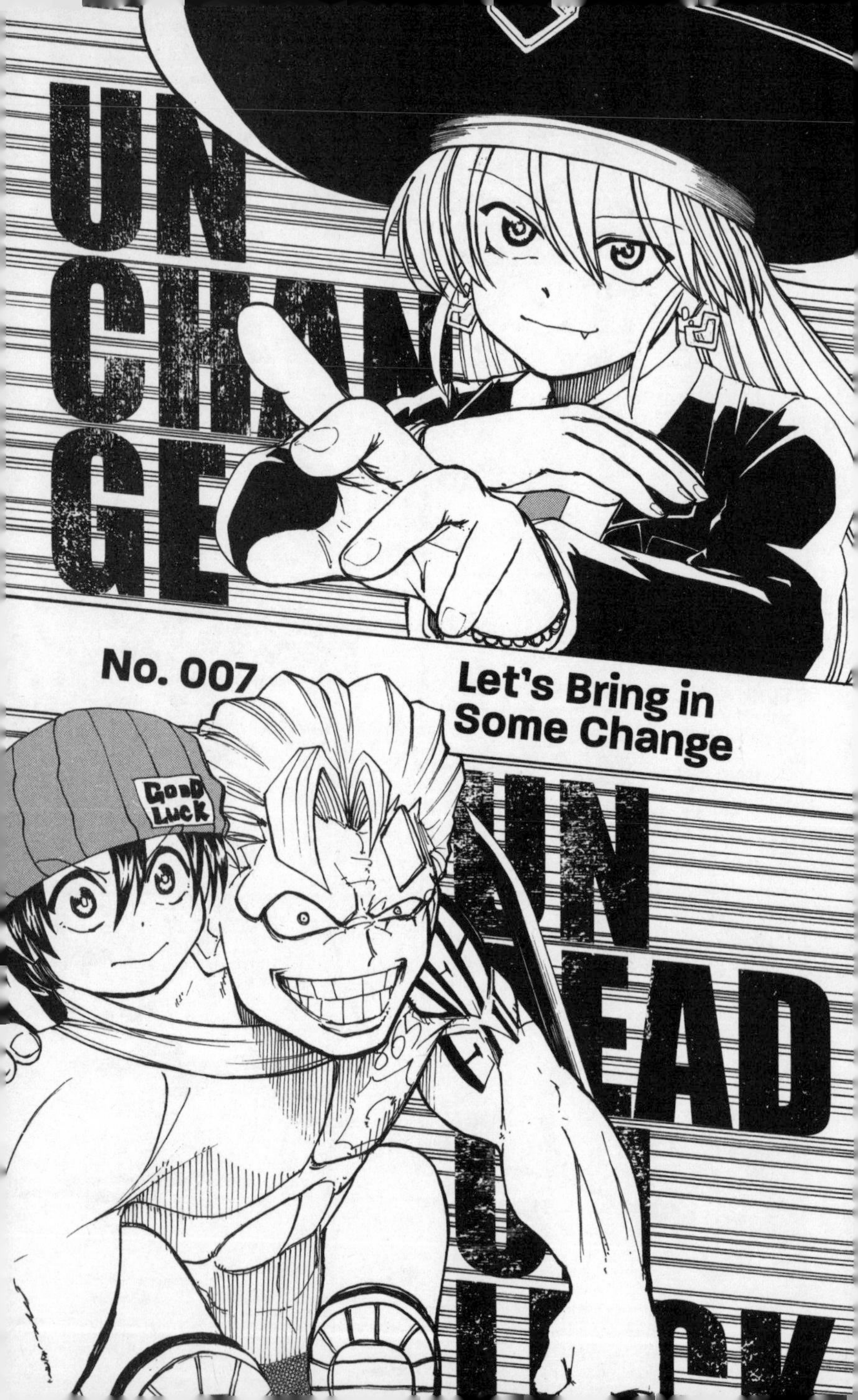
No. 007
Let's Bring in Some Change
GOOD LUCK

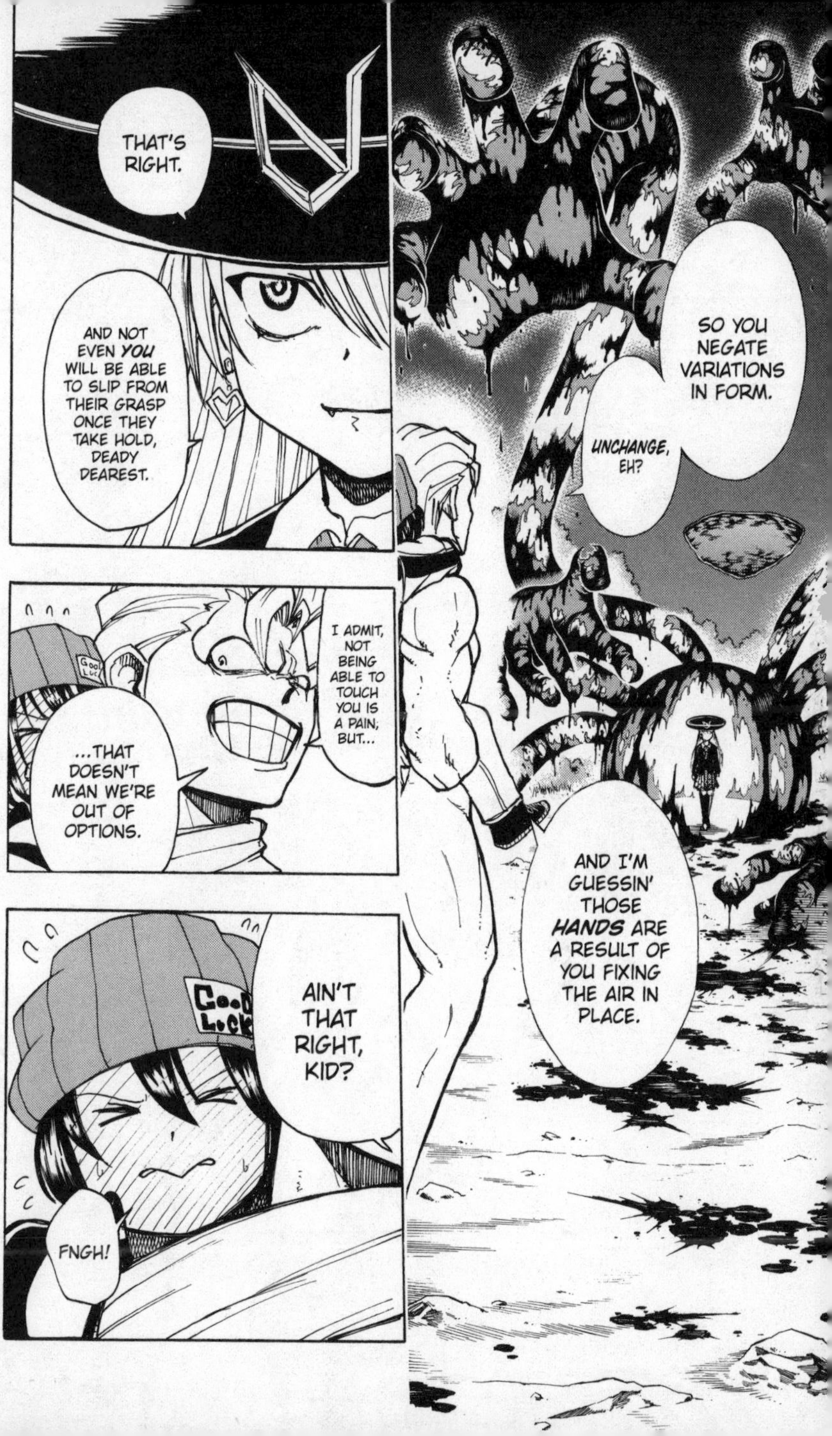
SO YOU NEGATE VARIATIONS IN FORM.
UNCHANGE, EH?
AND I'M GUESSIN' THOSE HANDS ARE A RESULT OF YOU FIXING THE AIR IN PLACE.
THAT'S RIGHT.
AND NOT EVEN YOU WILL BE ABLE TO SLIP FROM THEIR GRASP ONCE THEY TAKE HOLD, DEADY DEAREST.
I ADMIT, NOT BEING ABLE TO TOUCH YOU IS A PAIN; BUT...
...THAT DOESN'T MEAN WE'RE OUT OF OPTIONS.
AIN'T THAT RIGHT, KID?
FNGH!

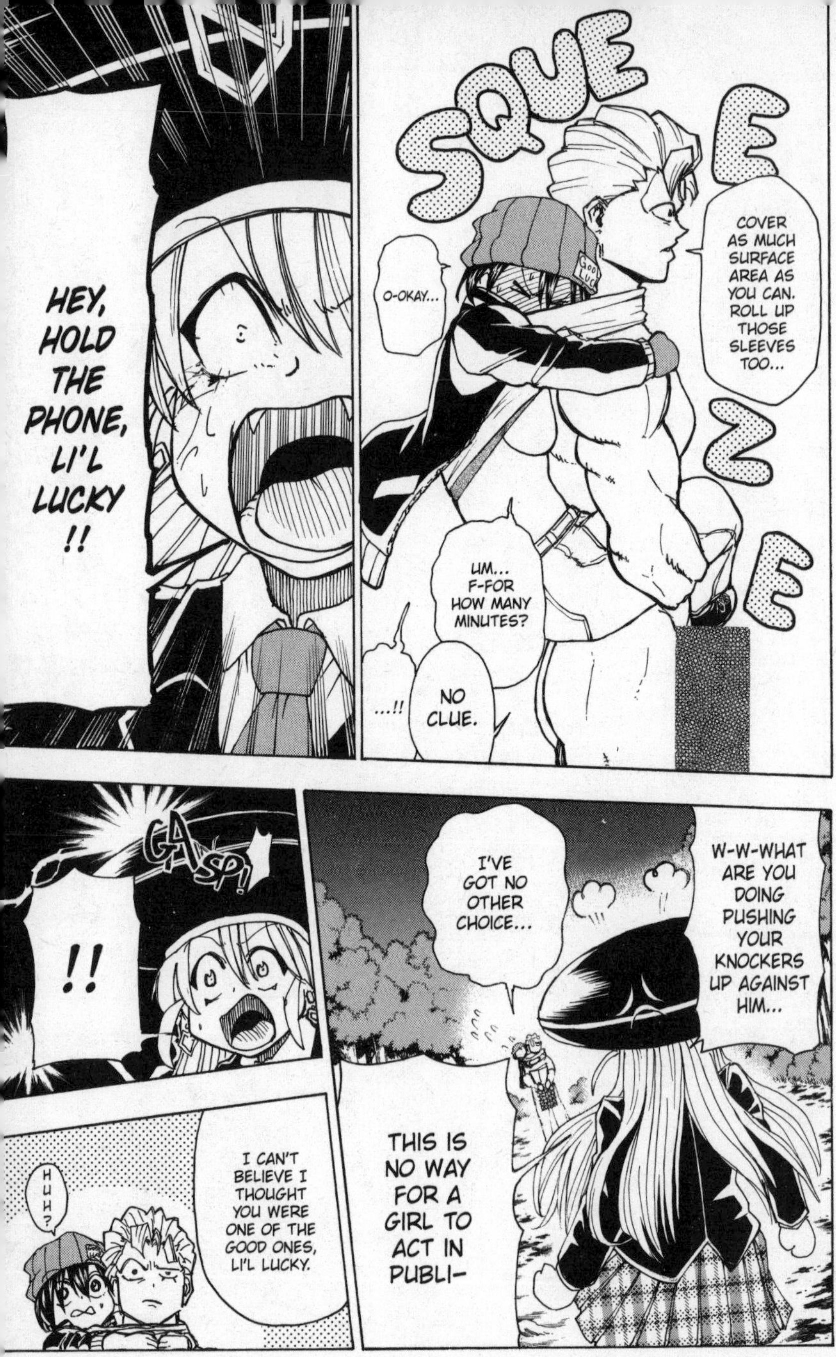

SQUEEZE
COVER AS MUCH SURFACE AREA AS YOU CAN. ROLL UP THOSE SLEEVES TOO...
O-OKAY...
UM... F-FOR HOW MANY MINUTES?
NO CLUE.
...!!
HEY, HOLD THE PHONE, LI'L LUCKY!!
W-W-WHAT ARE YOU DOING PUSHING YOUR KNOCKERS UP AGAINST HIM...
I'VE GOT NO OTHER CHOICE...
THIS IS NO WAY FOR A GIRL TO ACT IN PUBLI-
GASP!
!!
I CAN'T BELIEVE I THOUGHT YOU WERE ONE OF THE GOOD ONES, LI'L LUCKY.
HUH?

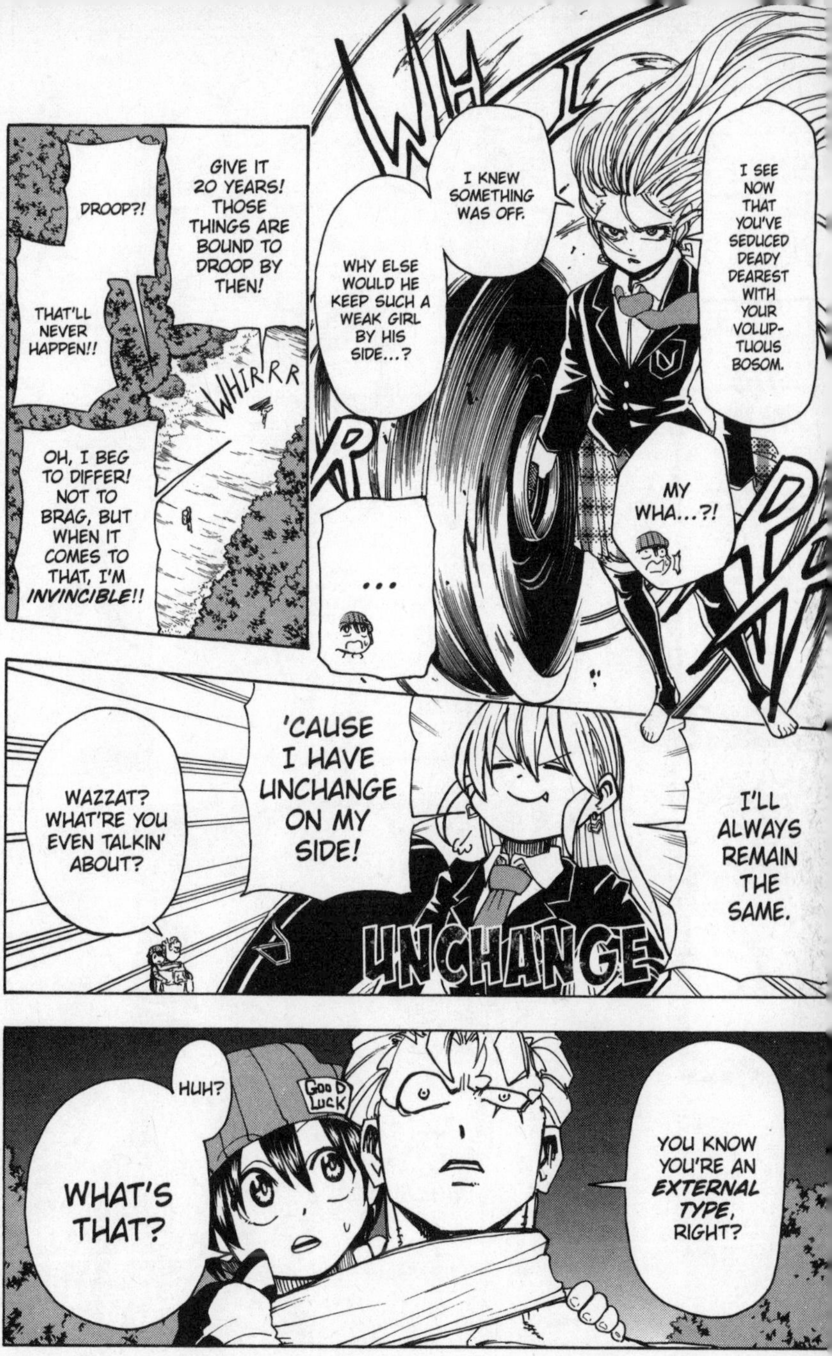
WHI
I SEE NOW THAT YOU'VE SEDUCED DEADY DEAREST WITH YOUR VOLUP-TUOUS BOSOM.
I KNEW SOMETHING WAS OFF.
WHY ELSE WOULD HE KEEP SUCH A WEAK GIRL BY HIS SIDE...?
MY WHA...?!
...
GIVE IT 20 YEARS! THOSE THINGS ARE BOUND TO DROOP BY THEN!
DROOP?!
THAT'LL NEVER HAPPEN!!
WHIRRR
OH, I BEG TO DIFFER! NOT TO BRAG, BUT WHEN IT COMES TO THAT, I'M *INVINCIBLE*!!
I'LL ALWAYS REMAIN THE SAME.
'CAUSE I HAVE UNCHANGE ON MY SIDE!
UNCHANGE
WAZZAT? WHAT'RE YOU EVEN TALKIN' ABOUT?
YOU KNOW YOU'RE AN *EXTERNAL TYPE*, RIGHT?
HUH?
GOOD LUCK
WHAT'S THAT?

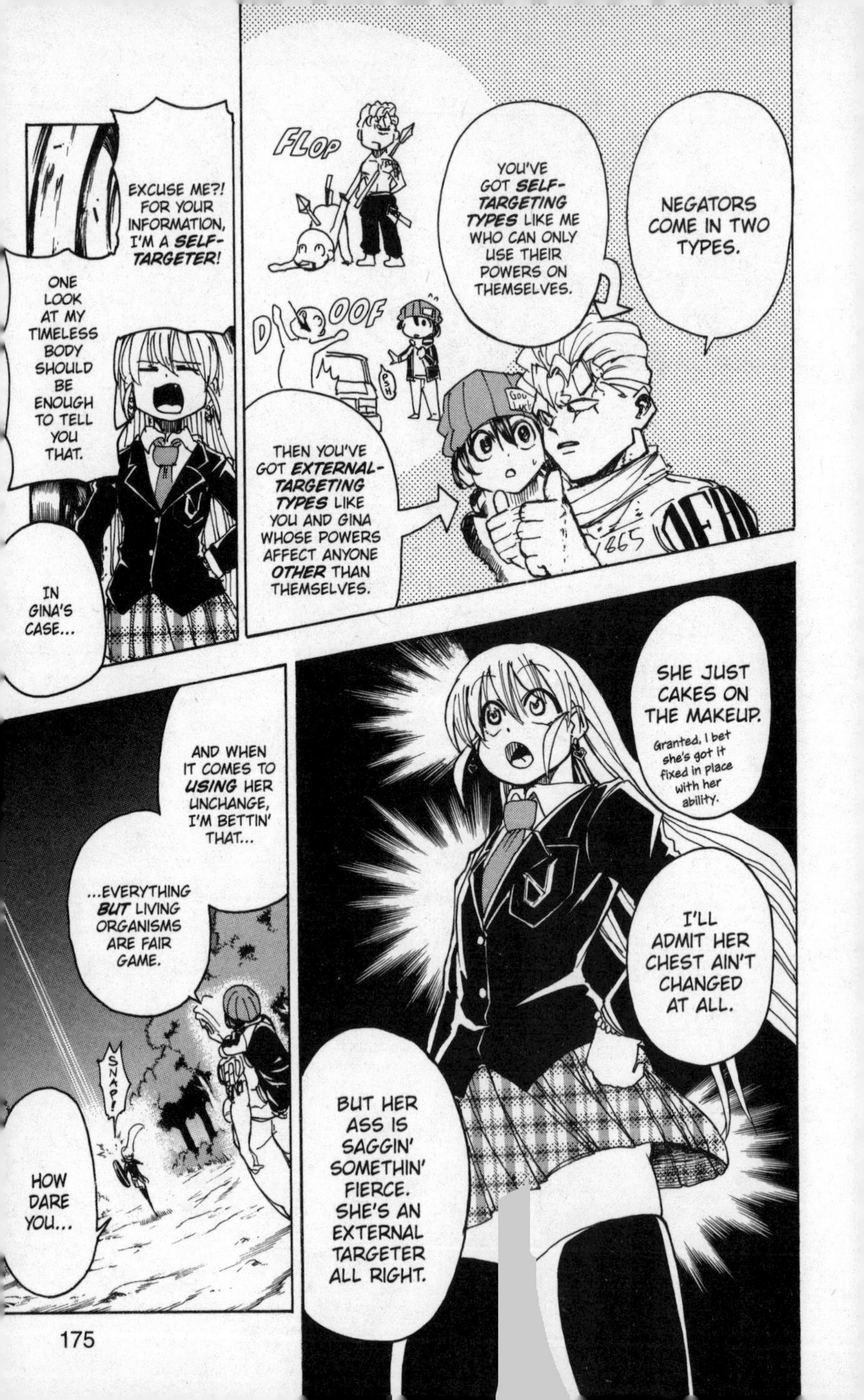
NEGATORS COME IN TWO TYPES.
YOU'VE GOT SELF-TARGETING TYPES LIKE ME WHO CAN ONLY USE THEIR POWERS ON THEMSELVES.
FLOP
DOOF
THEN YOU'VE GOT EXTERNAL-TARGETING TYPES LIKE YOU AND GINA WHOSE POWERS AFFECT ANYONE OTHER THAN THEMSELVES.
EXCUSE ME?! FOR YOUR INFORMATION, I'M A SELF-TARGETER!
ONE LOOK AT MY TIMELESS BODY SHOULD BE ENOUGH TO TELL YOU THAT.
IN GINA'S CASE...
SHE JUST CAKES ON THE MAKEUP.
Granted, I bet she's got it fixed in place with her ability.
I'LL ADMIT HER CHEST AIN'T CHANGED AT ALL.
BUT HER ASS IS SAGGIN' SOMETHIN' FIERCE. SHE'S AN EXTERNAL TARGETER ALL RIGHT.
AND WHEN IT COMES TO USING HER UNCHANGE, I'M BETTIN' THAT...
...EVERYTHING BUT LIVING ORGANISMS ARE FAIR GAME.
SNAP!
HOW DARE YOU...

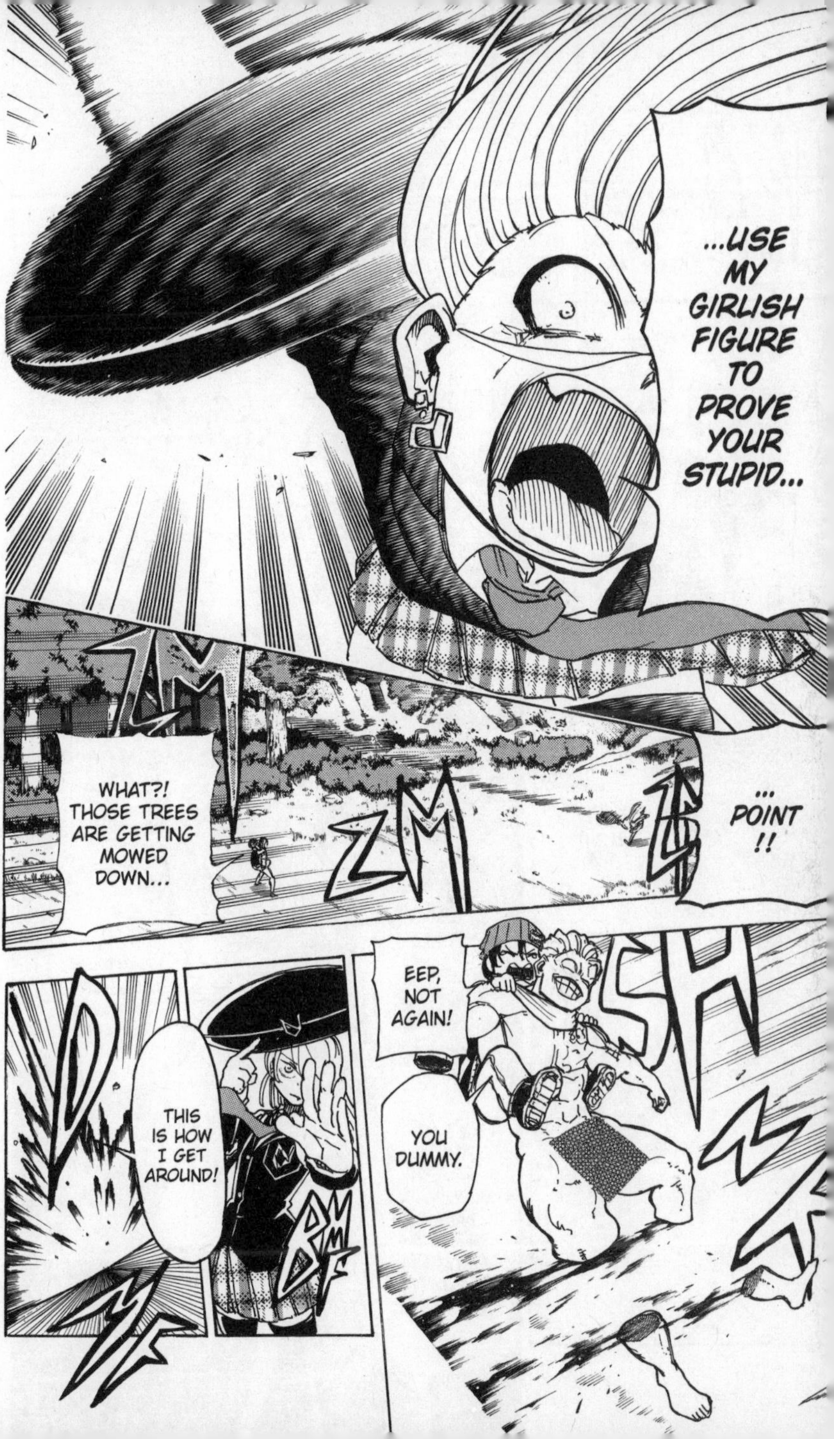
...USE MY GIRLISH FIGURE TO PROVE YOUR STUPID...
...POINT !!
WHAT?! THOSE TREES ARE GETTING MOWED DOWN...
ZM
ZM
EEP, NOT AGAIN!
YOU DUMMY.
SH
THIS IS HOW I GET AROUND!
BMF

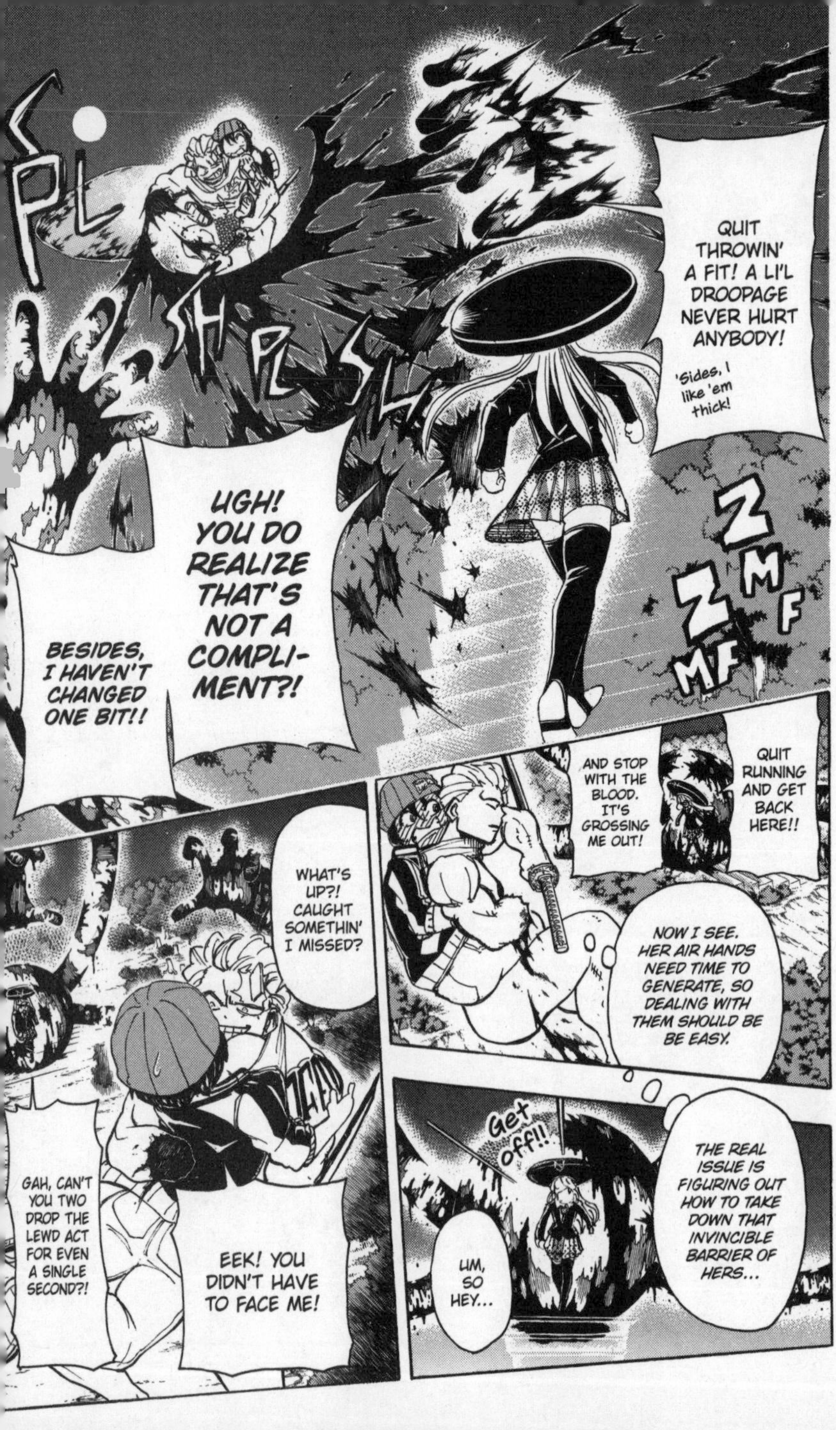
QUIT THROWIN' A FIT! A LI'L DROOPAGE NEVER HURT ANYBODY!
'Sides, I like 'em thick!
SPL
SHPLSH
ZMF ZMF
UGH! YOU DO REALIZE THAT'S NOT A COMPLI-MENT?!
BESIDES, I HAVEN'T CHANGED ONE BIT!!
QUIT RUNNING AND GET BACK HERE!!
AND STOP WITH THE BLOOD. IT'S GROSSING ME OUT!
NOW I SEE. HER AIR HANDS NEED TIME TO GENERATE, SO DEALING WITH THEM SHOULD BE BE EASY.
THE REAL ISSUE IS FIGURING OUT HOW TO TAKE DOWN THAT INVINCIBLE BARRIER OF HERS...
Get off!!
UM, SO HEY...
WHAT'S UP?! CAUGHT SOMETHIN' I MISSED?
EEK! YOU DIDN'T HAVE TO FACE ME!
GAH, CAN'T YOU TWO DROP THE LEWD ACT FOR EVEN A SINGLE SECOND?!

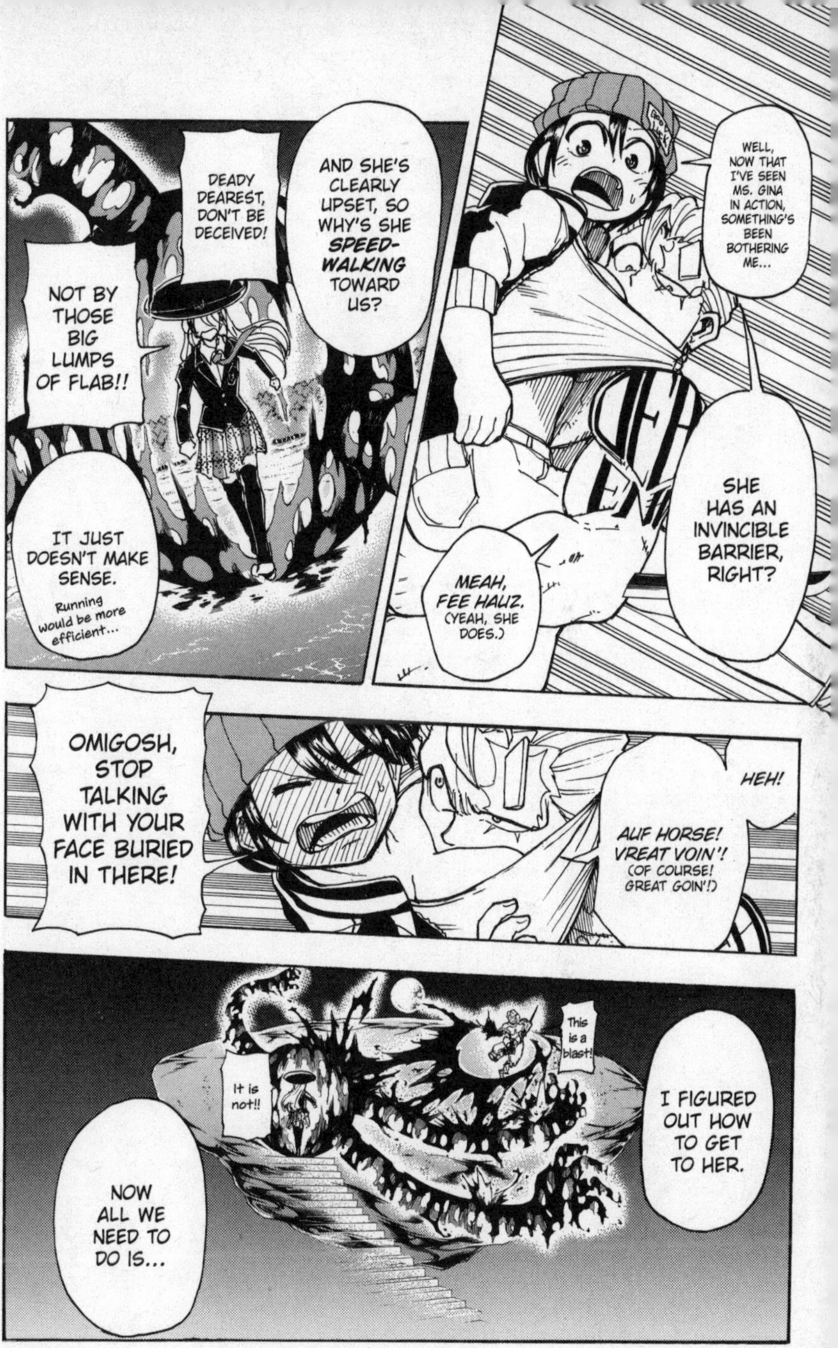
WELL, NOW THAT I'VE SEEN MS. GINA IN ACTION, SOMETHING'S BEEN BOTHERING ME...
SHE HAS AN INVINCIBLE BARRIER, RIGHT?
MEAH, FEE HAUZ. (YEAH, SHE DOES.)
AND SHE'S CLEARLY UPSET, SO WHY'S SHE SPEED-WALKING TOWARD US?
DEADY DEAREST, DON'T BE DECEIVED!
NOT BY THOSE BIG LUMPS OF FLAB!!
IT JUST DOESN'T MAKE SENSE.
Running would be more efficient...
HEH!
AUF HORSE! VREAT VOIN'! (OF COURSE! GREAT GOIN'!)
OMIGOSH, STOP TALKING WITH YOUR FACE BURIED IN THERE!
I FIGURED OUT HOW TO GET TO HER.
This is a blast!
It is not!!
NOW ALL WE NEED TO DO IS...

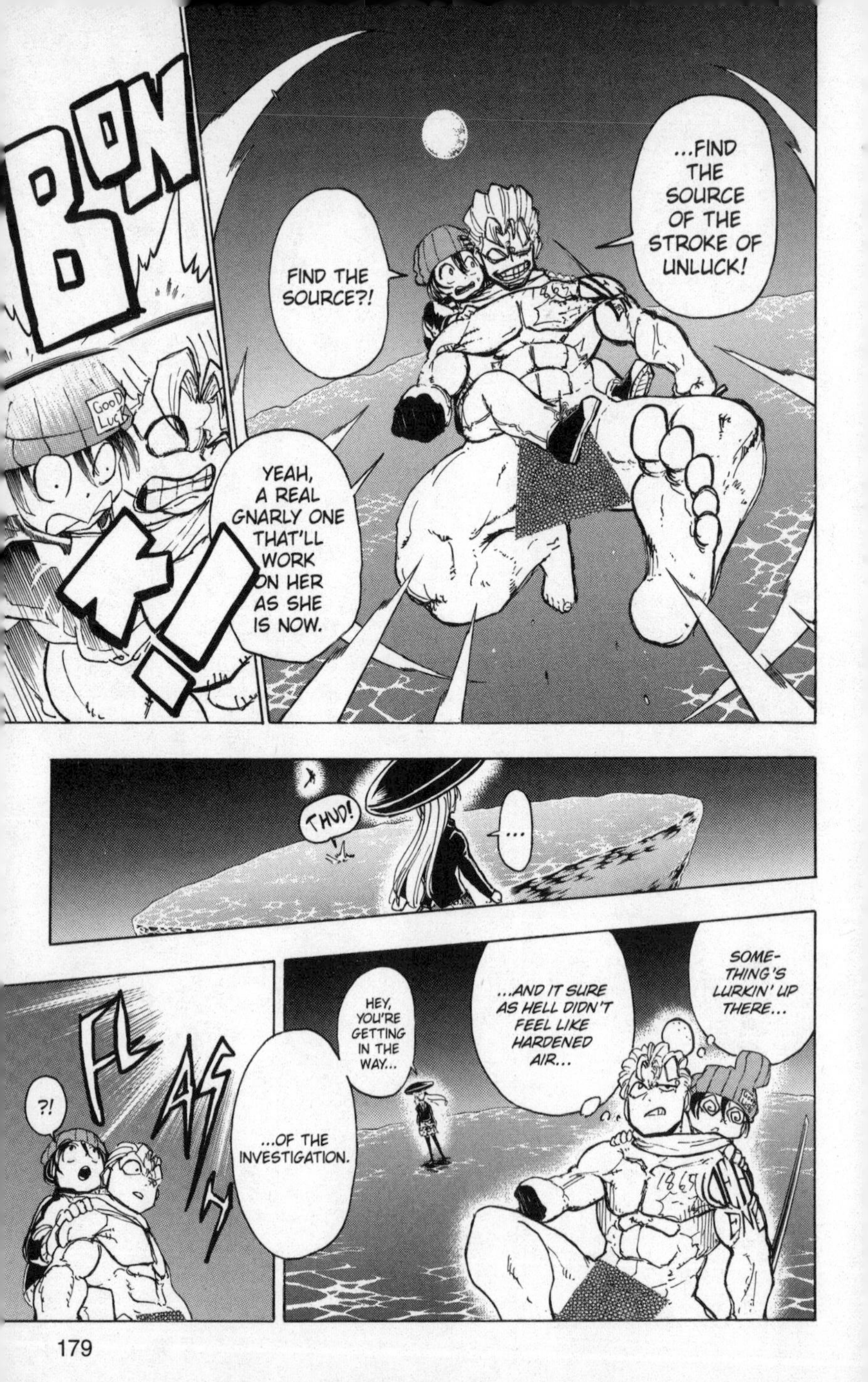
...FIND THE SOURCE OF THE STROKE OF UNLUCK!
FIND THE SOURCE?!
YEAH, A REAL GNARLY ONE THAT'LL WORK ON HER AS SHE IS NOW.
BOOM
GOOD LUCK
THUD!
...
SOME-THING'S LURKIN' UP THERE...
...AND IT SURE AS HELL DIDN'T FEEL LIKE HARDENED AIR...
HEY, YOU'RE GETTING IN THE WAY...
...OF THE INVESTIGATION.
FLASH
?!

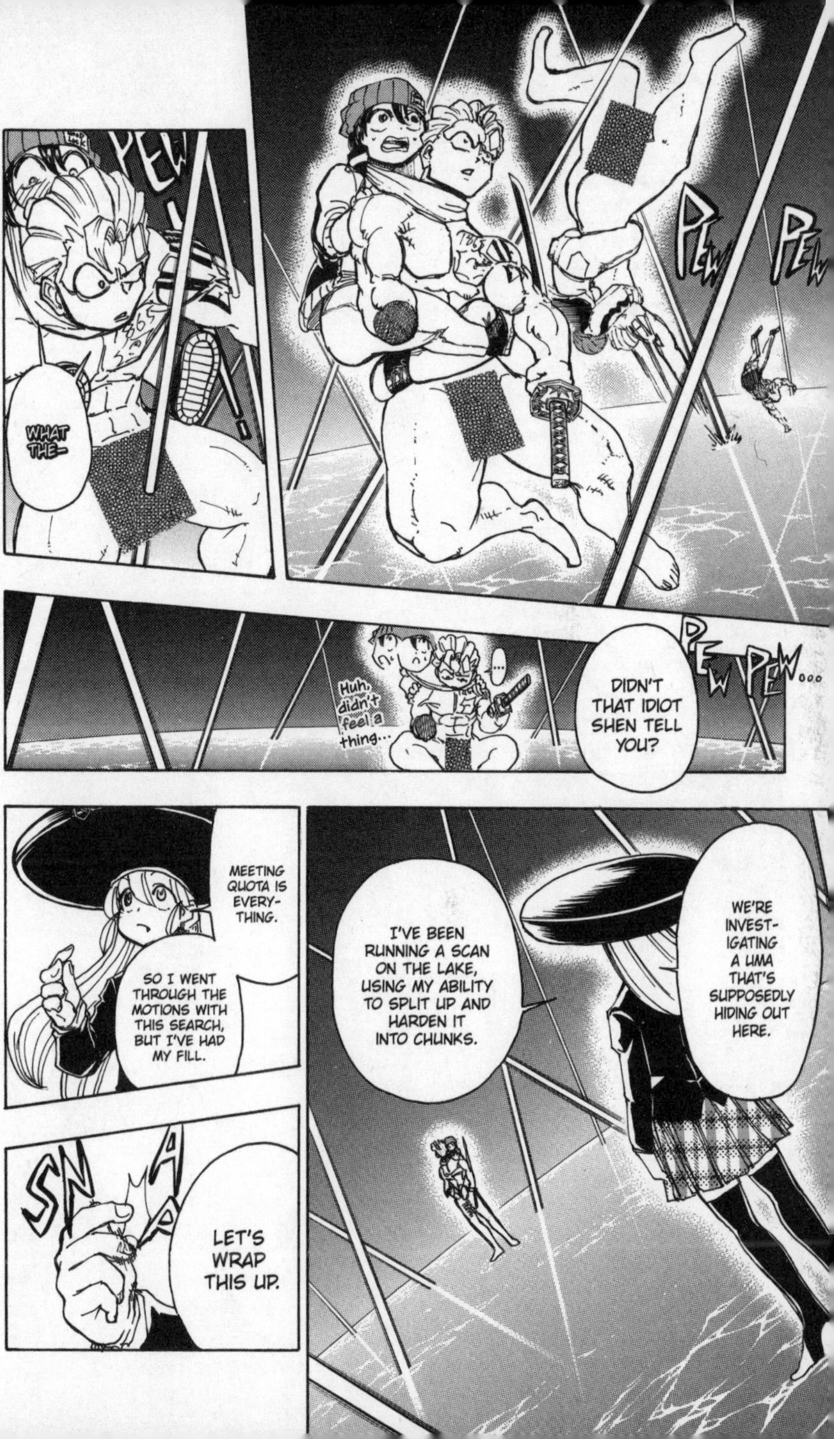
PEW PEW
PEW
WHAT THE-
PEW PEW...
DIDN'T THAT IDIOT SHEN TELL YOU?
...
Huh, didn't feel a thing...
WE'RE INVEST-IGATING A UMA THAT'S SUPPOSEDLY HIDING OUT HERE.
I'VE BEEN RUNNING A SCAN ON THE LAKE, USING MY ABILITY TO SPLIT UP AND HARDEN IT INTO CHUNKS.
MEETING QUOTA IS EVERY-THING.
SO I WENT THROUGH THE MOTIONS WITH THIS SEARCH, BUT I'VE HAD MY FILL.
SNAP
LET'S WRAP THIS UP.

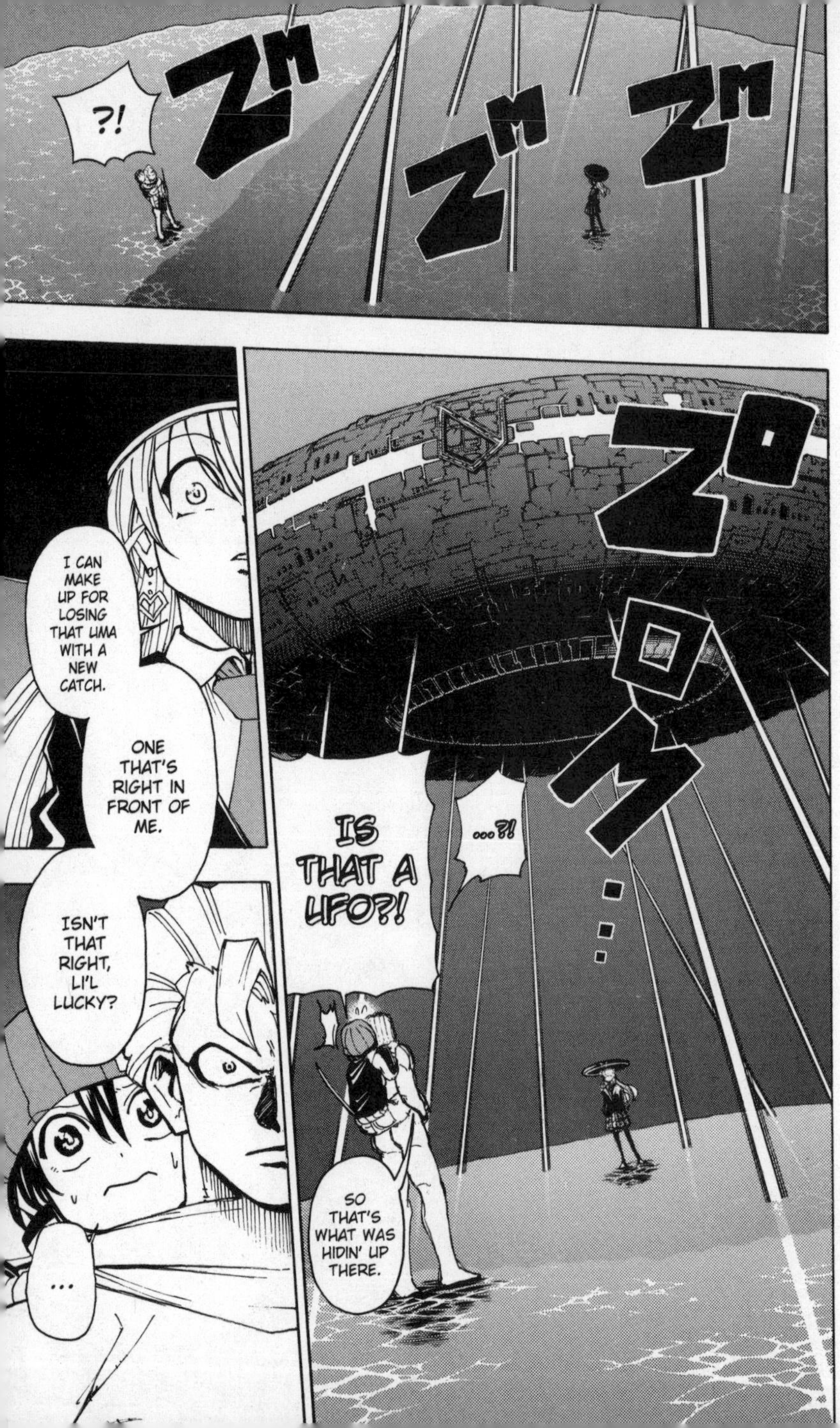
ZM
ZM
ZM
?!
ZOOM...
...?!
IS THAT A UFO?!
SO THAT'S WHAT WAS HIDIN' UP THERE.
I CAN MAKE UP FOR LOSING THAT UMA WITH A NEW CATCH.
ONE THAT'S RIGHT IN FRONT OF ME.
ISN'T THAT RIGHT, LI'L LUCKY?
...

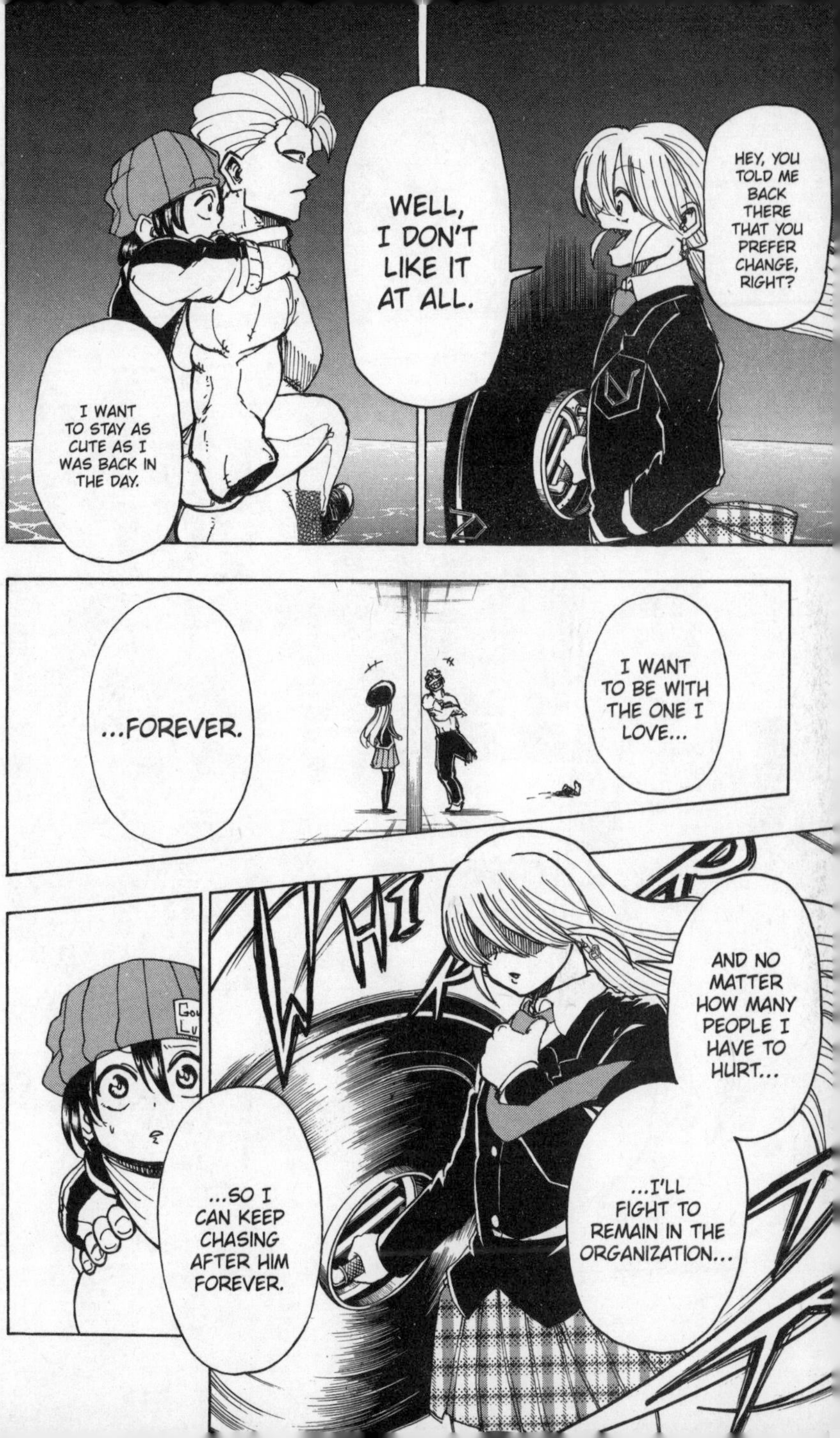
HEY, YOU TOLD ME BACK THERE THAT YOU PREFER CHANGE, RIGHT?
WELL, I DON'T LIKE IT AT ALL.
I WANT TO STAY AS CUTE AS I WAS BACK IN THE DAY.
I WANT TO BE WITH THE ONE I LOVE...
...FOREVER.
AND NO MATTER HOW MANY PEOPLE I HAVE TO HURT...
...I'LL FIGHT TO REMAIN IN THE ORGANIZATION...
...SO I CAN KEEP CHASING AFTER HIM FOREVER.

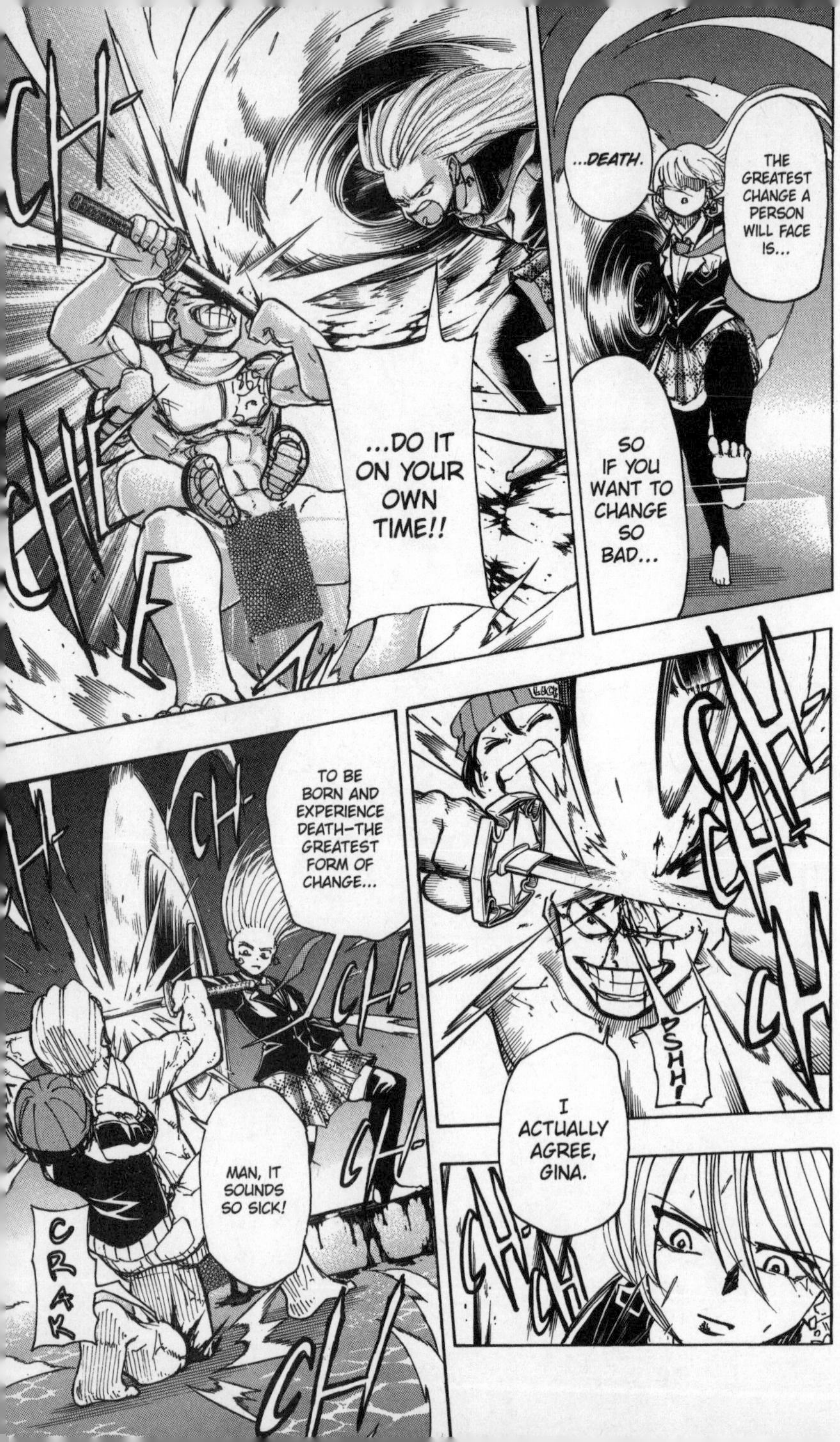
THE GREATEST CHANGE A PERSON WILL FACE IS...
...DEATH.
SO IF YOU WANT TO CHANGE SO BAD...
...DO IT ON YOUR OWN TIME!!
CH-
CHE
SHH!
I ACTUALLY AGREE, GINA.
TO BE BORN AND EXPERIENCE DEATH—THE GREATEST FORM OF CHANGE...
MAN, IT SOUNDS SO SICK!
CRAK
CH-
CH

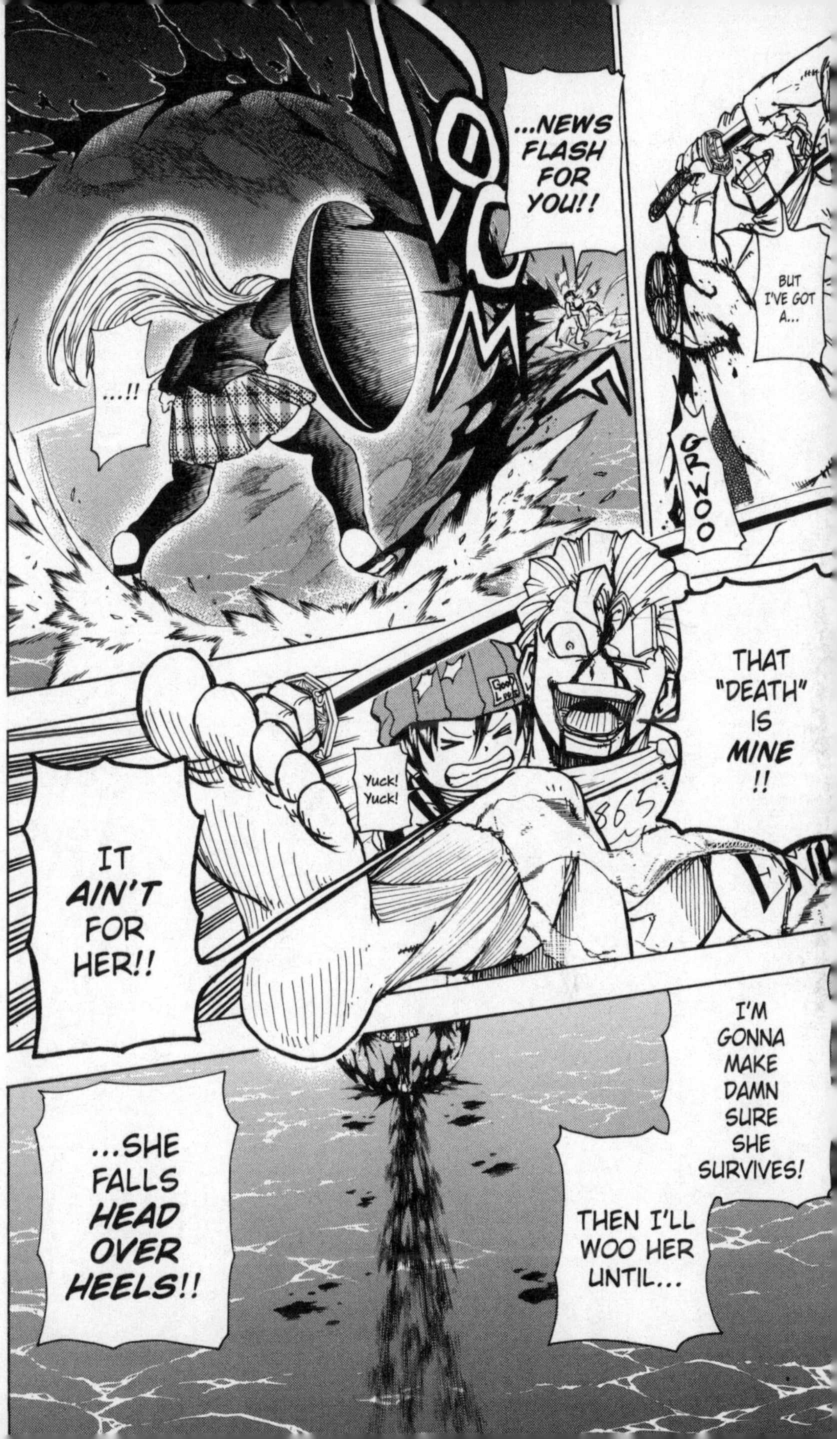
BUT I'VE GOT A...
GRWOO
...NEWS FLASH FOR YOU!!
DOOM
...!!
THAT "DEATH" IS MINE!!
Yuck! Yuck!
IT AIN'T FOR HER!!
I'M GONNA MAKE DAMN SURE SHE SURVIVES!
THEN I'LL WOO HER UNTIL...
...SHE FALLS HEAD OVER HEELS!!

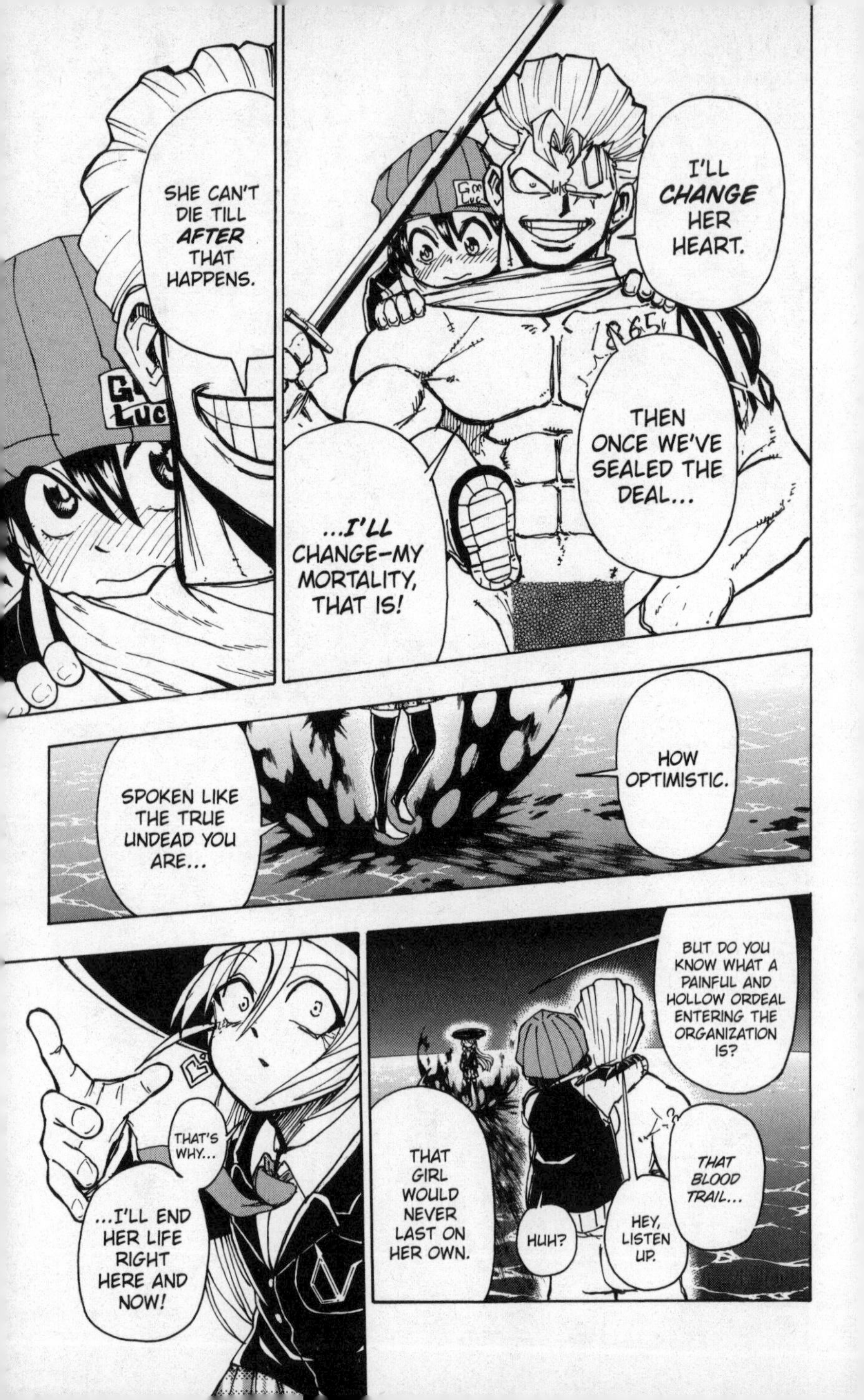
I'LL *CHANGE* HER HEART.
THEN ONCE WE'VE SEALED THE DEAL...
...*I'LL* CHANGE—MY MORTALITY, THAT IS!
SHE CAN'T DIE TILL *AFTER* THAT HAPPENS.
HOW OPTIMISTIC.
SPOKEN LIKE THE TRUE UNDEAD YOU ARE...
BUT DO YOU KNOW WHAT A PAINFUL AND HOLLOW ORDEAL ENTERING THE ORGANIZATION IS?
THAT BLOOD TRAIL...
HEY, LISTEN UP.
HUH?
THAT GIRL WOULD NEVER LAST ON HER OWN.
THAT'S WHY...
...I'LL END HER LIFE RIGHT HERE AND NOW!

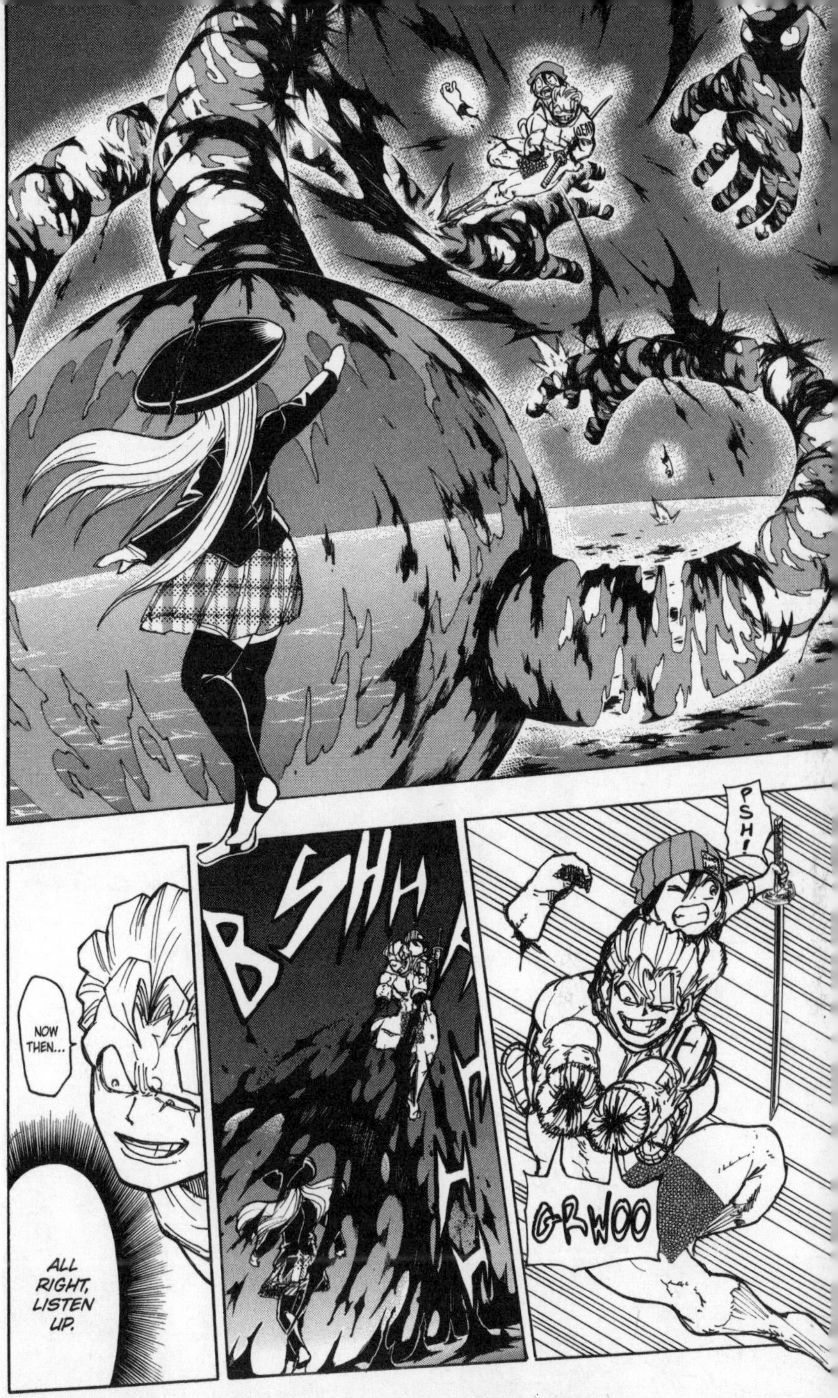
PSH!
GRWOO
BSHHHH
NOW THEN...
ALL RIGHT, LISTEN UP.

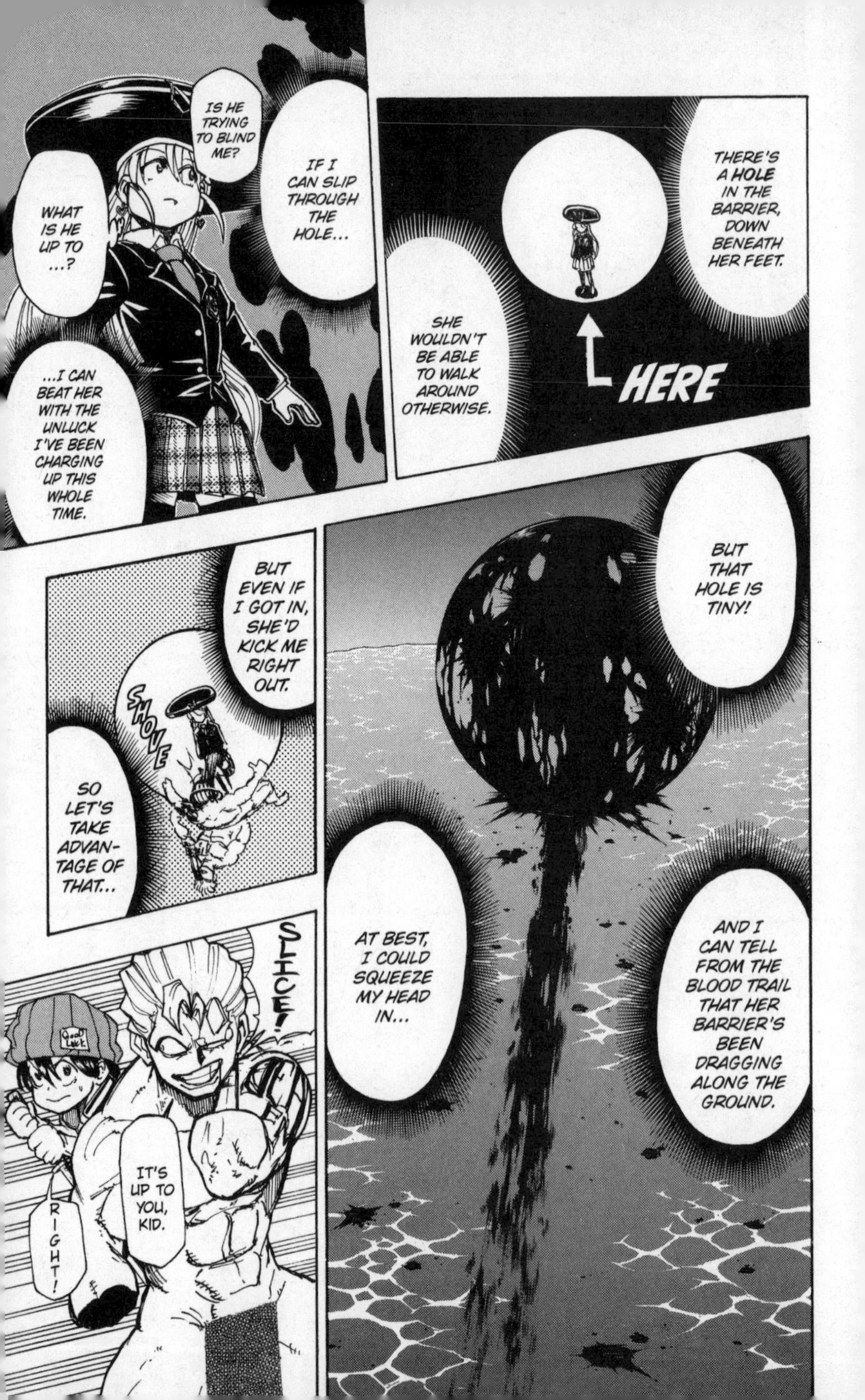
THERE'S A **HOLE** IN THE BARRIER, DOWN BENEATH HER FEET.
SHE WOULDN'T BE ABLE TO WALK AROUND OTHERWISE.
HERE
IF I CAN SLIP THROUGH THE HOLE...
IS HE TRYING TO BLIND ME?
WHAT IS HE UP TO ...?
...I CAN BEAT HER WITH THE UNLUCK I'VE BEEN CHARGING UP THIS WHOLE TIME.
BUT THAT HOLE IS TINY!
AND I CAN TELL FROM THE BLOOD TRAIL THAT HER BARRIER'S BEEN DRAGGING ALONG THE GROUND.
AT BEST, I COULD SQUEEZE MY HEAD IN...
BUT EVEN IF I GOT IN, SHE'D KICK ME RIGHT OUT.
SHOVE
SO LET'S TAKE ADVANTAGE OF THAT...
SLICE!
Good Luck
IT'S UP TO YOU, KID.
RIGHT!

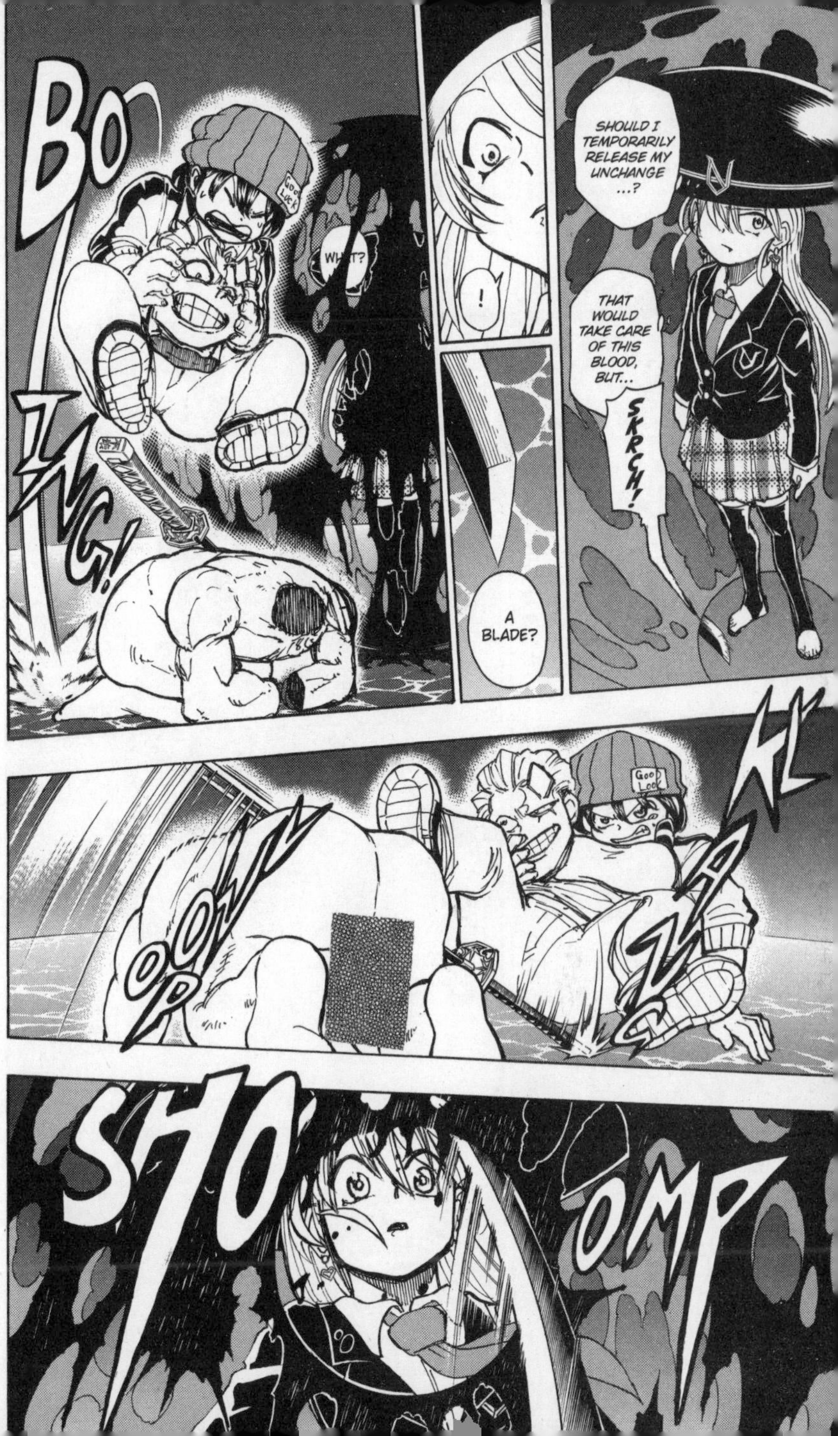
SHOULD I TEMPORARILY RELEASE MY UNCHANGE ...?
THAT WOULD TAKE CARE OF THIS BLOOD, BUT...
SKRCH!
!
A BLADE?
BO
WHAT?
ING!
KLANG
POOOW
SHOOMP

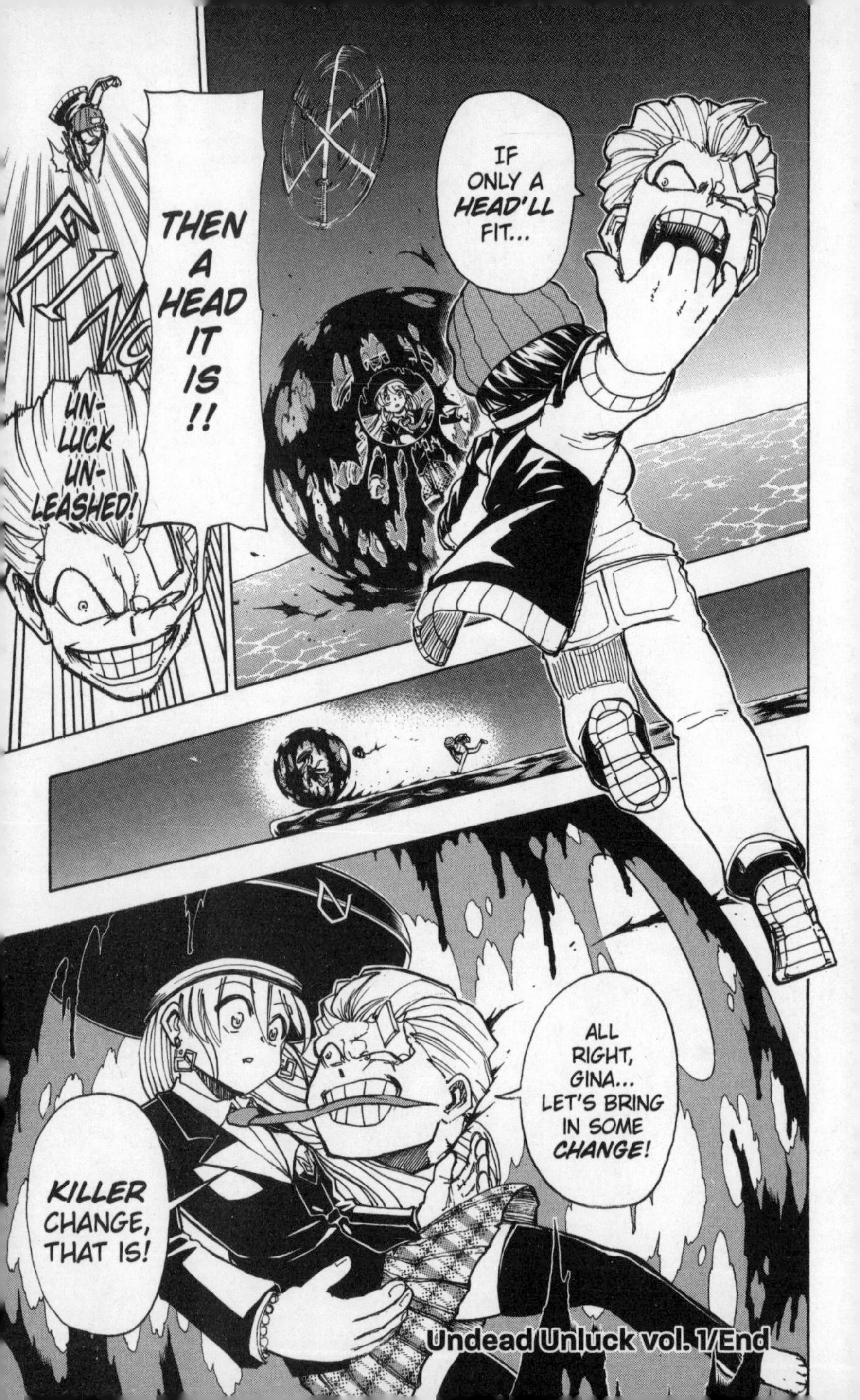
IF ONLY A HEAD'LL FIT...
THEN A HEAD IT IS!!
FLING
UN-LUCK UN-LEASHED!
ALL RIGHT, GINA... LET'S BRING IN SOME CHANGE!
KILLER CHANGE, THAT IS!
Undead Unluck vol. 1/End

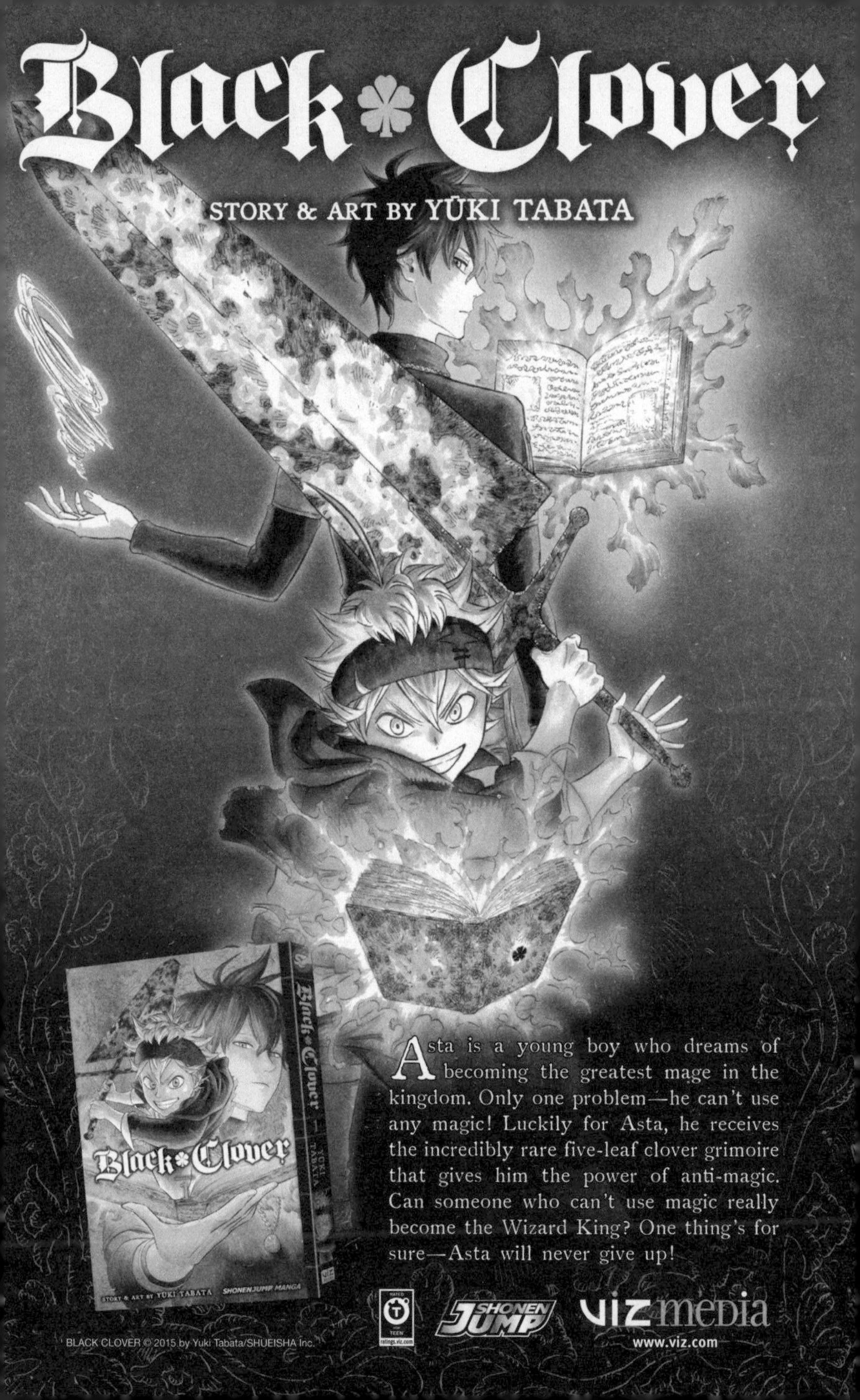

Black Clover

STORY & ART BY YŪKI TABATA

Asta is a young boy who dreams of becoming the greatest mage in the kingdom. Only one problem—he can't use any magic! Luckily for Asta, he receives the incredibly rare five-leaf clover grimoire that gives him the power of anti-magic. Can someone who can't use magic really become the Wizard King? One thing's for sure—Asta will never give up!

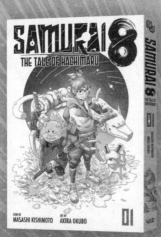
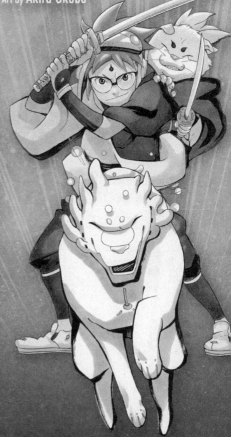

This is the LAST PAGE

You're reading THE WRONG WAY!

W9-DHI-314

UNDEAD UNLUCK reads from right to left, starting in the upper-right corner. Japanese is read from right to left, meaning that action, sound effects, and word-balloon order are completely reversed from English order.

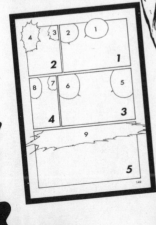

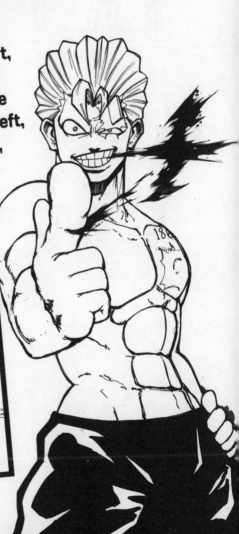